ALL YOU KNOW IS FACTS

Books by Martin Mayer

Nonfiction

ALL YOU KNOW IS FACTS
DIPLOMA: *International Schools and
University Entrance*
EMORY BUCKNER
THE LAWYERS
SOCIAL STUDIES IN AMERICAN SCHOOLS
(former title WHERE, WHEN AND WHY:
Social Studies in American Schools)
THE SCHOOLS
MADISON AVENUE, U.S.A.
WALL STREET: MEN AND MONEY

Fiction

A VOICE THAT FILLS THE HOUSE
THE EXPERTS

ALL YOU KNOW IS
FACTS

MARTIN MAYER

1817

Harper & Row, Publishers   New York, Evanston, and London

Parts of this book were first published in the following: *Esquire, Fortune, Harper's Magazine, High Fidelity, Horizon, Life, Musical America, The New York Times Magazine, Opera News,* and the *Saturday Evening Post.*

FIRST EDITION

LIBRARY OF CONGRESS CATALOG CARD NUMBER: 68–28210

M-S

For Ellen,
the best editor

Contents

Preface

Ambience; or,
Who Put the Overalls in Mrs. Murphy's Bouillabaisse,
and Why

SOMETHING more than twenty years ago, on a spring afternoon in
Cambridge Common, a young lady and I were passing time in that
humid haze of tenderness and self-importance which is the atmosphere
of a student love affair. I recall, uncertainly, that we were talking
about poetry. This was a subject she was "studying" and I was not,
but W. H. Auden had come to town not long before to give a reading, and I had done a piece about him for the wartime version of the
Harvard *Crimson*. As I reconstruct the conversation, my lady made
some reference to a poem of Auden's, and I told her when and where
it was first published and what collections it was in and probably
something about alterations between first publication and first collected edition. As I was drawing breath to continue her enlighten-
ment, she rose to her feet in uncontrollable annoyance and said in the
most cutting voice she could command, *"You!* All *you* know is facts!"

Well, I can tell you, I was upset; and for a long time, too. Today,
though, if the "bad" word *facts* can be changed to the "good" word
information, I will own the criticism calmly. I believe in information.
Often, when I am boring all around me by putting together *viva voce*
the pieces of some puzzle I am to describe in print, people will ask
for my opinion of some part of the story, whether I think it's a good
thing or a bad thing, and I have terrible trouble answering them. I
cannot even be trusted to give a simple answer to the reasonable and
despairing question about what some piece of data *means,* because I
can usually see (and can rarely refrain from explaining) several possible meanings, none of which should be ignored. My job as I understand it is to get the picture right; and if you get the picture right
people select from your prose partial and directed perceptions similar
to those they select from reality; and that's fine.

Once in Milan, my wife and I stood fascinated for ten minutes before the best pitchman we had ever seen. He had a box full of those papier-mâché clowns that were for years the peddlers' stock in trade, and as he jiggled a string tied to the middle finger of his right hand the clown danced a wondrous shuffle on the sidewalk. In his left hand the peddler held a penny whistle, on which he blew a South Italian tune which could have made the paving stones dance, let alone a paper clown. Somewhere in a doorway, of course, there was an accomplice holding the other string which made the dance possible— but it seemed to us that the least we could pay for the entertainment the peddler had given us was the purchase of one of his clowns. I teased him a little by asking him in shattered Italian whether the clown would dance for me as it danced for him, and he assured me that it would. Then I asked him about the music. "Ah," he said, making a bow, "la musica—la musica, fate voi stesso."

Here, then, dancing as best I can make them dance, are some of the pieces of papier-mâché human perception calls reality. The music you must make for yourself.

According to a recent statement by a magazine editor (I am no good at names unless I write them down, but "Podhoretz" clongs distantly, like a bell in a *schul* on the road to Mandalay), the art form of our times is the nonfiction magazine piece. I should like to believe this, given the great prestige of art and artists, but I can't. My definitions of art are no better than the next man's, but I have written novels and short stories as well as nonfiction prose, and I find a significant difference between the two kinds of work. When I read over the next morning the fiction I composed the night before, I am never really confident that it does what I want it to do, while the adequacy of a page in an article seems to me as measurable as the height of a column of mercury in a glass tube. The writing of magazine articles, in other words, is not an art but a craft. Sometimes, when people ask me what I do for a living, I say that I make chairs and sell them to people who buy chairs.

Almost all the furniture on display in these pages was originally hand-carved to the order of editors—in fact, I cannot think of half a dozen pieces in the last ten years which have grown out of my sug-

gestion to an editor rather than an editor's proposal to me. Much of
my magazine work therefore relates to subjects—finance, advertising, education, law, television—on which I have written or am known
to be writing a book, because it is in these contexts that an editor is
most likely to think of my name. Several editors, however (especially
Harold Hayes of *Esquire,* William Emerson and Otto Friedrich of the
Saturday Evening Post, Jack Fischer and later Willie Morris of *Harper's,* and Lewis Bergman and Harvey Shapiro of the *New York
Times Magazine*), have regarded me as an available general reporter; and these assignments are, of course, the most fun. The outstanding example in these pages, I suppose, is the little profile of the
hairdresser Kenneth Battelle, a piece with negative specific gravity,
which began as one of the bright bubbles that shimmer implausibly
behind the stern Carolina cracker façade of Harold Hayes.

Writing for magazines, at least as I do it, is an economically irrational occupation, in which gross income from a job bears little relation to either the quantity or the quality of the work required. Some
of the pieces in this book sold originally for $300; others for $5,000.
There are many instances of low-priced pieces which took considerably more time and effort than high-priced pieces. In general, I accept assignments from editors subject to satisfactory conclusion of
negotiations with my agent, Emilie Jacobson of Curtis Brown, with
whom I have worked since we were both kids, nearly—sorry, Emmy
—twenty years ago. The aim of the negotiations is to push the editor
to "a good price for that magazine," and I rarely have turned down
what looked like an interesting proposal because the money was inadequate. To me, the luxury of free-lancing is to be able to accept or
reject assignments because I do or don't wish to work on the subject,
not because the job is or isn't profitable. One cannot carry this flag
into every battle—enough money can make any subject interesting,
and sometimes a fascinating subject is just impossible at the price.
(I looked for two years, for example, for the funding to carry the
costs of a major piece on Arthur Judson, who once managed the New
York Philharmonic and Philadelphia Orchestra simultaneously, while
also managing the conductors of nearly all the nation's other major
symphony orchestras. A. J. was willing—just barely willing—to help

out, to provide access to a significant and quite unknown piece of American social history in several dozen cities. But only *Harper's* wanted it, and *Harper's* couldn't come within $5,000 of paying half the costs.) Still, there are several articles in these pages which yielded less than one-fifth my average price for the time they took. Self-image: a small thing, but mine own.

My academic background is in economics, and I have the economist's habit of mind—or "discipline," to use today's fashionable and confusing lingo. I see the world in terms of choices, alternative uses for scarce means, in terms of processes rather than purposes, of real events at the margin rather than imagined changes at the center, of elasticities and substitutions, of those continuities which, as Justice Holmes put it, are never a duty, merely a necessity. Thus I have written relatively little about politics, which strikes me as a fundamentally accidental phenomenon. I would not for a moment deny the occasional immense importance of political decision or leadership luck (what is important is most often bad luck); but usually, it seems to me, the ranges of political choice are narrowly restricted by economic and social reality—even when the political change calls itself a revolution. I write about substructure not only because it is more interesting but also because it is, to me, more significant.

I like as much of my information as possible to emerge from interviews, so that data can be flavored by personality. Setting up appointments, for someone like myself who has no secretary, can be a great pain in the neck; and here valorous deeds are done by the despised and rejected of men, the flacks at the larger organizations. Books, scholarly journals and government publications provide background. I try to read them during (rather than before) the interviewing period, as a source of new questions, to diminish the repetitiousness in a series of interviews. I very rarely read previously published magazine articles on a subject, to avoid imitating other people's organization and emphasis—and also to make sure that I don't eliminate what may be the best and most readable organization simply because I happen to have learned that another magazine has already used it. Nobody remembers a magazine piece, anyway.

Interviews, when they go right, are conversations. Preparing a magazine article is like plotting a mosaic: one needs bright bits of stone, but probably not too many of any single color. An hour's interview will produce anywhere from half a dozen to twenty pages of notes, which will in turn produce perhaps three or four sentences of a final piece. Thus it is a great mistake to try to make every moment count in an interview: most moments are necessarily wasted. Serendipity accounts for the best stuff in almost any magazine piece.

Solidly grasped, the jargon of the field to be discussed becomes a power tool for drilling information out of anybody. You will always do best if you try to get your respondent talking in his own way about that aspect of the subject which most interests him. At worst, a man who is talking about what interests him can be guided to what interests you by questions which deflect the midstream of his discourse, a much easier task than getting him started at the beginning along channels he is for any reason less than eager to follow. There will be plenty of time to discard the jargon and the parochial approaches when the notes are spread out before the typewriter.

Note-taking, for me, is mostly a question of catching characteristic phrases, speech rhythms and sentence structure: content takes care of itself. In general, I feel an obligation to make my first selection of what I may possibly use from an interview while I am face to face with my victim. I disapprove profoundly of the tape-recorded interview, which leaves the writer free at a later time to select from full text anything which serves his later purposes. If what a man says does not seem important enough to write down at the interview itself, he is entitled not to see it appear as one of the handful of quotes attributed to him in a finished piece. Though I have a personal, primitive kind of shorthand available to me at moments of pressure, I almost always write out in full script (omitting the neutral words, the Alberti bass of the conversation) whatever I feel may be valuable later. If I fall behind, I direct the conversation into a backwater which does not greatly interest me while writing down what does. My memory for speech is deadly at any range up to about five minutes, excellent for individual sentences and for the gist of a statement up to about an hour after the end of the conversation, if for any reason it is impossible for me to make my notes while chatting.

Normally, I write one article at night while "researching" another during the day. (Jerome Wiesner, while President John F. Kennedy's science adviser, defined the word *research:* "to look again: we didn't find anything the first time.") Because the two pieces are usually very different in intellectual focus and personality, and because chunks of my time go to music criticism (I write a monthly column about music for *Esquire*), a very long day is possible without fatigue—one subject serves to relax the mind from contemplation of the others. I write on an electric typewriter and cannot easily understand how people have ever managed to compose in longhand. With the typewriter, instant rewriting and interstitial editing are routinely simple, and I can literally charge at a difficult sentence by retyping the sentence before and pushing on with new momentum at whatever the barrier may be. This running-jump approach is my normal operating procedure: picking up an article the next night or the next morning, pencil in hand, I read over everything already written before proceeding to the next page. Opening pages tend therefore to be somewhat more finely written, because I have gone over them more often.

Many pencil marks are made once the foundation of a paragraph is in gesso, because even in the hands of the great artists in its use—a Bernard Shaw, a Max Beerbohm, a James Joyce, an Evelyn Waugh, to assert the standards of judgment by chronological rank—English is a word-order language; and improvements in an already precise English sentence grow more often from reordering its elements than from changing them. If the words are in optimum order, even very long sentences will not fatigue the reader: the preceding sentence has seventy-two words, but I think it reads easily enough. Writing it took twenty-five minutes.

I work virtually every night of the year: I tend to grow irritable, like a cow which has not been milked, if I cannot relieve myself each evening of the burden of prose I have been accumulating all day. I enjoy writing, and never hang my head over a problem (I do hit my head, though, with a gibbonlike gesture that amuses friends and has given me a callus on my scalp which the great photographer and dermatologist Henry Sarason says is like the calluses longshoremen get on their hands). Finished copy emerges at the rate of three pages a night, twenty pages a week. As Maupassant once pointed out, three pages a night adds up to an enormous amount of verbiage in a year.

I retype my own articles, partly because I am usually fighting a deadline and the packages you carry get home first, partly because retyping gives me a last look and a last chance to edit before submission. I can retype, with a clean top copy, at a rate of about twelve pages an hour, and if the writing business ever goes sour, I guess I can make a living as a typist. (My wife was recently asked $2 a page for a manuscript of hers; at that rate, which I doubt that anyone actually pays, I could cut down on my typical work week and still take home $50,000 a year.) Up to recently, I was too sick of any piece I had just finished to read over the final typescript before sending it in to the editor who assigned it. But I have been growing soft, and just as I find I can no longer bring myself to type in a hotel room after two in the morning or in an airplane on a night flight to Europe, I now become uncomfortable unless I have proofed the ms. before sliding it into the envelope. I also tend to read my stuff in print now, which I never used to do at all. This may indicate that I am beginning to take myself seriously, which would be a nuisance for a number of people, especially myself. Can a young man trust himself over forty?

Most pieces—not all—require some further work after their first submission. In general, the difference between the professional and the amateur magazine writer is that the professional knows his stuff can be improved and the amateur doesn't. (There are, of course, some famous and highly paid amateurs.) The difference between a professional and an amateur editor is that the amateur tries to do the improving himself, while the professional finds the right way to get the writer to do the work. In the timeless war between the rim and the slot, class solidarity now places me in the phalanx at the rim; but I have sat in the slot and I respect the difficulties of the job.

Some famous editors had no notion of how to help a writer improve a piece (Lester Markel of the *New York Times Magazine,* for example, would say, "I don't know why, but, Martin, I'm disappointed"; and my one long-distance contact with Henry Luce, on the Princeton admissions piece reprinted here, produced only the Delphic

"Mr. Luce says it needs a fix," which it didn't.) *Esquire's* Hayes, perhaps the last of the personal editors, gets himself emotionally involved in his reactions to a piece, communicating not an objective critique but a cry for help. (One of his best letters began, "I can sense your impatience with me . . .") Friedrich of the *Saturday Evening Post*—a friend, mind you, since 1944, and himself a writer of great accomplishment—gets me talking about the subject of the piece and then says, "Why don't you use *that";* he also proposes specific reorganizations, not so much in the hope that they will be followed as in the realization that consciousness of *any* viable alternative organization can break a writer out of the bonds of his own first perceptions. George Bush of *Better Homes and Gardens,* by his superb sense of (and respect for) the reasons why his readers buy his magazine, can induce in even the intellectually snottiest of Harvard graduates a feeling for the honesty of a simpler stylistic orientation.

What I write is determined nearly always by the subject and my own abilities, not by the "market" for which the piece is destined. In general, I try to write what I would like to read about a subject, and I will write the same piece on that subject for any magazine—certainly for *Esquire, Harper's,* the *New York Times Magazine* and the *Saturday Evening Post,* which are my most frequent markets; for *Life* or *Redbook* or *McCall's,* each of which has bought a single piece; and probably for *TV Guide,* which has bought half a dozen. (Several of the articles here were commissioned by one of these magazines and published by another of them.) In a job for *Fortune* or *Commentary* I would feel myself more at liberty to use the shorthand of finance or sociology (respectively); and in jobs like the pamphlets I have written for the Advertising Research Foundation I can of course assume acquaintance with the lingo and a sense of which questions are significant. For *Better Homes,* as noted (and it should also be noted that the only prize of any substance I have ever won, a University of Missouri business journalism award, was for a series in *Better Homes*), I am to a degree under tutelage. The hard job is trying to remember what I didn't know when I started.

Expertise for these purposes is less difficult to acquire than people realize: there is a great difference between knowing something well enough to do it and knowing something well enough to write about it with respectable authority. Every piece of nonfiction writing conveys different levels of meaning to different readers. By quoting accurately from the conversation of practitioners, I can bring into an article (especially, of course, into a book) nuances of expression which are probably more meaningful to my best-informed readers than they are to me. This is not modesty: it is, I know, a great deal, and requires a great deal of work, to understand what in a man's presentation will be most significant for his colleagues. But few people realize how much can be learned, for purposes of reportage, by careful listening to what a man is trying to say as well as to what he is saying.

This book is published on the fifteenth anniversary of my departure from the last job I held, as an associate editor of *Esquire*. All eighteen articles, which appeared originally in nine different magazines, are drawn from the last decade's work. Some pieces of which I am most fond have been eliminated because I used or plan to use the material in a book; a few have been included for reasons of the historical interest of the subject. Most are here because I believe them to be my best work; and that is, in context, reason enough. A magazine, Arnold Gingrich once said, is rather like a circus. If anybody likes *all* the acts in a circus, it's a lousy circus. Like the circus patron, the magazine reader will put up with a good deal which doesn't interest him much in return for a few things he thoroughly enjoys. I think a book of articles is like that, too. Anybody who finds that Verdi's *Falstaff* or the liquor industry or a city school district or mutual-fund selling is not his bag is welcome to turn a few pages and try the next bag.

I am grateful to many people for these fifteen years. Writing for magazines has been for me by every measure an extraordinarily rewarding life. I have done what I consider serious work, in a field where one can be virtuous and still have cakes and ale. I have seen the world, the here and now and there and then, and more of the future than most men have the chance to meet. I have been able to involve my wife in my work, and we have often delighted in the opportunity to take our sons with us on our travels.

Beyond the joy of the varieties of experience, there is also a moral quality about the work I do, which I should like to honor. A writer, in the lovely phrase of Eugene Manlove Rhodes, gets his scars on the front of his face: he must live with his mistakes as other men, by and large, need not. It is a public life which rests on reputation, where reputation is written in canon with performance. Caesar's wife could have had no better than a meteoric career in my business.

The late Joe H. Palmer once told the story of an outside man who gave a slow pill to the wrong race horse, and later protested "almost tearfully" that it had been an honest mistake. I will make that minimum claim, untearfully, for myself and for the others of my totem. Some of my errors of fact still have the power to make me blush; some of my errors of judgment still make me wince; and I can recall a dozen moments of indiscretion or anger in conversation or correspondence which I would very gladly take back. I should like to be able to do what I do better than I now do it. But I can honestly say that I have done the best I can. In ten books for my own signature and two for the signature of others, in more than 150 articles and perhaps 200 critical pieces on music and books, I can think of nothing in my work of which I have reason to feel ashamed. In writing, as in other aspects of life in this society, the reward for postponing immediate gratification turns out to be, in a word, freedom.

1

A Quiet Thursday
in the Life of Mr. Kenneth

[Perhaps because it is so different from the sort of thing I am supposed
to do well, this article is for me the best piece of work I have ever done
for a magazine; it is also, as I noted in the preface, one of the most imaginative assignments ever made by the resourceful Harold Hayes of
Esquire. It is improved by one bit of artifice: in fact I spent several days
hanging around Kenneth's scissors, and made a composite single day out
of the best of the conversations. Not long after the article was published,
Kenneth left Mme Daché and went into business for himself. He has continued to flourish: the base price for a cut is now $25. The unnamed
"Great Lady" of the article was, of course, Jacqueline Kennedy.]

KENNETH BATTELLE, known to his business associates, clientele and
several million American females as "Mr. Kenneth," is a boy from
Syracuse not yet forty but already at the top of his trade. As chief
hairdresser and supervisor of the beauty salon at the ladies' retooling
emporium of Mme Lilly Daché, he commands a fee of $15 for a
haircut and "styling"—which means that after he finishes cutting
he will instruct an assistant in exactly what he wants done with what
remains. Anyone who calls him out of town to cut and set her hair
will pay $1,000 for his day, and his fee for a demonstration-lecture
to fellow hairdressers is $1,500. Few of his clients, however, feel that
they have received anything less than value for money; indeed, before
his reputation became so large as it is today, many of them tried to
give him a tip on top of the price—and were brushed aside, for Mr.
Kenneth does not accept tips. "Remember," says Lillian Ross of *The
New Yorker,* who first came to his chair to scoff as a Talk-of-the-
Town reporter and stayed to become a weekly customer, "you are
dealing here with an artist. An artist with a scissors."

Apart from the scissors, which he wields left-handed, Mr. Kenneth
is an artist in his own appearance. He is a slight man of medium

1

height who holds himself almost stiffly erect. His suits are beautifully tailored to his posture, the jacket sloping from prominent shoulder blades to a distinct waist accented by pockets cut on the diagonal, the well-pressed trousers, never a wrinkle, narrowing to bottoms without cuffs (a hairdresser whose trousers had cuffs would always be cleaning hair out of them). A vest of the same material, perhaps ornamented by brass or jeweled buttons, peeps out from between the narrow lapels of the jacket; and from the vest, triumphantly transfixed by a jeweled stickpin, a rather wide tie rises to a Windsor knot. A silk handkerchief billows slightly from the breast pocket of the jacket. Above it all, balanced, it seems, just a little precariously, is a round head somewhat too large for the dimensions of the body, a round, symmetrical, handsome face, and carefully combed thinning brown hair, always just short of requiring a cut. The smile is boyish and casual, yet cool and always the same.

But artifice stops, rather short, with the static composition of the lady's hair and the hairdresser's body. Neither in manner nor in approach to the job is there anything arty about Mr. Kenneth. "Most people," he says in a soft voice, speaking in the deliberate rhythm that marks all his activities, "think this is a frothy business. I don't. I think it's a service business. People come to Kenneth—this isn't, I hope, as vain as it sounds—people come to Kenneth because they think Kenneth can do something for them. Usually, they're pleased. I hope it's because something *has* been done for them. But sometimes, right after I've cut their hair, when it's just lying there wet, they'll say, 'It looks better already.' This business is in part illusion. You have to feel what people expect you to be, and then be it."

Most customers come to Mr. Kenneth for the soft, voluminous, very feminine hair style associated with his name and with that of a Great Lady who must not be mentioned. In fact, however, he does all sorts of cutting and styling, suiting his work to the hair, the face, the lady's expressed desires. He feels that everybody likes "something different" (he changes the décor of his own apartment several times a year), and he always knows another way to solve the old problem. He rather enjoys a little chit-chat with the girls—secretaries and suburban housewives, as well as regular customers from the *haut monde* and *demi-monde*—but he believes and wants to believe that the strength of his position rests on the quality of the work he does. Even on a day when he has cut thirty or forty heads of hair, working until nine at night though the salon has officially closed at six, he cares how each of his customers looks when she says her hair was cut by Mr. Kenneth. First of all, he is a craftsman, and when he comes to work in the morning he looks forward, almost cheerfully, to a day's exercise of his craft.

On Thursdays the salon opens at ten, but out-of-towners and new customers often come in early, the long and the short and the tall wandering through the store-front boutique of Mme Daché's narrow, nine-story home-and-business building on Fifty-sixth Street between Madison and Park Avenues. The salesladies ignore these anxiously premature patrons; the senior of the group, a vigorous, dumpy Italian lady with gray hair, is speaking nervously on the telephone: ". . . *più non posso. Okayokay? Okay. Ciaociao.*" In the windowless room directly behind the boutique stands the long curved desk which is Forward Command Post for the salon; here a staff of three or four soberly efficient ladies answers the telephone, keeps track of who is coming in when for which hairdresser, prepares the bills and collects the money. On Thursdays and Fridays, with the social affairs of the weekend just over the horizon, ladies have "standing appointments" with their special hairdressers and enter every week at the same hour by ritual. As a matter of policy, Mr. Kenneth tries to take everybody who walks through the door, whether or not she has an appointment, but on Thursday a girl at the desk may have to tell a newcomer that none of the hairdressers is free until noon. "Bonwit's is open," the girl says cheerily, "or Bloomingdale's . . ."

Mr. Kenneth arrives on the hour and takes a quick look at his own appointment list, for curiosity's sake. Then he walks up the carpeted stairway, which rises with a not-quite-clean French elegance to the main salon on the second floor. At the head of the stairs is a rather splendid circular room, mirrors around the wall reflecting not only the hairdresser's chairs before them but also all the other mirrors and chairs, so a customer can see who else is here and be seen by those whose attention she may crave. Two more hairdresser's chairs, with their associated sinks, face a free-standing mirror inside the circle near the rear, giving a touch of theater and increasing the apparent size of an already large room. The colors are pink and white.

Mr. Kenneth passes by the main salon without a look—he may not enter it all day, though he usually makes a visit or two. (He usually does *not* look in on the third floor, where the more esoteric beauty operations, from hair dyeing to waxes that remove hair to assorted massages, are carried on in the semiantiseptic surroundings of an uninspected private hospital.) Mr. Kenneth turns away to the rear, to a rectangular room about the size of a normal bedroom, which has been cut up by gray transoms to make five partially enclosed working areas, each with chair, sink and mirror. A customer is already in one of the chairs, head tilted back, neck resting on the contoured edge of the black sink, long blond hair soaking in the sink. Like every Daché customer, she wears a pink cotton wrap, usually in lieu of her street clothes, which are hanging downstairs. Mr. Kenneth ignores her and turns into the "dispensary" area to the left, where maids work at kitchen sinks. In the windowless dispensary room, he hangs his coat on a tree. This room, lined with bottles in boxes like a section of a supermarket, is Mr. Kenneth's only hope for privacy; here he can retire, very occasionally, to smoke a cigarette and to sit perched on a white kitchen ladder. One of the girls has, by custom, brought Mr. Kenneth something for breakfast—a bacon-and-egg sandwich wrapped in aluminum foil to keep it warm. He eats half the sandwich, rewraps the rest, drinks a cup of coffee, looking out on the still-quiet hallway between his room and the big salon. "It's a long day; nobody wants to start it."

Another customer is already in process of shampoo; Mr. Kenneth glances out, picks up comb and scissors, and approaches his first of the day, who is now sitting up, a pink towel falling with her hair behind the back of the chair. She is a newcomer, but Mr. Kenneth knows her name from the appointment sheet, greets her by it, and removes the towel.

"My problem," the lady says with a commendable and almost successful effort at composure, "is babyfine hair, as you can see."

"Uh-huh." Methodically, stroke by stroke, in an andante rhythm formed of almost square gestures, Mr. Kenneth combs out the lady's hair.

"I'm from Baltimore. Usually I wear a bubble."

With ritual motions, Mr. Kenneth combs up all the hair that starts above a line at the base of the scalp, and pins it to the top of the head. "You wear a bubble because it's fine, you want to make it more voluminous?"

Slowly, twenty or thirty strands at a time, Mr. Kenneth combs the back hair straight down, shifts the scissors to his left hand, and cuts a straight line. "When it's fine . . . you have to cut it bluntly . . . all these things. . . . It's easier short . . . but like all things . . . you get tired of it. . . ." The back finished, he loosens some hair from the top and repeats the ritual, working first on the rear, then on the right side, then on the left. "How's the hairdressing in Baltimore?"

"How *is* it?" The lady pauses. "We have a couple of good places. Not like here, of course."

"Uh-huh." Mr. Kenneth works very seriously, his mouth formed into a slight pout, giving equal attention to each strand of hair. Behind him, one of his assistants, a rather small young man with staring gray-green eyes (all Mr. Kenneth's assistants are smaller than he is), watches with emotions that are not to be fathomed by an outsider.

"Do you approve of permanents with this sort of babyfine chewed-up dyed hair?"

"I don't think your hair's so bad."

Ladies are now arriving to meet appointments for which Mr. Kenneth is already late—his calendar is as trustworthy as an airline timetable in a foggy winter. The second customer has finished shampoo (Mr. Kenneth works with clean, wet hair) and is seated in the chair in the next area. In a gesture of solicitude, he steps to her side and pumps the chair somewhat higher, then returns to his first.

"Now," he says, "you're going to comb it this way," and he runs his hand over her head from right to left.

"I always comb it the other way. Is that because that's the way my mother did it?"

"When you go that way, it lies flatly—nature of the hair, the way the hair grows. Comb it this way, you get more lift. I believe lift is very important."

She waves her hand over her hair. "Feels so strange."

"Oh, you'll get used to it," Mr. Kenneth says, and summons to his side a very pretty young Swedish girl in a black dress. They both stand behind the lady, and Mr. Kenneth pushes her hair. "Now, she has very fine hair," Mr. Kenneth says to the Swedish girl, "and I don't want it to look fuzzy. Get it very high *here*. I don't want any of it clinging. And if you'll do me a very large favor, before you spray it, bring her back to me, let me see it, if I want to change it . . ." The Swedish girl leads the lady away to the main salon, and Mr. Kenneth moves on.

Next is a regular customer, a lady in her thirties with light freckles and pale-blue eyes, not in the least nervous. She greets him with, "How was your trip?"

"Around the world? Very wild. All those airplanes. Waiting to get into the palaces."

Mr. Kenneth methodically, again, cuts hair, pinning up, taking a few hairs at a time, getting the line straight. Another of the young men comes by, and Mr. Kenneth speaks to him:

"Did you get to theater on time?"

"Yes, just barely. I showed her one of your hairdos—the one in *Glamour*."

"With the hair coming into the eye?" says Mr. Kenneth. "The funny picture?"

"Yes. She thought you'd be insulted because she laughed."

"Funny, that's the way she wears her hair. Remarkable that she can't see it . . ."

Yet another, an older woman; then a striking lady who could be either a model or a society belle, and turns out to be both. With semi-proprietary boldness, she interrupts Mr. Kenneth: "If you *do* have time, I've got to pose for a couple of things—you wouldn't be very impressed, it's not your sort of thing."

"What is it? Sears and Roebuck's catalogue?"

"Oh, no—I'm co-chairman of this committee, and I have to pose with my co-chairman. Fifteen Kodas."

"Oh, dear."

"I told you it wasn't your sort of thing."

Miss Daché herself, red-haired, short, not slim, important, comes down with a transparently thin model to be togged out with Cleopatra jewelry for a newspaper fashion page. "Can you do her?"

"I don't think so."

"Miss Preston herself is coming for the picture."

"It looks like a major undertaking."

The model, who has been examining her straight black hair and everything else about herself in a mirror in the next booth, says to Mr. Kenneth, "Did you say it looks mangy?"

Mr. Kenneth pauses to survey a just-released lock of hair from the head of his older customer; then, under control, replies, "No, I didn't say that. I didn't say that at all. I said 'a major undertaking.' Setting. We don't have time for that."

Miss Daché wheedles. "Miss Preston herself."

"Do it in hats," says Mr. Kenneth. "I'd rather not do it at all than do it and have it not look right."

"Of course," says Miss Daché coldly.

"Do it in two different hats," says Mr. Kenneth brightly, ruffling the hair of the customer to examine its appearance with somewhat more body. Miss Daché and the model disappear.

"My husband *adored* the way you did my hair last time, it was *such* a success."

"That's good news. . . ."

"What are they doing in Paris?"

"I don't know—yes, I do. The Cleopatra thing."

"I don't know how Cleopatra wore her hair."

"Neither do I. Oh, no, I do. Long hair. Ella Cinders . . ."

". . . In Nassau, the most *divine* place. Most marvelous golf course in the world. Most wonderful tennis. This man from Chicago bought it all up, he sells lots around it, very beautiful, very expensive. What are *you* going to do in Barbados?"

Mr. Kenneth says, wearily, "I'm going to try skin-diving."

A model parades into Mr. Kenneth's area, wearing something the management of the boutique would like to sell to some customer of the salon. Mr. Kenneth greets her, and she turns to him a face of blond impassivity. "A mute," he explains. "She can't talk."

". . . I just got back from Las Vegas," says a lady from East Orange. "All the chorus girls have long hair."

"I don't think fashion is going to be made," says Mr. Kenneth, "by what the chorus girls are wearing in Las Vegas. . . ."

Theatrical types arrive and chatter: "Terrible about Ernie. . . . No dough left at all. . . . They were such terrible gamblers. . . ."

". . . Marilyn's in town, you know."

"Yes, she was here. . . ."

"What made you come in?" says Mr. Kenneth to another suburban customer. "I'm always curious."

"Actually, it was magazine articles. . . ."

The manicurists are working on hands; the maids are sweeping; assistants, with all chairs occupied in the big room, are setting hair in Mr. Kenneth's booths, wrapping carefully combed strands around big wire-mesh rollers. He is now with a regular customer, a young lady of very considerable means and position, intelligent, eternally nervous.

"Now that we've straightened it, we'll have to curl it."

"That's what my sister does—she has it permanented and dyed and cut."

"Oh, my God—amazing she has any hair left."

"It always looks good."

"*She* must have a good hairdresser."

"Are people ever going to wear their hair in page-boy again? Nobody does today."

"I think that's fairly fortunate."

"Do you really think lemon juice works if you squeeze it on your hair and sit in the sun?"

"It sounds pretty drastic. Ought to do something."

"You're sure you're not getting it too short?"

"No, no. Yes, by your standards. No, by mine."

"Some people look so good with very long hair."

"Who?"

"All those people out in the big room."

"They're all seventeen."

"I have a friend who isn't seventeen—she's twenty-nine, and it looks marvelously."

"If you say so. No, really, I'm sure it does."

The store model returns in another outfit, escorted by a saleslady. Relenting, the model says, "Good morning, Kenneth."

"See," he comments, "she *does* talk."

"I put a dime in her," says the saleslady, and steers her out into the big room.

Escorted by the Swedish girl, the first customer returns, her hair now a great golden aura about what turn out to be excellent features. Mr. Kenneth combs out and sprays her hair himself, and the odor of the spray fills the room. "Cancer in a bottle," comments another customer. The lady from Baltimore looks at herself in the mirror with honest and surprised admiration. She says, "I wish I had a picture of this."

Mr. Kenneth says, "Oh, it looks *good.*"

"You don't have a picture of this, or a name?"

"I don't have names for hair-combs."

"Because once I get home . . ."

"Hair-combs just happen. . . ."

"For you. . . ."

"Gregory, tell Mona to come look how it's changed, will you?"

The customer says, "Well, I certainly thank you," and rises from the chair.

"Come again, when you're in New York," says Mr. Kenneth.

The nervous regular, now sitting and waiting for the man who will set her hair, has been studying the mirror. "Mr. Kenneth, may I ask you a question?"

"Yes."

"What about a bang?"

"No."

Out in the big salon, the ladies are chatting, examining themselves and their neighbors, nibbling on sandwiches catered by Robert Day-Dean's, reading books they have brought themselves or magazines from the catholic selection in the racks—*Publishers' Weekly,* the

Atlantic and the Italian *Epoca,* for example, as well as the usual ladies' and movie magazines. For them the time is passing, quickly or slowly or as usual, depending upon individual temperament. For the people who work in the salon, however, each minute is another nibble in the hide of the great enemy, The Day, which here as in a factory or in Arnold Wesker's kitchen must be lived through and discarded, taking with it some piece of oneself. The great break in occupations does not in truth come between blue collar and white collar, but between those jobs which provide their own time focus and those which trap the worker in the patterned hell of the clock-face.

For the worker in a beauty salon, the irritant routine of The Day, with its predictable cycle of crisis and relaxation, is heightened by the unpredictable piecework character of the pay. A hairdresser will receive a basic salary of, say, $100 a week, plus (at Daché) a commission of 25% on everything over $200 spent by customers for his services during the course of the week. In addition to this payment from the boss, the hairdresser receives tips, which may vary anywhere from fifty cents to five dollars per customer, though the extremes are rare. The appointment calendar may or may not be full, but it is calibrated in half-hours, each tense with the conflict between output and tip.

Much of Mr. Kenneth's manner of work is an escape from The Day, which he knows and hates. Taken into the Navy after a year at Syracuse University, he returned home as the eldest child of a divorced mother, with four younger sisters to see through adolescence; and he worked four years as a clock-bedeviled hairdresser ("fifteen hours a day," he recalls, probably with some exaggeration, "six days a week") "until my sisters were, like, eighteen or twenty." Then he went to Miami to try his luck, and hated it. Nine months later he was in New York, working at Helena Rubinstein's.

"I was bottom man on the totem pole," Mr. Kenneth says, "so I got all the discount customers—former employees of Rubinstein, fashion people, assistant beauty editors. Nobody else wanted them, because the commissions were lower. They would ask me to work magazine and newspaper stories, setting hair for photographers, and nobody else wanted that, because there were no tips. But you become a better hairdresser. You get the chance to invent things, then you come back here and bring them down for street wear, so to speak. And when I moved here, after five years at Rubinstein, I found myself with a fantastic clientele, this strangely powerful group of customers. The assistant beauty editors had become the beauty editors."

During the years at Rubinstein's, Mr. Kenneth also got in the habit of volunteering to come to the houses of certain cherished customers and brush their hair just before a major social function. He does it still, once or twice a week, and makes no charge for the service: "Then I never *have* to do it." Like everyone else who has done well in the world, he believes others should follow his tactics, and he urges his juniors to undertake newspaper and magazine dates, and to visit customers' homes. "But I suppose," he says, "they have more private life than I do."

To a degree, Mr. Kenneth has beaten The Day by making it all part of his private life. He is free of the appointment calendar; he works on each customer as long as he, of his own free will, wishes to work. Very prominent people indeed can wait while he cuts a secretary's hair; though his income is now something more than $50,-000 a year, he recalls very well how much money $15 was when he had to work for it by The Day. At the same time, he enjoys his ability to float on the levels to which his talents have taken him, the ability to make jokes with, literally, any woman in the world.

It is all a private matter: celebrity in itself means little to Mr. Kenneth, except as a source of business. Not long ago a rather formidable gray-haired lady marched up to him while he was working and called "Kenneth!" in a voice that made him jump. "Kenneth, why don't you ever visit your old high school? All our other famous graduates come back. Gordon MacRae comes back. Why don't you?"

"Then I remembered she was my old history teacher," Mr. Kenneth says. "I asked her if she wanted her hair done, but she said, no, she just wanted to be sure I would visit the old high school, like the other famous graduates. Like Gordon MacRae. I thought what a funny idea she had of fame."

This Thursday is a winter's day, at the season when many of the women who gladly put down $15 for a haircut (plus $6.50 for a shampoo and set) are off in warmer climates; and as the afternoon wears on, the crush in Mr. Kenneth's quarters diminishes. A look at the calendar shows only eighteen appointments for the whole day. Even so, everybody waits.

"Go to René," says an English lady to a customer announced as on her way to London and seeking a local hairdresser. "He'll keep you waiting, but not *quite* so long as Kenneth."

"Oh," says Mr. Kenneth, "do you go to René?"

The English lady, small, black-haired, middle-aged, will talk only about the weather. She is en route home from a month in Jamaica, and she does not josh with hairdressers. She is amused by the experience of a cut by Mr. Kenneth, who carefully refrains from telling her of any of the other English customers he has had that week. After she has gone to the big room, however, one of the American regulars asks about a titled customer then being lavishly entertained in New York.

"Goodness, yes," says Mr. Kenneth. "I've never heard of anybody who is having so many parties, breakfasts, lunches, teas, dinners, balls, given in her honor. It's almost like being the Duchess of Windsor. I had a customer yesterday who said that if she were asked to one more party for Lady B. . . ." Mr. Kenneth pauses to examine a lock of hair, and the customer finishes his sentence for him: "she'd go." Mr. Kenneth smiles, and says, "Yes, I suppose she would."

". . . I had lunch in the Modern Museum. Have you ever done that?"

"Yes," says Mr. Kenneth. "And I think it's awful."

"Did you see the Chagall windows?"

"Yes."

"I picked up a Chagall seven years ago at Parke-Bernet."

"Now, don't tell me how much you paid for it and how much it's worth today. I can't *stand* that."

"Did you see the Rembrandt at the Met? The one they paid the two million dollars for?"

"Yes, and I didn't like it much. I wish they'd bought the Fragonard, the one that went to Washington."

"We ought to have you on the Fine Arts Commission, Kenneth."

"I don't want to get on the Fine Arts Commission. I've got my own Fine Arts Commission, right here—all you lovely ladies. No, really. When I go home, every night, I write five hundred times, 'I should be grateful to spend my days the way I do.' I write it five hundred times, every day."

"The difficult thing with those sales," the lady says thoughtfully, "is that your insurance goes up."

"Not too many people have that problem," says Mr. Kenneth, and turns to an assistant. "William, while you're waiting, give it a turn here. Quite straight *here,* quite straight . . ."

There is a handsome lady from South America, a newcomer in New York from Caracas for two weeks. "Your name . . . is Kenneth. . . . I hear . . . a lot . . . about you. The best newspaper . . . in Colombia . . . *El Tiempo.* . . . They say . . . a lot . . . about you. Very good things."

"Uh-huh," says Mr. Kenneth.

"Have you . . . been . . . in South America . . . sometimes?"

"No, but I know about that newspaper."

"You know . . . in the Caribbean . . . it is very hard . . . for good combs . . ."

There is a very long-haired girl with a round face, in her twenties, somebody's secretary, as Mr. Kenneth quickly ascertains.

"Everybody thinks my hair is bad."

"Do you think so?"

"I wouldn't have worn it that way so long if I'd thought it was *that* bad."

The pinning is quickly finished, and the girl says, almost in terror, "You *are* going to cut it?"

"Yep."

The first snips produce foot-lengths of varicolored hair on the floor. "All I know," says the girl miserably, "is that you're cutting it. . . . What's *he* doing, taking notes?"

"He's working on a book on dandruff, and he's very disappointed, none of our customers has dandruff."

But to his assistant, later, Mr. Kenneth makes a point of saying,

"I like her hair; she has pretty hair," and the girl goes off cheerful for the rest of her ordeal, which includes dyeing.

There is the older lady, who hasn't been in for several weeks. "If you cut it too short, they'll say, 'Who gave you that lousy hairdo?' "

"Tell them, 'I got it at Macy's . . .' "

"Did you fire Michael, Kenneth, or did he quit?"

"What did they tell you?"

"They told me he was on an extended vacation for his health."

Mr. Kenneth laughs. "You make up your own mind."

And someone elegant comes in to kill a few minutes in a shopping day and have a cup of coffee with a friend who's in the chair. "Kenneth, I want to tell you I've had *more* compliments."

"And what a hard time you gave me. Now, you come back once a month," Mr. Kenneth says, and makes a clipping gesture.

"I will. Once a month. And anything you want to do, Kenneth. Anything. All the way."

"You always manage to make me blush," says Mr. Kenneth calmly. "Nobody else can do that."

Liquid is rolling off her friend's specially shampooed hair. "You're dripping all over the place?" Mr. Kenneth says in a kindly way. "No charge." It is the last appointment of the day.

At only a few minutes after six on this easy Thursday, Mr. Kenneth in the same andante puts on coat and gloves, and the silk scarf with a wool lining, and walks down the stairs. He talks over the day briefly with the indispensably businesslike lady who runs the desk —for Mr. Kenneth is the general manager of the salon as well as its chief hairdresser, and he is supposed to know the *Gestalt* while he cuts the hair; he used to have to read figures every night, but now he just takes them home every weekend. Mr. Kenneth gives a final, squared-off wave and a final boyish smile, and is off. Upstairs, his assistants, tied to the clock, are finishing The Day.

2

Monument to the Muses:
The Building of Lincoln Center

[This article was commissioned by *Horizon*—specifically, by editors William Harlan Hale and Eric Larrabee—for delivery in the spring of 1962 for publication in the July issue. Though Philharmonic Hall was not to open until September, the editors wished to be sure they would not be scooped on what was, inevitably, the biggest arts story of the year. As a result, the piece was already on press when the first acoustical tests were made in the hall. Because my information on this aspect of the story was necessarily incomplete, the editors decided to cut from the long manuscript the thousand words on the acoustical design of the hall. I was thereby saved considerable embarrassment when the hall opened, because I had been as convinced as the architects that the auditorium would be excellent for music, while in fact it proved a fiasco. I have restored that section, partly for the intrinsic interest of the material and partly because hubris *should* be punished. I have also opened a few other minor cuts which the editors made for reasons of economy or (ahem!) cowardice. The statistics are as of 1962. They are updated, and preliminary answers given to a few of the questions raised in the article, in an afterword.]

LINCOLN CENTER for the Performing Arts, which will declare itself open in September with a series of gala performances in a new 2,600-seat concert hall, is the first effort the business community has ever made to play Medici on the American scene. A vast enterprise, covering fourteen acres of land previously occupied by tenement housing on the West Side of Manhattan, the Center when completed, probably in 1967, will contain permanent homes for the New York Philharmonic, the Metropolitan Opera, and the Juilliard School of Music, as well as a repertory theater, a 2,800-seat ballet theater, a library, a museum and a park with an outdoor bandstand. The total cost of the physical facilities will be at least $132 million and perhaps more than $140 million; and another $10 million will be placed in "a fund for education and artistic advancement," to give the Center itself some

15

role beyond that of landlord. Contributions from federal, state and local governments will make up $40 million of the total, assuming nothing goes wrong at the last minute at City Hall; the rest will have been raised (the Center is still more than $25 million short) from foundations, corporations, private individuals, and in one dramatic instance of foreign contribution, from the West German government.

No home for public spectacles has been built on so grand a scale since the fall of the Roman Empire. The enormous job of organizing, sustaining and directing this effort has brought together, at meetings held at least every other week for the past seven years, a remarkable assemblage of New York corporate and financial executives—among them, Clarence Francis, former chairman of General Foods Corporation; Arthur A. Houghton, Jr., president of Steuben Glass; C. D. Jackson, vice president of Time Incorporated; Devereux Josephs, former chairman of New York Life Insurance Company; David Keiser, chairman of North American Sugar; and, as chairman and presiding mover and shaker of Lincoln Center, John D. Rockefeller III. Committees of advisers have proliferated below this golden Board, but the Grand Design comes almost exclusively from businessmen and their lawyers. Neither artists nor their traditional patrons, the hereditary landholders, have been represented at the moments of major decision; one looks in vain on the Board for the great New York *rentier* families, Astor, Goelet, Vanderbilt, Whitney, *et al.,* who once were the uncontested custodians of culture. There is a philosophy here—even if it does not have much to do with art— as well as a set of buildings. And behind both philosophy and buildings lies a remarkable piece of social history.

The genesis of Lincoln Center can be traced to 1928, when Otto Kahn of the Metropolitan Opera went to John D. Rockefeller and his son, and asked them for $2 million to pay for a grand plaza to stand in front of the new opera house he planned to build in the block bounded by Forty-ninth and Fiftieth Streets, Fifth and Sixth Avenues. Having brought Rockefeller into this area, which is now Rockefeller Center, Kahn's new opera house vanished into the gathering gloom of the Depression. The site intended for the opera house became the RCA Building. For some years, the Rockefellers kept a candle in the window for the Met, holding open the land on which the Eastern Air Lines building now stands. By the mid-1930s it became obvious that the Met had no future but bankruptcy and reorganization, and would be lucky to hold onto its unsatisfactory 1887-vintage opera house below Times Square; and all plans were abandoned.

But a new opera house is the grandest of building projects, and people bitten by this vision are liable to recurring seizures in which they see sketches, grand foyers, stage equipment, opening nights. Wallace Harrison, then a tall young architect who had begun to move in Rockefeller circles, now a big, raw-boned, almost Lincolnesque senior statesman of architecture with the United Nations as well as Rockefeller Center behind him, kept in a place where he could easily get at them the preliminary sketches he had made for Otto Kahn's opera house. And the Rockefeller family was still interested in a center for the arts, despite the agony associated with the first non-arts Center ("Nobody will ever know what that place cost the old man," Harrison said recently; "he sold Standard Oil at two dollars a share to pay for it"). While Rockefeller Center was in the planning stages, the family had picked up a good deal of land directly to the north. This location was now seen, especially by John D., Jr.,'s son Nelson, as the ideal place for an arts center, with opera house, concert hall, costume museum and (the one structure that was actually built) a museum of modern art. "I remember," says Harrison's associate Max Abramovitz, "all the arguments about traffic flow, arcading streets, and so forth—all the things that have come up again recently."

In the changed political climate of the late 1930s, however, this sort of complex could be built only with government cooperation, which at first seemed easy enough. The Met was no longer a wholly private enterprise; the boxholders who had previously owned the house had sold out to a new Metropolitan Opera Association specially chartered by the state legislature. And La Guardia, whom former ushers of the house can remember sneaking in to catch an act of an opera between other matters, was the closest New York has ever come to a musician as mayor. "It was touchy," says Charles M. Spofford, a partner in the Wall Street law firm of Davis, Polk, Wardwell, Sunderland and Kiendl, who was then a freshman member of the Met board and is now Vice-Chairman of Lincoln Center. "The Association was new. Opera has a reputation as an aristocratic affair, not popular in the 1930s. But La Guardia wanted to leave New York two legacies, an airfield and a music center, a home for the opera. We had talks with him about a new Met and a hall for an associated orchestra, hopefully the Philharmonic. In 1939 we had several meetings in the summer City Hall out at the World's Fair."

This project required, however, the help of Robert Moses, then parks commissioner and general supervisor of public improvements. Moses, though a lifelong Republican, was at that time bitter about all the rich so-and-sos who were trying to block public-works projects. He took the position that opera was a dying art form being kept alive for the social amusement of people with whom La Guardia should not associate. "I think the Mayor buried the plan," Moses said recently at his offices on the World's Fair site, striding about hugely and speaking with his typical flooding energy, "because of some comments I made about the boxholders."

Spofford, too, now had the bug, and when he returned from the war and was elected president of the Metropolitan Opera Association he kept before his board the prospect of a new theater. C. D. Jackson of Time Inc., who had just joined the board, was made chairman of a New House Committee. The majority of the board was against the idea ("a combination of nostalgia and conservatism," Jackson says; " 'I love every inch of the gold curtain and I want to be buried in it when I die' "). But an engineering survey, on which the Met spent $25,000, convinced the board that the old house could not be brought up to modern standards of comfort or theatrical efficiency, and Spofford and Jackson were authorized to try.

Spofford's first idea was a site inside Central Park at Columbus Circle, and in 1947 he took the proposal to City Hall, then occupied by William O'Dwyer, with whom he had served in Italy. O'Dwyer was interested, but inevitably referred the plan to Moses, who was now involved with city planning and slum clearance and no longer opposed to public help for a new Met—though not at the expense of park land. "We convinced him," Spofford recalls, "that this could be a vehicle for enabling opera and some of these other institutions to find their way to the community, like the libraries and the museums—provided we could do it in conjunction with the city. Moses said, 'Let's see if we can't work it into Title I' [the Federal Housing Authority slum-clearance program, through which federal funds can be used to help cities condemn and purchase land for urban renewal]. We got on Moses' Title I mailing list."

While Moses was searching for a slum suitable for an opera house, Spofford and Jackson examined the real-estate market. "We looked at the Third Avenue car barns," Spofford recalls. (This site, in the east Sixties, now holds Manhattan House, a giant luxury apartment building.) "There was a scheme to put us on the tail of the Seagram Building. Somebody wanted us to go to the top end of the park at One Hundred Tenth Street. But when you began seeing where the plots of land were, you knew the only way you could do it was Title I."

Moses' first proposal was a piece of land just south of Washington Square, where the middle-income apartments of Washington Square Village now stand. Jackson explored this idea thoroughly, had traffic studies done and questionnaires distributed to find out whether people could or would get to a Met on that site. It was rejected finally as "too tricky, too expensive, too remote." Moses said the other day that one of the directors of the Met had told him, "Nobody goes down there any more."

Presently, in 1951, Moses became involved in two capacities—as head of the Slum Clearance Commission and the Triborough Bridge Authority—with the Columbus Circle site on which the Coliseum now stands. Again the Met, like the boll weevil, went looking for a home—on what was, in fact, the perfect site, both for the opera and for the city. Now it was Moses' turn to abandon the idea, for reasons that have never been fully explained. Moses says, "There was never any chance of an opera house at the Coliseum. Nobody really took it seriously." Jackson did. "I took it seriously enough to get half a million dollars out of John D. Rockefeller, Jr., as a pledge to buy the land." But Moses was not prepared to go along, and let them know it, in March, 1952, through the delicate device of a statement to the press.

Once the Coliseum plans were completed, Robert Moses turned his mind to the half-mile-long site north and west of it, centering on the spot where Broadway and Columbus Avenue cross to form Lincoln Square. Here, in this run-down, mainly Spanish-speaking neighborhood, he would bring about a masterpiece of slum clearance. Moses called Joseph Hartfield—senior partner of the Wall Street law firm of White & Case and a powerhouse on the Met's board—and offered him a site in the middle of the area that the city was planning to condemn and purchase. Max Abramovitz, a gentle and straightforward architect who is Wallace Harrison's partner, remembers that he, Spofford, and Hartfield rode the subway up to Sixty-sixth Street to look around: "Somebody said, 'What a hell of a neighborhood,'" Abramovitz recalls, "but here was all that land for virtually nothing."

With rising acrimony, the Met Board debated Moses' offer for more than a year. The site was in many ways unsatisfactory—an intersection that had a tendency to jam up even without an opera house on one corner, convenient to four bus lines but only one subway, surrounded by rather unappetizing structures. Then, in April, 1955, Moses got on the very top of the high horse he keeps for such emergencies and told Spofford this was the Met's "last chance"—it was Sixty-fourth Street or nothing, and the Met had better be ready with a million and a half dollars to buy the land by July first, or it would be nothing.

Spofford and Irving Olds, also a White & Case partner as well as chairman of United States Steel, set to work raising money. Wallace Harrison again began to make drawings for an opera house, and to sit in on meetings with members of the Met Board and Moses. "We were riding back from one of those meetings in a car," Spofford recalls, "and Wally Harrison said to me, 'You ought to get hold of Arthur Houghton, and bring the Philharmonic in.'"

Of all the major symphony orchestras in the United States, the New York Philharmonic alone played in a hall that was owned by a profit-making corporation. Because Carnegie Hall also contained profitable studios, its owners could afford to lease the auditorium for a relatively low rental—indeed, when the orchestra moves into the new Philharmonic Hall in Lincoln Center its rental costs will rise at least $40,000 a year over what they were in the last years of private ownership of Carnegie. The orchestra's lease, which ran from year to year with no provision for cancellation except on three years' notice, gave the Philharmonic an illusory sense of security. The land occupied by Carnegie Hall, running along Seventh Avenue from Fifty-seventh to Fifty-sixth Streets, just south of Central Park, was prime real estate, and could be sold for development (or even for a parking lot) at a price greater than the capitalized annual earnings of the building. Yet, despite some ominous rumblings from within the corporation that owned Carnegie, the board of the Philharmonic-Symphony Society refused to worry. In 1950, when C. D. Jackson called Floyd Blair, then president of the Society, to ask whether the orchestra might be interested in joining the Met at Washington Square South, Blair could say no without even telling his board about the call.

In 1955, the Philharmonic was served with its three-year eviction notice, but given an option to buy the building if its board so desired. "They were very fair," says David Keiser, president of North American Sugar and of the Philharmonic-Symphony Society, a small, friendly man with a perpetual squint, who was almost forcibly removed from the Juilliard School by his parents many years ago because he was needed in the family business. (William Schuman, now president of Lincoln Center and formerly president of Juilliard, says Keiser was the only student in the history of the school "who had to leave for reasons of affluence.") "The owners of Carnegie gave us a long time. Even when they sold the hall to a developer, it was on a deal whereby the Philharmonic could purchase from him within six months, if we changed our mind."

Fortunately, the real-estate deal fell through—and Carnegie Hall was eventually saved from the knackers by a special act of the state legislature. For the Philharmonic had decided, quite early in the game, that it did not wish to buy Carnegie Hall. "The price asked," says Arthur Houghton of Steuben Glass, chairman of the Philharmonic, and occupant of Manhattan's last really enormous town house —"was quite substantial. The building was many years old, and quite frankly not architecturally distinguished. And acoustically it was *not* one of the great halls. We decided to look into the possibilities of building our own concert hall. We didn't have the resources to buy a prime corner site, but perhaps we could buy something in the center of a block, where we'd have to build only one façade. I asked Wally Harrison to come over. He built *this* building"—the reference is to the green Corning tower at Fifty-sixth Street and Fifth Avenue, where Houghton has his offices—"and he built our Corning Glass Center upstate. I asked Wally to make preliminary drawings and estimates. While I was talking, a peculiar expression passed over his face. He said the Met had just approached him for a similar job, and perhaps I should get in touch with Chuck Spofford, see if we couldn't do something together—perhaps under one roof."

Spofford and Houghton dined together at the Knickerbocker Club, and quickly decided they needed a Rockefeller.

The problem was: *Which* Rockefeller? John D., Jr., was too old, and not well; Nelson already had political plans, and had been around the barn once too often with the Met, anyway; David was too busy working (quite successfully) to fill the giant shoes Winthrop Aldrich had left at the Chase Bank; Laurance was totally occupied building the American electronics industry and making embarrassingly large profits. Spofford's best bet, clearly, was John D. III, the eldest brother, a spare, modest, cautious man with bright blue eyes, who looks like photographs of his grandfather and who shares his grandfather's complete lack of interest in music. Spofford waited, and approached Rockefeller in Pennsylvania, at a conference on foreign relations in which they were both participants.

On his return to New York, Rockefeller called twenty or thirty people whom he knew to be interested in music, and asked them whether they thought the city needed a new opera house and a new concert hall. Receiving their encouragement, he agreed to head what came to be called the Exploratory Committee for a Musical Arts Center. "He is the kind of guy who does one major thing at a time," says C. D. Jackson. "He accepted *moral* responsibility for Lincoln Center."

Both the Met and the Philharmonic would have settled for new halls for themselves, but as Rockefeller consulted more people he saw the possibility of something much grander. Lincoln Kirstein, director of the New York City Ballet, was an old friend, and from Kirstein Rockefeller knew that there was no adequate theater for the dance in New York. Acquaintances interested in the theater had complained to him about the fact that New York, unlike the great European capitals, had no repertory theater. And by temperament and family tradition, Rockefeller felt that the reviving Center project should be linked to educational purposes as well. "We began," Houghton recalls, "by talking about two buildings or one big building. Suddenly the thinking got explosive."

In early fall, 1955, the committee—which now included, among others, Kirstein, Olds, Harrison and Devereux Josephs of the New York Life Insurance Company—began a schedule of luncheon meetings every other Monday, fair weather or foul, in all seasons. "We asked ourselves," Rockefeller remembers, "Do you stop with music? Or do you do all the performing arts? Or all the other arts as well? Then we asked, Do you bring education into the field? One of the factors was this need for bridging the gap between the performing groups and the teaching groups. After we had talked over all these matters for some time, I made a recommendation, a formal motion, at one of our meetings, that we do just the performing arts, and that education should be brought in. I remember Irving Olds said—it pleased me tremendously—'John, I thought we'd already all agreed on that.'"

Columbia University had recently announced its plans for an arts center. Rockefeller approached Columbia and also its neighbor on Morningside Heights, the busy Juilliard School of Music. "Over the period of the conversations," Rockefeller recalls, "Juilliard got more and more enthusiastic about joining Lincoln Center, Columbia less and less." Eventually an agreement was reached with Juilliard whereby the school will institute, with money from Lincoln Center's special fund, a full-scale theater program. "The other institutions," says William Schuman, the president of Juilliard who has since become president of Lincoln Center itself, "moved because they needed new buildings. We're moving because we believe in the idea."

Three institutions were now lined up, and Rockefeller was certain it would be only a matter of time before Kirstein's ballet company made a fourth. There remained the problem of the repertory theater, later solved by the formation of a new institution under Robert Whitehead of Producers' Theater, who received a $500,000 grant from the education fund to set up shop. The theater, named after Mrs. Vivian Beaumont Allen, the May Company heiress who gave $3 million toward its construction, will seat 1,100 in a wide, shallow auditorium. It has been designed to Whitehead's specifications ("nobody else will be able to use it") as the perfect setting for something that he says "must become an art theater—in the sense that the Brecht Theater became that, or the Théâtre National Populaire in Paris, at its best." Finally, to fill the other building the committee projected, the New York Public Library agreed to move its Music Division from the central building on Forty-second Street to a new home amid the sounds of Lincoln Center, in a museum of the performing arts.

By June, 1956, when the exploratory committee went out of business and Lincoln Center was incorporated, most of the major decisions had been made. The original Sixty-second-to-Sixty-fourth Street site had been expanded to Sixty-fifth. (Later, when the architects announced that it would be impossible to cram all the buildings into eleven acres, the Center acquired a piece of the next block to the north, for Juilliard. "John Rockefeller was in Asia somewhere when we found we had to have that land to the north," Houghton remembers, "and Bob Moses had said he'd never give us another foot. But he came up for the evening and had a few drinks, and at the end of the night we had the land.") The approximate size and function of every building was known, and the committee was ready to begin making definite arrangements. Lawsuits hung in the air, because Fordham, a Jesuit university, was to take up a piece of Moses' Lincoln Square Urban Renewal project and the existing tenants were invoking constitutional separation of church and state. The federal authorities were feuding with the city authorities. The New York Board of Estimate was delaying its approval. But there was going to be a Lincoln Center; the time had come to call in the technicians.

Oddly enough, nobody at any time seems to have questioned the central conception. "Everybody agreed," Spofford says, "that it was not only a good, it was a great idea." Nobody suggested that an arts center might be regarded as just a touch provincial for a cosmopolitan city—that in London, which has the world's busiest (though not the world's most interesting) concert, opera and ballet season, the halls are so far apart it takes a good taxi ride to get from one to any other; that even in Vienna, which has built a tourist trade on its residents' alleged musicality, the Staatsoper and the Konzertsaalen are separated by the city's best hotel and some blocks of Ringstrasse. Jane Jacobs' worry about "decontaminating" a city's culture, isolating it away from the real life of the place, was still some years in the future—though the Finnish architect Alvar Aalto, who was asked to contribute an idea for a site plan, felt something of the sort: he shocked Harrison, who is still disturbed when he thinks of it, by a drawing which showed Lincoln Center as "a closed fortress against New York."

The members of the exploratory committee found it only natural to assume that the whole of Lincoln Center would be bigger than the sum of its parts. They shared what Houghton calls "a feeling of exciting dedication," in an atmosphere far different from the dreary wrangling that characterizes the boards of the institutions themselves, and he found an analogy: "It's the kind of opportunity the Lenox and Astor Libraries and the Tilden Trust took when they joined together to build the New York Public Library." Raising money for all of the institutions together was clearly easier than raising it for any of them separately. To the Center's executive vice-president, Edgar B. Young, with years of experience at the Rockefeller Foundation, here was a chance to break the traditional patterns of philanthropy, the insistence on medicine and education, and lead both foundations and corporations to the idea of contributing to the performing arts. But there was never any guarantee that this excitement would persist. Moses, soured by the long delays, puts his finger on a sore spot when he says, "What is the relationship between Lincoln Center and its constituent elements? That's never been decided."

The problem has turned out to be a real one. It rose to the surface this past February [1962] with the announcement of seven nineteenth-century-style potpourri programs at benefit prices to launch Philharmonic Hall in September. Harold Schonberg, music critic of the *New York Times,* a supporter of Lincoln Center, expressed in print "the sinking feeling of a lover discovering that his beloved has false teeth." Rockefeller was disturbed. "Lincoln Center got jumped," he said, "for programs we didn't choose. One of the fundamentals is that the constituents are independent entities responsible for their own artistic programs and financing." Not until five years after the incorporation of Lincoln Center did the committee begin serious consideration of exactly *how* the whole was to be made larger than the sum of its parts.

Meanwhile, the show was on the road.

During the spring of 1956, members of the committee, including Rockefeller himself, traveled to Europe to visit concert halls, theaters and opera houses, new and old, and to talk over problems with European managers, architects and artists. In October of that year, theater experts, acoustical consultants and architects were assembled in New York for the first of several grand conferences. Among the architects were all those later assigned to buildings—Harrison (Metropolitan Opera; chairman of the group), his partner Abramovitz (Philharmonic Hall), Pietro Belluschi (Juilliard), the late Eero Saarinen (repertory theater), Skidmore, Owings & Merrill (library-museum), and Philip Johnson (dance theater, later called New York

State Theater when the state put up the money)—plus Alvar Aalto of Finland, Sven Markelius of Sweden, Marcel Breuer and Henry Shepley. They agreed on the proposition that the site was too small, and on very little else.

The architects' arguments were distressing to Rockefeller, who believes in consensus. "The major influence in this whole thing," says Harrison, "has been John's view of perfection." The committee had also felt a need to pick up a wholly outside opinion, from an organization that would not be involved in operating or building Lincoln Center. Money was appropriated for a full-scale "feasibility study," and the Philadelphia firm of Day & Zimmermann, consulting engineers, was assigned to the job.

With the Day & Zimmermann report, submitted on the last day of 1956, a shadow of innocence and naïveté falls across the prospects of Lincoln Center. Day & Zimmermann were basically builders of lofts, warehouses and factories; and except in the case of the opera house, they had to operate virtually without instructions from their clients. They examined Carnegie Hall and existing theaters of approximately the seating capacity suggested for the other Lincoln Center halls, calculated the number of cubic feet occupied by each such building, and then applied a price of $2 per cubic foot, which was about what it cost to build stripped-down movie theaters in the Philadelphia area in 1956. ("They forgot about air conditioning," says Abramovitz, "about the problem of isolating noises, about room for the people in back, offices, rehearsal rooms . . .") They came up with a figure of $55 million for the land, the garage, the service plant and all the buildings.

Day & Zimmermann thought the new concert hall could be built for $4 million (Abramovitz has brought it in at $15.4 million); the dance theater for $5 million (estimates, in May, are $18.3); the education plant at $5.5 million (now $16.2 million); the repertory theater and library-museum at $2.9 and $2.8 million (now $8.2 and $7 million, respectively). Only with the Met, which Day & Zimmermann estimated at $23.6 million (now $35.4 million), did the Philadelphians get as high as half the now-projected costs. A $55 million estimate has risen to $132 million, and even the latter figure is still subject to possible upward revision, though only over Edgar Young's dead body.

The same astonishing blend of ignorance and optimism flavors the sections of the report that calculated operating expenses and revenues. The Met was assured, for example, that Lincoln Center could supply for $263,000 the maintenance services which cost almost $700,000 at the old house. Projected rental charges on Philharmonic Hall were calculated on the assumption that the house would be used 470 times a year, though Carnegie had been rented only 310 times the season before. Proposing an operetta season in the new opera house to provide summer rentals, Day & Zimmermann suggested as a production that might fill the house for fourteen weeks the operetta *Rosalinda* by "J. Straus"—obviously unconscious of the fact that *Rosalinda* was merely an Anglicization of *Die Fledermaus,* which the Met had been playing throughout the previous season.

At a distance of five years, it is impossible to understand how the directors of Lincoln Center could have accepted the Day & Zimmermann report as their blueprint—but they did. The fund-raising target was set at $75 million, which Day & Zimmermann had recommended, to allow $19 million for contingencies and the education fund. And later, when the arguments began to arise about the size of the halls and their seating capacity, the Day & Zimmermann operating figures were always there as evidence that the Met and the Philharmonic could be virtually self-sustaining in Lincoln Center.

The Lincoln Center now in construction is bigger and better than anything contemplated by Day & Zimmermann, and the board has managed to keep its patience through all the increases in costs. ("It always happens," says Rockefeller rather sadly, commenting on the quadrupled cost of Philharmonic Hall. "It happened with this little Asia House we built, too. It's like in a family. Somebody's very sick, you know he isn't going to recover, but when he dies it's a terrible shock.") At every turn, the architects have been able to appeal to the sponsors' pride in what they are building. When the architects insisted, the board bought more land. When they pointed out that Day & Zimmermann had contemplated nothing more than the reproduction of the cramped existing facilities, the board authorized bigger buildings. ("I told them," Abramovitz recalls, "that I felt it was a shame that in the richest country in the world people should have to go out into the street for a smoke during intermission.") When the architects adjusted the scale of the buildings for aesthetic reasons, the board authorized an increase in the size of Philharmonic Hall after the foundations for a smaller structure had already been completed.

About half of Day & Zimmermann's amazing underestimate can be accounted for simply by the increased ambitiousness of the project. "It would have been disastrous," says Houghton, "to do anything less than what is magnificent." At every turn, until Edgar Young insulated them from the Board, the architects were able to argue that penny-pinching *here* would ruin the idea. Month after month the architects came to the building committee with improvements; and protesting they would ne'er consent—they were businessmen, practical people, they had to keep an eye on what was financially feasible—the committee quickly consented.

"Imagine six architects, all working on a single site—six architects, compromising!" Thus Philip Johnson, architect (with Ludwig Mies van der Rohe) of the Seagram Building, where he keeps his office. "We each imposed it on ourselves. We could have done a World's Fair, each man his own building, without regard for the others, but it wouldn't have been good for the project."

Nonetheless, beyond agreeing to hold the same cornice height, to use facings of light beige travertine from Italy, to keep first stories to the same height in all buildings, and to have austere exteriors planned around plain shafts of columns, the architects found it hard to make a unanimous recommendation to the building committee. Even when expanded, the site was awkward. Moses had set his little park and band shell immovably in the southwest corner, making an L-shaped pattern of buildings, which none of the architects wanted. Not long after the European architects departed, Harrison sold the committee on his original plan of a central plaza at Columbus Avenue, with the Met behind it and two other large buildings at either side. But there was still continuing debate over where each of the buildings should be spotted.

Meanwhile, 1957 disappeared into history and 1958 wore on with victorious lawsuits, fund-raising, purchases of land, careful relocation of tenants, and—on July 21—the first demolitions on the site. The Philharmonic was supposed to be ready first, but it could not be built on the southeast corner, because a large warehouse still stood there, immune to proceedings under the slum-clearance laws and demanding a separately negotiated purchase. (The warehouse was owned by Joseph P. Kennedy, who exacted a price more than double the assessed valuation.) Presently, the northeast corner of the site was clear of buildings, and it became obvious that this location, always plausible, was where the Philharmonic had to be.

For the architects, the Lincoln Center buildings have been a staggering job. Harrison has given the bulk of his time to the opera house for more than six years, and the drawings are still far from finished. Moses says, "I used to drop by Harrison's place at West Hills, after a party, at one in the morning, on Saturdays, and I'd find Wally and Wong, who ran the drafting room, down in the root cellar, making drawings and looking at models."

The Philharmonic's requirements, as Abramovitz recalls them, were simple in the extreme: "They wanted a hall at least as good as Carnegie, and three thousand seats." Then Abramovitz's acoustical consultants—Leo Beranek of the M.I.T.-based firm of Bolt, Beranek & Newman, aided by Hope Bagenal of England—told him the two desires were incompatible. Given modern fire laws and modern comfort—the need to place seats at least three feet apart back-to-back and to make them wider, "to take care of M'sieu's knees and Madame's behind," as Edgar Young puts it—the acoustical consultants were not prepared to recommend a hall larger than 2,400 seats.

"The only really successful hall built in this century is Symphony Hall in Boston, completed in 1900," says Leo Beranek, a small man with graying hair, wearing a gray suit and a black-and-gray tie, and exhibiting a mild manner quite different from what one would expect after hearing architects talk about his dogmatism. "It was a copy of the old Boston Music Hall, only it was forty feet longer. But this kind of court ballroom architecture has gone out. We decided to try and find out on a reliable statistical basis what made some halls good and some halls bad. We studied about sixty halls, here and abroad, halls used by good orchestras, halls in which enough musicians had performed so we could get enough comments. The first thing we found was that running through the whole interview system was a general negativeness toward large halls. Then we used modern acoustical measuring tools to find out what made halls sound good or bad."

Beranek found three highly significant factors dividing the good from the bad—acoustical intimacy, reverberation time at different frequencies, and loudness. Acoustical intimacy is the feeling of music in the air, rather than just music from the stage. Beranek believes it is created by having a very short time lag between the direct sound wave that comes to the listener from the stage and the first reflected sound wave that comes to him from the walls or ceiling. Thus, in many halls, seats somewhat to the side are better than seats in the center. The ideal plan is a narrow hall, like Symphony Hall in Boston. Failing a narrow hall, acoustical intimacy demands sound reflectors hanging down from the ceiling; the new Philharmonic Hall will have 106 such "clouds" floating over the audience.

Reverberation time is the length of time before a sound made on the stage dies away to inaudibility in the hall. Beranek's statistical analysis of the opinions of conductors, performers and critics tells him that there is no one ideal reverberation time—opera and symphony are best at different timings, and baroque, classical and romantic orchestral music each have their own ideal reverberation time. After listening to Beranek's presentation and consulting its own list of performing artists, the Philharmonic building committee—Houghton, Keiser, George Judd, the manager (after Judd's death, Carlos Mosely) and Leonard Bernstein—requested a reverberation time of at least 1.8 seconds. In Beranek's analysis, "lively" sound is a function of the volume of air in the hall divided by the total acoustical absorption of everything else in the hall. People are the worst sound absorbers: for each extra member of the audience, occupying perhaps six cubic feet of air space in his person, acoustic considerations demand several hundred additional cubic feet of space in the hall.

Loudness is simply a function of how far away from the source of the sound the listener has to sit; anything much more than 200 feet away, Beranek argues, will give the listener the feeling that the music is being played in the next county.

Adding it all together, Beranek told Abramovitz that interior dimensions of 750,000 cubic feet, with an audience of 2,400, was as far as he could go in safety. Several years of argument back and forth —every time Beranek disapproved an idea, Abramovitz would call Hope Bagenal in England, only to hear the old man say softly, "Oh, Max, don't do it; I've done it, and it was awful"—pushed Beranek only to 850,000 cubic feet and 2,600 bodies. "I would push him until I saw he was afraid," Abramovitz remembers. "I never push a consultant beyond the point of fear." Beranek confirms the recollection: "Max was always watching my face," he says, "even more than he was listening to what I said."

Abramovitz learned from Beranek that the acoustics he had studied years before was all wrong, that a fan-shaped auditorium, which the 1930s had regarded as ideal, failed to reflect sounds back to the listener in the center and thus lost "acoustic intimacy." But Beranek adopted certain of Abramovitz's ideas: that sight lines were important acoustically ("if you can see, you start off with the possibility of good sound") and that distance from the stage was crucial in a big hall. From these central conceptions, Abramovitz developed a number of designs, and did plaster models to see how they would look. "I started with a repeat of Carnegie, improving sight lines. Then an amphitheater. Then one big balcony. Then four or five shallow balconies, like Radio City. Then I realized there was something to these rectangular halls. Then Karajan suggested a pattern like the Santa Cecelia in Rome, with the audience behind the stage. I began asking conductors how they would feel about balconies behind the stage, but most of them didn't like it. Finally I evolved the step-down along the sides." The finished hall has three shallow balconies, each of them extending along the sides in a descending slope, so that the front of the first "balcony" is on a level with the floor of the parquet. The surfaces of the interior walls, and the sides of the balconies, are concrete, for sound-reflecting reasons—Abramovitz at one point wanted wood, but Beranek would allow only thicker wood than the budget would tolerate.

Everything about Philharmonic Hall had to be cleared with Beranek; and the other architects, watching the complications Beranek created in Abramovitz's designs, vowed they would have none of it. Acoustics is not an exact science; different consultants go in different directions; some of Beranek's apparently most precise formulations work only after some extra curves have been fitted to the data—Philadelphia's Academy of Music, for example, crams about 3,000 people into a hall of only 550,000 cubic feet, without great losses in the liveliness of the sound. Johnson, the free spirit of the group (perhaps the free spirit of New York), went to Denmark and got an acoustical consultant who would approve the "baroque theater," with balconies disguised as antique boxes one row deep all along the walls, which he and George Balanchine wanted for the dance. Harrison has worked with Beranek, who insists on a canopy coming out over the opera audience just above the top of the proscenium arch, to reflect sound immediately into the orchestra seats; and with Danes, and with Germans, and with a man at Bell Labs who has a machine which, in theory, can simulate the sound of a hall from architectural descriptions. But there is no escape from the acoustics engineer: the three big buildings are for musical entertainment, and the first question, even before appearance, must be how the music will sound.

The problems the acoustical consultants set the architects were as nothing to the problems they set for the directors of Lincoln Center. The two original constituents, the Philharmonic and the Met, are both sellout attractions these days, but they are both on the ragged edge financially because their necessary expenses are so great. Both institutions required considerably larger seating capacity if they were ever to hope for escape from large annual deficits. In the end, however, despite what Spofford describes as "quite a hue and cry within the boards," Lincoln Center had to be governed by Rockefeller's "view of perfection."

This "orientation to quality," as Edgar Young describes it, will leave the performing institutions with leases that must cover maintenance costs on luxurious buildings, and seating capacity inadequate to meet the bills unless seats can be sold at substantially higher prices, which nobody wants to see. Assuming that the New York City Center winds up in the New York State Theater, which both Rockefeller and Moses insist must happen, the total additional subsidy required to operate the four performing institutions will run around $3 million a year.

But the decision to build for quality, even at the risk of bankruptcy, is of a piece with the original decision to build a Center. This grand union of the performing arts would, it was argued, create a new pattern of charitable contribution in the United States, elevating the performing arts to a status beside medicine, museums and education in the pipe rolls of the kings of industry. In the end the leaders of Lincoln Center again put their trust in Business: It would provide. "These men of affairs," says William Schuman admiringly, "are basically men of faith."

In May, 1959, Lincoln Kirstein resigned as a director. Lincoln Center, he said, is nothing more than "a question of clean facilities. I was led to believe it was a heroic, idealistic effort, and it turns out to be a real-estate scheme. I'm not interested in real estate."

Kirstein believes Lincoln Center has priced out of his reach the theater that was being built for his New York City Ballet; and he finds it scandalous that a committee willing to approve expensive enlargements of buildings should send him begging to the state and the city for the $400,000 annual subsidy he would need to operate in the New York State Theater. "There's no generosity anywhere here," he says, "no real patronage." Kirstein wonders what Lincoln Center expects to do with the New York State Theater, which will have an interior cubic volume almost exactly as large as that of the old Metropolitan Opera, and will thus be much too big for the kind of attraction (Old Vic, D'Oyly Carte, Viennese operetta, etc.) Reginald Allen, the Center's executive director, has talked about putting on that stage. (Philip Johnson, rather cynically, agrees: "The whole trick in designing this theater," he says, "is to make it look full when it's two-thirds empty. I don't have the vaguest notion what they can use it for; the last theater this size in New York had to be torn down because it was always vacant.") Kirstein feels he has been asked to lead the City Center to the New York State Theater on terms that would force the opera and ballet companies to play for a sellout every night. "I'm not interested in normal operations," Kirstein says. "I'm interested in surplus. The distinction of an institution lies in how wasteful it is, wasteful in ideas, talent, art." Kirstein foresees a Lincoln Center in which the constituents, struggling annually against horrifying deficits, dare not risk a new opera, a new play, a new idea.

Of all the people who have been involved in the direction of Lincoln Center, two alone have given their whole lives to the arts: one is Kirstein and the other is William Schuman, the composer who became president of the Center in 1962. Schuman's view of the Center is that it will be "a dynamic and constructive force in the arts." Obviously, these two men hear different drummers.

Cut away from their old roots, Schuman expects the constituents will have to develop new habits. "Lincoln Center will sponsor projects to strengthen the constituents and bring other activities into the Center. We will educate the public to new works, whether they prove provocative or provoking. We will sponsor the first major American festival of international scope, music, opera, choral, dance, theater and film. There will be a Lincoln Center Teachers' Institute. We will bring to the Center every summer four to six hundred teachers, who will come a minimum of two summers, perhaps three, the teachers of speech to act under a Harold Clurman, the pianists to study with a Rosina Lhevinne or a Beveridge Webster, the teachers of dance to do ballets under a Balanchine, a Tudor, a Limón. The core of Lincoln Center will be the fund for education and artistic advancement, which will require continuous fund-raising, to establish a situation where we don't have a hand-to-mouth existence. But the money will be there."

Maybe so. The odds against Schuman and the Center are high, but they are not prohibitive. The shining existence of this monument to a belief in Culture may indeed draw new foundation and corporate contributors to the performing arts, on a continuing basis. Failing adequate private support, Lincoln Center will be able to make a stronger case than any single institution for city or state or federal subsidy—in fact, federal subsidy has been much in the minds and the mouths of the directors of Lincoln Center for the past eighteen months. ("What was once a dirty word," C. D. Jackson says, "is now a thoughtful proposition.") Finally, Lincoln Center has something going for it which cannot be weighed in any known balance—the excitement of new halls. Even in an age when rockets aim for the moon, there is for anyone at all sensitive to these matters a great thrill, a leap of the heart, at the first sight of the mastery of space represented by a large concert hall or opera house. Perhaps this thrill will act upon creative artists, performing artists and audiences with such power that all merely practical considerations will triumphantly be swept aside.

The future is, as always, in the hands of the artists. It may be twenty or thirty years from now before New York will know whether or not to thank the powerful, dedicated, oddly impractical businessmen who have created for their city this monument to their respectful, distant and refreshingly innocent confidence in Art. Lincoln Center, as the businessmen planned it, has no built-in aesthetic purpose. The artists may find one.

[It is hard today to remember a time when there was no Lincoln Center: whatever else has happened, the place has become an inevitable focus in the lives of those of us who put any amount of time into the performing arts. I make at least sixty trips a year there. Though this piece still seems to me about right in its attitudes and in the questions it asks, the fact is that the perspective from which it was written has been irrevocably lost.

[Financially, the picture is much blacker than I had thought possible. The buildings (Juilliard is not yet finished) now look to cost $200 million, not the $140 million Edgar Young had set as an absolute ceiling. Much of this additional cost reflects faulty planning: to take the most convincing (if inexpensive) example, Philharmonic Hall opened with three men's urinals in the main floor ladies' room. The extra deficit from operating in Lincoln Center rather than in the more modest older halls is $3 million *for the Metropolitan Opera Association alone,* and counting the deficits of the institutions formed for the new buildings (the summer festival, the pops season, the musical comedy company, the "film component" and the coming "chamber music component" as well as the repertory theater) Lincoln Center has added more than $6 million to the annual cultural burden on the city's charitable resources. If one adds to this figure the interest on $200 million, the extra contributions required by the Lincoln Center operation can be calculated to a figure larger than the total receipts of all New York's opera companies, symphony orchestras and ballets from all sources (subscription, box office and charity) in the season before Philharmonic Hall was opened. Wow!

[Even after two complete acoustical remodelings (one of which involved covering all the walls of the auditorium with wood), Philharmonic Hall is still acoustically uneven and something less than first class. I rather like its looks, though—which is more than I can say for the disastrously gaudy Loew's Lincoln Center which resulted from the pulling and hauling between Wallace K. Harrison and the board of the Met. Saarinen's repertory theater has also been a disappointment—indeed, I think some of the troubles of the companies which have successively failed in this structure trace to the unwisely wide and shallow auditorium in which they must play. But intellectual pretentiousness and artistic amateurishness would probably have doomed the companies which have played here regardless of their surroundings. Apart from the splendid library-museum, the one solid success has been Johnson's New York State Theater. Backstage is inconvenient (Johnson couldn't care less about theater *qua* theater, and it shows), but the house has comfortable entrances, surprisingly accessible continental seating and a glorious huge silver-and-gold assembly room on the level of the first gallery, with *loggie nello stile di* New Orleans overlooking it from each higher level. The décor of the interior is pretty high camp, but it works.

[And because its artistic direction was capable of taking advantage of this elegant new theater, the New York City Opera has enjoyed a great flowering at Lincoln Center. A team of conductor (and general manager) Julius Rudel, designer Ming Cho Lee and director Tito Capobianco—plus singers like soprano Beverly Sills, mezzo Beverly Wolff, tenor Placido Domingo and bass Norman Treigle—has given the City Opera productions of an international quality enhanced by the glamorous setting. At the old City Center in the silly Mecca Temple, attendance ran about 60 to 65 percent of capacity; at the New York State Theater, the City Opera has been virtually sold out for every performance. Deficits are up substantially because of the cost of running the theater. ("In the old house," Rudel says, "if there was trash in the hall I'd call the janitor and wait for days, or clean it up myself. Here I don't dare leave my office without looking both ways, for fear I'll step on a maintenance man.") But there can be no doubt that the benefits of the new surroundings have out-weighed their costs.

[If the institutions can secure sufficient contributions to cover the lux-uries of Lincoln Center, however, there may be no reason for an outsider to worry about finances—after all, it's only money. At a social evening not long ago I ranted about the way Lincoln Center had endangered the financial stability of the New York Public Library, which went right up to moving day before it could raise the million dollars required to shift its music and theater collection to Sixty-fifth Street. Mark Schubart, William Schuman's brigadier first at Juilliard and now at Lincoln Center, said sensibly, "That's the way you raise money—at the last minute, when you can prove you need it desperately." And that's right.

[The fear that the institutions would have to play commercial repertory to pay their bills has proved unfounded: Bernstein's fancy modern-music series with the Philharmonic came in Lincoln Center, Rudel has tri-umphed with several contemporary works, and even the Met has been more ambitious in its new theater than it was in the old. The Lincoln Center summer festival has brought various new goodies, including the Hamburg and Rome opera companies, and has put on month-long con-cert series at prices people can afford. Meanwhile, the separate manage-ment at Carnegie Hall, forced to find events to fill its auditorium, has been splendidly imaginative in adding to the variety of the city's musical life.

[Lincoln Center has expanded the audience for the performing arts and the range of entertainments available. If the new audience is mostly gauche, imperceptive and unresponsive—well, we all started there our-selves; the appetite comes with eating. And if the new entertainments are of variable quality, it seems fairly certain that more of the good eventually produces more of the best. In short, some of the questions raised in the last section of this article have been answered favorably to Lincoln Center by the passage of time; and on the others, the books are still open. Kirstein is back on the board; and Schuman by and large has done what he said he would do.

[One name is necessarily missing from this article, but should not be missing from the book: Morton Baum. Pianist, tax lawyer and former politician from the La Guardia days, Baum was the guiding genius of the City Center of Music and Drama from its incorporation in 1941 to his death in 1968. Indeed—to tell a tale not available for publication in 1962—a proximate cause of John D. Rockefeller III's involvement in Lincoln Center was Baum's flat refusal to have him as chairman of the board of the City Center.

[Baum had been frozen out of the planning for Lincoln Center, and it was only because of his vast skill at in-fighting that the New York State Theater ultimately became home for the City Opera and the City Ballet. His death means, among other things, that the details of this story will never be known. Baum's files, as the board of the City Center found to its horror after his death, were under his hat. One incident, however, did leak from the negotiations to bring the City Opera to the State Theater. The representative of the Met said that if the two houses were to play at the same time in adjacent buildings, the City Opera would "of course" have to give up such universally popular operas as *Traviata* and *Bohème,* "which the Met does so much better." Baum, not batting an eye, said there wouldn't be any trouble about that; division of labor was a good thing; and in the new arrangement the Met would "of course" give up *The Marriage of Figaro* and *Don Giovanni,* "which we do so much better." The Met dropped the point.

[Unpaid and as nearly anonymous as he could be—he would never sit still for an article about himself—Baum worked himself to death at the age of sixty-three. His funeral was attended by a unique assemblage of the city's artistic, political, financial and legal life. Peace to his vain and restless and honest spirit; and may his memory long be green.]

3

The Disembodied Voice . . .
of the Times Lit. Supp.

[A by-product of the months my family and I spent in London while I was working on *The Schools,* this article is one of the few pieces I have written that grew from my own suggestion to a magazine. My wife and I (especially my wife) had been faithful readers of the *TLS* for some years—it was and still is, among other things, the only place where a New Yorker can read about what is going on at, say, the Morgan Library, or in the scholarly collections of American state universities. We wanted to know where it came from.

[At the time of writing this piece, I was less than convinced by the arguments for anonymous reviewing, but the subsequent arrival of *The New York Review of Books* persuaded me that the *TLS* is right. The New York version of the London original has obviously felt itself compelled to carry reams of unedited copy because of the important people who signed the stuff. Though the tone of scholarly reviewing has been better in *The New York Review of Books* than in either our older book-review media or our scholarly journals—and though *The New York Review* has honorably tried to pay more for reviewing than other people pay—it seems to me that the vices of this sometimes vicious publication would have been greatly minimized, without penalty to its virtues, if its founders had adopted the principles of the *TLS.*

[The *TLS* has not changed greatly since the publication of this article in *Esquire* in 1960. Arthur Crook is still its editor. Stanley Morison is dead. Alan Pryce-Jones wound up traveling not to Guatemala but to the Ford Foundation, which, predictably, proved itself unable to find significant use for his talents. The Astor family no longer owns *The Times.* The article brought me a friend—Alfred Knopf, who called one day out of the blue because he wanted to meet the author.]

EVERY FRIDAY morning there appears, in small quantities, on newsstands all over the British Isles, a weekly newspaper of sixteen to twenty-four newsprint pages slightly larger than those in an American tabloid, devoted almost exclusively to unsigned reviews of current, serious books. The books need not have been published in England —indeed, they need not have been printed in English. For the *Times Literary Supplement,* now in its fifty-eighth year of publication, takes as its province the printed word of the entire world. Almost one hundred of its almost five hundred anonymous reviewers live outside England; almost 12,000 of its almost 40,000 copies are purchased outside the British Isles. Partly because of its contributors' anonymity, partly because of its position as a subsidiary to *The Times* of London (a newspaper which, in the words of its official historian, "exists to instruct and inform Members of Parliament"), the *TLS* is universally regarded as the voice of "The Establishment" on questions of books and scholarship. Wherever people wish to know the opinion of The Establishment—that amorphous, amusing, highly intelligent, unidentifiable body of Englishmen who are assumed (perhaps erroneously) to rule the British realm—the weekly *TLS* is awaited with fear or hope, but always with impatience; and devoured with disgust or delight, but always with respect.

It is difficult to imagine an American university without copies of the *Times Literary Supplement* arriving in the morning's mail, impossible to imagine a faculty club which does not give at least part of its luncheon conversation to disputations based on some new or recent article in the *TLS.* Over the course of a year, the *TLS* will at least touch—probably hammer—on some aspect of everybody's academic specialty. No subject is too arcane, no book too abstruse, no criticism too nasty for the *Times Lit. Supp.* Occasionally the lead review—"the front," which starts on the center three columns of the five-column front page and runs on to a length greater than this article—will be devoted to a current book of general interest, like Montgomery's *Memoirs.* More usually, however, the front will be a long essay, hung like a criminal on the gallows-piece of a recent book, about the personality of Watteau or the philosophy of Wittgenstein, German views of the atom bomb, the quality of some medieval Persian poet or nineteenth-century Polish raconteur, the errors of historians in dealing with South American revolutions, or artistic patronage under the Abassid Caliphate. Often there are only three or four men in the English-speaking world with a considerable knowledge of the subject under discussion. One of them has been rash enough to write a book about it; one of the remaining two or three has been called upon by the *TLS* to exercise, anonymously, the rights of criticism.

In addition to the lead-off "front," each issue of the *TLS* carries in its heart an only slightly shorter "middle," an evaluation of a life's work, usually that of a novelist or poet though historians, artists, philosophers and scientists are always sneaking under the barriers. The ostensible excuse for the essay is a new book by or about the man in question, which will be mentioned in a footnote for orientation purposes. But the middle, like the front, is not really a book review. It is an attempt to change (occasionally to confirm) the conventional assessment of the total contribution made by some writer or thinker, or to ballyhoo some relatively unknown contemporary or historical, native or foreign litterateur. The recent upsurge in the reputation of the late Nathanael West, for example, traces largely to a middle in one of last year's *Supplements*.

If the book in question is bad (or the reviewer dislikes it), there are various recognized ways of dismissing it: "Professor Kinsley's book is presumably intended for readers who are not well acquainted with [the medieval poet William] Dunbar. They may rely upon his text, his notes contain much useful information, and his glossary is sound; but it would be a pity were they to take some of his critical opinions too seriously." This, of course, is an opening ploy; if the reviewer chooses to ignore the book until the end, he is more likely to write about what an outrage it is that the work of this great Uzbek poet has never before appeared in English; and how unfortunate it is that this first translation should be so clumsy and incompetent. Such short volleys from the firing squad are among the features which have made the *TLS* famous, but it must be said that they are relatively rare. More frequently, the reviewer even in a front or middle will express a fleeting gratitude to the author of the book for introducing to a wider audience, or ably commenting upon, the subject under discussion. Then he goes on to give his own opinions.

Though the front and the middle are the star attractions of each issue (and are separately billed, under their own titles rather than under the titles of the books discussed, on the front-page table of contents), three-quarters of the space in each week's *TLS* is devoted to relatively straight book reviews. Even here, however, the reviewer is expected to provide more than a mere opinion as to whether or not his readers will like the book. Each book will be dealt with, not as an isolated glob of reading matter, but as part of the world's continuing enterprise of scholarship, invention and creation.

The reviewer of a biography, for example, will analyze the author's sources and compare his product with previous biographies of the same man. The reviewer of a novel will discuss other ways in which a similar theme has been handled, suggest influences and proclaim originality. Standards of prose composition and book production are both set very high. Thus, the reviewer of Fleur Cowles' tribute to Salvador Dali comments that "The 'writing' is unfortunately full of crude and slovenly jargon, of inept metaphors and similes . . . and in consequence the book, in spite of its essential frivolity, makes difficult reading." When art books are under discussion, the reviewer is expected to scrutinize plates with the greatest care; nowhere else has the art world's preference for good black-and-white rather than inferior color found such powerful expression. And heaven alone will defend the publisher who has failed to supply adequate footnotes and index to a book of serious scholarship.

Each issue contains a short poem or two, with its author's name below it, and half a dozen or more signed letters. On the first page, below the logotype and atop the front, will be an illustration three columns wide, usually an art reproduction or a line drawing, with credit to the artist. Every so often, there will be a signed scholarly article on one of the rear pages, almost always a bibliographical note or a discussion of some unpublished material recently come to light. Special numbers—on children's books or theology, The Modern Novel or France since the War—may have names appended to articles. Otherwise, everything is anonymous. The grapevine carries rumors, people assume the worst or the best—but only rarely does anyone *know* who is responsible for any specific contribution to the *Times Lit. Supp.*

Many of the contributors of the past have come to light, either because *The Times* (which owns copyright on all reviews) has given them permission to reprint their essays in their own books, or because they have been identified in histories of the *TLS* itself. The list is, to say the least, imposing. It includes, among others, Henry James, Edmond Gosse, Edith Wharton, John Galsworthy, Max Beerbohm, historian George Trevelyan, Walter de la Mare, Robert Bridges, Walter Raleigh, T. S. Eliot, Middleton Murry, Virginia Woolf, John Buchan, Arthur Quiller-Couch, James Frazer (of *The Golden Bough*), Dean W. R. Inge, and musician Donald Tovey. It shakes an American's complacency to try to conjure up an American periodical which could command the services of such talent, for almost no payment, without even the prestige-value of a name at the bottom of the contribution.

"We don't have *anything* like it," is the repeated wail of Americans who read the *TLS*. Which is, of course, quite true. In sum, the American scholarly periodicals and "little magazines" cover as much territory as the *TLS,* but each surveys only its own quarter-section. Our unspecialized book-review publications are organs of the publishing industry; by contrast, the *TLS,* though it carries a moderate amount of book advertising, is an expression of the intellectual community.

"The United States," says Stanley Morison, who was editor of the *TLS* until 1949, "is a big country, all those pretensions—but it doesn't have a damned thing with which to instruct its elite." Proceeding along the trail of this insight, Morison in his years at the helm directed the *TLS* toward specializing in American books, a policy which his successor Alan Pryce-Jones followed eagerly until his retirement from the editorship this summer. Indeed, Pryce-Jones' last official function as editor of the *TLS* was the supervision of the special number on "Imagination in America," now on the newsstands in this country.

Of all the newspapers and magazines published in the United States, only the Sunday sections of the *New York Times* and *Herald Tribune* review as many *American* books as are covered in the *TLS*. No publication anywhere reviews so much of the output of the American university presses. American bibliophiles find in the *Times*

Lit. Supp., not in their own press, the news of an exhibition of Dickens' manuscripts at New York's Morgan Library, of rare bindings in the Baltimore Fine Arts Museum, of Holbrook Jackson incunabula at the Free Library of Philadelphia. There is thus a sense (a most important sense) in which America has—the *Times Literary Supplement.* From which, conclusions follow.

The entrance to *The Times* of London is a small but not undignified opening onto Queen Victoria Street just off the Thames near Temple Bridge. A uniformed elderly gentleman at a window takes your name and directs you to a small waiting room across the hall, where plain leather-covered chairs and an uncomfortable couch wait to receive visitors. On the wall hangs a framed piece of parchment, printed in red and black letters:

THIS IS A PRINTING OFFICE

CROSSROADS OF CIVILIZATION

REFUGE OF ALL THE ARTS
    AGAINST THE RAVAGES OF TIME

ARMOURY OF FEARLESS TRUTH
    AGAINST WHISPERING RUMOUR

INCESSANT TRUMPET OF TRADE

FROM THIS PLACE WORDS MAY FLY ABROAD
    NOT TO PERISH ON WAVES OF SOUND
    NOT TO VARY WITH THE WRITER'S HAND

BUT FIXED IN TIME,
HAVING BEEN VERIFIED IN PROOF
FRIEND YOU STAND ON SACRED GROUND

THIS IS A PRINTING OFFICE

A messenger boy who may or may not be interested in these sentiments leads the visitor from this confine to a small elevator featuring another sign to the effect that any messenger boy who uses it except when he has a visitor in tow will be canned. One flight up, then out into a broad but dirty corridor bordered by heavy closed doors;

down two steps at the end of the corridor, around a corner, up two steps and then another corridor; at the end of this one, down a flight of stairs, sharp left and left again, out of the maze and into one of the three moderately large rooms that constitute the offices of the *Literary Supplement*. The desks and tables are big and shabby, cluttered with apparently random piles of books and papers and correspondence. The windows look out on nondescript nineteenth-century loft buildings. The prevailing brown tone is not relieved, except on closer look, by the line drawings and *gouaches* that hang on the once-cream walls—signed by Picasso and Beerbohm and Wyndham Lewis.

In these offices every Thursday the staff of the *TLS*—usually four or five people—meet to select thirty to fifty of the week's three to five hundred new books, decide on the prominence the review of each book shall receive, and discuss which member of the reviewing stable shall be invited to munch this particular load of hay. "The selection of the books is the art of the *Supplement*," says Arthur Crook, who was Morison's and Pryce-Jones' assistant and on August first—much to his own surprise—became editor of the *TLS;* a round-faced, nervous, conservatively dressed young man wearing long black hair and black horn-rimmed glasses. "Of course, publishers are not loath to call your attention to a book they regard as important, and our reviewers, who are kindness itself, may know what's about to happen. Still, we always have this enormous effort of *keeping up.*"

During his ten years as editor, Pryce-Jones kept up mostly by traveling, flitting from Portugal to Germany, America to Scandinavia. "If you're interested in books," he says, "it's invaluable to know the people who are interested elsewhere. You have to read the essential books yourself, and you get a sense of which books they are. You also get a sense that you *needn't* read some books—even though everyone is raving about them. And you hear things. Every once in a while someone will say, 'Do you know there's a very good school of Turkish historians now?' Or, 'The Persian novel is looking up.' So you go ahead and do a roundup on the subject."

Crook's gentility and serious mien might be found in a scholarly library in any country; Pryce-Jones, by contrast, is that uniquely

British phenomenon, the intellectual man-about-town. Tall, and erect except when deliberately slouching (he was a lieutenant-colonel during the war), Pryce-Jones is to be seen at London occasions in full morning regalia or tails, depending on the time of day; or in a stiff collar over a striped shirt at the office or in a salon; always moving gracefully, smiling a full gleaming smile, talking brilliantly and as rapidly as the ear can follow. The manner wears a boyish complexion; and Pryce-Jones, who was fifty last year, looks at least ten years younger than his age. His social prominence in London is in most respects a personal accomplishment—for, while he was born to money and local position (Eton and Magdalene College, Oxford), he was also born Welsh. Recently a visitor rudely asked him whether it was possible in London to live down a Welsh origin. "No," he said. "But one can rise above it."

About three hundred of the paper's almost five hundred reviewers are men and women who work at universities; another two dozen or so are completely unknown youngsters. The *TLS* feels no need to apologize for extending the prestige of its anonymity to the opinions of juveniles. "Of course," Crook says, "you don't try them out on *the* book." A continuing organ like the *TLS* must constantly rejuvenate itself, and Crook believes that younger writers are to some extent entitled to a review from within their own generation. (The current staff looks back shuddering to reviews by the elders of thirty years ago, praising the work of the young "Mr. I. Compton-Burnett" and "Miss Evelyn Waugh.") All contributions from young reviewers are carefully examined, and often rather heavily edited, by a senior member of the staff. Usually the young reviewers apply for work at Printinghouse Square, but occasionally, as Crook puts it, "someone at All Souls will say, 'Look out for this chap'—and we'll go after him." England being what it is, most of the young contributors are recent graduates of Oxford or Cambridge, but the *TLS* tries not to be prejudiced. "A boy sent us a poem," Pryce-Jones recalls, "the son of a tailor in Brighton—no education really—and it turned out he could write."

Reviewers for the more important books will be chosen by the staff after lengthy arguments about just which man would be *perfect* for this subject. Then Crook goes out and gets his man. ("Fortunately," Morison says, "Crook is very persuasive on the telephone.") What the *TLS* can offer such distinguished reviewers is—simply—a guarantee that their reviews will be printed, and therefore seen by what is intellectually the most accomplished readership in the world. The money involved is usually less than fifteen dollars—conceivably as much as thirty dollars for the six-thousand-word front—and of course a writer gets no publicity value whatever out of an unsigned *TLS* review. But, unlike the American reviewer (who senses that the book-review section to which he is contributing has sent out twice as many books as it expects to cover, and will publish only what it regards as the best entries), the man who has received an assignment from the *TLS* knows he will see his opinions in print. The reviews may be edited (usually to make them more lively and less "anonymous" in tone), but they will not be killed. The *TLS* reviewer also knows that he will not be harried by deadlines. "I'd far rather get a really competent review from someone who can't be hurried," says Pryce-Jones, "than a sort of journalist's job."

In the old, old days many of the subsidiary reviews were written by the staff of *The Times*. Stanley Morison, who edited the official history of *The Times* as well as the *TLS,* feels that the entire enterprise was made possible by two American promoters named Hooper and Jackson, who bought the *Encyclopaedia Britannica* around the turn of the century and then assigned members of *The Times* staff to rewrite it. These relatively lucrative assignments turned a newsroom into a den of scholars and made it possible for the *TLS* to summon experts from down the hall when highly specialized books had to be reviewed. Today only the "short notices"—a page or two of paragraph-length comments on two or three dozen books appearing under the title of "Books Received"—are "done within the building." Even these perfunctory notes display remarkable care and expertise—as when, for example, the notice-writer notices in Frank Schoonmaker's *German Wines* the "odd omission [of] any reference to the new and still controversial Scheurebe grape . . ." Morison says, "You couldn't run a paper like *The Times* without having educated men around."

The last and one of the most important functions of the *TLS* staff is the selection of the signed part of the paper, especially the letters to the editor. Any author who wishes to complain about treatment at the hands of an anonymous reviewer will be allowed—nay, encouraged—to do so; and the author of the review will reply, over the signature "Your Reviewer." These interchanges make a kind of shadow play, with the author taking the role of flushed grouse, the reviewer portraying the expert huntsman (who sportingly uses rather small shot), and the *TLS* acting as pointer. The author rarely escapes, and there is some question as to why, as a supposedly intelligent bird, he should rise to such unequal battle. "When you're criticized," Crook says rather smugly, "your pride is so hurt that you feel diminished in the eyes of the public. If you have such a grievance you have, we feel, a right to debate it out with the reviewer."

Some of the letters are, in effect, news stories of the intellectual world—from an archaeologist who has made a discovery somewhere east of Suez, or a literary scholar who has dug up some new letters from Smollett to his mother, announcing their finds. Others are the traditional I-am-working-on-a-biography-of-the-late-Lady-Margot-Metroland-and-would-appreciate-any-information-from-anyone-who-knew-the-deceased. What most fascinates readers of the paper, however, are the letters of pure controversy (sometimes touched off by books or reviews, sometimes not), in which members of the academic community bare their knives and strike for the viscera of their colleagues.

In the early days of the *TLS* these fighting letters were usually from ecclesiastics. "We thrived," says Stanley Morison, "on theological venom." In the 1920s, the *TLS* opened its pages to the Baconians, and since then Shakespeare has had a lineage edge on God. More recently, led by Leslie Hotson, the Sherlock Holmes of Elizabethan scholarship, the cryptographers have shifted their attention from authorship to chronology and meaning. One series of letters, which appeared on and off for nearly a year, dealt exhaustively with the contention that the "crescent moon" mentioned in the Sonnets referred to the Spanish Armada, which would date the composition of the poems and perhaps help identify their "Dark Lady." Letters of textual analysis, debating the merits of variant readings, may dissect poets more recent than Shakespeare; one not long ago went as close to modern times as A. E. Housman. The oldest poets, however, arouse the strongest passions. "We'll never have to worry about the future of the *Times Literary Supplement*," says Morison, "as long as we have the Bible and Shakespeare, Dante and Milton."

This emphasis on letters-to-the-editor is, of course, part of the paper's inheritance from its parent *The Times*. The *TLS* was founded in 1902 because there was not room enough in the daily paper, especially while Parliament was in session, to give the kind of literary coverage the editors wished to supply. For the first twelve years of its existence, the *TLS* was simply given away with Friday's *Times,* a separate section folded inside the paper. On other days the front page of *The Times* announced "Price 3d." On Fridays the legend ran, "Price with *Literary Supplement,* 3d." Even after the *TLS* became a separate publication with its own circulation and revenue, *The Times* continued to exert all the rights of ownership. In 1922, indeed, Lord Northcliffe, who owned *The Times,* decided to kill the *TLS* and issued orders to that effect. Fortunately, his bureaucracy was inefficient, and he himself was not in sound enough mental health to remember tomorrow what he had said yesterday, so the *Supplement* glided past this worst of its crises.

The *Lit. Supp.* is still heavily dependent on *The Times,* which owns, houses, prints and distributes it, and picks up its annual deficit. How large the deficit is could not be discovered even by an accountant studying the ledgers. "You can't work out the overhead," Pryce-Jones says. "You *could* say that we could rent these rooms to *Le Figaro,* but they might be standing vacant. What would *The Times* presses and pressmen be doing if they weren't printing the *Literary Supplement?*" Such sophistries aside, however, there remains, unquestionably, a deficit. The *TLS* sells 40,000 copies at sixpence each in Britain and six dollars for 52 by subscription postpaid to the United States (a price advertised on the front page of each issue). Even at English wage scales, such driblets of coppers do not pay the costs of weekly publication. "But the deficit isn't large," says a business executive of *The Times,* "and the Astor family [which

owns the paper] is more than happy to pay it, considering the prestige the *Literary Supplement* brings *The Times*—especially in America."

"The operation runs itself," Pryce-Jones said recently, "and very
smoothly, too. We have business contacts with the daily paper, of
course, and we do have to keep in touch to make sure there are no
contradictions. One is independent, but one doesn't want to cut completely across the policy of *The Times;* one doesn't want to run a
review arguing that the North Koreans were right. If we turned ourselves into a paper promoting, for example, the cause of the Labour
Party or the Vatican—it would create an unwanted sense of strain."
Stanley Morison, who has personally promoted both socialism and
Catholicism, feels that the *TLS could* carry opinions contradictory
to the policy of *The Times*—"though it depends on how the reviewer puts it. When I was editor," Morison added somewhat grimly,
"nobody said anything in the *TLS* that I didn't agree with."

It was Morison more than any other individual who gave the *TLS*
its current look—in more ways than one, because he designed the
type as well as edited the paper. A big, bent old man with broad
shoulders and long white hair, he moves around London and Yale University peering through rimless glasses with a historian's curiosity,
anxious that nothing shall escape his powerful, original, eccentric intelligence. A typographer originally, adviser to the Cambridge University Press and editor of *The Fleuron,* he joined *The Times* when he
was over forty and devoted most of his time with the paper to the
writing and editing of its official history. He began to influence the
policy of the *TLS* in the later 1930s, which was financially the worst
hour in the *Supplement's* history.

"I was full of the right remedy," Morison recalled recently, sitting
at a table in his roomy apartment overlooking the Thames, "and I
succeeded in imposing it on the then-new editor. I wanted the paper
made more popular and readable. More pictures. A 'book of the
week.' Crossword puzzles. Competitions. We did it, and I was completely wrong. Circulation and revenue dropped off immediately. Because I was the man responsible for the disaster, they turned it over
to me as editor; that's the way things happen."

As editor, Morison established the two policies which distinguish the *TLS* today—the concentration on esoterica, and the unremitting attention to foreign books. "Before the war," Morison says, "unless a book was published here, it wasn't reviewed. That was because we didn't know the people. But the world has become ideological. The pedigree of ideas is now much more important than persons or the pedigree of persons.

"When I took over, the important ideas were coming from the existentialists, in France. I filled the paper full of philosophy, made it a headache to read, every week. Circulation went right up. Mind you, I also paid a lot of attention to the fact that it had to be solid, but not unreadable. We have a number of chaps who review for us who are devoted to the *TLS* because it taught them how to write. That's another of the virtues of anonymity."

Pryce-Jones was Morison's first choice as a successor. A traveler and linguist who had spent most of the 1930s in Austria, he could be trusted not to reduce the *TLS* back to its prewar, narrow English focus. Himself a writer—author of essays, poems and a first-rate book on Beethoven—he would continue the course of instruction in prose composition which Morison had started among the contributors. And he was willing, though not without argument, to accept Morison's thesis that the magazine had to be genuinely severe in intellectual tone if it was to survive. "When we make it really dry— 'Was Pascal Really Right?' " Pryce-Jones said the other day, "—then circulation goes up. I find it hard to believe, personally, but it seems to be so. People pay for it to get something to put their teeth into."

The qualities that made Pryce-Jones Morison's perfect choice also guaranteed that he would not wish to stay in an office at Printinghouse Square for the rest of his life. A few years ago—nobody knows exactly when—Pryce-Jones found he was rather bored with the job; and being a man who loves talk, he was not able to keep the information secret. This year he turned fifty and celebrated the tenth anniversary of his editorship. The conjunction of events convinced him it was time to leave. "I want to go to the country," he said recently, "and write large, unreadable books. Do rather long things for the paper—special jobs like fronts and middles, and foreign books.

Brush up my Czech. One can easily get into an ivory tower, and one must keep the exits free. I'll keep an office at *The Times*—in a place like this there tends to be a hutch into which an extra rabbit can be fitted. Until Kenneth Tynan returns from New York, I'll review plays for *The Observer* [a London Sunday paper owned by a collateral branch of the Astor family and printed by *The Times; The Sunday Times,* so-called, a small-scale equivalent of the better American Sunday papers, is *not* connected with *The Times*]. And I'll be available for assignments. If there's another revolution, for example, I want to be able to go to Guatemala for *The Times,* or anywhere else where they can use someone who is amused by foreign languages."

In choosing Crook to be Pryce-Jones' successor, *The Times* in effect gave a vote of confidence to the policies the *TLS* now follows. His selection was urged by virtually all the editorial officers of *The Times;* but the choice must have come as a disappointment to those —and they were many—who hoped that a new broom would enter the old cellar and, to the tune of *The Sorcerer's Apprentice,* flood the anonymous reviewers from their dry holes. Crook is as anonymous as the nonexistent masthead, in person and by conviction. "It's the paper," he says, "not the individual. . . . You get all these hackneyed things about team spirit, but I believe them. One is always being got at and being asked who reviewed something, and always one must risk offense . . ."

Actually, there was never any serious prospect that the *TLS* would give up the policy of anonymity. Attacks on the principle have been almost continuous throughout the history of the paper (it was H. G. Wells who spoke of "the anonymous greasers of the *Times Lit. Supp.*"). But *The Times* itself is an anonymous newspaper, carrying reports not from persons but from "Our Correspondent." Last spring [1959], when the Big Four foreign ministers were playing their daily game of parcheesi in Geneva, *The Times* upset the table by announcing that Mr. Selwyn Lloyd, who was dealing for Britain, was presently to be summoned by his government to other, less arduous duties. The story created questions in Parliament, and chatterings in chancelleries all over the world, but *The Times* never revealed the identity of the correspondent who had sent the news. If so ancient and respected a paper will place its own name—rather than that of an individual—on this sort of unconfirmable story, it is not likely to blanche at the prospect of accepting as its own the opinions of an anonymous book reviewer.

The heaviest barrage of fire against the policy of anonymity was touched off about two years ago by F. W. Bateson in the quarterly magazine *Essays in Criticism*. Briefly, Bateson's thesis was that anonymity acted as a cloak for academic malice, for the anti-Americanism prevalent in British intellectual circles, and for "beginner's confidence, alias cheek." Bateson argued that the identification of the reviewer enables the reader of the review to weigh the authority behind criticisms and to discount for known bias. Even pseudonymity would be preferable to anonymity, because the constant reader would pick up a knowledge of each critic's angle of approach by putting together the reviews published under each pseudonym.

Letters of vigorous attack were published by the *TLS* during the next two months, under the running title "The Disembodied Voice." The Oxford historian H. R. Trevor-Roper (whose knowledge of Homer had been questioned in a recent review) came up with a fine request "not only that justice be done but also that it be seen to be done." A defender who signed himself "One of Your Reviewers" stepped into Bateson's trap by arguing that good scholars writing under their own names cannot "honestly say in public what they think of one another's book." (Bateson's comment was: "Thou shalt not kill—except from behind.") But Pryce-Jones, operating through the "leading article" (editorial, to Americans), was able to repel the invasion singlehanded.

"The concept of a commando-group of beginners," Pryce-Jones wrote, "reckless, shameless, nameless, raiding campus and quad alike, is one associated almost entirely with signed reviewing. It is the named reviewer whose ego is at stake, and whose further employment will probably depend upon the injection of personality which he can add to his considered opinion.

"The anonymous reviewer has to submit himself to exasperating limitations. He belongs to a symposium, not all of a single mind, yet linked by the fact that the members can appear in a single paper without any gross violation of logical propriety. He has to organize his style so strictly that some of his best effects may be lost in the process. He may find himself part of a *Front Impopulaire,* condemned by associates whose views he rejects to the undeserved obloquy of strangers. His criticism will be wholly disinterested, since the general public will not know he has written it."

In conversation, Pryce-Jones makes the case less obdurately and more practically. "If we dealt only with literary books," he says, "the situation would be different. As matters stand, the point of it is that it suits our book to be able to go to people who would not wish to write over their own names—generals, admirals, foreign office people. If HMSO [Her Majesty's Stationery Office] publishes Japanese documents, the only man able to comment on it may be the man who was our Ambassador in Tokyo at the time—who certainly would not write under his own name." Occasional bits of malice and ignorance are not too high a price to pay for this opportunity—provided they can be kept occasional. "That's an advantage of anonymity," Pryce-Jones says. "We can always call a reviewer and get him to change that third paragraph."

In his final editorial on this subject, Pryce-Jones suggested that "in a world where the exhibition of personality for its own sake has become a hallmark of the age, there is something to be said for the display, as a change, of corporate personality, for the merging of the individual name, famous or no, into a collegiate entity. . . . The collector of autographs can, after all, visit our neighbors." Gentlemanly to the end, however, he permitted the last word to be said in one of the most famous of *TLS* letters to the editor:

SIR,
Most of us have long ceased bothering about the anonymity of your reviews because we have long ceased reading them, knowing that they are likely to be for the most part unlearned, worthless, misleading, brutish and flat. The two reasons for continuing to take the paper are the book lists, which are the quickest means of learning what is being published, and the correspondence, of which one reads only the signed letters.

                                                    B. A. WRIGHT

Only an Englishman could write such a letter: an American wouldn't have the nerve. There can be little question that the *TLS,* like The Establishment generally, enjoys tweaking Jonathan's nose— as a previous generation of Continentals enjoyed twisting the Lion's tail, and for the same reasons. And anonymity makes the occasional supercilious anti-Americanism of the *TLS* more difficult to bear. *Ad hominem* objections are not unknown in American criticism, but there is a great difference between the plain blunt dislike of your American book columnist and this delicately scented blackball emitted, anonymously, from within the confines of a club. One of the great problems of anonymity—not discussed, unfortunately, during the Great Controversy—is that anonymous praise always seems the work of an individual, while anonymous condemnation seems the opinion of an institution. Bitterness about certain *TLS* reviews (for example, the one ridiculing Marchette Chute for dedicating a book to the New York Public Library) is so strongly felt at American universities that Bateson could seriously advocate an end to anonymity as a step which "would do much to repair Anglo-American academic relations." To even the most bitter Americans, however, the *TLS* is one of the great institutions of the civilized world, whatever its faults—while many Englishmen occupying the same sort of intellectual position regard it as just another damned magazine.

Publications suffer—or enjoy—this kind of sea change all the time. Your Frenchman admires *Der Spiegel;* your German worships *Le Monde.* But the French equivalent of the German who reads *Le Monde* will talk of the paper as a nasty piece of work by a bunch of disappointed intellectuals who would like to be running the government. In England, the elite devour *The New Yorker* every week, without salt, and it is virtually impossible to convince even people who have visited America that *The New Yorker,* with all its excellences, has not been *intellectually* fashionable in the United States for at least a dozen years.

To say that one has stopped reading the *TLS* is a recognized social gambit in London. One of the most eminent of modern English novelists shakes his head sadly over "all that old Alan Pryce-Jones stuff." During the spring it was widely rumored (and believed, half joyfully, half masochistically) that *The Times* was preparing to turn over the *TLS* to one of C. P. Snow's "new men," a young Fellow of All Souls, Oxford, who happened to be a barrister but whose interests were almost exclusively "science and Russia," and who would remake the paper stem to stern. Talk against the *TLS* is so commonplace and so strong at a certain kind of English cocktail party that a young American scholar, visiting London this spring, finally turned on her host with the words, "We're always told not to criticize the Royal Family in front of Englishmen. Well, you be careful about criticizing the *TLS* in front of Americans."

This support from across the Atlantic was by no means what Stanley Morison had in mind when he lifted the *TLS* from the ruck of provincialism after the war—but it has probably been one of the most important factors in the continuance of his policies. The history of intellectual publishing shows that within a nation fashions in ideas are scarcely more durable than fashions in clothing; the *Geist* of the *TLS,* as Pryce-Jones called it, is for the moment out of date at home. But English is bigger than England. It is spoken today by more people than any other language in the world, and for many of the most articulate and intelligent of these people the voice of the *TLS* continues to ring true, regardless of the London fashion.

One man's parochialism is another man's catholicity. In living demonstration of the point, the *TLS* comes out each Friday, unchanging, serenely above all battles but its own, on your newsstand in England, by post to the world of ideas.

4

Avis v. Hertz

[In an odd way, a writer benefits from accumulations not unlike a manufacturer's invested capital. I have in my files nearly every note I have ever taken, and in my head, of course, the operating procedures of all the fields I have written about. Bill Bernbach (Avis) and Norman B. Norman (Hertz) had been half of my chapter on styles of advertising copy in *Madison Avenue, U.S.A.,* and it had done both of them a degree of good. We were all, in short, glad to see each other. I had talked with both of them again when I wrote a rather uncomfortable piece called "Madison Avenue Revisited" for the *Saturday Evening Post;* and at that time, indeed, both of them had talked about the Avis-Hertz fight. So when Willie Morris became editor of *Harper's* and called my agent to ask if I would do a piece on that subject, I knew exactly where in the mine I would find the ore. Having been around before does not save much time on an assignment—you still have to see all the people you would have had to see if you started fresh—but it does provide comfort, like a chauffeur-driven limousine, and it makes possible some added fun as well as a degree of authority in the writing.]

LOOKING BACKWARDS, it seems clear that the first shots were fired in 1959, when the Norman, Craig & Kummel advertising agency proposed to men all over the country that they should "Let Hertz Put *You* in the Driver's Seat." Before that, "Drive-Ur-Self," as most car-rental agencies called it in the days of Confident America, had been a natural descendant of the local livery stable and a commercial service to perhaps 200,000 business travelers, operating well below the normal levels of public attention. The center of the business was long-term truck leasing to corporations. The new ads made rent-a-car look like a notable growth industry, a customary adjunct of air travel, and a pretty sexy thing to do.

"You have to keep in mind the impact of this thing on the people here," says Jerry Shapiro, operations manager for Hertz Rent-A-Car, who was the account supervisor at the agency when the campaign began. "They went from trade magazines to the flying man,

Suzy Parker, Richard Avedon. There were cartoons in *The New Yorker*. The people they met at cocktail parties asked them how they got the man in the car, how they got Hollywood to make that movie, *Good Neighbor Sam*. Then, later, the discomfort was that much worse, because the whole cocktail party experience had been so new." Shapiro paused and considered his conversation. "I call this airplane talk," he said. "It's what I wind up saying to the guy in the next seat, after I tell him what I do. . . ."

What created the discomfort at Hertz—the irritating jokes at the cocktail parties and the predictable comments by the guy in the next seat—was of course the widely disseminated suggestion by the Doyle Dane Bernbach advertising agency, that men looking to rent cars should go to Avis, because "We try harder." Instead of promoting the attractions of car rental, the Avis campaign searched out the gripes—the lost reservation, the waiting at the counter, the full ash-tray and the empty gas tank, the dirty car, the streaky windshield wiper—and assured the customer that Avis would never do that to him, couldn't afford to do it, because Avis was "only Number 2."

Carl Ally, who took over the Hertz account in 1966, still grows angry (perhaps a little synthetically) at what Bernbach was doing to his current client. "The ads were saying Number 1 doesn't care," he says, "saying by innuendo that Hertz was a somnolent and sloppily run organization. They'll give you a dirty car with a bad windshield wiper, won't honor reservations; they have surly personnel. Our people were being maligned in public and nobody was defending them; we had a morale problem."

From Bill Bernbach's point of view, all this is nonsense. A soft-spoken, plump, white-haired, ingratiating genius from Brooklyn, Bernbach feels that he simply presented to the public the problem his client had presented to him: "Avis," read his first ad in January, 1963, "is only Number 2 in rent-a-car, so why go with us?" The first proofs of this ad went out to the researchers, Bernbach recalls, "and they told us not to run it. If you're Number 2 that means you're not Number 1, and that means you're not the best. But what the re-searchers had tested was not our campaign—our campaign was that we tried harder."

What looked on the other side like denigration of the Hertz personnel looked to Bernbach like a shot in the arm to Avis personnel. "The greatest stimulus for efficiency," he says, "is purpose. We went around to those different installations in different cities, called meetings of mechanics and car washers and counter girls, showed them the ads and said, 'You can make us or break us—if ever anybody needed anybody, *we* need *you*.' It made them important people, did wonders for them." Meanwhile, of course, the David-and-Goliath image appealed to a long-standing American prejudice: "A week after the first ads ran," Bernbach says, "I got a call from one of the Avis executives, who was in Chicago. He said he *had* to call me. He'd just rented a car at the airport. And while he was waiting on line at his counter one of the businessmen ahead of him nudged another one, gestured to the Hertz counter, and said, 'Look! *Our* line is bigger than *their* line. . . .' "

Over the next four years, the car-rental revenues of the Avis system (the company itself plus the local licensees who wave the Avis flag) appear to have gone from about $40 million to about $105 million; the Hertz system car-rental revenues, from about $120 million to about $190 million. While the dollar gain for Hertz was slightly greater than that for Avis, the upstart took an annually increasing share of the market—especially at the airports, where the Avis business is heavily concentrated and where the rivals are in direct and easily measured competition. Because airports are publicly owned and the rent on car-rental stations is calculated as a percentage of monthly gross revenues, the figures on who does what volume are discoverable. Until 1965, indeed, Hertz distributed comparative figures at the leading airports as a service to the financial press; but then the service stopped.

Bernbach had endless fun with his campaign. "We try harder" buttons were issued in forty-odd languages—eight million of them in 1964 alone. A series of ads warned the Avis management against the dangers of waxing fat. A copywriter complained in print that he had found cigarette butts in an Avis car he had rented; an ad featuring a picture of the Forum ("Look What Happened to Rome") asked "Will success spoil Avis?" Number 1 was never identified, except in one particularly flamboyant ad which showed a check on which the name Hertz had been crossed out and the name Avis written in above. "*You* remember it," says Hertz's Jerry Shapiro. "*I* remember it. We used to open the magazines every month and wince."

Finding an answer was an almost agonizing problem for Norman B. Norman, a classically aggressive advertising executive who has managed to remain lean and hungry while growing rich and gray. Only once did he yield to management pressure to hit back, and then it was with a little fable about the tiger and the pussy cat ("To tell the difference between the tiger and the cat take a look at the kitty"), which simply demonstrated that Hertz was Number 1, all right. A specific product guarantee—a $50 credit for anyone who found anything wrong with a Hertz car, even butts in the ashtray— failed to stem the wave of public sympathy for the struggles of little Avis against great big Hertz.

A few years ago, in the middle of the battle, Norman analyzed Bernbach's approach, and called it "Chinese humility. It's always *nebbish,* always apologetic. 'Think small' for Volkswagen. 'We try harder.' He uses it even when he has the top product. [The reference was to Bernbach's Rheingold Beer campaign in New York, with the slogan 'We must be doing something right.'] When you have a product that fits, it's brilliant. It's very hard to fight."

In the spring of 1966, Carl Ally sold Hertz the idea of a wholly different counterattack, and Norman was taken away from the problem, though not from the pain. Ally's approach was pure belligerence. "Somebody at Hertz," he says, "told me he wanted me to be careful about attacking the underdog—to use the rapier, not the bludgeon. I said, 'I'm not going to use either—I'm going to use the six-gun.' You know what the underdog is doing? He's gnawing your ankle. You shoot him."

The first Ally ad carried the blunt headline, "For years, Avis has been telling you Hertz is No. 1. Now we're going to tell you why." Bernbach, who had been waiting rather eagerly for this moment, re-plied with an ad which showed a large tower of coins toppling onto a smaller tower. "You've probably noticed," the ad read, "the big change in No. 1's advertising lately. No more jolly man flying into the driver's seat. Instead, they've come out with a get-tough-with-Avis campaign. Why? Because No. 1's share of the rent-a-car business is getting smaller. . . . If Avis isn't stopped, we'll be No. 1 by 1970."

By all classic advertising doctrine, Bernbach was a clear winner once again. Hertz had run ads with the name Avis in the headline, while Avis was still speaking merely of Number 1. And when Ally called off the war a few months later, he was forced to use Bernbach's phraseology: and his ad, showing smiling Hertz and Avis girls with their arms around each other's waists, carried the headline, "You were expecting maybe another get-tough-with-Avis ad?" Avis executives say rather wistfully today that the Ally campaign gave another year's life to an advertising approach which was dying a natural death. Nevertheless, it was much easier to maintain interest in the needling Bernbach had given Hertz than in a straight-out fight, and it can be argued that the brutality of the Ally approach was Hertz's earliest available exit. In any event, the advertising war is now over: this spring, though there will probably be occasional long-range shelling, both companies will be peacefully touting the quality of their own service in their advertising, and rent-a-car will settle down to a condition of competitive coexistence.

So far, the story that was played out in public. But there is more to it than that.

Wall Street first took an interest in the rent-a-car business in 1953, when General Motors, which had no special need for additional troubles with the Justice Department, sold its Hertz division to Omnibus Corporation—a holding company controlled, oddly enough, by John Hertz, who had sold his car-rental operation to GM twenty-eight years before. Omnibus' bankers were Lehman Brothers, and the repurchase of Hertz had nothing whatever to do with sentiment. Quite apart from the fairly obvious future of the industry, which was sure to expand with the growth of air travel, car rental in 1953 offered two of the financial market's favorite lures—a tax gimmick and a chance to employ a high degree of "leverage" (that is, to control large quantities of capital through a small investment).

The tax gimmick came from luxurious allowances for the depreciation of the cars, which left their proprietor with an operating loss to be charged against income. When this bookkeeping loss was recovered by selling the vehicle on the used-car market for more than its now-depreciated cost, the resulting profit was taxed at a much lower rate, as capital gains.

The leverage factor was Lehman Brothers' creation. Prior to the banking firm's intervention in 1953, bankers had considered the cars part of the capital of a car-rental business. A business can, of course, borrow some of its capital costs, but only rarely as much as 50 percent. Lehman persuaded a syndicate of commercial banks (including the First National of Chicago, Manufacturers Trust in New York and Union in California) that the cars were inventory rather than capital. To help a retailer carry inventory—especially easily resalable inventory—banks will lend a far higher proportion of the cost of the goods. In the case of Hertz, considering that the company as a volume purchaser could buy the cars for only a little more than wholesale price, the banks could safely lend nearly 90 percent of the cost. An investment of $2 million could then control a $20 million fleet of cars. To simplify drastically, a rate of profit on total investment only one percent greater than the going interest rate would produce a 10 percent profit on the company's own money—and most of that could be taken as capital gains rather than as income for tax purposes. Yummy.*

Among others who heard the same drummer was a Detroit car dealer named Warren Avis, whose local rental service was being submerged by a Hertz office which could rely on reservations teletyped

---

* In recent years, there has been another advantage of being inside the car-rental business—its validity as an economic forecaster. Renting downturns warning of recession and upturns heralding recovery have been noted three months before the trend shows up elsewhere, both at Avis and at Hertz, where president Rodney Petersen, who used to be an economist, has proposed the inclusion of such data in Department of Commerce business summaries. It will be noted that these fluctuations are shared across the board, and are quite independent of advertising pressure.

from other cities. With others similarly situated, Avis put together a sort of federation of independent renters which bore his name and was promoted with the stirring slogan, "All of a sudden I see Avis Rent A Car wherever I go!" The two strengths of the operation were an exclusive franchise at the Eastern Airlines terminal in Miami (so profitable that Avis could lease it to locals for $200,000 free and clear every year) and the entrepreneurial drive of Boston's Richard S. Robie, an old-timer in car rental who was en route to more diversified investments. (Robie was intensely receptive to new ideas, like schemes for one-way, rent-it-here-leave-it-there arrangements. "Let's try it," he would say to the filling-station people. "You can always go back to pumping gas.") In early 1955, Robie acquired a controlling interest in the Avis system and moved its headquarters to Boston. A year later, in a rather mysterious episode which nobody on either side likes to talk about, Hertz bought out Robie.

Old-timers at Avis say that Hertz stripped their company of many of its strongest licensees during the four months that Number 1 in effect owned Number 2. Old-timers at Hertz say nothing of the sort occurred—except that Avis did, of course, lose the Robie establishments themselves. Both agree, however, that it was a very sick rent-a-car company which Hertz threw back onto the market in mid-1956. Nor was Avis's condition improved by the fact that the hand which seized the bargain was that of Boston's Dumaine interests, themselves submerged in the sea of troubles around the failing New Haven Railroad.

One of those who worked on the Dumaine acquisition was a young Providence lawyer (Harvard Law School, '50) named Winston V. Morrow, Jr., now president of Avis, who joined the company as counsel in early 1957. It was not a cheerful experience for Morrow. "We had," he recalls, "a very weird central administration. Every way there was of losing money, we explored. I used to say my favorite subject in law school had been creditors' rights and remedies, and it fitted right in at my job."

To cash in on the benefits Lehman Brothers had seen, the car-rental companies had to operate through wholly owned branches rather than through licensees, who typically contributed nothing to a national operation except the smallest possible piece of the system-wide advertising and telecommunication costs. The system Hertz inherited from General Motors had relied on licensees even in markets like New York, Boston and Washington; under Lehman's guidance, the company went from 31 cities with company-owned operations in 1953 to 529 a decade later. In 1957, Hertz and American Express launched a joint venture (now liquidated and consolidated into a wholly owned Hertz International) which established car-rental facilities all over Europe. Avis under the Dumaine regime limped slowly behind, acquiring a few former licensees and entering the European market by means of profitless licensing arrangements abroad.

The fact was that, despite the leverage and the tax break, car rental was an appallingly difficult business in which to make money —especially in opposition to the established Hertz. Airports charged extraordinary rentals for a few square feet of terminal space and limited reserved parking facilities. (At many airports, in fact, the total fees from the car-rental agencies are greater than the total fees from the aircraft which are their reason for being.) Half the car-rental company's inventory is on the road, nobody knows where; the other half is idle on high-priced floor space in the city while unsatisfied customers are clamoring for service at the airport. Hertz estimates no fewer than 1,500 "transfers" a day in New York alone to bring the vehicles to the offices where the customers are. "How this garage business got so complicated, I don't know," says Hertz president Rodney Petersen. "But it did."

Poorly supervised or carelessly chosen managers can steal the company blind through cash rentals and padded maintenance bills. Bad weather wrecks a day's business at the airport, a weekend's business in the city, a season's business at a resort. Profit margins are forever at the mercy of the used-car market—and as the rent-a-car agency is the livery stable of the modern world, the used-car operator is the horse trader. "The moment you forget that you're in the business of dealing in used-car futures," says Avis's Morrow, "you're in trouble."

Greyhound lost something more than $10 million in a brief venture into rent-a-car; National, the surviving third nationwide operation, was in and out of bankruptcy through its whole career until Greatamerican Insurance bought it late in 1967.

In 1959 the bottom dropped out of the used-car market, and in 1960 the Supreme Court definitively disallowed the tax gimmick which had made rent-a-car attractive to high-bracket investors. Hertz switched top management, and Avis began to slide toward the knackers. Though Hertz's domestic aggressiveness had decreased substantially as the result of an anti-trust consent decree (the company agreed, for example, to stop seeking exclusive franchise rights at airports), Avis was unable to take advantage of new openings. Then, in March, 1962, the Wall Street house of Lazard Frères, which had noted Lehman's substantial profits on its Hertz business, bought the collapsing Avis system for something less than $5 million.

Lazard promptly threw out the existing management and installed the duo who had built the Hertz international business—Donald Petrie, another ex-lawyer, who had run the actual operations, and Robert Townsend, who had handled the financial end at American Express. At Avis the two men changed roles, Petrie joining Lazard Frères (of which he is now a partner), and Townsend (now retired) assuming the presidency of the company. Morrow had quit Avis that January in disgust, and was in the middle of negotiations for a job at Hertz when Townsend and Petrie called him back to be their vice president and general manager.

Through 1962, Avis and Lazard took their inescapable lumps in large and planned doses. Licensees were bought out, local operations and central systems were reorganized, new girls were hired and given bright-red uniforms, an aging fleet was disposed of for what it would bring, and at the end of the year the stations were stocked with brandnew Fords. Previously concealed losses were uncovered and debited and much of the next year's anticipated loss was written off in advance, until the books for 1962 showed a bone-crushing deficit of $3.2 million—but the books for 1963 were pretty well guaranteed to show a profit. Part of the deal in the large purchase of Fords was a big contribution by the auto maker to what would be a vastly expanded 1963 advertising budget.*

Following its standard procedure, Lazard originally offered the Avis business to Bernbach only on condition that he employ an ad man Lazard had chosen as the right supervisor for the account. When Bernbach flatly refused, Lazard's André Meyer said, "Well, my man told me you wouldn't do it," and signed up on Bernbach's terms, which included virtually complete control by the agency of the content of the campaign.

"We try harder" hit a marketing situation where Avis was equipped with bright shiny new cars and personnel, while Hertz was on an eighteen-month cycle of vehicle replacements with Chevrolet, still recovering from management shakeups, and saddled with union seniority agreements at its rental stations. Though nobody doubts either the reach or the grasp of Bernbach's advertising—"all those people who sent me envelopes full of cigarette butts didn't get the idea by themselves," Morrow says—the fact is that his campaign was backed in 1963 by that strongest of selling forces, a superior product. "No. 2" was in truth big ol' Lazard rather than li'l ol' Avis (and in July, 1965, while Bernbach was running lyrical ads about Horatio Alger and hailing the American creed of "No. 2ism," it became a division of giant ITT)—but it really was trying harder.

"In terms of prices," says a banker with a large stake in Hertz, rather cautiously, "Avis has been very *good* competition." Even National in its agonies has gone no further than giving Green Stamps to customers. About half the volume at the airports comes from men who walk off the plane without any reservation and choose among counters. (This risks not finding a car on Tuesday nights and Wed-

---

* Avis later left Ford and went to Plymouth, which was prepared to give the rental company cars on a six-month lease—once the tax gimmick disappeared, there were advantages in financing through manufacturers rather than through banks. Ford went to Hertz, and General Motors, rather puzzled, found itself dealing with National. Avis has now returned to purchasing rather than leasing most of its cars, but its supplier is still Plymouth.

nesday mornings, incidentally, but it's pretty safe the rest of the week.) Nothing could be more certain to draw these customers than a big sign on the desk displaying a lower price list, but an open war in rental prices would (like the gas price wars which break out sporadically at neighboring filling stations) cost much more than even an advertising budget which runs 8 percent of gross revenues.

Price competition is not nonexistent—in late 1967, when Avis and National raised prices on standard cars at a dozen airports, Hertz caused to be placed in the newspapers on the financial pages the fact that it was not following suit, and envelopes containing bills to corporate customers were stuffed with an announcement that Hertz was holding the price line (at least for the time being). But public display of bargains, which is normal procedure in other retailing, has been restricted in car rental to the local budget and discount operators, whose inability to deliver or pick up at airports and hotels has kept them a minor factor.

To some extent, the high order of competition in the Hertz and Avis ads expresses the companies' economic inability to compete in any other way. The girls at the counter can't do it themselves—"You put two girls working side by side," says Avis's Morrow, "they don't compete—they cry." Since 1964, there has been little if any to choose between the two companies in the service offered. Rosser Reeves, then of the Ted Bates agency, once described the dilemma of the modern advertising man in terms of the client who walks into the office, puts two identical half dollars on the desk and says, "Mine is the one on the right. You prove it's better." Bernbach's answer became almost a part of folklore.

What made the competition by advertising nasty and colorful in the car-rental business was in part the talent of the ad men, in part the incestuousness of the relationships—the hiring of Hertz executives to revitalize Avis, the long-standing semi-friendly rivalry between Lehman and Lazard. (RCA bought Hertz a year after ITT bought Avis, partly because the Sarnoff family, which is advised by *both* Lehman and Lazard, had made so much money in Avis convertible bonds.) But as service industries become increasingly important in the economy, we shall probably see many campaigns like these, particularly in situations where one of the competitors has a dominant role.

For what Bernbach was saying at bottom, as Norman shrewdly points out, was that there isn't any difference between car-rental services. It was fortuitous that in 1963 Avis, on a much smaller scale, was in better shape than Hertz. The paradigm for this sort of campaign was Sterling Getchell's famous "Look at All Three" for the upstart Plymouth, or Bernice Fitzgibbons' "Nobody But Nobody Undersells Gimbel's" ("Nobody" meaning "Not Macy's"). The beneficiary in 1967 was National, where the lines were shorter still—indeed, it was the trend lines at the airports which made money-losing National a marketable company last fall. Bernbach's own recognition of the phenomenon is implicit in his criticism of Ally's counterbarrage: "If you're the top person you should never acknowledge your opponent by name. It's like Nixon and Kennedy—Nixon made Kennedy an equal."

Nobody got hurt in the Avis-Hertz war, except psychically. Car rental was expanding so rapidly that even severe inroads on the Hertz share left Hertz a rapidly growing concern. Jerry Shapiro of Hertz says, "Norman and I and Gene Kummel used to sit around at the end of the day and say to each other that no industry can be healthy with only one company making money. If car rental had the future we thought it had, there just had to be competition coming up. We *wanted* competition. But we didn't want it to come *this* way. . . ."

5

How to Get into Princeton

[About two years before this article was commissioned by *Life, The New Yorker* had run a long piece on the work of the Yale admissions department. Thus, though Henry Luce was a Yalie of the bluest stripe, the *Life* staff had to look elsewhere when they decided there was sufficient interest in this upper-class and Eastern problem to justify a thorough article in a national magazine. I had never worked for *Life*, but the subject was one I knew something about, thanks to *The Schools*.

[Anyway, Loudon Wainwright, the articles editor of *Life*, called and asked if I'd be interested; and of course I was. Because of *The Schools*, and thanks to very generous and efficient and articulate cooperation at Princeton, it was an easy piece to write. My first draft was ponderous, but suggestions about reorganizing and tightening, especially from Wainwright's assistant David Maness, made the revision go easily, too. So I had no reluctance at all about coming in to the offices of the magazine on the day in 1962 when the issue in which it was scheduled was to go to press. The senior editors of a staff-written magazine are used to having the writer of an article on the premises to make any last-minute changes; and *Life* was paying enough to cover the cost of that day, too.

[The way *Life* works, apparently, is that an article is slotted into an issue on the recommendation of the articles editor, and the higher authorities do not read it until the last minute. Anyway, I was placed in a vacant office with a nice view (fortunately, I had brought a book), and I sat and waited while the piece rose through levels of authority like a captive balloon. An assistant managing editor wanted two sentences changed, and I changed them. Then "Mr. Graves," the managing editor, wanted two paragraphs changed, and I changed *them*. Wainwright was away somewhere, and the communications from on high were relayed to me by Maness, after his private conversations with the authorities involved. Unfortunately, "Mr. Luce" was in town, which meant that after I had made the corrections Mr. Graves wanted, the manuscript went all the way upstairs for one further, final reading.

[It was almost six o'clock when Maness came into the room I was occupying, an odd but clearly unhappy expression on his face. I asked what was wrong. "I don't know," Maness said. "But as I interpret what Mr.

Graves thinks Mr. Luce said . . . " And I suddenly realized that not only was I not to hear directly from the author of the criticism, I was not even to hear directly from anyone who *had* heard directly. Maness thought better of his effort at interpretation. "All I know," he said finally, "is that Mr. Luce says it needs a fix. We're taking it out of this issue. You go home, and we'll call you."

[About a week later Wainwright called. "Mr. Luce wants to know," he said hopefully, "why you chose Princeton. . . ."

[As it had been *Life,* not myself, which had chosen Princeton, the question was too hard for me. Wainwright and Graves still liked the piece, paid full price for it, and eventually cut it cleverly to one-quarter of its original length and (with my consent) ran the torso as a quickie in the front of the book.

[Princeton admissions director C. William Edwards had read the full piece, and felt that a lot had been lost in the cutting. (So did I.) At his urging, the *Princeton Alumni Weekly* called and asked if they could buy the serial rights to the original for fifty dollars. I was delighted to sell them the piece, and what follows is the story as it ran in the *Princeton Alumni Weekly.*

[The brief discussion of SAT scores and their significance is oversimplified—500 was the average for 1942, and by 1962 the average score had dropped under pressure of numbers of candidates to about 450. The word "theoretically" was supposed to cover this problem, which is too complicated statistically to explore in a magazine article, or in a book of magazine articles.

[None of the men in the Princeton admissions department in 1962 was still there in 1968.]

"THEODORE FALK," said a voice of authority. "Ted is at Upper High School in Iowa," replied a nasal, younger voice, reading data from a file card. "He ranks sixth in a class of 441, his CSG is 2, we give him a 2-plus character, 2 over-all."

"He has a 655 verbal and a 740 math," said a third, much deeper voice, reading a typed sheet that was obviously the product of IBM data-processing machinery. "English 628, Latin 618, Social Studies 707."

The authoritative voice picked up again, reading from papers in a gray-brown file folder. "The school says he's superlative, a conscientious student, truly outstanding. He's had four years of English, four years of Latin, four years of history, four years of math, three years of science. The only grades he ever received that were not the highest given by the school were in physical education. Principal says he's one of the finest pianists ever to graduate from the school. Teacher says he's studying the *Aeneid* this year and it has awakened his imaginative instincts. He played on a sandlot baseball team that won national recognition. Alumni think he's great. He's good—let's take him."

The three men were sitting at a long gray Formica-top table under steam pipes and an exposed sprinkler system in a basement room of a nineteenth-century dormitory called West College, beside Nassau Hall on the Princeton campus. They were the Admissions Committee— Director C. William Edwards and his assistants Thomas H. Eglin and Gregory Farrell—and they had just admitted a boy to Princeton's Class of 1966 (his name and school, of course, are fictitious). All three men are Princeton graduates (classes of '36, '54 and '57, respectively), and all three have had some high-school teaching experience to help them estimate the value of the documents in the file folders.

At other private colleges all over the country (but especially in the East), other admissions officers were going through similar rituals, weighing objective evidence, bringing into play whatever resources of instinct seemed appropriate, attempting to deal perfect justice in a world where, as President Kennedy recently put it, "Life is unfair." Princeton's admissions office is merely one heavily visited salt lick in the great stampede that races each spring through all the "prestige colleges." But the Princeton case is remarkably pure. Princeton was the first college to announce "a policy of selective admissions" (back in the 1920s, when it really didn't mean much), and Princeton Professor Carl Brigham was the pioneer in measuring the qualities of candidates for college admission. As one of the Big Three, Princeton casts its net nationally, seeking extraordinary students from all sorts of schools in all sorts of places. Unlike Harvard or Yale, however, it is a classic residential college in a town that even today—for all the growth of its suburban housing and research industry—would scarcely exist without the educational institution. If he has a bad day at Harvard or Yale, a boy can escape into a subway or a bus and almost immediately find himself away from school; at Princeton, unless he has the time and money for the fifty-mile trek to New York, he is immured in his college.

Upon Edwards and his colleagues in the basement room devolved the responsibility of making sure not only that Princeton would be happy with the boy, but also that the boy would be happy with Princeton. Edwards worked at the job in shirtsleeves.

Theodore Falk's folder went atop a pile representing candidates already admitted, and a new folder came off the top of the stack of F's.

"Harold Fall!"

"Hal," said Eglin reading, "is a valedictorian, first in a class of 176 in Michigan. CSG, 3-plus. He's 2-minus character, 2-minus over-all."

"Verbal 541," said Farrell, "math 648, English 497, advanced math 537."

"He's their valedictorian," Edwards said, "but they're not crazy about him. Somewhere between average and unusually good. Class president, drama club, business manager of the paper. They send one of these damned personality checklists, with the checks a little on the right side. I can never figure out what we're supposed to make of these. Wants financial aid but he's never held a summer job. Brad Craig (director of the Bureau of Student Aid) sees him, doesn't like him at all—'Glib, cocky. Wanted to make an impression and did: a negative one. I don't think he'd add a thing to Princeton.' Alumni like him. Teacher says he's a perfect gentleman but his powers are limited. He's *out.*"

The numbers which Eglin read were Princeton's own; the set Farrell read came from the College Entrance Examinations Board and represented standardized test scores. The "character" and "over-all" ratings, on a scale from one to five, reflected Edwards' judgment of the boy after a preliminary reading of his application. "CSG" stands for "Converted School Grade," and is an estimate of the value of a boy's high-school work in Princeton terms. The lower the number, the better the score, as in golf; 2-plus, which sounds like more than 2, means better than 2 (i.e., between 1 and 2), and virtually guarantees admission.

The College Board scores, required as part of an admission's application by nearly all the private colleges, represent grades on multiple-choice tests given simultaneously all over the country half a dozen times a year. A score of 800 is perfect; 500 is theoretically average. About 700,000 high-school seniors took some of these tests during this past year. On any one test, only about 16 percent scored over 600, and fewer than 3 percent (about 4/5 of one percent of all the nation's seventeen-year-olds) could boast a score over 700. Two sorts of tests are given—Scholastic Aptitude (SAT), which is supposed to measure "developed ability" to do college work, and Achievement, which is supposed to measure how well a student has mastered a specific subject. The Aptitude tests come in two varieties, verbal and mathematical, and it was these scores that Farrell read first; all the others were Achievement scores.

"Terence Falmouth!"

"Terry is number two in a class of twenty-three at Private Academy. CSG, 3-plus. 2-minus character, 2-minus over-all."

"Verbal, 711; math, 657. English 637, Latin 537."

"They think he's a superior boy. 'Happy to recommend Terence.' He's been working fourteen hours after school, but he still finds time for the paper. His IQ is 117. Teacher says 'his work in the classroom leaves little to be desired.' He gets an 'average' from the alumni. I guess we'll hold him." This folder went on still a third pile, the largest of all, for boys who would be looked over again, in greater detail, later on.

Nobody who works at college admissions can completely ignore the cabalistic numbers Eglin and Farrell read from the file card and the IBM paper. They are the only direct comparisons between candidates, and they must mean *something*. Still, the experienced admissions staff will regard them as evidence rather than proof. Terence Falmouth's 711 verbal score is very good indeed, better than the score of the average admitted candidate, but it guarantees him nothing. A man like Edwards, who over eighteen years read some 50,000 folders at Princeton, sees a great number of boys every year and speaks with many school principals and headmasters. He necessarily develops a semi-conscious sense of the human qualities expressed by the pieces of paper, much as a professional bridge player develops a sense of whether the queen is or is not below the jack. He would have to be right far more often than simple probabilities predict— which is all anybody can honestly claim for the "objective" test scores themselves. Moreover, he feels personal responsibility for each decision, which is more than a standardized test can say. In only one area, at the top of the scale, did Princeton limit Edwards' discretion in deciding to admit or refuse candidates. Princeton policy, established in 1959, declares that verbal or mathematical aptitude scores of 780, or an average SAT of 750, mark a boy as potentially extraordinary; and no candidate with such scores may be refused by the admissions staff without further review by a faculty committee. Whenever such scores showed up on a boy's record, Edwards said, "he makes the team."

"Richard Falton!"

"Rich is up there in Bangor, Maine, he's second in a class of 242. He has a 147 on the Merit (the test given by the National Merit Scholarship Corporation; 147 is an excellent score and qualifies a student further for a crack at a scholarship). We don't have a CSG."

Edwards, reading over Farrell's shoulder, said, "He's making some team!"

"Math team—782. Verbal—711 . . ."

Edwards lit a cigarette and browsed through the folder. "He wants to be an engineer. . . . The school puts in one of these career inventory tests. *Look* at that!"

Eglin looked at the scores reported on the "career" test. "According to the psychologists, he's going to be a nurse."

"Very poor score for policeman, I see," Edwards added. "Well. He plays first horn in the orchestra. They write a book about him. He's spent two summers studying math, science, music. He's sports editor of the yearbook. He's played varsity football, baseball, basketball, track. Taking three Advanced Placement courses this year. Guidance counselor says he comes from a good home background, from a reading family—sounds a bit of a prig. But I don't think we're going to find a better engine [for engineer] kicking around. He's *in. . . ."*

This year, Edwards and his associates processed some 4,000 such folders. On April 16, the letters went out with the news—admission for 1,200-odd, refusal for about 2,700, an ambiguous position on an Alternate List (with advice to plan on entering some other college) for the rest. In September, about 800 strong—those of the accepted who decided to go to Princeton rather than somewhere else, plus perhaps a handful from the Alternate List—a new freshman class will sleep in the dormitories of Old Nassau.

The Ancient Mariner chose one of three, at random, and happened to get Coleridge. The "prestige colleges" of the Ivy League choose one of three (at Harvard, one of four) with the greatest possible care and delicacy, and worry about what they get. Admissions departments at the most prominent private colleges today face problems that are various, endless and beyond solution. They cannot with anything like full confidence select from the large community of "qualified applicants" that smaller group who will make the most of a liberal arts education and move to distinction as adults. They cannot hope to please coaches who want the raw material for winning sports teams, or faculty members who regard only a certified genius as a plausible student (provided he is really smart). They cannot even predict to safe tolerances how many of the boys they accept will in turn accept them.

For eighteen years, Princeton's Edwards lived amongst these problems with a kind of grim insouciance, refusing to worry about what could not be helped. He is a barrel-chested, earnest but by no means humorless man with a round face and close-cut gray hair. Born in Boston and reared in California, he taught American history before the war at the Noble & Greenough School in Dedham, near Boston, served in the American Field Service and returned to Princeton in 1945 to help organize the special veterans' program for students who flooded in under the GI Bill. When veterans turned out to be like other students (only better), Edwards' job was merged into the admissions department. Of the admissions directors at the major Ivy

League colleges, Edwards was the only one who dwelt atop the volcano from the first shocks of the late forties to the continuous lava flows of 1962. On April 23, a week after the announcements went to the boys, he resigned as admissions director, partly because he felt obliged to help out with his family's business in California, partly because "I don't think I could live through another admissions season.

"Before 1946," Edwards says, "the only question the admissions committee had to answer was, could he or couldn't he? A boy who wanted to come to Princeton simply took his College Board exams and validated fifteen Carnegie Units. (A Carnegie Unit is a high-school course, in any subject, that meets every day for at least forty minutes.) At that point, the bells rang, the lights flashed, and you were in. In 1946, for the first time, there were more qualified boys than the admissions committee could accept. Since then, instead of setting up standards for admission we've had to make comparisons, choose among boys all of whom meet the standards. What we're trying to compare, too, are very different attributes and abilities."

The changes in the admissions job are startlingly large. Harvard, which now turns down three-quarters of its applicants, took almost two-thirds of them as recently as ten years ago. Princeton used to get four-fifths of its applications from a relatively few private preparatory schools; this year two-thirds of the applicants (and a majority of the entering class) were drawn from 1,561 public high schools. Quality has risen even more rapidly than numbers. At Princeton, this year's average applicant had a scholastic aptitude verbal score of 604. (Nine girls sent in applications, with an average SAT-V of only 530, "which proves," says Greg Farrell, "that girls who apply to Princeton are dumber than boys who apply to Princeton.") The class that actually entered Princeton ten years ago had an average SAT-V of 585, a figure not much higher than the average score of this year's *rejects*. Edwards believes that about 3,000 of 1962's 4,000 applicants could handle Princeton work: "These days, it's a breath of fresh air to read a folder from a boy who really isn't qualified."

Under the admissions procedures set by the Princeton faculty in

1959, about 150 boys a year qualify virtually automatically through test scores or school records which place them scholastically in the top half of one percent of the nation's high-school graduates. (Most of these boys have applied to more than one college, and they will be accepted everywhere; fewer than 70 of the 150 will come to Princeton.) Once those who "make the team" are past, a boy must show something more than pure academic ability. Of those candidates whose College Board scores place them in the top 3 percent but below the top half of one percent, two-fifths will be turned down.

"I looked for something that stuck out," Edwards says. "The boy has written a violin concerto, or run a hundred yards in 9.7, or taken a program heavy with Latin and Greek, which is rare these days." A candidate for Princeton's engineering school, which is supposed to get a fifth of every class, received special consideration, because engineers are hard to find—the brightest boys tend to look on themselves as mathematicians and physicists, not engineers. A boy from a backwoods high school got a second look, too, on the theory that he must have a strong reason for wanting Princeton. High priority went to a Negro applicant who was clearly qualified on all counts. (But the admissions department does not always know an applicant is a Negro: Princeton requires no photograph with an application, and alumni interviewers may be too shy to mention the fact. A few summers ago a boy nobody at Princeton knew was a Negro turned up in the freshman class, to Edwards' delight. Few Negroes apply to Princeton; before the Civil War, it had a large Southern population, and reputations last long in education. Last year Princeton made a special effort to learn why some Negro boys accepted for the class of '65 had finally decided to go to another college; from one, the answer came back, "I don't think I want to be Princeton's Jackie Robinson.")

And, of course, the son of a Princeton alumnus—the "legacy," in admissions terms—would be accepted unless there was a good reason to turn him down. "Good reason," inevitably, is variously defined. "The faculty," says Tom Eglin, "feels that any idiot whose father went to Princeton can get in. The alumni feel your boy has to be a genius to make it." About two-thirds of Princeton's legacies were taken in 1961, but the proportion was lower this year. Legacies account for about one-fifth of each class.

Selection of next fall's entering class began, in effect, in May, 1961, when most college-bound juniors took a set of the College Boards, partly for the chance to pick up achievement scores in subjects they had been studying all year, partly for the same reasons that a trainer exercises a horse a few days before a big race. At Princeton, nobody paid much attention; the staff was wholly occupied fending off plaintive or violent or even vicious attacks from the parents of boys who had been refused admission, from the schools, and from the alumni interviewers who had, sometimes passionately—"Please, Bill, please, for God's sake"—recommended them.

The new year proper started in June, when letters requesting application blanks for the class of 1966 arrived in quantity. Each letter launched a gray-brown file folder which would end up, much fatter, on the table in the basement room. Soon the first interview reports were in the folders, though not by the choice of the admissions staff. "Summer used to be a time of peace," Edwards recalls, "but there is no more peace. Last year, we interviewed, on a quiet hot July Tuesday, maybe twenty boys coming in to see Princeton with their parents and to see us." Meanwhile, staff members took care of some housecleaning, preparing for the dean's office the annual small "danger list" of boys just admitted despite certain academic or psychological weaknesses, writing reports to President Robert Goheen, to the alumni and the College Board, and entering on the CSG ledger books, to the credit or debit of the schools which had sent them, the grades of last year's freshman class.

In October, the forms were sent out—to each candidate, an application for admission to the freshman class, a handsomely illustrated booklet called *Undergraduate Education at Princeton* and a copy of the current undergraduate catalogue with course descriptions; a form for a "principal's report" on the boy, calling for a full academic record, a few checklist items, an over-all one-word rating, and a page worth of personal comments; and another form, accompanied by a stamped, addressed envelope, to be given to a favorite teacher for a more intimate (and sometimes more literate) appraisal than Princeton can expect to receive from the usual principal or guidance counselor. Then the admissions staff followed the forms, visiting schools of every kind in nearly every state, interviewing upwards of 2,000 boys. "The glamour jaunt," Edwards says, "is Hawaii"—though it would be a little less glamorous for Greg Farrell, who taught in a Honolulu private school for two years, then signed on a merchant ship and sailed the South Seas for a year before returning to Princeton to join the admissions staff.

Eleven men from Princeton traveled to interview candidates last year, but seven of them did most of the work—Edwards, Eglin, Farrell, Joe Bolster of the Alumni-Schools Committee, Craig of the Financial Aid office, Registrar Howard Stepp, and John Boorn of the Class of '61. Edwards hires a new graduate for his interviewing staff each year, to make sure there would be someone who had recent contact with the undergraduate mind. Boorn, a darkly handsome football player and honor student, serious and highly observant below a casual manner, took the job for a year because it was interesting; he will move on next fall to work in architecture.

Edwards, Eglin and Farrell were, in effect, empowered to admit a boy at the interview. Visiting a school they knew, with a principal or headmaster whose opinions they had learned to trust, and with school grades and the May test scores before them, they rated each candidate A, B or C, and told the school, which usually told the boy. "An 'A,'" Edwards says, "was a commitment from us. We promised to admit the boy. It didn't guarantee him a scholarship, and it wasn't a demand bid—Princeton isn't like some schools, where the boy has to hold up his right hand and say he's not applying elsewhere. But if they know Princeton is their choice, we'd like them to withdraw other applications."

The folders representing boys with A's were read at the selection meetings with a preliminary announcement by Eglin that "he's riding on an A." Fairly often, a boy did not look quite so good against the great mass of applicants as he did when the only immediate comparison was his classmates. After reading one folder, Edwards commented, "Well, he's not very exciting, but he has an A, so I'm afraid he's in."

A visitor to this session, Dean of Students William Lippincott, took his pipe out of his mouth and asked, "If a guy goofs badly, can you de-A him?"

Edwards said, "We can de-A him"—and, in fact, a boy Princeton wanted badly to admit lost his A this year, though not necessarily his ultimate admission, when he was expelled from boarding school for getting drunk. But only complete academic collapse or severe misbehavior will take away a boy's admission once the interviewer has given him an A. Edwards wanted to abandon this system, but all the other Ivy League colleges use it, and he could not move alone without risking the loss of boys who might decide against Princeton because another college gave them a guarantee when Princeton wouldn't. The A rating is not even very effective as a recruiting device: of 353 A candidates in 1961, 97 went somewhere else.

Each Princeton interviewer operated his own way. Eglin read a boy's folder before an interview, to get material for questions. A rather small man with a high voice and youthful features, he affected an almost tentative manner, leaning forward over his desk and taking notes as the interview proceeded. Farrell, by contrast, never looked at a boy's folder until the interview was over, to make sure his judgment would not be influenced by test scores or grades. He leaned back as he asked questions in his deep voice, and examined the candidate through rather formidable horn-rimmed glasses; and he never put a word on paper until the interview was finished. He pushed for an answer from a boy where Eglin would move on to something else; Eglin was more interested in hearing the sort of question a boy would ask about Princeton, Farrell more interested in hearing a boy talk about himself. Eglin gave a little edge to an athlete, Farrell to a boy who seemed to have been reading something which interested him. Yet both maintained as informal an atmosphere as could be managed under the circumstances—and both liked many more boys than they disliked. And because they were both immersed in the same pool all year long, looking about from closely comparable vantage points and seeking similar fish, they agreed about a boy *as a Princeton candidate* more often than they disagreed. They also played squash together at lunch time.

Edwards himself stopped interviewing in January, locked himself in with the folders, jotted preliminary impressions of candidates and wrote letters for additional information where he wanted it. Edwards and the others, who also read as many folders as they could, sometimes added to the card Eglin would read at the meeting a note in red pencil to remind them of something that struck them as they glanced through the folder. These notes were not necessarily confined to the profound or the technical; at one session this year, for example, Eglin after reading the numerical data turned to Edwards and said incredulously, "Does this say *fat*, Bill?"

"Oh yes," Edwards said, unperturbed. "This is the fat boy. Guidance counselor thinks he should demonstrate self-control by losing weight."

"Good Lord, yes," Farrell said. "I saw him. He weighs more than three hundred pounds. Walks like a penguin."

Farrell read the scores, which were high, and Edwards began with, "He wants to be an engineer." Eglin muttered, "One fat engineer, coming up. . . ."

Edwards, Eglin and Farrell began the "first round" this year on Monday, February 19, and for three and a half weeks they simply read through the folders, moving from A to Z. Sessions ran from 8:30 to 5:30 weekdays, with an hour for lunch, and from 9 to 4 Saturdays. Eglin kept a running record of the results for each half day; on February 23 for example, the committee moved in the morning from CAR to CLO, took 20, rejected 33 and held 30 for further consideration; that afternoon folders moved off the table from CLO to CRE, with 13 Ins, 33 Outs and 40 Holds. No case was given extended consideration in the first round, and no arguments arose; the purpose of the first round was to get the top and the bottom out of the pile, and if there was any disagreement about a boy he was obviously neither top nor bottom.

The way to move quickly without being unfair is to adopt a prejudice about a boy early in the reading, then look in the documents for a reason to reverse it. Edwards began one reading by saying, "Here's a boy who's got top scores and he's a valedictorian, but he's also applying to the Naval Academy and he can't spell it.

He writes about himself, '*I* was elected president of my class, *I* won the science prize, *I* worked at the college labs on Saturday, *I* did this, *I* did that.' Teacher says he's a bit of a snob, which I can well believe. You saw him, Greg, and you say—you say he's great."

"I remember him," Farrell said a bit grimly. "He's a real good boy."

"I won't argue with you, Greg," Edwards said. "He's in."

Again, Edwards began reading a folder with the words, "Here's a Princeton son who sees the handwriting on the wall—he's applying to ten colleges. He got thrown out of the Blank School, and he's finishing up at XYZ Academy, that refuge of last hopes. Even there he ranks 47 out of 68. They love him, of course. They always do. Clearly qualified for Princeton work, superior boy, etc. Let's see what Fred has to say at Blank School." This comment was to be the nail in the coffin, but Fred of Blank liked the boy, felt that he was a rather shy soul who had done poorly because of pressure from a heavy-footed, aggressive father, and with increased maturity might be a credit to Princeton. Edwards read ironically an alumni interview which spoke of what a great guy the father was, then said, "I guess we'd better hold him."

The end of the first round this year saw 926 admissions, up from 784 the year before. At this point decision-making stopped briefly while the committee tried to predict how many of those accepted would in fact attend Princeton—a vital matter, because the college has room for only so many, and cannot afford the loss of tuition income if there are too few. (Two years ago, Amherst guessed low by 30 percent and had to bunk boys three and four to a room when the acceptances came in; last year, as a result, all the Ivy League colleges admitted too few and had to go to their Alternate Lists.) Each folder from the Admit pile was run through again, and each boy was assigned a probability rank, from 1 (sure to come; last year 92 percent came) through 5 (sure to go elsewhere; last year 18 percent came). After all the entrails were examined, the omen was 618 freshmen from 926 admissions.

Meanwhile, upstairs in the Financial Aid office, Bradford Craig had calculated "the gap"—the scholarship, loan or student job help each of the admitted candidates would need, over and above what he could make in the summer and what his parents could contribute, to pay the $3,000 a year which even a frugal boy must spend at Princeton. About 40 percent of every class needs some help. Craig guarantees to close the gap completely for every boy admitted on the first round, and will do his damnedest to find money for those admitted later. If the special scholarship and loan funds are inadequate, he will try to con the treasurer out of an appropriation for scholarships from Princeton's general funds; $55,000 came from this source in 1961–62. In all, Princeton this year gave its undergraduates $1,204,000 in scholarships, $350,000 in loans, and $260,-000 in wages for student jobs.

When Edwards and his colleagues returned to folder-reading, they had on the wall in front of them a giant chart, listing all the schools which sent candidates this year and the CSG and test scores of the boys already accepted and rejected from each school. Where a boy was admitted with school rank or test scores below a boy who was rejected, the committee re-examined both cases, to make sure there had been good reasons for the decisions. Then the second round began, and the folders from the Hold stack were read, again in alphabetical order, for placement in new In, Out and Hold groups.

Now everything took longer. Principal's and teacher's comments were parsed, interview reports studied, academic records analyzed to prove an upward or downward trend, or to see just how tough a high-school schedule this boy had been willing to carry. With the chart before them, the committee knew the geographical distribution of those already accepted, and might drop a small weight on the scale to help a boy from an area still sparsely covered. From now to the end—which in some years has required four rounds—was nasty work. By definition, there was something to be said for, and something to be said against, every boy whose folder had been held originally. Selection among them could not be much more than a reflection of personal taste in qualities and disabilities. Each of the committee members had his own favorites among these candidates, and argued for their acceptance; sometimes the others would yield to the strength of his feelings, sometimes not.

As the number of folders on the In stack neared the total the committee could admit, each man had to fight for his candidates, because another decision to hold would in fact be a rejection. Even after a special round for prospective engineers had eliminated all the candidates in that category, there were still five hundred folders being held for further consideration when the books were closed. "We never rejected them," Edwards says. "But they weren't in, so they were out."

Seen from the outside, the admissions staff at Princeton looked like a gourmet at table in a great restaurant, unable to choose because all the descriptions are so appealing. From inside the faculty, however, the view was different. At all the Ivy League schools the professors are complaining that the entering classes are just not good enough. Yale and Dartmouth have set up faculty committees to investigate the work of their admissions offices, and a Harvard committee grumbled to not much purpose about admissions policy in a report published two years ago. Since 1959 a subcommittee made up of the faculty members of the full Committee on Admission has worked closely with Edwards' department. In addition to reviewing policy, this committee, headed by Charles C. Gillispie, who is professor of the history of science (and a Wesleyan graduate), recommends the action to be taken on applicants whose records indicate they fall in the category of the extremely bright but seem to have emotional problems. The full committee makes final decisions every year on about twenty marginal cases in addition to applications referred to them by Gillispie's subcommittee.

"The committee was set up," Gillispie says, "because the faculty was dissatisfied with the entering class. We wanted to see if the admissions staff was preferring 'well-rounded students' to hard workers. We found that wasn't true; I think that, given the applications, a group of faculty members or trustees would choose about the same class the admissions office chooses. But we still feel we might have a brighter class than we do. We want to know why seniors in school apply to Princeton—and, even more important, why they don't apply. This matter of our clientele and its quality appears to be a question

of Princeton's image. We want to see what we can do about changing the image if it's inaccurate—and what we can do about changing
the University if, as I think is true, some of the image *is* accurate."

Edwards was not certain that a faculty or trustee group would,
in fact, make the same choices that he and his staff made—and not
entirely sure that he regarded the comment as the compliment Gillispie intended. But he was conscious of the continuing need for re-
cruitment, even under current conditions of admissions pressure, and
he recognized the image problem. Indeed, he couldn't escape it. Competition for top candidates is intense, a year-round irritant at every
admissions office. (It is restrained to intangibles, however: during
the week before the announcements were mailed out, the financial
aid officers of the Ivy League colleges and M.I.T. met in Boston to
make sure each school's scholarship offers were in line with what its
rivals were offering the same boy.) Part of Edwards' annual report
to President Goheen was a rundown on where the boys went who
decided against Princeton—in 1961, there were 119 who went to
"our most serious competitor," Harvard. Some years ago Princeton
fretted over a boy first-class in both swimming and school, who was
receiving weekly letters from the Yale swimming coach about the
progress of the athletic season; and Harvard this year sent Princeton
a cold letter inquiring whether any special inducements had been
given to a prize-winning young scientist and musician to make him
tell a Harvard recruiter that he just wasn't interested, he was committed to Princeton. "We're dealing in both a violent buyer's market
and a violent seller's market," Edwards said. "We don't go out and
stand on a soapbox and wave orange-and-black banners, but we do
try to present Princeton in the most favorable light. You can't begin
to estimate the harm F. Scott Fitzgerald did us with his idea of
Princeton as a country club."

The recruiting work of the admissions office is done mostly
through an Alumni-Schools Committee headed by Joe Bolster ('52),
a rather small, serious young man who combined coaching the cross-
country track team with service on the admissions staff before taking
his present job in 1959. Bolster keeps in touch with Princeton clubs
and individual alumni all around the country. These informal repre-

sentatives, armed with kits from Nassau, make sales pitches at "college nights" in the high schools, badger principals and guidance counselors for the names of outstanding boys, and line up interviews for visiting members of the Princeton admissions staff. Recently, several clubs have established prizes at their local high schools to give a top student a free trip to Princeton during his Easter vacation.

By all known measurements, this recruiting has been successful. More apparently superlative candidates apply to Princeton each year, and the entering class can honestly be advertised as the best ever. Yet among the most sensitive and intelligent of college admissions officers and deans, in and out of Princeton, the worry has been growing that the measurements themselves are not much good.

Interviews, for example, are notoriously weak reeds; if there are two interviews in a folder and one is a rave, the odds are about even that the other will be neutral or negative. Not long ago, the Harvard Business School studied its admissions policy in the light of students' subsequent achievement, and came out with the opinion that in judging at this level of quality most interviewers are wrong more often than they are right.

Princeton's CSG rating, too, is full of holes, like a wall against which a target has been placed for beginning riflemen. It attempts to predict only freshman grades, which are perhaps the least important single measurement of what a boy will take from his college education; its prediction of senior grades and honors has never been statistically checked, but is known to be fairly poor. The mathematical formula on which CSG is calculated gives great rewards to the boy who finishes in the top 3 percent rather than the top 10 percent of his class, though the "rank orders" which supply this information are often rather trivial calculations.

And College Board scores, partly because of the elaborate machinery with which they are produced, look much more "scientific" than they really are. At best, they measure a narrow range of attributes. "Ten percent of extra energy," Wilbur J. Bender wrote in his final report as Dean of Admissions at Harvard, "is probably worth at least 150 points on the SAT score. And judgment may be worth 200." Many other kinds of aptitude tests are possible, and some of them would give quite different results for many candidates. Two of last year's winners of National Merit Scholarships, awarded largely on the basis of a different aptitude test, scored *below the national average* on SAT-V; 140 of them had scores below the SAT-V average of Princeton's entering class.

The elements of error in all the factors—test scores, grades in school, principal's comments, interview reports—often reinforce each other rather than cancel out. All such measurements may reward priggishness as much as talent. While its difficulty and quality are usually overrated, college work does require an independence not always rewarded or even admired in the high schools—and very possibly penalized by the standardized tests. To the older generation, today's students sometimes seem a little too predictable. "We have too much mark-grubbing," says Merrill Knapp, Dean of Princeton College, "by boys who have come to Princeton only because they want to go to graduate school."

Such as it is, however, today's admissions wheel is the only wheel in town; and it isn't crooked any more. The days are gone when an admissions officer risked his job if he took too many Jewish boys from the Bronx or Polish boys from Buffalo. Princeton's procedure, moreover—the In-Hold-Out decision, repeated until the class is full —leaves room on later rounds for gambling on the boy with lower test scores but some remarkable accomplishment in biology or French or music. Most of the boys the Princeton faculty really wants will come through on the first round. Some extraordinary students, and some extraordinary young men, will remain in the Hold pile, but there is as yet nothing in their records to mark them off. A selection at random among the folders in the Hold pile would serve, almost as well as the battles in the committee, to protect the interests of Princeton, the intellectual community and the nation. The painful choosing among apparently equal candidates which characterized the third round of folder-reading was a mark not of Edwards' care but of his humanity.

Except that the whole business is necessarily inhumane. Most of the Princeton rejects are Golden Boys in their own community. "Somebody's written glowing, enthusiastic letters," Edwards said.

"They think this is the best boy in town, or in the school, the best boy in years. They're probably right. The boy knows it, it's part of his personality. Of course, an awful lot of them don't really want to go to Princeton. But there are others. If you stop to think what this reject letter will mean . . ." "Somebody," he added a few days after his resignation, "has got to find a better answer than I know."

So, on April 16, the letters went out, not only to the boys themselves but also to their schools and to the alumni who had recommended or interviewed them, who must be kept informed and encouraged to try again.

Harold Fall, who had been rejected, received a letter beginning, "It is with sincere regret that I must inform you that the Committee on Admissions was unable to include you among those selected for . . ."

Terence Falmouth, who was on the Alternate List, was told, "It is with sincere regret that I must write you that our Committee cannot admit you to Princeton at this time. . . . While this may not be the final action or decision of the Committee, I must urge you strongly to gain admission at some other college or university. . . ."

Theodore Falk, who had been accepted, did not receive a personal letter. He got a bulky envelope, including a Certificate of Admission, a postcard to be returned promptly to inform Princeton whether or not he was coming, a statement from the Undergraduate Honor Committee explaining the Honor System, and a form announcement of how much financial aid Princeton was prepared to give him. Atop the package of papers was a printed statement with the Princeton seal in orange and black: "To the Class of 1966:

"It is with very great pleasure that we send you the enclosed certificate of admission!" . . .

6

Bayard Rustin

[It is odd these days to think back to the time—1964—when Bayard Rustin was regarded as an outrageous radical and revolutionary. But the *Saturday Evening Post* needed some courage to run this very favorable piece at the time; and I got a fair amount of mail, from the South and from California, including a number of photostatic copies of the official vice squad report of the homosexual episode for which Rustin went to jail.

[That episode made more trouble for me than for anybody except Rustin himself. It is disposed of in the piece in one-half of a sentence, but it is here. I liked and admired the man, and I believed in the causes for which he was fighting. But the fact was that his career had been warped—indeed, deformed—by the extreme vulnerability in public life that comes with conviction on a morals charge. To tell Rustin's life story and leave out this fact (which nearly all of his old friends mentioned when talking about him) struck me then and strikes me still as fundamentally dishonest. Rustin's friends, however—and some of my friends who didn't know Rustin—thought I was a fink. So be it.

[The Randolph Institute has been formed, and Rustin is its director. Norman Hill is his Assistant.

[I had never met Rustin before I was assigned by Otto Friedrich to write this piece. He had dinner at our house between the time the piece was finished and the time it ran. I have not seen him since.]

DURING the middle two weeks of April, newspapers all across the country featured stories about a threat by civil rights demonstrators to tie up all traffic en route to opening day at the New York World's Fair. The day arrived, but not the thousands of cars which were supposed to "stall-in" on the network of highways leading to the Fair. Indeed, traffic moved better on that April 22nd than it had on any day for years. One of the civil rights leaders who had publicly supported the stall-in was cornered by reporters and asked to explain the failure. He praised the organizer of the abortive demonstration, then added, "But let us face the facts—he is no Bayard Rustin. If Bayard had promised two thousand cars, there would have been at least a thousand there."

The comment was a tribute to experience, and to talent. Bayard (pronounced "Buy-erd") Rustin, who first came to national attention as Deputy Director and general manager of last summer's March on Washington, has been professionally engaged for a quarter of a century as an organizer of mass movements and demonstrations. Now fifty-four, his stiff brush of hair turning gray over what is still an astonishingly youthful and athletic figure, Rustin is regarded by most civil rights leaders as the indispensable back-office man for any major effort which involves people on the streets. "Nobody will try massive action today," says Norman Hill, the young national program director of CORE, "without trying to get Bayard into it."

Rustin is a free lance in a romantic tradition associated with cheap novels and bad television rather than with real life: he is a fighter whose talents are always available to A Good Cause. Usually, the Cause is civil rights or pacifism, though Rustin has also set up picket lines to support strikes, to protest British imperialism, to denounce German anti-Semitism, etc. He is affiliated permanently with only one organization—the War Resisters' League, which lists him as Executive Secretary on leave to work for others. He has no job. A Quaker group in New York sends him a little money every month, but basically he lives on the fees he is paid for organizing demonstrations.

As the creator of what he likes to call "social dislocation," Rustin specializes in imagination and invention. The man is an artist as well as an organizer—he made his living for some years as a nightclub singer, working with Josh White and Leadbelly at New York's Café Society, and he could make a living tomorrow as an interior decorator specializing in antiques, which he collects with a knowing and loving eye. To Rustin, a demonstration is not just a matter of getting a lot of like-minded people together in one place. It is a piece of theater which will be a memorable experience for the spectators (which is what most people are); and it is an opportunity to find a soft spot where concerted action can make a dent in society.

In this spirit, Rustin in 1947 planned and organized the first Freedom Ride (he called it the Journey of Reconciliation; got arrested in North Carolina; served thirty days in a chain gang and then wrote a series of newspaper articles which led to the abolition of the chain gang in that state). In 1955–56, as the resident idea man of the Southern Christian Leadership Conference, he developed the bag of tricks which sustained Martin Luther King's bus boycott in Montgomery, Alabama. On the pacifist side of his career, he set up the first Aldermaston Ban-the-Bomb marches in Britain in 1957, and led the very courageous (if perhaps foolish) bunch of marchers who set off across the Sahara in 1960 to try to stop the first French nuclear test explosion.

Perhaps the most remarkable of Rustin's contributions has been the discovery of ways to persuade the authorities to cooperate in demonstrations against them. One of the reasons the March on Washington went so smoothly was that Rustin planned it out, step by step, with the Washington police, who were too surprised to do anything but follow his instructions. Setting up the first New York school boycott in February, Rustin achieved such excellent liaison with the police that they loaned him a sound truck to use in managing the crowds before the Board of Education. For another school demonstration in May, Rustin worked directly with the Board of Education to choose the schools most suitable for a "study-in" by colored children, and to arrange the reception of the illegal visitors. Once these magic tricks have been demonstrated, they seem reasonable enough —the authorities and the nonviolent demonstrator both wish to avoid serious trouble on the big day, and because their interests are momentarily identical they ought to be able to work together. But before Rustin began waving his wand, nobody had even imagined that American bureaucracies could be made to cooperate in their own destruction.

When Rustin signs up to organize a demonstration, he first tries "to analyze the objective situation" (a favorite phrase, left over from his Communist days in the 1930s) and to prepare a written manual, with at least a heading and a cost estimate to cover every contingency. "He's a very clear thinker," says Moe Foner of the Drug and Hospital Workers Union, for whom Rustin organized a citizens' committee in support of a strike against New York private hospitals. "He sees the problem from A to Z. Lots of people can tell you A should be done, but Rustin can tell you to do this and this and this to *get* A done. He learns fast—he came into the school boycott at three o'clock on a Saturday morning, and by Sunday he spoke as though he'd been running boycotts twice a week for years."

At work, Rustin spends most of his time on the telephone and in small meetings, hunting out the people who can be counted on to do a piece of the job. Doing one job for Rustin almost invariably leads to doing others; he keeps a record of all positive contacts in a file of 3-by-5 cards, and he is shameless about soliciting help for a demonstration. (Recently he called a reporter who knew him only through interviews to ask rather fretfully if the reporter could find him a free sound truck.) The shabby temporary offices pulse with young volunteers moving in and out, never fewer than a dozen or so, and sometimes several score, of all sizes, shapes and colors. The March on Washington was managed out of New York headquarters —and if there had been any organized protest against the Senate filibuster that would have run from New York, too—mostly because Rustin can get so much of the work done in New York by young volunteers, and it makes a difference in a movement forever starving for funds.

The young flock to Rustin partly because his disheveled personal life and work habits match so well with theirs—like them, he can spend one week working eighteen hours a day, and the next week in total idleness—and partly because he is willing to give them responsibility and let them make mistakes. One of the few on salary is Tina Lawrence, Rustin's remarkably pretty secretary (when he has a secretary; in between jobs, she says, "he sends me CARE packages"). Miss Lawrence remembers fondly the moment in the planning of the first school boycott when Rustin emerged from his office with the solution to the problem of what to do with the children on the day they didn't go to school. The idea was a number of "Freedom Schools," to be set up in church basements and club houses. Rustin described them briefly to Miss Lawrence, and then, she recalls, "He just said, 'My dear, I want you to coordinate all these Freedom Schools, and I don't care how you do it. Just give me a master list of who's teaching in each one.' You get this feeling," Miss Lawrence adds, "that he has faith in you."

Rustin enjoys educating his young volunteers in the intricacies of American social protest. "You work for him a week," Miss Lawrence says, "and unless you're a total idiot you learn something—economics, politics, the legal structure of the country. It's like a class Socrates might have conducted, except for the hours. You'll finish up something at three in the morning, and he'll say to you, 'Now, I heard you talking earlier about automation and what it was going to do to the Negro. What did you mean by that word, automation, and what do you think should be done about it?' And he won't let you go home until you come up with a bright idea."

As a result of her first year's education from Rustin, Miss Lawrence organized a group called East River CORE, which made the front pages of the newspapers by dumping garbage on the Triborough Bridge and tying up homeward traffic to Long Island for two hours on a spring day. They consulted Rustin before they moved, and Rustin advised against their demonstration, on the grounds that it was too complicated, didn't really relate to what they were protesting against (segregated schooling), left no possibility for negotiation, and might actually harm someone by delaying an ambulance or a fire engine. When he finished, Miss Lawrence said, "Do you want us to drop it?"

Rustin said, "Do I convince you?"

"No."

"Then do it," Rustin said. "The only way you'll ever learn anything is by making mistakes."

When the big day came, Miss Lawrence was on salary on one of Rustin's projects, and he came out at about four in the afternoon to dictate a memorandum. "I can't," said Miss Lawrence, shaking her long black hair at him. "I've got to go sit on a bridge."

"Oh, that's right," Rustin said, grinning. "I forgot. Well, good luck, my dear." And he returned to his office to scribble out the memo himself.

The upshot of the Triborough Bridge demonstration was as Rustin had predicted, a set of screaming headlines in the papers about the dangerous militants of East River CORE—and nothing else. Commenting on this sort of demonstration, A. Philip Randolph, the seventy-five-year-old president of the Brotherhood of Sleeping Car Porters, once said, "It's easy to get people's attention; what counts is getting their *interest.*" But Miss Lawrence learned, and when the World's Fair "stall-in" was dominating the newspapers, East River CORE alone among the New York chapters of CORE stood by the national leadership in opposing the plan. Reporters were intrigued by the apparent shift in position, but there were no headlines in the paper about it; and that was a lesson, too.

Rustin insists that every demonstration he runs shall be related immediately to a specific objective. Freedom Rides and lunch-counter sit-ins are the ideal, because they call attention directly to the evil being fought and at the same time establish a strong bargaining position for the negotiations which must be the result of any successful demonstration. Schools, jobs and housing, the Negro objectives in the North, are less easily demonstrated for. Though he opposed the "stall-in" as pointless, Rustin went out to the World's Fair on opening day and got himself arrested for blocking the entrance to the New York City pavilion. "We couldn't let that Fair open without a protest," he says. "A Fair celebrating American affluence, with a third of the country living in poverty." But he felt awful the morning after, because the demonstration was what he calls "grasshopping—just a demonstration, no purpose to it."

The lesson comes from Gandhi, who was Rustin's particular idol, and from A. Philip Randolph, who has been Rustin's mentor and protector since he broke with the Communist Party in 1941. Though his name doesn't get in the newspapers much, because he speaks only when he has something important to say, Randolph is still, as he has been for a generation, the most significant and effective of the Negro leaders. Almost singlehanded, Randolph secured what are still by far the most important governmental actions affecting the American Negro—Franklin Roosevelt's Executive Order 8802, outlawing discrimination on government contracts, and Harry Truman's desegregation of the armed forces. Randolph won the first by threatening a

March on Washington at a time of international crisis, and the second by urging Negroes not to register to be drafted into a Jim Crow army —an action far more "militant" than anything the new razzle-dazzle leadership has ever dared. "I remember," Randolph says, smiling happily, "an FBI man at the meeting where I said that, and he came up to me and said solemnly, 'Is that your statement,' and I said, 'Yes.' He told me not to go away, he was coming back with somebody else, and I said I was staying right there; and he came back with somebody else, but I never heard from either of them again."

Alone among the Negro leaders, Randolph has a permanent chair among the seats of the mighty, on the executive council of the AFL-CIO. To give this position a little more leverage, he organized in 1960 the Negro American Labor Council, which he leads. He was the only person ever considered by the civil rights groups to be director of the March on Washington, and it was at his insistence, over the more or less violent objections of everyone else, that Rustin was made deputy director. Norman Hill of CORE explains Rustin's position simply: "The man who has always pulled things together is Randolph, and Rustin is close to Randolph."

The other leaders objected to Rustin's prominence for one reason: they were scared. Even today, after everything has turned out well, they will begin any conversation about Rustin's appointment with the words, "Knowing how vulnerable he is . . ." Probably nobody else in American public life is so easily attacked as Bayard Rustin. He was an organizer for the Young Communist League; refusing to go to a Conscientious Objector camp, he served twenty-eight months in Lewisburg Penitentiary for draft evasion in World War II; and while most of his twenty-three arrests are the battle stripes of a cause, one, in California some years ago, was on a morals charge. This incident cost Rustin his job as Race Relations Secretary for the Fellowship of Reconciliation, and some years later forced his departure from the Southern Christian Leadership Conference when Adam Clayton Powell for political reasons of his own began a campaign of innuendo about "Rustin's sinister influence" on Martin Luther King.

A politician wishing to accuse Rustin of "disloyalty" can easily convict him out of his own mouth—twenty years ago, Rustin said and wrote comments about the United States which make Malcolm X look like a narrow-minded piker. "I tell you, brother," Rustin says today, "I fought against it for years, against being American—in my speech, my manner, everything. My experience was like Jimmy Baldwin's, really—it's a hard thing for a Negro to accept, being American, but you can't escape it."

"There's a limit to how big Bayard can become," says George Houser, director of the American Committee on Africa, who has worked with Rustin since they both took jobs at the Christian pacifist Fellowship of Reconciliation in 1941. (They came from entirely different directions—Rustin from the Communist Party, which he had just left; Houser from the Union Theological Seminary.) "If Bayard ever gets on a high perch, it's too easy for some Southern senator to knock him off it."

The man who could be knocked off the perch was born in West Chester, Pennsylvania; his faintly English accent was deliberately acquired during the time he was trying to escape being American. "I come," he says, "from a very working-class background. I was illegitimate, as so often happens in the Negro community, and I was brought up by my grandparents. My father was from the West Indies. My grandfather was a caterer and extremely poor, but there was always enough to eat because of leftovers from the banquets. Sometimes there would be no real food in the house, but there was plenty of *pâté de foie gras* and Roquefort cheese." From an early age, Rustin helped prepare banquet dishes, which left him with skill as a cook and pride in his skill. Most of the time these days he has to eat hotel food or the product of the short-order cook in the hash-house, but every so often he likes to whip up something startling for friends. On his travels, which now include most of the globe, he picks up ideas and techniques for dishes as well as for demonstrations. "After six months in India," he says, "I could make a curry as well as any Indian alive."

Like many other intelligent working-class Negroes before and since, Rustin went drifting about the country after graduation from high school (where he was on state-championship football and track teams). He returned sporadically to Pennsylvania, and accumulated three years at two of that state's Negro colleges—Wilberforce and Cheyney State Teachers. At both, he helped pay his bills by singing. "The quartet we had at Wilberforce must have been pretty good," he recalls. "After I left, the group went on without me, as The Charioteers."

During his drifting, Rustin wandered into the Communist Party, and when he came to New York in 1938 it was as an organizer for the Young Communist League. He enrolled at City College, where for three years "I did just enough work to stay matriculated"; his real job was recruiting evening-school students for the Party. He continued to pay his bills by singing, but now he was in the big time, at Café Society. "He was really very good, you know," George Houser says. "He had an audience appeal. If he'd wanted to play it that way, he could have been a Belafonte."

Those first years in New York, Rustin gave most of his earnings to the Party and lived in Harlem with an aunt, moving about the ghetto from one tenement to another. He was and still is immensely excited by the sight of great masses of colored people in one place, whether it is Africa or One Hundred Twenty-fifth Street on Easter Sunday— "so many people, all so happy, so beautiful. In Harlem," he says, "I thought I'd find this wonderful community, all these colored people bunched together. And at one level, there *is* a strange sense of community—but on another level, there's an absolute isolation and loneliness. There's such a preying upon one another, a kind of necessary preying, but it's terrible."

Hatred for the social system that creates Harlems still drives Rustin's attitudes and actions. For all his experience, he is still shocked by what he calls "the breaking-in"—the incessant burglarizing by which some Negroes live off other Negroes. (And nothing is sacred—the typewriters and mimeograph machines at the offices of the March on Washington were stolen several times, and had to be redeemed at pawn shops.) Among the by-products of this hatred is Rustin's contempt for the Black Muslims, who have no social or economic program. "Prostitution and dope addiction, people being thieves and liars," he says, "this is a *disease*, growing out of a social situation. Maybe the Muslims have reformed some prostitutes and drug addicts, though I've spent time with them and I haven't seen any. But for every five prostitutes the Muslims convert, the system in Harlem makes fifty more."

This hatred kept Rustin in the Communist Party through the Trotsky trials and the Hitler-Stalin pact, which shook out much of the membership. What drove him away, oddly, was the event that made Communism respectable for other Americans, the German attack on Russia in 1941. "In the Scottsboro case and such things," Rustin says, "the Communists had given the appearance of great interest in civil rights. Then, I was brought up a Quaker, you know, by my grandmother, and the Communists had become the great peace party. I was working on the campaign against segregation in the armed forces, and the Communists were all for it. Then Hitler attacked, and they became a war party. The line was, 'Everybody in the armed forces. People's war. Second front. No domestic issues; forget about discrimination in the Army.' "

For Rustin, leaving the Party meant a break with all his friends, his work, his purpose in life. He remembers not knowing what to do with himself for a week, until an acquaintance suggested that he go talk with A. J. Muste at the Fellowship of Reconciliation. Muste showed Rustin that there could be a profoundly radical, violently nonviolent movement apart from the Communist Party, and introduced him to the people with whom he is still working. Indeed, CORE was founded in Chicago as a secular arm of Muste's religious Fellowship; James Farmer and George Houser, its original leaders, were both on the Fellowship payroll. Rustin served at the beginning as the organizer of the New York branch.

The shock of leaving the Party was followed a year later by the shock of a long jail sentence on the draft charge, and between the two of them they made Rustin a less exclusively political being. Though he seems from the outside to be wrapped up in the cause, his activist friends are often disturbed to find that he has private tastes far removed from politics and meetings and demonstrations. His exotic apartment, his love for music and his wide-ranging tastes in books give his friends the belief that, as one of them says, "Bayard will give himself unstintingly to the specific project, but for the long-term follow-through, I think he gets bored with it."

Rustin lives in four and a half rooms in a new (predominantly white) middle-income housing development south of Penn Station on New York's West Side. His apartment is not like the others in this development, or in any other development. It is profusely decorated with religious paintings and *objets,* ranging in size from small metal crucifixes and miniature African wood carvings to six-foot-high stone and wood German sculptures of saints, resting on Gothic pedestals. (Except for a huge pair by the door to the terrace, which rest on antique cabinets converted to stereo speakers.) The furniture is carved dark wood of a German High-Renaissance style, with crimson plush cushions for the chairs. Outside, looking very odd on the dusty austerity of a middle-income terrace, is the one piece of non-Christian art in the place—a small erotic bas-relief from the Tantric tradition of India.

Most of Rustin's antiques are German, because they were acquired through an elderly Berlin refugee named Leon Medina, who had a shop on New York's University Place and was probably Rustin's dearest friend during the dozen years following the war. Rustin called Medina "Papa," accompanied him to auctions, helped him with refinishing jobs, and acted as his purchasing agent with unlimited authority on trips out of the country. "The best pieces" Rustin owns were left to him by Medina's will.

The original acquaintance with Medina and the interest in German antiques trace back indirectly to Rustin's twenty-eight months in Lewisburg. "The awful thing about prison," he says, "is the being bored"; and to avoid it, Rustin taught himself to play the guitar. Finding that most of what was available for the guitar had been written for lute, he built himself a lute and learned to play that. Emerging from prison, he went browsing for furniture that would go with the lute, and stepped through Medina's door.

Rustin's enthusiasm for lute music carried through in another direction, too. People visiting his apartment for the first time are always surprised (and sometimes rather discomfited) to find that the phonograph is playing a Renaissance Mass or a Bach suite for orchestra rather than the expected jazz or folk songs. "Music," says a sinister character in Thomas Mann's novel *The Magic Mountain,* "is politically suspect"; and Lenin once told Maxim Gorky that he could not listen to music too often—"It affects your nerves and makes you want to say stupid nice things." Rustin in a way confirms the comments: "When you're dealing with people all the time and nothing is ever settled," he says, "it's a great pleasure to strike a C-chord and know it's a C-chord."

Rustin's friends worry about his future. "He was *much* younger three or four years ago," says Tom Kahn, a lean, intense young man whom Rustin recruited from the Socialist Party for the first Youth March for Integrated Schools in 1958, and who served as Rustin's aide-de-camp ("the man who picked up the pieces") through the March on Washington last year. "The March took an enormous amount out of him. I worked sixteen hours a day with him, I'm a lot younger than he is, and it drove me crazy. But the leaders regard him as possessor of inexhaustible childish energy which never has to be compensated for."

Except for Randolph, in fact, the leaders speak rather coolly of Rustin: "If you want to work with Bayard, you have to know how to *use* him," says the director of one group. "Bayard Rustin is not a Negro leader," Whitney Young of the National Urban League once explained with some care, "because a Negro leader is the head of a Negro organization." ("That tells you," Tom Kahn says bitterly, "what is wrong with the Negro movement"—but Rustin himself agrees entirely with Young.) Since the March on Washington, however, Rustin has seemed so useful that he is invited as a courtesy to the policy meetings of the leadership group. He was in Washington in April, for example, at the meeting where the leaders decided not to do anything loud about the filibuster against the Civil Rights Bill. Rustin thought the decision was wrong, and said so; but he had to accept the verdict, if only because he came to the meeting representing nobody but himself.

On the other hand, Rustin's independence enables him to call his own shots, and to work for the cause as a whole rather than for any one jealous piece of it. He claims that his lack of affiliation has actually been a help. "If you have five organizations working together," he says, "each of them has to raise money and maintain an image. They can't let somebody from another organization lead their demonstration. But I can be available to all of them." Tom Kahn thinks the argument is silly, because nobody can be an effective fighter without a firm footing and a corner of his own. "Bayard," Kahn says drily, "has always been a great one for making a virtue of necessity."

Rustin probably will have an organization to lead in the near future—an A. Philip Randolph Institute, which is to be established, probably by trade-union money, to perpetuate Randolph's name, to act as a service center and clearing house for civil rights groups and to push such groups toward the non-Communist Left which Randolph has fought for since the days of Eugene Debs. Randolph has approved the plans. "I'm interested in Bayard having some sort of organizational base," he says in the magnificently deep voice that has caught the attention of AFL conventions for more than forty years. "But the Negro American Labor Council is a little too prosaic for Bayard. He moves quite expeditiously and these people want to sit around in committee and talk about it for a day. We have to invent something for Bayard, something which would give him a social situation that requires continuous creative action. This Randolph Institute might do that."

It might do more. "Now that the movement is confronting serious and basic questions in American life," says CORE's Norman Hill, "you can't be effective without an institutional base. And someone like Rustin, who is capable of building up a mass of followers, is always suspect to the leaders if he doesn't have a place where he fits." Hill thought a moment about the Rustin problem, which he has lived with since 1958, when he stopped off between Haverford College and graduate work at the University of Chigaco to absorb some education from Rustin. "At the least," Hill said rather heartlessly, "a Randolph Institute would give Bayard the chance to say, 'This in fact is where my office is . . .' "

7

The Routine Murder in New York

[Another Harold Hayes idea for *Esquire.* I accepted the assignment in part because I was beginning work on *The Lawyers,* and the gears seemed to mesh. Some years later I learned that the role of the District Attorney's office in these matters is greater than I had known, and that because of Frank Hogan's fierce desire to prosecute only guilty people the homicide squads have to prove their case pretty thoroughly to the homicide division of the New York County D.A.'s office before indictments are sought. (It was an assistant D.A., not a defense lawyer, who showed that George Whittemore had not in fact murdered Janice Wylie.) Supreme Court decisions have since outdated the paragraph about questioning of suspects, but the clearance rate for homicides has not greatly changed: murderers, on the whole, still wish to confess. It should not be necessary to add that this desire to confess is wholesome when the person confessing is in fact guilty, and that civil libertarians have rocks in their head if they believe murderers have some kind of right to escape punishment. This said, there still remains a vast difference between voluntary and involuntary confessions.]

ALONG the East River for more than half a mile stretches one of the world's great medical complexes—New York University medical school and its associated University Hospital, the congeries of buildings that make up Bellevue Hospital, and a huge red Veterans' Administration hospital. About halfway down, forming the southern border of the gleaming white N.Y.U. quadrangle, stands a new seven-story building which announces its difference from its neighbors only by a black shield beside the doorway, proclaiming that this is the office of the Chief Medical Examiner of the City of New York. A policeman, not a nurse, sits at the desk in the modest entrance room. On the rear wall, in steel letters on red marble, runs a legend: TACEANT COLLOQUIA EFFUGIAT RISUS HIC LOCUS EST UBI MORS GAUDET SUCCURRERE VITA. The policeman directs visitors to a translation in Gothic script, hung in a frame in the hall around the corner: "Let conversation cease, let laughter flee, this is the place where death de-

103

lights in helping the living." The Chief Medical Examiner's office deals in nothing but corpses.

The Latin is on the wall at the personal request of the C.M.E. himself, Dr. Milton Helpern, author of the internationally standard text on forensic medicine, Kentucky Colonel, past president of the New York County Medical Society, recipient of honorary degrees from virtually every major medical school in the Western world and of awards from countless other organizations, including the New York Funeral Directors Association. "I don't know where that Latin quote comes from," he says. "It's medieval. It sometimes has a calming influence on excited people, and we get some very excited people here." Dr. Helpern is the model of the old-fashioned country doctor (though he is a New Yorker born and bred); he wears half-glasses down on the nose, brushes a disorderly shock of white hair across a wrinkled brow, and smokes a corncob pipe. He may be a calming influence himself, in what is by no means a calm community.

About 90,00 people die in New York every year. The great majority, of course, are what the clinicians call "naturals"—another poor soul liberated by one of the ills to which mankind is prey. Nearly 30,000, however, approach the category of "sudden, suspicious or violent" deaths, which are investigated by the C.M.E. Of these 30,-000, no fewer than 6,500 are taken for autopsy. In 1964, C.M.E. records showed more than 600 of them as homicides, making New York the murder capital of the world; London, by contrast, had only 66 homicides in 1963. The murder *rates* are higher in Chicago and Los Angeles, but their populations are smaller. In New York, the number of murders is rapidly catching up with the number of deaths from automobile accidents; the Borough of Manhattan already shows about 300 murders a year as against fewer than 200 deaths by auto.

Obviously, there has to be a system. "You can have the most marvelous equipment," Dr. Helpern says, "this wonderful building, all the talent we have working here, and it's no good unless somebody sends you the customers." The system operates by law—under the New York City Charter, it is a misdemeanor for anyone finding a dead body not to report his discovery instantly to the C.M.E. Since most people in New York have never even heard of the C.M.E., it is hard to imagine a prosecution for violation of this section of the law—but another section requires the police to report to C.M.E. all corpses that come into their hands, and here is where the matter usually starts. A medical examiner arrives at the place where the body was found and looks it over *in situ* before loading it onto the wagon for the trip to the office refrigerator.

Hospitals also report all deaths to C.M.E.; they are not allowed to release the body to an undertaker without C.M.E. clearance. Often the hospitals themselves request an autopsy, because the staff is puzzled, because there is something students or researchers might learn from some judicious slicing, or because the hospital wants to guarantee C.M.E. support in the event of a lawsuit. "You have a terminal cancer patient," an officer of a big hospital explains, "and two days before he dies he falls out of bed. Well, you want C.M.E. to certify that he died of cancer and that the fall had nothing to do with it, to make sure you don't get stuck with a negligence case."

A death does not become a homicide in New York until C.M.E. certifies it as such. "Sometimes," Dr. Helpern says, "you can't tell whether it was homicide, suicide or accident—the police have to clarify that. The body in the river is going to look the same whether he was pushed in, fell or jumped. And, of course, if a fellow was shot six times, you don't have to establish the cause of death. But you want to know, Was he intoxicated? What did he last eat? You want to know the caliber—a few days ago there was a fellow in Queens, and the report said it was a .32 or a .38, but we found it was a shotgun. That's important."

C.M.E. does not solve murders. In the words of Deputy Inspector Henry Guttenplan, head of the police Bureau of Technical Services, "The jurisdiction of the medical examiner is to establish a cause of death; he is not charged with apprehending the perpetrator." (This is the authentic police style; rookies are not allowed on the street until they have learned to say "da poipatraiter" rather than "the killer" or "the thief.") As part of discovering the cause of death, however, C.M.E. collects all the evidence that might have a bearing on how the victim came to be a corpse, from clothing to pill bottles to submachine guns. The police ballistics squad compares the bullets dug out of the body by C.M.E. against the gun impounded by C.M.E. New York has a well-equipped police lab which takes up nearly a whole floor of its spanking new Police Academy building; and here, too, there is a shield and some Latin: VERITAS PER SCIENTIAM. (The shield is kept in a storage room dominated by boxes with gay pictures of clowns; the boxes hold the Qualatex balloons used in the drunk-ometer tests.) Lab work in New York is sophisticated enough to prove through X-ray diffraction analysis that the silencers on some captured guns were made on a lathe in the home workshop of one of the Gallo gang. But nearly all the molecule examination required by a murder investigation is done at the "forensic pathology labora-tories" at C.M.E.

New York's medical examiners are highly critical of the coroner system which operates almost everywhere else in the United States. "You can't let the undertaker or the local butcher make the deter-mination of whether or not a death is a homicide," says Deputy Chief Medical Examiner Dr. John Devlin. "It's not just that people get away with murder, it's that people are tried for a murder nobody committed. All the process of law is a farce unless it's proved be-yond doubt that a murder *has* been committed." To take care of this matter, and also to help the public health authorities, New York has given C.M.E. an exceedingly elaborate medical research installation, including an electron microscope, infrared and ultraviolet spectro-photometers, nuclear magnetic resonators, and so forth. "You get a body and do an autopsy," Dr. Devlin explains, "and you don't find anything. You think, my God, maybe he was poisoned. You say, send me some brains, some liver, some kidney, they go to the dis-tillation rooms and out to the departments looking for a general unknown. There's a lot of that," Dr. Devlin adds darkly, "a lot."

C.M.E. has a number of cases every year in which investigation reveals that the man hit by the truck was dead before the truck hit him, or the man who apparently died from a stroke had been stabbed with an ice pick some days before in a friendly fight which he never reported because he felt okay when it was over and the guy who did it was his favorite drinking companion. There are also cases, though, where the police arrive to find blood all over the room—and the medical examination determines that the blood came from the future corpse thrashing about in the throes of carbon monoxide poisoning or a heart attack. Occasionally, particularly when the victim is a Bowery bum, C.M.E. has serious trouble making up its mind, because the autopsy reveals five different causes of death. And with 6,500 corpses to be looked at in a routine manner every year, C.M.E. also makes some bad mistakes—a diagnosis of natural death, for example, in a murder to which a man later confessed; and when the body was dug up, sure enough, it was full of knife holes. Good medical examiners are hard to recruit; C.M.E.'s wages are low, and a highly specialized training in pathology is desirable. "If he's just an ordinary doctor," Dr. Helpern says, "you just can't train him— you know, he can't play the piano."

By law, C.M.E. must remain open round the clock, every day of the year; and the District Attorney's office must have an Assistant D.A. of the Homicide Division on duty twenty-four hours a day. The most likely time for a murder in New York is Saturday night between ten and midnight; the most likely place is the northern half of Manhattan; and the most likely weapon is a knife, though the variety here is considerable. On a table at Manhattan North Homicide Squad, under the bulletin board featuring an illustrated Holy Name calendar (a fish for every Friday), stands a bound ledger labeled "Book of Homicides," with the basic data about each murder in the district inscribed in neat policeman's handwriting, six murders to a page. Two pages produced seven causes of death—Stab, Shot, Pipe, Gun (hit over head with), Abortion, Fist, Hot Coals.

Most cases come to the attention of the modern police force through the earpiece of a telephone; even if the body is discovered by the uniformed cop on the beat, investigation does not formally begin until the plainclothes detective at the precinct house has been notified. Each of New York's eighty precincts has its own detective squad. The detective who picks up the phone (this activity is called "catching squeals") is the man on the case, and will hold this distinction forever. When a suspect is formally charged with the murder—an action that can be taken only by the District Attorney's office, and not by the police themselves—this detective will be "the arresting officer." A detective in New York is a patrolman with talent, or perhaps with friends. Any patrolman may be assigned to a detective squad at any time, and any detective may be busted back to the uniformed force. Such changes of status do not appear in the Police Commissioner's printed reports; they are considered purely administrative and internal. Detective salaries run from $8,126 to $10,140, as against patrolmen's salaries of $6,355 to $7,806 [in 1964], so the matter is important to the individuals involved. Of the city's 23,000 patrolmen, some 3,500 work as detectives, about 150 of them in one of the eight special homicide squads.

The call to the precinct detective is merely the first of many. If nobody else has done so, the patrolman on the scene calls a hospital and orders an ambulance; and it is usually an ambulance doctor who pronounces the victim dead. He then goes away with the body, which is more than can be said for the rest of the crowd that now begins to arrive in response to the telephone calls, the radio messages from police communications center and the signals on the grapevine—the precinct detective, the assistant medical examiner, the homicide squad detective, the police photographers in their special van, the ballistics squad, the latent fingerprint squad, relatives, friends, newspapermen, and ordinary bored New Yorkers. The patrolman at the scene has been looking around for witnesses and for possible evidence (one of the ways a patrolman gets to be a detective is by handling himself well at a homicide). When the precinct detective arrives, the patrolman turns the case over, with a report of everything he knows; and the precinct detective fills in the homicide detective. "This goes on forever," says Lieutenant John Robb, commanding the homicide squad of Manhattan South, "as the higher echelons come in, and you keep relaying the facts to them."

If there are witnesses (and sometimes even when there aren't, just to stay on the safe side), the precinct detective calls the District Attorney's office. In Manhattan, a dozen lawyers work on homicides for Assistant D.A. Alexander Herman, and every day one of them takes the twenty-four-hour assignment, from nine in the morning to nine the next morning; he doesn't have to stay in the office, but the switchboard has to know where he is at every moment. "It's four in the morning," says Herman, a lean, tan, irritated lawyer who has made his career in homicides, "and you're available—you're in bed. Sometimes it's just that they've found a body, and you ask some standard questions—were his pockets inside out, that sort of thing— and then curse the cop out for bothering you and go back to bed. If they've got witnesses, you rout out a stenographer and go to the scene or to the station house. When I used to go out on cases, I was never out of a station house in less than three hours. If I have a street brawl, or a stick-up in a public place, lots of people who think they saw it, it'll take me five, six hours in the station house. There are always the two detectives, local and homicide, and sometimes ten or twelve more, plus a couple of bosses who get in the way. Sometimes I've been out on three and four cases in a night, never got to sleep. You can count on it New Year's Eve."

The case which demands the immediate presence of the D.A. is the easy one, from the police point of view. The most common is probably what the homicide squad calls "the grounder," because it's easy to field—husband and wife, or boy friend and girl friend, have got into a screaming fight, and the neighbors hear it and call the cops, who arrive to find one dead and the mate holding a smoking gun or bloody knife. (There is remarkable sexual equality in these matters: in 1963, there were exactly twenty-eight each of wives killing husbands and husbands killing wives.)

For many detectives, "the floater," the body in the river, is the most hateful case, largely because of the elaborate formal procedures involved in preserving the stinking mess and identifying it before a routine investigation can be begun. "What do you do first in a homicide?" asks a detective sergeant. "You canvass the neighborhood where you find the body. What are you going to canvass with the floater—the fish? Look. If you really know the *Manual of Rules,* and a floater washes up in your precinct, you know what you do? You push it back into the river, and hope it comes up in some other precinct."

The "D.O.A.," Dead on Arrival, presents annoyances almost as great as the floater's. What it means is that the ambulance got to the scene before the cop; and the ambulance doctor and his helper have been destroying possible evidence ever since. A more serious matter is the delay between the crime and the hospital's telephone call.

The police "clear" a higher percentage of homicides than of any other crime (about 90 percent—and Captain Paul Glazer of the headquarters staff says that in half the others "we know who did it. We have the information but we don't have the evidence; and there's no point arresting him, because then when he gets off he's got double jeopardy working for him.") Lieutenant Robb of Manhattan South argues that the homicides get solved because, "number one, we spend a lot of time on it; and number two, the homicide gets discovered shortly after it's committed, so you can put your time and effort into it immediately."

The detectives called to a homicide work on it straight through, without a break, until they lick it or they drop. "When a man catches a homicide," says a detective, "you know what happens to him? He goes thirty, forty hours without sleep. You get so tired you don't know what people are saying to you, but you've got to stay around, or something happens and you lose continuity. I love homicide, but the hours are terrible."

If the body is found where it was killed, the detective can go to work immediately, checking the locality and the people who live in it, the people who might have been with the victim when the crime occurred. The floater and the D.O.A. complicate the problem by creating a need to find the scene of the crime before routine canvassing can begin. In the case of the floater, days may elapse before the victim is even identified, and the detective's first rush of energy must be dissipated hanging around C.M.E., badgering the Bureau of Criminal Identification for news about fingerprints or laundry marks, making a pest of himself at the Bureau of Missing Persons, checking about among his stable of informers to find out who if anyone is missing from the crowd of New Yorkers who are regarded as likely candidates for a watery grave.

Murders that are not solved within the first two weeks tend to drag out. If the case is particularly irritating to the community (like the Wylie murder, the two girls brutally butchered in a fashionable apartment; or the Gallagher case, the Columbia physicist found dead

in Central Park), the detectives originally assigned to it will continue
to work on nothing else for an indefinite period of time. During this
period, they are very much their own boss, setting their own schedules and working whatever roads seem promising to them. Other
cases go on the back burner, though no homicide is ever closed until
a grand jury indicts, and the detective responsible is supposed to be
working on it even during a routine tour (in homicide, the routine
tour, in a car or at a desk, is usually a ten-hour day four times a
week or a fourteen-hour night five times in two weeks). Once a
week, the lieutenant in charge of each homicide squad will run down
with his men the outstanding cases in his area, to find out what was
done on them the week before. Some cases have been passed on
several times from retiring detective to rookie—for example, the
murder of financier-playboy Serge Rubinstein in his Fifth Avenue
mansion. "The problem with that case," says a detective who has
worked on it, "is that everybody you interview had a good reason to
kill the son of a bitch."

Apart from gang killings (which are matters of somewhat limited
concern to the police, unless they involve "civilians"), the most likely
unsolved murder is that by the burglar who panics when disturbed.
"He has no motive for killing the victim," says Lieutenant Francis
Sullivan, commanding Manhattan North Homicide, "he has no knowledge of the victim, he hasn't been in that neighborhood for a year,
and now he'll never go back." Lieutenant Robb, who came to homicide work from the relative simplicities of the Safe-and-Loft squad,
is outraged by the unique anonymity of the New York murder case:
"Lots of times," he says, "our homicides are people *who never laid
eyes on each other before!*"

In the absence of tips from informers or fingerprints, detectives
must rely mostly on descriptions from people who may (or may
not) have been witnesses to the murderer's escape route—hence the
canvass. These descriptions are not necessarily trustworthy: "A wit-
ness in fear for his own safety," says Lieutenant Sullivan, "will exag-
gerate certain features of face, size, and so on." Nevertheless, the
Bureau of Criminal Identification employs four policeman-artists
(more properly, illustrators) to draw pictures based on such descrip-

tions. Witnesses may also spend hours plodding through police photo files to identify men who "look like" the man they saw. Discouragingly often, these pictures turn out to be of men who are currently in jail, but sometimes a burglar on parole will find a surprise waiting for him when he next reports to his parole officer.

In a homicide of any difficulty at all, the evidence against a suspect is highly circumstantial, and often the significance of the scientific data is that they do not *eliminate* this one. If the blood on the suspect's coat matches the victim's type and not his own, nothing is proved—but if it *doesn't* match the victim's type, it makes excellent evidence for the defense (provided the defense attorney knows enough to ask about it). Among the cases of which C.M.E. is particularly proud is the murder of a French prostitute—"a two-hundred-dollar-a-night gal," says Dr. Devlin. "She was sixty. I did the autopsy, and when the police asked me how old she was, I said, maybe thirty-five, meaning she could be younger. She'd been out that night with an engineer, he'd gone up in the elevator with her at midnight and come out at three in the morning, and she was found bound and smothered. We did an analysis of the semen on her leg, and it wasn't his—he was nailed, but it wasn't his!" Sometimes, of course, technical evidence can be good enough to shift the burden of proof onto the suspect, whatever legal theory may say—if the murder gun has his fingerprints on it, he needs a really beautiful explanation.

Normally, however, what solidifies the cops' belief that they have their man is the suspect's own statement during questioning in the station house. There is a good deal about any crime that can be known only by the man responsible, and most suspects talk. Murder suspects are rarely if ever beaten up by the police in the station house (drunks and bums sometimes are, if the orders are to keep a neighborhood free of such presences); they talk because their act is on their minds, and they want to justify it. A detective tells about a case that started as a floater, which became a seventeen-year-old girl with a name and a boy friend who had killed her:

> He said she told him she wouldn't do it that night because she had the curse, and he said she'd have to do it anyway. She locked herself in the bathroom, and he got his shotgun and threatened to shoot

through the door if she didn't come out; and when she wouldn't come
out, he said, the gun went off accidentally. All her fault. He loaded
the body in a paper carton and took it off to the river. You hear all
this talk about the girl in Queens who was yelling, and thirty-eight
people heard her and nobody called the cops. Well, this box with the
girl in it was heavy, and it was a little small, and every time he put
it down when he was carrying it to the river a leg would flop out or
an arm or something. *Hundreds* of people must have seen it—but
nobody called the police. Once we had the story, of course, it was
easy to check.

Murder stories get checked fairly often. They must be accepted
first by the district attorney's office: "Since we're lawyers," Alexander
Herman says rather tartly, "we know what a legal case is; so we direct
the arrest." Then a grand jury hears them, and decides whether or
not the evidence justifies prosecution; and, finally, the whole business
is thrashed out before a judge and jury. Both the precinct and the
homicide detectives work closely with the D.A. at every step in the
proceeding; the gathering of evidence is by no means completed with
the arrest. Every time the case is called in court, even if everyone
knows that the only purpose of the hearing is a postponement, the
homicide detective must be present. "You sit around all day," says
one detective sourly, "just so you can escort the prisoner from the
courtroom door to the defense table—any uniformed cop in the court
could do it, but you have to be there." Departmental rules demand
that the detectives be present throughout the ultimate trial; and a
"Murder One" (first degree, with a possible death penalty) never
takes less than three weeks in New York. Even a lazy man can get
bored sitting around a courtroom or repeating the same story over
and over again. The loudest complaints uttered by homicide detectives (and especially by their supervising officers) are about this waste
of time at the conclusion of a case.

Nevertheless, homicide seems to be a popular duty with the New
York police. The average age of the squads is high, not much (if at
all) short of forty; and in a bureaucratic, paramilitary organization the
popular jobs can always be identified by their association with seniority. Creature comforts are minimal, and the homicide detective
probably works longer hours over the course of a year than any other

man on the force. Manhattan South is housed three sagging flights up in one of the old rabbit warrens corruptly built as precinct houses at the turn of the century; Manhattan North is in a new building, but homicide's floor, which the squad shares with the locker rooms, is the only one not air-conditioned in the summer, and this year's economy drive took the poor cops' Coke machines away to save the cost of the electricity. A firehouse is on the other side of a thin wall, and the bells ring all night long. Still, the work is intrinsically interesting.

"When I was with the Eighteenth Squad," says Lieutenant Sullivan, "we had nine thousand cases a year, mostly petty larceny. On a precinct squad, you get nine or ten cases on a tour, and you don't have much incentive to follow up. The ordinary man is very much inclined to give everything he's got to a homicide." Most homicide detectives also relish the relative independence of the post: though pressure from on high can get pretty heavy on occasion, the day-to-day work is done alone, in plain clothes, in unmarked cars, without much supervision from the Department's serried ranks of sergeants, lieutenants, captains, deputy inspectors, inspectors, deputy chief inspectors, assistant chief inspectors, etc. There are few opportunities for graft, but the New York policeman's reputation as a grafter has been much exaggerated, certainly since Commissioner Valentine cleaned up the force for Fiorello La Guardia. And to the degree that "service" is the satisfaction of the cop (a degree much greater than is commonly realized), the homicide squad offers certainty—whatever arguments people have about the role of the police in the society, everybody agrees that catching murderers is a contribution.

Nobody who works on any aspect of murder investigations in New York wants to be accused of brilliance. "You can't just take a dead body and commune with it and come up with the answers," says Dr. Helpern, who is the most liable to such accusations. "We don't go in for the bizarre stuff. It's all hard work, a lot of investigation." Perspiration is the fashion—and, indeed, the fact. "We spend hours and hours," says Lieutenant Robb, "digging and digging to find witnesses. You're no better than your witnesses." Deputy Inspector Guttenplan of Technical Services wriggles at the popular notion of what his boys do. "This business of a lab cracking a case," he says, "it doesn't happen. Well, maybe it does happen, but not often. We're a service unit, that's our philosophy; we're part of a team."

New York has no Hercule Poirot or Inspector Trent; there is no roving staff of detective geniuses at headquarters who can be summoned to say, "Aha!" The case is handled where it occurs, by that part of the machine which scratches its metallic mesh across this turf. When someone is specially assigned, it is likely to be for organizing ability—like Lieutenant Sullivan, a blond, crew-cut young man with a violent New York accent, who was in charge of the arrangements for guarding Khrushchev and Castro when they were in New York for a United Nations meeting, and is now refining the procedures at embattled Manhattan North.

Murder and the communications network switch on the machine, the gears grind, and nine times out of ten the answer pops out the slot. It can even be argued that we don't want brilliance in this operation, for brilliance is best defined as the ability to make unlikely connections. Given the enormous power of the police over the individual—the fact that, as the late Charles P. Curtis of Boston wrote, "no one who has been indicted and formally charged with crime is really presumed innocent by anyone but his friends or well-wishers or someone who happens to know that the government was wrong"— we may all sleep more soundly in our beds for the knowledge that our detectives rely on system rather than on intuition. Anyway, despite popular mythology to the contrary, cops are a lot smarter than crooks: the average IQ in the prisons is about seventy-five, and most murderers are even less intelligent than the run of criminals.

If the classical legal philosophers and criminologists were right— if, as Bentham and Lombroso argued, crime is deterred by the certainty of its punishment rather than by the severity—New York's 90 percent clearance rate should have stopped murder by now. Instead, the numbers have more than doubled in the years since the war, though the population of the city has been stationary. Perhaps the last, thudding word has been said by the Police Department itself, in last year's release of the data gathered by its Statistical and Records Bureau. "While the figures indicate that most homicides occur on the spur of the moment and that the increase tends to show a disintegration of moral values, the Bureau stated: 'The motive for murder is buried deep in the mind of the murderer.' " There's something reassuring—at least a little reassuring—about that.

[A nice New York cop story related to Lt. Sullivan's UN duty tells of the radio call that Khrushchev was on his way to lunch at the Guinean Mission—and the surprise of the clerks at the Italian Mission when they looked out the window and saw hundreds of policemen.]

8

A High Order of Talent:
Bernstein's Falstaff

[I am not an "opera buff," but I am a sucker for opera, which is for me incomparably the greatest of art forms. And I admire *Opera News* and its editor Frank Merkling. In the fall of 1963, Frank called in a promissory note that I would write something for him, and we went over the possibilities for the forthcoming season. By far the most interesting to me was the projected *Falstaff;* and I cannot imagine ever again enjoying so greatly the gathering of information for an article. The production described here was mounted, of course, in the old Opera House at Thirty-ninth Street.]

OF ALL human activities, with the one exception of war, an opera production brings together the greatest variety and disparity of talents and temperaments in search of a single goal. From the hammering together of sets to the hammering out of an ensemble, an endless number of activities must be performed in tempo, in collaboration, and well-nigh perfectly by all concerned. The basic abilities required are physical, which means that they may be common to people who have nothing else in common. (Opera is full of people who are forever touching, slapping the back, embracing—because they must work closely together, and they have no other means of making contact.) The direction of the enterprise, however—the management of the theater, the planning of the music and the drama—presents almost exclusively intellectual problems, requiring for their solution an unusual mixture of systematic intelligence and human understanding. Behind a triumph like that of the Bernstein-Zeffirelli *Falstaff* lies a long trail of decisions by many people other than the principals.

It all takes time, too. Rudolf Bing and his associates knew before the end of 1961 that the Metropolitan Opera was going to stage *Falstaff* in March, 1964. By May of 1962, Leonard Bernstein was signed to conduct the opera and Franco Zeffirelli to design and direct it. (The two men came as a team. They had long since become friends in Italy, and they wanted to try working together; at one time they planned to do a *Falstaff* for television. Neither was available without the other.) Singers were chosen for them through the rest of 1962 and into 1963. Neither Zeffirelli nor Bernstein had asked to be consulted in the matter of casting roles. "It's not that kind of opera," Zeffirelli says in lightly, crisply accented English. "If I am asked to do a *Tosca,* I want to know who's the Tosca; if I am asked to do a *Falstaff,* I want to know who's the conductor."

In the end, the cast included three principals who had performed *Falstaff* with Zeffirelli before—Regina Resnik as Quickly, Fernando Corena as the alternate Falstaff, Luigi Alva as Fenton. Gabriella Tucci had sung Alice to great acclaim at La Scala. Most of the rest were new to their parts; it would be a first Nannetta for Judith Raskin, a first Meg for Rosalind Elias, a first Falstaff for Anselmo Colzani, Mario Sereni's first Ford in nine years. And it was the Metropolitan's first *Falstaff* since 1949. There was a lot of work to do.

By January, 1963, technical administrator Herman Krawitz and artistic administrator Robert Herman had made up fairly firm schedules for *Falstaff.* Zeffirelli came in that month with sketches for the sets and costumes. Krawitz, a blunt, chubby, talkative refugee from the theater, looked over the sketches for technical feasibility and passed them on to Mr. Bing for approval ("He *never* delegates the final approval," Krawitz says). There were three other new productions this season, and the costume shop would not be done with *The Last Savage* until this January twentieth, so the costumes were farmed out to the expert Karinska; Zeffirelli went to her shop overlooking the theatrical shabbiness of West Forty-fourth Street and talked fabrics and decorations. Wigs were ordered from Florence, as they have been for five years. The rest, Krawitz decided, could be done by the Metropolitan's own set- and prop-makers, in the big old loft building half a block from the house.

When Zeffirelli returned to America in May with the finished drawings (which he made himself), he went over to the shops and met Tex Lawrence, the lean, mustachioed director of scenery construction, grandson of the man who ran its carpentry department sixty years ago. "All we talked about was the things that made it impossible to do what he wanted," says Lawrence, who made his living for ten

years as a commercial fisherman in Mexico and cultivates the fisherman's attitude of total discontent. "Everything was too big to go on
this stage." The *Falstaff* sets may well be the largest ever built by the
Metropolitan. They had to be intricately hinged to get down the elevator, and they will have to be entirely rebuilt to a different scale for
the Spring Tour. Zeffirelli found them still a little small but graciously took the blame on himself: "It's this damned problem of
thinking in meters and then designing to a foot scale."

The new *Aïda* and the new *Manon* were set up on the stage in
August, and by September the shops were beginning to work on *Falstaff*. Zeffirelli returned to New York again, to discuss scene painters
and a shoe man and to talk with Richard Hauser, a lanky, often un-
shaven young man who heads the staff of six that builds hundreds
of new props every year—from swords to furniture to candelabra to
drinking glasses—mostly out of foam rubber, wood and molded
Fiberglas. "There isn't anything we can't make," Hauser says proudly
—and then adds, "for a designer who's here to tell us about it."

Despite the precision of Zeffirelli's drawings ("he's a great technician," Hauser says), Krawitz was calling and cabling him through-
out the fall, the cables invariably beginning with the words "UR-
GENTLY NEED," which serve in the opera world as a substitute for
Krawitz' signature. He expects to send such telegrams on every show.
"No production is a *problem*," he says, "in the sense that people
usually use the word. We're geared to put on operas. But it's custom
work—it's not like pressing ashtrays, every one comes out the same.
You have to be ready, that's all. For example, I fought with Bob
Herman to get the main stage for a technical run-through on Friday,
February fourteenth, so we could hang the nets and drops and get
ready to set up. And I put two Sundays in the budget for overtime,
so we could start setting up for Zeffirelli on the sixteenth. If we hadn't
had the Friday onstage and the budget, we might have had a 'problem.' "

Herman, a lithe young man who came to the Metropolitan from
Carl Ebert's workshop at the University of Southern California, was
meanwhile scheduling singers, rehearsals and performances—a jug-
gling activity that requires a very steady hand. Many featured artists

are engaged by the performance. Rehearsal time has half value, because casts do not hold together for rehearsals. Just before the company went on the stage, a visitor commented to Zeffirelli on how glorious the ensembles had sounded in smaller rooms. "Yes," he replied.
"Sounds good—sounds different, too, every time, because the singers
are different. In five days I've had three Pistolas, three Megs and two
Falstaffs."

These rehearsal substitutes were the "cover cast" Herman chose
mostly from the roster of singers signed up for the entire season, who
can take over if somebody falls ill or fails to show up. They all have
to be coached in their roles, so the conductor does not find himself
stuck with lessons in words and music when he wants to work on
interpretation. For *Falstaff,* Herman chose Martin Rich as *maestro
sostituto* (to use the Italian phrase, more accurate than "coach") to
get the company ready for Bernstein. A rather small man from a
German background, with precise gestures and a steady beat, Rich
is listed on the roster as an Associate Conductor. He would serve as
Bernstein's "cover" at the Metropolitan, taking five performances on
the Spring Tour when Bernstein was occupied elsewhere. Rich had
never worked on *Falstaff* before but had always wanted to do so.
In addition to the covers, he would be expected to work with the
regulars who were new to their roles; "They have to know it *cold,*
because it's a comedy—they shoot around the stage."

Rich's main helper was assistant conductor Victor Trucco, who
would be the prompter in the pit and meanwhile worked all ensemble
rehearsals. A firm man with a gray crew cut, Trucco contained in
his person all there was of a Metropolitan Opera tradition for
Falstaff. No member of the management had been around the last
time the work was done, no singer in the cast had sung his or her
role here before, and the parts from which both the singers and the
orchestra worked were brand new, untouched by any previous conductor's markings. But Trucco had been prompter for Beecham's
performance in the early 1940s, and for a Reiner performance on a
trip to Philadelphia. He was there in case anyone grew curious.

As the end of January approached, the chorus got to work in the bar at Sherry's, their normal daytime habitat. Associate chorus master Thomas Martin sat at a tiny, roll-away piano, his back to the bar, where a waiter in a gray coat methodically stowed ice cubes and swabbed wood, not listening or not hearing. The chorus sat in a semicircle around the piano, a pair of klieg lights behind them on high stands to illuminate their scores. They do not appear in *Falstaff* until Act II, Scene 2, and they don't have much to do then—but what there is is tricky. In the big fugue that ends the opera, they would have to take their cues from the solo voices, and Martin, coaching them, played the vocal lines rather than the orchestral accompaniment. "But you have to count, too," he warned them. "I'm pretty sure the solo cues will come, but if they don't, *you* will retrieve the situation." The chorus nodded, almost in unison.

Every theatrical production has its moments of exaltation and its moments of depression. In *Falstaff,* the first week of February proved to be the gloomy time: everybody found himself working more and enjoying it less. Zeffirelli had signed to arrive on February first, but he had a first night at Covent Garden on February fifth; he would not appear until the night of the sixth. Tex Lawrence looked at the frames for the sets stretched out on the floor of his shop and said, "Unless he's unlike every other designer I've ever met, he won't like them. Sometimes it seems we have to build everything twice."

Rich was multiply harassed. Silvio Varviso's sudden illness, which Rich had saved from theatrical disaster by jumping into the pit and taking over in the middle of *La Sonnambula,* meant that he also had to lead several performances of *Ariadne auf Naxos* while completing preparations for *Falstaff.* The singers had learned what a coach could teach them, and Rich had been unable to reach Bernstein to find out what he would want in key passages. Finally, Bob Herman sent Bernstein a Krawitz-type URGENTLY NEED telegram, and Rich got half an hour of the maestro's time. The singers were snappish. Rich interrupted an ensemble rehearsal in the Guild Room to caution a singer that a passage must be "in tempo."

"Why?" came the reply. "Verdi wrote *senza misura.*"

"Because it sounds better this way," Rich said.

Another singer muttered, "It'll all be changed, anyway"—and Rich patiently said, "It probably will be. I don't know what Maestro Bernstein wants."

The bottom was reached on Monday, February tenth, when Bernstein was scheduled to begin work—and did not come. (Later he explained that he had been just too worn out; the week before had seen the most preposterous of the avant-garde pieces in his Philharmonic series, plus a children's program to be taped at 6:30 Saturday morning. "I needed the day," he said, "to get the Verdiana blood flowing." The management had known he would be late, but the musicians and the artists had not.) Rich took the first orchestral rehearsal, a general run-through on the roof stage. The orchestra was annoyed at the idea of a rehearsal just to read through a score. "Look," one of the men said, "we are an *opera* orchestra, we can read anything and follow anybody."

That afternoon's ensemble rehearsal had some of this nagging quality, too. Tucci and Alva were delayed, as well as Bernstein; with the exception of Resnik, who had loyally flown in late Sunday (after a Saturday-night *Carmen* at the Paris Opéra), the faces were familiar. So was the procedure. Though Trucco was there, sitting beside Rich and prompting in a harsh, penetrating voice, the singers still worked from open score. When Bernstein came they would have to work from memory; they did not need their parts now, they needed the cues from each other, which could never be really secure until they were part of an interpretation. They kept wanting to change seats, to be next to the person who would give them cues. Rich could not tell them where they would stand in relation to each other on the stage. *Falstaff* is such fun to sing, the business of putting together the bits of ensemble mosaics is so pleasurable when it works, that the session kept cheering up—but there was a felt need.

Zeffirelli was in the house, though the singers did not know it. Herman had agreed to give Krawitz's department all of Zeffirelli's time in the first days, to take care of the physical production. Late that afternoon, Zeffirelli insisted on breaking away from designer's chores; he came to the Guild Room, quietly opened the door, stepped deftly in and stood against the wall. Behind him, looking fretful, came

Krawitz's earnest young assistant Michael Bronson, armed with clipboard and pencil. The ensemble proceeded through the final fugue, and Zeffirelli waited, listening, a slight man in slacks and loafers, high-necked dark sweater over an open white shirt, the long Donatello face broken by a smile. As the fugue ended, he called "Bravo!" and darted into the semicircle of seated singers at the end of the room—and there was a joyous call of *"Eh, Franco! Come sta?"* Then he was gone again, to look at props. He would not actually work with the cast until Wednesday the twelfth, but he was there, and it helped.

Zeffirelli is a fanatical worker who goes seven days a week because there are not eight, and he works late every night: "I am low blood pressure, I stay up until three or four in the morning, and I hate to get up early." Notoriously tardy (Bernstein says his wife refuses to ask Zeffirelli to dinner any more, because he is never less than an hour and a half late), he presented problems to the Metropolitan's scheduling. Bronson solved some of them by turning up at Zeffirelli's room whenever he was tardy—"I invest in buying him a breakfast," Krawitz said—and taking him off to look and correct.

At the heart of Zeffirelli's talent is a fantastic scanning ability that enables him to see more at a glance from a bad angle than others will see with a long, hard, straight-ahead stare. The mechanism works equally well close up (in the quadrilingual monkey cage of Karinska's, examining swatches of material for costumes) and at a distance (in the cavern of the auditorium, telling scenic artist Vladimir Odinokov what must be done to the drops and sets installed onstage for his inspection). It also works on moving targets. There is an extraordinary intensity about Zeffirelli watching the singers, flopped in a chair, muscles loose and jaw slack to concentrate all the formidable energy and intelligence through the pale eyes.

Zeffirelli's technique with singers is to show what he wants them to do, acting everything out with broad gestures ("Remember, this is the Met, not the Piccola Scala"), often doing it again beside the artist, to convey by empathy and touch the essence of the conception. Different artists react differently to the technique. Resnik, ferociously intelligent and articulate, must verbalize the instructions, describe to Zeffirelli what she has seen him do; and then she does it, with her own sharp humor. Tucci stands absolutely still, in her erect posture, staring dark eyes apparently unfocused, translating what she sees for the benefit of her own muscles, and she is right the first time. Raskin, who came to the professional stage from a conventionally abstract education at Smith, sees instantly what Zeffirelli wants, and believes that because she sees and understands it the kinetics will be automatic—with the result that she is wrong and knows it, and tries again, angry at herself and her offended vanity. Vocally, too, Raskin learns it before she can do it; but nobody minds hearing her try twice in that radiant voice.

Sereni had other problems: he had never been asked to work this way before. An amiable, broad-shouldered man with a ready smile, quietly concentrated at all times on the production of his own voice, he was delighted with Zeffirelli's tricks in acting out Ford but did not always see what they had to do with him. All Zeffirelli's acting was done, of course, with the rehearsal piano going in the background, to keep the timing right; Sereni would practice singing what his role called for, looking to Martin Rich's baton rather than to Zeffirelli, who would sometimes start singing himself to attract Sereni's attention and on several occasions called out, *"A me, Mario!"*

"Si, Franco."

"Guarda a me, per favore, non pensare alla musica!" (Pay attention to me, please, not to the music.)

But Sereni was immensely willing, susceptible to the strongest sort of instruction from Zeffirelli—and from Bernstein, who took the same pains over his phrasing that Zeffirelli took with his acting. In both sorts of sessions, too, Sereni had a kind of extrasensory support from the rest of the cast, who would quiet down and pay careful attention while he worked to follow both the director's and conductor's leads. By the end of their third day of rehearsing, Zeffirelli and Bernstein had created in the cast an extraordinary loyalty to themselves and to the quality of the forthcoming *Falstaff*. Sereni was now part of the team.

And Bernstein was the leader of the team. He had quickly dissipated any worries that he was not prepared, or did not care. Resnik came bouncing out of the first ensemble rehearsal, smiling hugely, to say, "It's like the old days of rehearsing with Reiner and Bruno Walter." Bernstein knew the score in every breath and phrase, and he had known it for two years. He had thought about what everything should sound like; he had firmly in mind the sweep of each act. For all its instrumental ingenuities and melodic beauties, the heart of *Falstaff* is in its shifting rhythms, and Bernstein is the world's master of that. He was dazzlingly effective with both the soloists and the orchestra.

Leonard Bernstein has put so much of his life into things other people do as well as or better than he—conducting Bach cantatas, for example, or writing Broadway shows—that we tend to forget how great a career seemed to stretch before him when he first came down from Boston more than two decades ago. La Scala, where he made his operatic debut in 1953, had spread word that he was one of the century's major opera conductors—but our recent experiences with Italian judgment of conductors have not been encouraging. Coming to work at the Metropolitan, moreover, dealing with people who did not know him in the flesh, Bernstein carried an odd handicap: he has talked about music too much to a middlebrow audience, and his manner in public has been condescending, often to the point of music-appreciationism. He had to prove to skeptical musicians that there was more to him than appeared on television.

It took him about half an hour. He arrived at the orchestra rehearsal on Friday the fourteenth in a black turtleneck sweater, mop of graying hair hanging forward over the famous good looks, and commented on how many of the orchestra members he had met before, when they were playing in Pittsburgh and he conducted there. The downbeat followed the greetings—and the opening staccato phrases of the opera echoed clumsily about the roof stage. Bernstein stopped and began working it over, now fiddles, now cellos, now horns—section by section, getting it right. He moved on, singing the vocal parts as an opera conductor must, still unhappy about faint imprecisions in the opening phrase; but now, rather suddenly, the orchestra cared. They knew he was listening, they knew he could tell the difference, they were no longer rehearsal slaves. They were professionals proud of their craft. Between 10:30 that morning and

1:30 that afternoon, with thirty minutes for a single break in the middle, the orchestra found out how good it could be. Rhythms became crisp, attacks solidified, and the string tone, all mud at the start, clarified as though a storm had washed away the dirt.

Preparing an opera (though not, oddly, a symphony), Bernstein has a beautifully clear beat, which he accents on occasion by stamping his heel on the podium. A lot rests on the beat, because his manner solicits rather than commands authority. Errors by the orchestra do not produce the conventional rap on the music stand and the imperious downbeat to resume; instead, Bernstein shakes his head sadly and mutters, "That was *terrible;* we'd better do it again." Strong effects are created by surprise rather than anger. Thus on the following Monday, as the orchestra finished the angry bombast of Ford's aria and moved to the lilting syncopation of Falstaff's re-entry, Bernstein stopped them. "This," he said with mock ferocity, "is the *divine* moment of this opera. If you screw it up, so help me God, I'll murder you. It's dramatic, it's elegant, it's Chaplinesque. Let's get it right."

Unlike most conductors, Bernstein takes obvious pleasure in praising an orchestra, and he does it as comes naturally. There is an occasional "Bravo," but he feels stiff with it; usually there will be a call of "Great!" or even *"Teriff!"* Toward the end of the first rehearsal, as the men followed his rubato in the scene between Fenton and Nannetta, he called, "Hey, that was *gorgeous!* I have nothing to tell you about that one. You follow so beautifully." It was hard work; the men were forever marking scores with Bernstein's instructions, cheerfully given: "I see what you were doing—you have that last note a quarter note. *Forget* it. Put a dot on it." Or, "Do you have this marked on 4?" When the answer came no, Bernstein pointed the baton and ordered, *"Schreib!"*

This casual approach means that Bernstein can get away with nothing. The result he is after must make sense to the men, or it will not come. At the same time, however, Bernstein's manner permits initiative to rise from the orchestra. Thus during the Ford-Falstaff duet he wanted a particular rough sound from the staccato strings, and he could describe it only as something like the croaking of a frog: "It should be biting, mocking. You might try it all with the downbow—there must be some little trick." Downbow did not work, but one of the men found the trick—the bow in one position, bouncing on the strings—and rapidly spread it around the orchestra.

Similarly, Bernstein had decided in advance where the second-scene ensemble of ladies had to breathe while echoing the last sentence of Falstaff's love letter, to make sure the *risata* (laughter) was loud enough at the end. At Friday afternoon's rehearsal, Janis Martin replaced Elias as Meg—because Elias was about to sing Olga in *Eugene Onegin*—and she did not pause where Bernstein wanted. He looked down kindly from the high podium. "You weren't here yesterday for the breathing lesson, were you?"

"No."

Bernstein explained what he was after, and Resnik interrupted. "We were working at it all morning with Mr. Rich," she said, almost desperately; she is too experienced a singer to believe that one can really tell a conductor how to do things. "We had to think so hard about the breathing we couldn't sing it."

Raskin leaned forward and said earnestly, "We can do it without the breath."

Bernstein said doubtfully, "And the ha-ha-ha will be loud enough? Well, let's try it and see."

The ladies roared through the phrase and shook the walls with the *risata;* Bernstein turned the point of the baton toward his breast, stabbed himself and slumped forward over the desk, clearly dead.

That Saturday afternoon, while the radio audience was listening to *Otello,* the *Falstaff* singers had their last rehearsal before going onstage, in the long ballet studio at the Fortieth Street side of the building. Martin was in the *Otello,* Elias in that evening's *Onegin,* so Meg was played by another alternate, Joann Grillo. Bernstein was dressed for this occasion in a suit and bright red tie, and he sat on a chair on a tiny little podium just large enough to hold it. Most of the afternoon was given over to the second act, especially the long, wonderful and (as Bernard Shaw once pointed out) wholly Shakespearean scene between Ford and Falstaff. Corena was the Falstaff (Colzani was being Iago onstage at that moment), and Bernstein worked on his interpretation of the ending of "Va, vecchio John." "These words are not *buffo*," Bernstein explained; "they're very pathetic. The audience should all cry when you sing them. It's so touching—a love song to yourself. We all do this." Corena sang it *dolce*. Bernstein said to Trucco, who was beside him, "He understands everything so well when you say it, Corena; it's marvelous." Corena almost blushed.

They took a break after the second-act finale, and Alva, a black-haired young man with a serious approach to his work, came to the podium to thank Bernstein for all he had learned in this first week's rehearsing. Bernstein, conscious that Alva had just sung Fenton in Rome with the great Italian conductor Carlo Maria Guilini, pulled him forward and kissed him on the forehead.

The sets went on the stage the next day, Sunday, with the supervisors present for love and the stagehands for Sunday overtime. Zeffirelli stood by and checked out the props; he watched the men roll out the heavy pieces and hang the lighter ones onto pipes to be lifted to the fly gallery. "I don't know how the tradition of big stages was lost," he said reflectively, his back to the asbestos curtain. "This one is really no bigger than Covent Garden. In the eighteenth century the stage was two, three times the size of the rest of the auditorium. Probably it was lost in the nineteenth century because of the concentration on the voices, which was a great thing in its time."

Lou Edson, the Master Mechanic, came by, and Zeffirelli stopped him to ask about the trap doors: "What do they look like?" Falstaff would have to escape through a trap before the laundry basket in which he was hiding could be picked up and thrown out the window. Edson pointed out a trap; Zeffirelli, his mind on many things, noted that it was too narrow to permit the passage of the padded Falstaff costume. In a fairly complicated conversation, he made arrangements for the frame around the platform to be cut open. Then the sets for Act I, Scene 1 ("the eleven scene," in opera lingo) were standing, the asbestos curtain was lifted, and the half-dozen supervisors walked with Zeffirelli on the rickety wooden bridge over the orchestra pit into the auditorium. Some of what Zeffirelli saw from the back of the hall he liked, but not all. He had long, serious talks with the scene painter about roughening the appearance of the walls, with Edson about rehanging the drops and with Lawrence about putting in more wood to replace painted canvas, particularly where his sketches had shown a railing for the loggia. Lawrence fought back, hard. "I'm listening to you," Tex replied at one point, "and with great patience, too, I must say."

Zeffirelli showed even greater patience. "I don't, you know," he said, "trust paint much myself." And Lawrence yielded. Later, an observer asked him why he had been giving Zeffirelli such a hard time; the points were clearly valid. "Oh, he was right," Lawrence said flatly. "Very logical and reasonable. I fight designers on principle. If you fight hard over what's logical and reasonable, you never hear from them about the other things."

Zeffirelli wandered all over the set, peopling it with the *Falstaff* characters in the attitudes he had taught the singers, and then gave Edson authorization to strike this one and put up "the twenty-two scene" (Act II, Scene 2). It was four in the afternoon; the stagehands had been working since ten; nobody was near going home.

The next day, Monday the seventeenth, the Metropolitan gave itself over entirely to *Falstaff* for the daylight hours. Bernstein was rehearsing the orchestra on the roof stage, Thomas Martin the chorus in Sherry's. On the stage the singers were working, with piano, on the second scene of the first act—the sets up, the props in place. In the greater spaces of the stage, it was harder to keep the complicated ensembles together. There were stairs to climb and descend, props to shove around, each of nine singers to be made rock-solid on what he would do eighteen days hence. Zeffirelli was all over the stage, demonstrating, accompanying, backing off, adding bits of comic business, setting up the love scenes for Alva and Raskin ("Remember, you are *sixteen*").

At two o'clock, after the orchestral rehearsal was over, Bernstein came down to sit in the auditorium and watch what Zeffirelli was doing. The two of them were, after all, engaged in a single enterprise, dependent on each other's timing. The breaks Bernstein could or should make at the many double bars, the length of each *fermata,* would rest to a degree on the action Zeffirelli had designed. At the same time, Zeffirelli's actions had to be in tempo with what Bernstein was doing in the pit.

Near three o'clock, when the singers and Zeffirelli had been working four hours on this one twenty-minute scene, the performance began to round itself into shape. Bernstein enjoyed watching it. Then there came a moment when the singers had to cross a fair amount of stage, and the rehearsal pianist maintained tempo through a passage Bernstein had just told the orchestra to mark *accelerando*. It was something Zeffirelli would have to know; Bernstein pulled himself out of his seat at the center of the auditorium and wandered across the bridge up to the stage. The action returned to the moment that had summoned him, and he beat the quickening time.

The Merry Wives of Windsor and their menfolk swept across the stage to the new tempo, plotting against each other. Facing the singers, their dark, sweatered backs to the auditorium, Bernstein and Zeffirelli shook their shoulders in rhythm together and nodded to each other—two men still youthful, the highest order of talent developed by the lyric theater in the postwar era, working together for the first time on the miraculous Shakespeare opera an old man wrote at eighty.

They were making an event in the history of the Metropolitan, perhaps in the history of opera—but they could do so only because some scores of others had also given this *Falstaff* the best they had. There would be plenty of credit to go round.

[An afterword is necessary here. In performance, despite the weaknesses of Colzani and Sereni, *Falstaff* was as great a triumph as all had hoped —indeed, I would regard it as the most successful single production of Rudolf Bing's time at the Metropolitan Opera, which dates back to 1950. The next season was Bernstein's sabbatical from the New York Philharmonic, and most of us expected that pride in this glorious production and loyalty to the cast would lead him to give up the few weeks which would be required to maintain the performance; but we overestimated his professionalism—he just wasn't interested. (In fairness, it should be said that Irving Kolodin believes the terms of Bernstein's sabbatical leave, never revealed, forbade him to do any conducting whatever in New York.) The performance passed into the hands of Kapellmeister Rosenstock, and then to worse. Three and a half years after its *prima*, I reviewed a revival of it for *Musical America,* as follows:]

Falstaff Plunges

SINGING her first Alice in Verdi's *Falstaff* at the Metropolitan Opera, Phyllis Curtin was heavily handicapped by the need to fit her fine talents into as coarse and clumsy a total performance as the Met has presented in the last few years. Considering the surroundings, Miss Curtin came out of the display creditably. There was not much she alone could do about the hodgepodge ensemble work of the second scene (remember how funny and delicate and delightful the wives of Windsor were, and the sparkle of the nonet?—well, forget it). And her occasional barking in the middle register was doubtless a deliberate part of the cast's disorganized search for comic effect. At the crucial moments—in the rather matronly lower register which reminds us that Alice is at least the age of the Marschallin, and in the trumpet A's and sustained C of the top line of the fugue—Miss Curtin sang with appropriate force and beauty.

But this *Falstaff* as a whole was unfair to an artist being reviewed and to an audience paying Met prices—not to mention poor old Verdi. The orchestra played raggedly for Bruno Amaducci, and much of the singing was (to be charitable) careless. The feeling that nobody had the production under control got so strong in the living-room scene that Judith Raskin, usually so careful to stay in character, began beating time against the laundry basket at *Gaie comari di Windsor,* presumably to help Miss Curtin, or maybe Signor Amaducci. Even the technical crew made little contributions—like letting Bardolfo unveil invisibly in the dark in the finale.

This production was a triumph in 1965. Its sets and costumes are still stunning, its props (saving only the unfortunate sight gag with the flower vase) are both charming and suitable. Musically, the performance deteriorated under Rosenstock, and has now simply disintegrated under an apparently novice conductor. Dramatically, everybody's timing is off, a condition complicated by the free-lance addition of all sorts of vulgar unfunny business. To treat a past accomplishment of this quality as something cheap to put on in the middle of the week is simply inexcusable. If *Falstaff* is to be kept in the repertory, it must be allocated some time for dramatic polishing and a conductor who can hold it together. How about (ahem!) Sarah Caldwell . . . ?

9

Community Control on Ocean Hill

[My first article urging the decentralization of the New York City schools was a piece in one of the earliest issues of *New York,* then a new throw-away within the *Herald-Tribune,* in the fall of 1962. The following spring I returned to the subject with a piece in *Harper's* entitled "Welcome to the City!," describing for the benefit of our new superintendent of schools the situation he would find on arrival. In the spring of 1965, in an article entitled "Close to Midnight for the New York Schools," I detailed from the vantage point of a semester in Switzerland, where I was working on a study of international education for The Twentieth Century Fund, the obvious deterioration of the institution which had created life chances for generations of raw immigrants but lost its nerve, its sense of high function, when confronted with the Negro and Puerto Rican in-migrants of the 1950s and 1960s. Finally, in the fall, 1967, I published a *vale* to the New York City Board of Education in the *Saturday Evening Post,* under the title "How Not to Run the Big City Schools."

[None of these was a piece of magazine work in the normal sense, be-cause from September, 1962, through June, 1967, I served as chairman of one of the city's local school boards. The *Post* piece, which is avail-able between boards (in Street, ed., *Innovation in Urban Education*), was autobiographical. The fact that I wrote it for the *Post* rather than for the *New York Times Magazine* was deeply resented on Forty-third Street, where my explanation that the *Post* paid ten (10) times as much was re-garded as poor excuse for treason.

[In self-protection, I promised to write a piece about decentralization and local school boards for the *Times Magazine.* Presently, after some weeks of unusually laborious writing, I produced something quite unpublish-able. By early 1968, everybody was agreed (at least on the surface) that decentralization was desirable, and the real issues in dispute were tech-nical issues. They could not be intelligibly discussed, I suggested, by peo-ple who did not know the difference between an administrative assistant to an assistant field superintendent and a deputy assistant administrator in a headquarters bureau. Magazine pieces cannot be written about such issues; and I could not write about the astonishing range of false issues which had been raised in early 1968 by decentralization's incompetent newfound friends, and which would lead eventually to a refusal by the legislature to take any significant action.

[Nevertheless, the *Times* wanted something from me on this subject, and I suggested a reportorial piece on what seemed from a distance the most likely to succeed of the Ford-sponsored demonstration units. The result was the longest article the *Times Magazine* has ever carried. It was bumped from three straight issues to make room for something the editors erroneously considered more timely, and then it appeared in the middle of a crisis which could be no more than touched upon in the second paragraph, because all but the first few paragraphs had already gone to the printer. But tragedy had been palpable when I wrote.]

THE OCEAN HILL-BROWNSVILLE "demonstration unit" is a group of eight New York City public schools—two on the intermediate level and six on the elementary level—which since September has been more or less independently managed by a "unit administrator" chosen by a nineteen-member locally elected "governing board." Both the administrator, Rhody McCoy, and a solid majority of the board are Negro, as are about two-thirds of the pupils in the eight schools. (Most of the other pupils are Puerto Rican; about a sixth of the teachers are Negro or Puerto Rican.) To help him administer, Mc-Coy has a standard district superintendent's staff of his own choice, plus the usual complement of principals inside the schools. The extraordinary attrition of school personnel in a neighborhood as rattled as Ocean Hill has enabled McCoy and his board to fill seven of these principalships (at least temporarily) with their own nominees—only three of whom, incidentally, are Negro.

Whatever else the Ocean Hill governing board has accomplished in seven months, it has held the loyalty of the neighborhood. On Manhattan's lower East Side, the board of a similar project has been publicly repudiated by the parent associations, which have requested the Board of Education to resume complete control over the neighborhood's schools. But the parents of Ocean Hill staged an effective boycott the two days before Easter vacation to demand that the Board of Education turn over to their governing board complete authority over the eight schools. And in seeking to dismiss from the

unit the sole surviving regularly appointed principal, plus five assistant principals and thirteen teachers—as they did on the day this
article went to press—the governing board spoke the hearts, if perhaps not the minds, of the Ocean Hill community. The attempted
dismissals have created an angry confrontation on the previously
rather abstract issue of decentralization of the school system, and
the outcome is still uncertain.

McCoy has his offices in a pair of apartments on the first floor of
a new middle-income high-rise development still in process of construction on Atlantic Avenue. Unusual things are supposed to happen here, and sometimes they do. The other day, in the dining ell
of the living room that serves the project as general office and reception area, about fifteen ladies sat around an old conference table and
listened while a consultant and saleslady for a publisher told them
how to use, and why to buy, a set of new remedial reading texts.

All the Negro ladies were clustered around the far end of the
table, and all the white ladies were at the near end of the table. At
11:30, the ladies at the front, who were teachers, left to go back to
their schools; but the seven Negro ladies at the rear remained. They
were "paraprofessional" aides, housewives who live in the neighborhood and have children in the schools, and this session was part of
the training program which puts them in classrooms for half a week
and in instructional sessions for the other half, preparing them for
permanent appointments as teacher assistants. Their schedule called
for them to remain at the office until noon.

McCoy, a short, squared-off man with a light-tan complexion and
a sandy mustache, who speaks softly around a thick-stemmed pipe
that is a virtually permanent part of his physiognomy, emerged from
his private office—the tiny middle-income-apartment bedroom—to
talk things over with his neighborhood ladies. They had various concerns, some very practical and immediate, like the fact that after
five weeks of working as trainees they had not yet received their first
pay checks.

Mostly, however, they were troubled by questions about their function and the function of their training, which to date had been almost
entirely inspirational rather than practical. The practical work was to

be done in Manhattan, at P.S. 148 in the middle West Side, a "600 school" for children with severe behavior problems, where McCoy, a product of Howard University in Washington, with a graduate degree from New York University, was acting principal before he received the call to Ocean Hill. McCoy explained that the P.S. 148 staff was already working with ten parents from the demonstration unit and could not handle more than ten at a time, and he was not going to bring them back to Brooklyn until the P.S. 148 people certified that they were ready to come.

"We want to be reasonably sure," McCoy said, "that when we turn this group into the classroom it will be effective—we want you parents to have the skills you need to work with children. We're working on the teachers, too—they worry about parents coming in with skills they don't have."

One of the mothers volunteered that she felt she was useful in the classroom right now: "We do pretty well without special skills," she said, "having went to New York schools ourselves."

Another of the paraprofessionals was puzzled: "She's the *teacher*. What do you mean she doesn't have the skills?"

McCoy nodded. "Well, an academic teacher may not be a reading specialist," he said. "You *will* have skills they don't have. And a teacher has a youngster who says 'street' without the final 't.' Well, the teacher just thinks, 'That's the way they talk in this culture.' You'll know he has a problem with final sounds, and when the teacher sends the kid to you, you'll work on final sounds. . . ."

Future historians will have no difficulty dating precisely the moment of decision that the New York schools could not be significantly integrated. It happened on the Sunday after Labor Day in 1966, when the president of the Board of Education, at the insistence of Mayor Lindsay and without consulting his board, announced that the new Intermediate School 201, on 125th Street, would not open that Monday with the rest of the city's schools, for fear of violent demonstrations by black militants.

This traumatic episode climaxed a year of mounting conflict between the school system and a fraction of the Harlem community, which resented the construction of this windowless fortress of a school on a site more than a mile from any significant English-speaking white community, guaranteeing a pupil population virtually 100 percent Negro and Puerto Rican. Conscious of support from a quiet but large (probably majority) fraction of Harlem, which wanted new schools near home more than it wanted school integration, the board had brushed off the protesters with soothing words— including what looked like a pledge to bring white students to the school from other parts of the city. When this pledge was dishonored, as it had to be, the militants exploded.

In what seemed to be a spasm reaction, the protesters announced that if this was to be a Negro school, they wanted a Negro principal, and they wanted a say in what the school would teach. This was a demand which parents who disliked busing their children could support; and after the board refused it, Mayor Lindsay's people in Harlem told him there would be trouble when the school opened. It turned out, however, that the militants' support in the community was far less than the Mayor's spies had claimed—the school opened a week late, and half the parents sent their children through a threatening CORE picket line marching to enforce a boycott. But something had to be done to get everybody (including the Mayor) out of the situation—and from the groves of academe a call arose for "community control" of the ghetto schools.

For some months the Mayor, the board and assorted professors struggled to give meaning to this phrase, to define the functions of the "community council" proposed to supervise the work of I.S. 201 and the elementary schools which feed into it. Leading Harlem political figures, after investigating the situation, refused to touch the question; McGeorge Bundy, recently arrived in town as president of the Ford Foundation and eager for involvement in racial questions, considered undertaking the conciliation of the battling groups, then yielded to better advice and backed away.

But the I.S. 201 crisis had triggered a widespread, if previously latent, sense of the need for the "decentralization" of what Superintendent Bernard Donovan recently described as the city's "monstrous and overbearing" school system.

New York City has roughly 1,100,000 children in its public schools, almost 900 schools and about 60,000 teachers and other instructional personnel to man them. Such a system is obviously too large to run from a single center, and indeed the Board of Education is divided administratively into thirty districts, each headed by an "assistant field superintendent." But virtually all moneys are allocated directly from the central office; all personnel are assigned to specific jobs from the central office and their working conditions are held uniform under terms of a citywide union contract; all attendance zones are drawn centrally, and a single curriculum is mandated on all schools, regardless of whether it seems to be producing results. Parents and teachers perceive this monolith as the property of neither the public nor the profession, but of "the system" itself; and everybody who wants to get anything done treks down to 110 Livingston Street in Brooklyn, where the system has its lair.

Decentralization of the decision-making processes in the city's schools, to bring education within the range of possible influence by the people who send their children and the teachers who work in the buildings, became in 1966–67 a slogan of great political appeal. Among those adopting it was a group of black militants and white radicals who appointed themselves a "People's Board of Education" and advertised their existence by sitting in the big swivel chairs of the members of the board for an uproarious twenty-four hours before the police cleared the room. This People's Board encouraged the formation of little people's boards to compete with the powerless but official local advisory boards in each of the system's thirty districts.

Formation of a people's board for Ocean Hill-Brownsville was part of this movement, but it was more soundly based, and its administrative grievance was more uncomfortable for the Board of Education. Although this depressed area made up about one third of District 17, there was in the fall of 1966 nobody from Ocean Hill-Brownsville on the existing local advisory board for the district. While officially denying that anything of the sort was in the works, the Board of Education began negotiating with the leaders of the unofficial People's Board with the idea of giving them a district of their own and some unspecified functions in its management. Meanwhile, the Board of Education was also negotiating with the chairmen of its local advisory boards to increase their influence by increasing the authority of the system's district superintendents—on terms that would require the superintendents to consult with the local boards before exercising authority.

A new element was introduced into this confused situation when the Lindsay administration proposed to the State Legislature a new gimmick to gain additional financial aid for the city's schools. This aid is calculated on the assessed valuation of the real estate within the school district. When New York City is taken as a whole, the value of its real estate makes it eligible for only the state's minimum per-pupil grant. But if the five counties are considered separately, the low values of real estate in the dormitory counties of Queens, Richmond and the Bronx produce extra state aid of more than $100 million a year.

The Legislature did not react kindly to the idea of appropriating additional state aid for New York City alone, and at one point threatened to insist that the city's school system be broken into five borough systems if state aid was to be given on that basis. Dissuaded from this course, the Legislature made new aid contingent on some alternative plan to decentralize the city's schools, to be submitted in time for the current session—and by the Mayor, not the Board of Education. The Mayor appointed a distinguished committee to produce such a plan, and McGeorge Bundy consented to chair it. The result was the Bundy Report, published last November, proposing the fragmentation of the school system into thirty to sixty almost autonomous districts, each to be run by a board of eleven local residents, six of whom would be elected (through an indirect process) by the parents of the district's school children.

Bundy's staff at the Ford Foundation, having kept in touch with the I.S. 201 situation, had come up with some ideas for "community control" which the foundation was prepared to finance. When the Board of Education reached agreement with its local advisory boards on a minimum (but not trivial) decentralization plan, which was adopted last May, a loophole was left for alternative experiments along the lines Ford was developing. In June, as the Bundy committee got to work on the overall decentralization question, Ford announced that "demonstration units" of decentralized school administration, dominated by the local community, would be established in four small areas of the city with the help of $163,000 from the foundation.

One of the four units was to command I.S. 201 and its feeder schools; one was in the Two Bridges area on the lower East Side, where a Yeshiva University school project and Mobilization for Youth had presumably prepared the community (this is the unit where the parents' associations have repudiated their board); one was around Joan of Arc Junior High School in the marginally integrated middle West Side, and one was Ocean Hill-Brownsville. The ground work already done by the people's board there made it possible to organize quickly in Ocean Hill-Brownsville (the Joan of Arc unit has not been organized yet, and the I.S. 201 unit was unable to agree on an administrator until late March). When the term began last September, the schools in Ocean Hill-Brownsville were under orders to report not to their district superintendent but to Rhody McCoy as unit administrator.

Juridically, the Ocean Hill-Brownsville unit is in an odd limbo. Except for $250 recently allocated by the Board of Education (with a stern and detailed prescription of how to account for its expenditure), the unit has no funds of its own. Anything it wishes to purchase must be funneled through the board's normal processes—which means, for example, that McCoy had to wait several months before he got authorization to have a telephone installed in his office, and that the Lord alone knows when some 10,000 new library books will actually be delivered.

The tables of organization for the unit's schools are set at Board of Education headquarters and may not be changed—though the new scheme of two teachers for each first-grade classroom is not working any better in Brownsville than it is elsewhere in the city ("It's like two women in a kitchen," a teacher said disgustedly the other day), McCoy cannot shift any of these underemployed and unhappy teachers to other duty. The citywide union contract controls all assignment of instructional personnel in the unit and severely limits the possibilities for in-service training of teachers. Mary Alice Riddle, an alert young (white) former first-grade teacher whom McCoy chose as his co-ordinator of Early Childhood Education, has so far managed to set up a single half-day "workshop" for each of the 175 teachers in the unit's primary grades—"though our No. 1 need," she says, "is brainwashing sessions, to give our teachers the belief that these children are worth teaching and can learn."

One substantial special power granted to McCoy is the right to recommend for the principals' jobs men who have not achieved the normally required standing on the competitive examination for such positions mandated by state law. Superintendent Donovan and the Board of Education must approve and actually appoint the new principals, but they have in fact done so for all but one of the recommendations.

This new power, however, may turn out to be illusory: in response to a suit brought by the association of the school system's supervisors, a trial court has declared the special appointments illegal (and most lawyers who have looked at the case find it hard to see how any court could rule otherwise, though the case is now on appeal and you never can tell). Moreover, the Board of Education has told the new Ocean Hill-Brownsville governing board that, even if the case is won, it intends to give the new principals tests similar to those it now administers, and to confirm only those who pass the tests.

The problems McCoy and his board and his principals must meet with their limited authority are a summation of the condition of the urban poor. Though there are decent blocks of single-family housing in the area, most of it is a collection of tenements once described by Alfred Kazin, who was born in Brownsville, as "New York's rawest, remotest, cheapest ghetto." Most of the housing is more than sixty years old, put up during the unbelievable five years 1899–1904, when, according to Moses Rischin in his book *The Promised City,* the population of Brownsville rose from 10,000 to 60,000, and 1,000 immigrants a month came off the boat to work in its sweatshops. Most of the school buildings date back to those days, too, and to say that they have not been well-maintained would be an understatement.

Nor have the schools changed much, as schools, from Kazin's time. "It was never learning I associated with [my] school," he wrote in *A Walker in the City* in 1951; "only the necessity to succeed, to get ahead of the others in the daily struggle, to 'make a good impression' on our teachers, who grimly, wearily, and often with ill-concealed distaste watched against our relapsing into the natural savagery they expected of Brownsville boys. . . . My belief in teachers' unlimited wisdom and power rested not so much on what I saw in them—how impatient most of them looked, how wary—but on our abysmal humility. . . . You made the 'good impression' by sitting firmly at your wooden desk, hands clasped; by silence for the greatest part of the livelong day; by standing up obsequiously when it was so expected of you; by sitting down noiselessly when you had answered a question; by 'speaking nicely,' which meant reproducing their painfully exact enunciation; by 'showing manners,' or an ecstatic submissiveness in all things."

The atmosphere has loosened just a little in forty-odd years; there are in most buildings tables and chairs instead of desks; more work is needed to maintain order; and the teachers' enunciation is no longer exact—any speech is now acceptable except the slurred sounds of the black South or the singsong of a Spanish accent. Otherwise, Kazin's description is still serviceable for the Brownsville elementary schools.

These schools are a failure by any known measurement. Well over four-fifths of the children in McCoy's unit read below grade level, most of them well below; and something like a quarter of the junior-high population is essentially illiterate. Both teachers and children are unhappily bewildered, then stoical, about the inability of the usual teaching process to show results. It is hard to get teachers to work in Ocean Hill-Brownsville at all—about half the staff are substitutes; half the regularly licensed teachers have less than two years' experience; there are several vacant positions in each school, and the daily absentee rate among teachers is about 10 percent.

Efforts to remedy the failures of the schools are further crippled by the almost unbelievable transiency of the students. Lou Fuentes, the new principal of P.S. 155 and the city's only Puerto Rican to hold such a position, came to the unit from Farmingdale, Long Island, where he had been a reading consultant (his background, incidentally, includes a term as principal of a white school in Georgia, where he was easily accepted, despite his tan skin, as some kind of foreigner). In Farmingdale, Fuentes had become a convert to the Initial Teaching Alphabet system of teaching reading to beginners, but he feels he can't introduce it in P.S. 155 because the children move in and out too fast—of the 1,100 in the school in September, fewer than 500 will still be there in June. New arrivals will have taken the place of the other 600.

What, after all, can a local governing board and a unit administrator and a handful of specially chosen principals do to cure pathologies like these? "Go see for yourself," said Rhody McCoy.

I.S. 55 is the showplace school, a brand-new building which opened February fifth with 1,450 students and a staff of 103. "The eyes of New York and the entire nation are on *this* school and *this* community," said a Special Notice mimeographed and broadcast through the community on the occasion of the opening. ". . . Let it be known that we will raise our children to cherish I.S. 55 and make it grow as a symbol of what people can do when given a chance . . . THIS SCHOOL AND ITS COMMUNITY IS NOW A PART OF HISTORY. THE RECORDS MUST SHOW IT AS A POSITIVE CONTRIBUTION."

Designed long before anybody was talking of community involvement, I.S. 55 is a square, brown, brick fortress with crenelated walls. It has no obvious main entrance—its dark-brown steel doors blend into the walls—and its windows are hidden in the recesses of the crenelation, behind dark-brown metal grids. It seems admirably designed for defense: one feels looking at it that a handful of teachers armed only with a few pots of boiling oil could hold off the neighborhood indefinitely.

The atmosphere inside matches the architectural impression, for this is a building where everybody—administration, teachers, children—is terrified of disorder. Seven to nine staff members are on hall patrol duty during every class period. Even when the halls are relatively empty, children are expected to stay on the right side of the permanent line down the middle, and to turn square corners. As anything left in a locker is stolen almost immediately, the children keep their coats and books with them at all times; but anyone who actually *wears* a coat in the halls is sent to a guidance counselor, possibly home for the day. Further problems are created by faulty acoustical planning which gave the classrooms hard-surfaced, ridged ceilings. The resulting extraordinary resonance blurs even precise speech and amplifies that screaming of teachers and children which gives junior high schools their characteristic zoo-like roar.

The school conducts grades 5 through 8 under the system's new 4-4-4 plan. Such organization supposedly permits individualization of instruction by mixing classes differently for English and math, creating small groups and forming teams of teachers. Every class has a daily period of Basic Skills—"to make sure they get spelling and writing," says principal Percy Jenkins, "and don't just read stories all day." The top groups in English achievement study French their last two years; most of the pupils in the school have classes in Spanish. There are twenty-four classes a week in "Afro-American and Puerto-Rican history and culture" to supplement the standard social-studies program. Next year Jenkins hopes to separate out "a real talent group," which will receive intensive instruction in music or art.

Within the classrooms, however, it is hard to find any signs of originality. For reasons professors of education doubtless think they can explain, each lesson is to be directed toward a single purpose, which the teachers dutifully write on the board. Thus, in a seventh-grade basic-skills class: "Aim: to gain an understanding of what America was like in 1492"—and underneath it four words, "unknown, nomads, united, primitive," each to be used in a sentence and defined. ("The tomb of the unknown soldier is in Washington.")

A teacher in a science class is performing for the students the classic experiment about saliva and starch, adding to the test tube without explanation "a substance we call Benedict solution, and when we add heat, if there's a little sugar, that solution is gonna turn green. . . ." On the board the children can read "Aim: What happens to food in the mouth?" In the African-culture class the teacher is playing a Miriam Makeba record with a pure nineteenth-century European instrumental background, and has dutifully written on the board, "Aim: to improve our understanding of African music." In an eighth-grade English class the visitor is greeted with the announcement: "Are you the gentleman from the *Times?* This is a very bad class . . ." The teacher says to the class, "Everybody copy," and writes on the board, "Aim: we will talk about foods and dishes typical of different nationalities." Then she explains to the class, "Typical means certain people eat foods typical of what they eat in different countries . . ." The resonant room hums with conversations. "I can't believe," the teacher says sharply, "that some people can find so much to talk about when there's nothing to talk about."

On other days, the visitor goes on to some of the elementary schools. In one he finds a sixth-grade class working in third-grade readers of the green-grass-grows-in-my-yard variety. "At first," says their businesslike Negro teacher, "they objected, and said they'd already had this material. I told them they needed something in which they could make *progress*. But, of course, their attention span is so limited. . . ."

In another school, by contrast, second-graders were getting reading instruction from pamphlet materials difficult enough to challenge third-graders. The visitor, pleased and impressed, sat down with one child and asked her to read from her book; and neither she nor any of the other children who clustered around could come anywhere near reading it. The school's principal was distressed; the teacher, who was not responsible for this material (it had been introduced by another teacher who had taken over the class during the regular teacher's daily "planning period"), paid no attention except to ask whether the visitor was being disturbed by the children who were crowding around.

When the visitor returned to McCoy's office a few days later, he said he thought things looked pretty bad.

McCoy said, "You mean the buildings . . ."

"No."

McCoy took his pipe out of his mouth and dropped his hands to the mass of papers on his desk. "Truthfully," he said, "I feel I can make changes. I'm a damned good educator and administrator. But everywhere I've ever been before, after a few months I've been able to show a success model. Here I can't show a success model yet. I know it. And it's killing me."

According to observers at Harlem's I.S. 201 (among them several Negro teachers who left that unit in February to come to Ocean Hill-Brownsville), the antics of a publicity-hungry governing board without professional guidance have in fact made some bad schools even worse. At Ocean Hill-Brownsville, seventy or eighty teachers have quit, as have the eighteen assistant principals in the schools for which McCoy imported new principals. (The Board of Education replaced the assistant principals from existing lists without consulting McCoy or his governing board, and they are now trying to fire three of the new men.) Yet it seems unlikely that McCoy has lost many people he really wanted to keep. What is wrong with the Ocean Hill-Brownsville unit today is not, as has been charged, that black-power fanatics have run down eight nice schools of the Board of Education, but that McCoy and his governing board have been unable to make significant changes in the way the schools work. They are no worse than they were; but, except perhaps in surface discipline, they are no better, either.

It is not for lack of effort. McCoy, who lives in Roosevelt, Long Island, arrives at his office every morning at 7:30; until recently all the principals met with him there at that hour every day. (Now there are only two preschool meetings a week, on the grounds that even a dedicated man does best if he isn't groggy from fatigue.) Most nights of the week McCoy has meetings of some sort—with his governing board, with parent associations in the unit, with citywide civic groups concerned about decentralization or poverty, with black education groups or with "one of the kangaroo courts that's already trying to evaluate us." Consultants of all kinds come from universities, from publishing companies, from Government agencies, from Ford. McCoy meets with them, involves his principals and to the greatest possible degree involves his teachers—he desperately wants the teachers to choose for themselves the materials they will use and the programs they will teach. But very little happens.

"I have a few things going," McCoy said the other day. "There are the paraprofessionals. At I.S. 55 I have two college kids, one of them from Pratt, one with three years at Middlebury; both have backgrounds like these kids, and they're trying to teach them self-discipline—if kids take a teacher's room apart, I'll never be able to find out whether the teacher's any good or not.

"I have to do three things. I have to create an atmosphere where a teacher can work. I have to select those teachers who need exceptional help, and select the master teachers to help them. (We're going to tape outstanding lessons by outstanding teachers, and make them available to other teachers.) Then I have to get rid of those teachers who don't work out. If I create an atmosphere of professionalism, and I give the teachers freedom, I can expect performance."

Eventually, McCoy envisages a system of teaching teams, with master teachers, licensed teachers and paraprofessionals working together. Some master teachers would have primary responsibility for subject matter, some would have primary responsibility for the overall adjustment and performance of a group of children. McCoy is eager to introduce new programs (several phonics programs are already in use in classrooms where teachers volunteered to try them; Robert Davis' imaginative Madison Project mathematics is being taught to paraprofessionals in the hope that they will then carry it into classrooms, and Lou Fuentes has been encouraged to set up classes in first and second grade which will teach children to read Spanish before they even begin to study English).

But the heart of the future McCoy projects for his schools is the restructuring of the teaching job. The notion of specially recognized (and rewarded) master teachers has been anathema to the profession for years; presumably the United Federation of Teachers would have to approve.

McCoy grunted. "We meet with the U.F.T.," he said coldly, "once a month."

Of the many tragedies in Ocean Hill-Brownsville, none is so grim as the mutual antagonism of the teachers' union and the demonstration unit. Its roots, of course, are deep in the failure of the children, for which the teachers wish to blame the community and the community wishes to blame the teachers. (These attitudes, incidentally, are entirely independent of the skin color of the teacher.) In theory, decentralization offered a chance to shift attention from who's-at-fault to what-can-we-do-together. Instead, tensions in the unit have heightened the teachers' hostility to the children and their parents, and the community leaders' feeling that the teachers are racists.

The U.F.T. helped to draw up the original proposal for the unit and demanded and received a representation of eight teachers and one union delegate on the governing board. But when the time came to elect permanent teacher representatives, the union refused to participate; the best that could be done was the calling of a rump meeting of a handful of teachers supporting the unit, at which four "provisional members" of the board were chosen.

By the first law of practical politics—that the weaker party is always at fault when something goes wrong—responsibility for the collapse of what once seemed a promising relationship must be placed upon the governing board and McCoy.

The first serious error was the board's nomination of Herman Ferguson to be principal of the new I.S. 55. This created considerable adverse comment in the press, because Ferguson was one of a group of black militants indicted on a charge of conspiracy to kill Roy Wilkins and Whitney Young. To the union, however, Ferguson was even worse than a suspect in a murder plot—he was a known saboteur of the union's cherished More Effective Schools program. As assistant principal of P.S. 40 in Queens, which according to the statistics was the most successful of the union-sponsored M.E.S. schools, he had denounced its principal, Harold Baron, for "practicing genocide on black children" and had stimulated a noisy CORE protest at the school. Because the children were in fact doing well, the all-Negro parent community was horrified by the protest. Ferguson's name was therefore mud with many people, especially with the union, and his nomination by the governing board was deliberate and senseless provocation.

The labor dispute that marked the beginning of the school year provided an opportunity to mend fences. The union leadership was uncertain how successful the strike would be in the face of the effort to break it by the Board of Education and the Mayor, and over the weekend before it began, U.F.T. officials offered the Ocean Hill-Brownsville governing board the union's support—at school headquarters, in the Central Trades and Labor Council and in Albany—in return for a gesture of support for the strike.

It was asking more sophistication than the governing board could supply. As the Rev. C. Herbert Oliver, chairman of the board, said the other day. "We felt we could not bargain with our children." The governing board denounced the strike and—from the union's point of view—sought to keep the schools open with scabs.

Whatever the political realities, however, anyone who actually visits the classrooms must sympathize first with the parents, who feel that too many teachers are just not teaching their children. The attitudes of many teachers, white and Negro, are contemptuous and punitive.

An unusually public and unforgivable example of some teachers' hard-heartedness came the last week in March, when a fire at 2:30 in the afternoon emptied I.S. 55 (and revealed something of the deficiencies of its ventilating system, as smoke from the one room actually blazing belched from the ducts into all the corridors). At three o'clock, out on the street, a few teachers simply turned over the keys to their rooms to their children, went over to their cars and drove away. Others dumped children's possessions in piles in the auditorium. In the bedlam which followed the reopening of the building, fights broke out among students, and a number of coats were stolen.

Principal Jenkins says that 80 percent of his staff behaved "magnificently," but the other 20 percent are still there. It was in response to this situation that the parents' associations of I.S. 55 and J.S. 271 staged their boycott on April tenth, to demand full power—meaning the power to fire teachers—for the governing board.

Much as he sympathizes with the feelings of the community, McCoy is committed to the proposition that when the new leadership takes hold, the teachers' performance will improve. "My principals have to *solidify* the staff," he says, "so we won't have a mass turnover in September and have to start all over again." Yet, lacking a success model, there may be limits to how long McCoy can hold the unit on a constructive course.

One faction of the board, led by Father John Powis, a young Catholic priest who feels that "the oppression has got even worse this year," already wants to close down the governing board and turn the schools back to the district superintendent. When the time comes for this proposition to be discussed seriously, the governing board will probably find its hands tied by its human commitments to the unit staff and principals who gave up secure positions elsewhere to come to Ocean Hill-Brownsville. But McCoy, who has dominated the unit as a good administrator always dominates a school system, may find his leadership potential severely restricted by the politics of the neighborhood.

In that event, McCoy's troubles are likely to be compounded by his feeling that because he is black and because he cares, he expresses in his person the will of the community. "I listen to the community," he says, "and I translate its wishes into programs. And it's part of my top-drawer operation here that I always have an alternative program to offer the board. I came here with years of experience in my hands, with sixteen or eighteen programs to try. The board understands that."

Mr. Oliver is not quite so sure. "Some members," he said cautiously the other day, "feel that they ought to know more about what's going to be brought to the board. All the principals so far have been McCoy's recommendations. There's a growing concern on the board—people want more consultation before candidates are brought to the board officially. He's often said, 'I don't know how to work with this board.' We're both learning."

On the subject of authority over the budget, the board and McCoy have worked out a charming contingency plan: "If the board gets the money," Mr. Oliver explains, "McCoy can't spend it; and if he gets the money, the board can't interfere. Of course, we haven't received anything yet."

The governing board feels itself abandoned by the Ford Foundation (which had once unwisely spoken of a possible $300,000 for paraprofessional training), rejected by the U.F.T. and despised by the Board of Education. ("If the board doesn't recognize us," says Mr. Oliver, "why should the teachers pay attention?") Nonetheless, the project enjoys considerable goodwill in all these institutions, and in the press: incidents which would be treated as sin if they occurred at I.S. 201 are dealt with as aberrations or ignored in Ocean Hill-Brownsville. And Ford will soon give McCoy another $275,000, through the Institute of Community Studies, to work on instructional programs.

Knowing all his people's troubles with the unit, U.F.T. president Albert Shanker said recently, with some courage, "I think it's just possible that McCoy may make it." Superintendent Bernard Donovan says, "I'd like to see McCoy succeed. I've bent over backwards to assist him—but I can't go as far as I'd like because of the law." (The members of the Board of Education may be less sympathetic than Dr. Donovan, who recognizes McCoy's professionalism.) McCoy's powers, as the equivalent of a district superintendent's, are indeed considerable—but because they do not include the right to allocate budget or assign personnel, they are insufficient. They should be increased; and if the law forbids it, the law should be changed.

Giving McCoy and his board their heads will not guarantee moderation and tranquility in the unit. Behind the impassive professionalism McCoy is deeply hostile to much of American society. His administrative assistant Eduardo Braithwaite could serve as Mr. Arbuthnot in a Frank Sullivan piece entitled "The Cliché Expert Testifies on Black Power" ("Africa, man, that's the center of *everything*"). Fuentes is a Puerto-Rican separatist, who regards mastery of English as far less important to his students than mastery of Spanish—wandering around his school with him is a true venture through the looking glass, to a world where a New York principal gets annoyed with a child who answers in English when addressed in Spanish. But the important question now is not what these children think as the result of the instruction they receive, but their ability to think at all.

There must, of course, be grave doubts whether McCoy can make a significant difference in education in Brownsville.

The resources required to make a dent in the troubles of Ocean Hill-Brownsville are wildly beyond the capacity of the community to provide, and McCoy knows it: "They ask this community which they have degraded for X years to come up now with all the answers to urban education. Well, we can't; and don't expect it. But as long as I am here, things will be done. We won't create miracles, but things will happen, and this project will not die."

All things considered, it is an impressive and credible pledge. The debate on the decentralization of the schools this year has been discouraging in its intellectual level and obviously unproductive of political action. Emphasis has been placed consistently on those issues which most frighten the professional staff, rather than on the new opportunities for more responsible and responsive professional work.

But whatever else the Legislature may do in this session, it should give McCoy a chance to make good on his personal promise, by authorizing the Mayor or the Commissioner of Education to suspend whatever sections of the education law may need suspending to give a functioning community school board the power to carry through its administrator's ideas. No experienced observer could give McCoy and his people more than an outside chance at rescuing from ignorance and futility any substantial proportion of the 9,000 unlucky children in his area—but nobody really believes that the Board of Education as currently owned and operated can offer any chance whatever.

[In the aftermath of the I.S. 55 fire, during the weeks while this article was sitting in type at the *Times,* McCoy lost control of his board, and the Ocean Hill experiment failed. At this writing, in October, 1968, the dimensions of the failure are unknown, and it is not impossible that some way of resuscitating the victim will be found. Reluctance to admit the initial failure, however, has already produced a citywide three-week teachers' strike, riots at Ocean Hill itself and related pieces of terrorism and nastiness (especially on the Lower East Side, where Lou Fuentes and some of his friends held the local school board physically captive for five hours and said blood would flow in the streets unless the local board and "the Jews" chose Fuentes as a district superintendent).

[The motion to dismiss the nineteen teachers and administrators was opposed by both McCoy and Oliver, and indeed violated a recently adopted bylaw of the governing board, that the board would not entertain charges against individual teachers unless they were brought by McCoy himself. And the individuals involved were not, in fact, the I.S. 55 teachers who had abandoned the children during the fire. They were union activists, skeptics on the issue of decentralization and people who had quarreled with the more aggressive members of McCoy's administrative staff. According to later statements by John Niemyer, president of the Bank Street College of Education and an independent fellow, who had somewhat reluctantly taken a watching brief from the Board of Education, the UFT was willing to accept its members' transfer out of the district, as of April, provided the whole affair was managed quietly. Instead, the governing board trumpeted its "dismissals" of the nineteen and its "power" to order such dismissals. I talked with McCoy on the phone that afternoon, not knowing the full background and feeling sympathetic to the cause; and I was surprised to hear him say, despairingly, "I want the record to show that this community behaved very well under severe provocation for eight months." He did not like the dismissed nineteen any more than the members of the governing board did, but he knew the "dismissals" were fundamentally self-defeating.

[The UFT responded by calling a strike in the unit, and about 250 teachers walked out. Parents stopped sending their children to school. The Board of Education held some aimless meetings, Ford (unwisely) confirmed its new grant, some part of the story ran every so often on the back pages of the newspapers.

[Of the nineteen "dismissed" staff members, one (the only Negro) was reinstated, and eight applied for transfer, which was gladly given. The other ten insisted on their right to their Ocean Hill jobs. The UFT offered a peace pipe (for which UFT president Albert Shanker has never received credit) by accepting outside arbitration of the charges finally, after long delays, produced against the ten teachers. (The governing board, obsessed with the academic *juvenilia* of "power," had proclaimed that it didn't need reasons for its actions.) The arbitrator, Judge Francis Rivers, himself Negro, ruled that no charges had been proved against the teachers. The governing board refused to accept the result.

[During the summer, most of the UFT members who had struck the district in the spring applied for transfer; only 100 were left in the district, and McCoy "hired" new teachers to replace the 100, whom the governing board had said would no longer be permitted to teach on Ocean Hill. The UFT could not now mount an effective strike against the district. But its contract, after all, was with the Board of Education. A governing board established by the Board and an administrator appointed by the Board were flagrantly violating that contract. The Taylor Act forbidding strikes by public employees was in all fairness and logic (though not, of course, in law) inapplicable to the situation, because the rationale of all such laws rests on the quid pro quo of job security in public employment. The UFT had no respect for the Taylor Act, anyway. Shanker announced that unless the 100 teachers were assigned to their old jobs at Ocean Hill, the union would close the city's schools.

[The Sunday before school was to open, Mayor Lindsay met with both sides at length and announced that the governing board had consented to being forced to take the teachers back (it had not consented to take them—just to being forced), so there would be no strike. No union leader, of course, could call off a strike on this sort of unsupported verbal assurance, and 54,000 of the city's 57,000 teachers stayed away on opening day. So did the great majority of principals and assistant principals, whose association—fear makes even stranger bedfellows than politics—supported Shanker. The Ocean Hill schools opened peaceably, as did the schools of the I.S. 201 complex (which had made its peace with the local UFT chapter); nearly all other schools were closed. Lindsay, with a gift for saying the wrong thing that would long ago have wrecked the career of a less pretty man, announced at a public meeting during the day that "there is no strike" and that "the Ocean Hill governing board pulled the rug out from under Mr. Shanker" by agreeing to be forced to accept the teachers. Nevertheless, the Board of Education the next day reduced the deal to writing, and on Wednesday the city's schools opened.

[In Ocean Hill, unquestionably egged on by members of the governing board and McCoy's staff, terrorists threatened and in a few instances physically assaulted the returning teachers. It was now obvious that some schools would have to be closed while the matter was thrashed out—either 8,500 children in Ocean Hill or 1,100,000 children elsewhere in the city were going to lose time in the classroom. Closing the Ocean Hill schools quickly and sharply, on an issue where the governing board was clearly wrong, would have provoked disturbances there and perhaps in one or two other trouble spots, but it would have put the pressure to make peace on the Ocean Hill governing board, which would have been held responsible by its own constituency, correctly, for depriving the local children of schools. Closing all the schools meant citywide exacerbation of racial tension. The choice was Lindsay's, and he chose wrong. On Friday, Shanker again closed the city's schools.

[For two weeks, the Mayor, the Board of Education (now, for the first time, dominated by Lindsay appointees), the courts, the Superintendent of Schools and the State Commissioner of Education flapped about rather aimlessly, while the union demonstrated that, by golly, there really is such a thing as the exercise of "power" in the affairs of men. (Normally, of course, the essence of what the sociologists have unfortunately called "power" is that it does not have to be exercised; but that's a subject for another place.) Various church groups, newspapers, community action boards, and civil rights organizations denounced the UFT; Oliver said Lindsay was holding down the community while the union raped it; McCoy said Shanker was depriving him of his manhood (thus revealing an interesting split of attitude in the Ocean Hill inner circle). The labor movement—including its Negro leadership, headed by A. Philip Randolph —stayed solidly behind Shanker, as did most of the non-Communist Old Left, rather to the surprise of observers who did not know that Brooklyn CORE, which now dominated the Ocean Hill governing board, had long been a heavy cross for national CORE to bear because of its Stalinist orientation. But all this was sideshow—the essential fact was that the city's schools could not reopen until the UFT had a deal.

[During the course of the strike, I found myself in an elevator in a mid-town office building with a man whose children were in public school in my old district, and who had come to almost every meeting of my local school board. "This is all *your* fault," he said, trying to be pleasant and not quite succeeding. But, dammit, it isn't my fault: the transmutation of decentralization to "community control" was done by the sociologists at the universities, not by those of us who understood the problem.

[The distinction is vital. Decentralization, which I promoted as vigorously as I could for five years, called for placing the locus of decision as close as possible to the schools themselves. It removed from the district super-intendent's arsenal of excuses for inaction the explanation that he was simply following citywide policy. *Accountability* to the "community" was inherent in decentralization—the district superintendent would be forever stuck with the need to explain and justify his actions to his local board. I would have been happy to see the boards with authority to dismiss their superintendent (for cause) at the end of a school year. And I wanted

great latitude *for the district superintendent* in the appointment of principals and the assigning of teachers (via district-by-district negotiations
with the UFT in the broad frame of a minimal citywide contract), because I don't see how you can hold a man accountable for the performance of an organization unless you let him pick the key people in that
organization. But apart from the power to dismiss the superintendent himself—and some sort of advice-and-consent role with the appointing power
on the choice of a new man—I wanted local boards entirely out of the
personnel picture. This is, in practice, the way suburban school boards
operate: when vacancies occur, they hire the man their superintendent
wants, because he, not they, has to supervise the actual work. And it was
the way Ocean Hill worked while the experiment worked—all the new
principals were McCoy's choices rubber-stamped by his board. What I
urged at the end of this article, as few readers seem to have recognized,
was power for the governing board to authorize McCoy to act in certain
areas, not power for the board to order him to act.

[Nothing—literally nothing—could be more damaging to the life chances
of slum children in a city like New York than the politicization of hiring
and firing in the schools. We see it happen every so often in the suburbs,
when the Birchites come in and start laying about them with their axes.
But the Birchites soon reform or get voted out; the suburban nexus is
attractive enough so good teachers and principals can be got once again
after the situation stabilizes; and, after all, the kids are not greatly im-
periled, because most of their useful education occurs in the home and in
their association with each other. In the ghetto a large fraction of what
hope there is for the child lies in the technical skill of his teacher.

[When we say the New York slum schools are failing, we mean that they
fail with major fractions of the children entrusted to them. They do not
fail with all, and it is simply untrue to say that "the schools could not
be worse." They could be; and they will be. On the other side (*pace* people like Jonathan Kozol and Herbert Kohl, whose descriptions of their
work read to this observer like the typical self-deceptions that are the
attraction and the curse of almost any good teacher), when we speak of
making the schools better we do not expect to rescue *all* or anything like
all the children who now fall through the sieve. We don't know enough,
and the troubles these children bring to school are too demoralizing, for
any sensible planner to hope for overwhelming success. New York's
original Higher Horizons program, before it got "democratized," hoped
for substantially improved academic performance by 50 percent of those
in the slum schools, which still strikes me as a reasonable target.

[Fifty percent, in any event, would assure the school of adequate "community support." The Bundy Report on decentralization contains one inexcusable folly—inexcusable because both Bundy and his assistant Mario Fantini recognized it as folly—in a statement by Professor Preston Wilcox to the effect that communities can "unite" around the issue of education. In fact, communities inevitably divide about the issue of education. People's attitudes toward a school are a function of how well they think their children are doing; and because different children do differently well, even in the slums, parents are *always* divided in their judgments of a school. Indeed, the inevitability of these divisions—and the high degree of fantasy ordinarily encountered in discussions of the quality of a school—is what makes it necessary to insulate the teacher's job from political pressures, to provide licenses and tenure and union grievance procedures. There is no large cadre of skilled teachers and brilliant paraprofessionals waiting to jump in and make the schools work in the ghetto (indeed, the people at McCoy's old school who were training the Ocean Hill paraprofessionals were astonished at his statement to the ladies that they would have diagnostic skills the teachers lacked; the most that could be hoped for, I was told, was minimal competence at carrying out a cookbook phonics program—which would be, incidentally, much more than nothing and distinctly worth having). The only hope is that the experienced people we have, with a leaven of eager newcomers and neighborhood helpers, can with better leadership and better materials and methods produce better results in the schools.

[Rhody McCoy knows the importance of professionalism in personnel policy; and Al Shanker knows that current Board of Education procedures are protecting incompetent personnel in a disgraceful and wholly unprofessional way. (In a debate the two of us had on decentralization in the spring of 1968, it was Shanker and not I who pointed out to an audience composed mostly of schoolteachers that only 12 of 57,000 teachers had been dismissed the year before, though everybody knew there were thousands of teachers who ought not to be teaching.) It is outrageously untrue to accuse McCoy of anti-Semitism (half the new teachers he "hired" to replace the UFT strikers were Jewish) or to accuse Shanker of bias against Negroes (the union's record on integration is impeccable). Both are wholly first-rate men. I think one can fairly say that McCoy, who as a teacher of tough kids had often strong-armed students, tolerated from the beginning an element of physical threat he should have condemned; and that Shanker, who has to run for election, allowed himself to be trapped by a wholly negative element in his membership. Still, someone like myself, who knows both men casually, must believe that the two if left alone could have worked together fruitfully, and that the scenario which cast them as enemies, written as it was in ignorance and haste on both sides, has turned sociology to tragedy.

[For one brief moment a rapprochement seemed possible. The deal worked out to end the second strike sweetened the pot substantially for Ocean Hill—while the governing board would have to take back the 83 teachers who still wanted back after the trauma of September, it would also be allowed to keep all the novices McCoy had "hired" to replace them. Shanker, selling the deal to the union's executive board, added rather courageously a statement that "Now we must all learn to work with Mr. McCoy." When Oliver told the *New York Times* that the governing board was rejecting the deal and would order McCoy to remove the 83 teachers from classrooms, McCoy denied that the board had done any such thing, and pointed out that the teachers were as of that moment at their posts. But then the governing board did meet with McCoy in executive session, and did issue the order Oliver had prematurely announced; and McCoy, having decided the previous spring that he would have no enemies on the left, opted for solidarity and destruction. *Sic transit spes mundi.*]

[PPS: Two days after the preceding paragraphs were written, unbelievably, the settlement was allowed to collapse. McCoy under orders from the "suspended" governing board told his principals to remove the UFT teachers from the classrooms—and was in turn "suspended," though he continued at his office as usual. The principals announced they would follow McCoy's orders, and they too were "suspended." At J-271 not only the returning UFT teachers but also the assistant principals who were assigning them were driven away with threats and curses. Superintendent Donovan closed J-271, and met with its teachers. McCoy, who clearly knew things other people didn't know, told the Ocean Hill parents the school would reopen presently, the principals would be back at their desks, and everybody should cool it. On Friday Donovan announced that J-271 would reopen Monday, and all the principals would return with full power to reassign teachers within their schools—but Donovan personally would see to it that this power was not used punitively. From a trade union point of view (though perhaps not in reality: nobody knows what private agreements Donovan had reached with McCoy), the school system had welshed. The UFT struck again, and at this writing the strike is in its fourth week. Doubtless the teachers have been stinkers. But everything they have done was their union's most probable reaction to each situation; and political leadership must stand responsible for predictable and avoidable disaster.]

10

Evergreen *in the Underground*

[This article was commissioned by Byron Dobell of *Esquire* in the late summer of 1965, and written that fall while I was on the road for The Twentieth Century Fund—in Paris, Geneva, Lagos, Monrovia, Yekepa, Accra, Dakar, Rio de Janeiro, São Paulo, Montevideo and Buenos Aires —whence it was shipped to New York by what looked like a most untrustworthy hotel porter. It did arrive, though, and everybody at *Esquire* said they loved it; and it never ran. Grrr.

[Going through my files in connection with the preparation of this book, I found a Xerox copy of the manuscript, read it, liked it, and decided I wanted it for these pages. *Esquire* released all rights, and at lunch with Otto Friedrich I mentioned that I had a three-year-old piece about Barney Rosset which I was very pleased with, and would the *Saturday Evening Post* like to see it? Friedrich replied that he and his colleagues had often thought of commissioning a piece about Rosset, but the project had seemed too chancy: they'd be happy to look at one for nothing. A couple of weeks later I had a cheerful call from Don McKinney of the *Post;* and the article was revised and updated on Shelter Island in the summer of 1968.

[Various morals can be drawn from this story. At one extreme might be You Can't Keep a Good Piece Down; at the other, The Rich Get Richer. . . .]

MAIL CALL in Kunming, China, one day in 1943 brought Lieutenant Joseph Passantino a letter from Chicago, where he didn't know anybody. Passantino, now a New York commercial printer, reconstructs the letter roughly as follows: "My son Barney writes me that you and he have become great buddies in China, so I imagine you already know how impulsive and enthusiastic he can be. Sometimes he becomes so excited he gets himself into trouble. . . . As his father, could I ask you to keep an eye on him, and be like a big brother to him? . . ."

Passantino was already trying. He and his friend Barney were the commanders of two units of ten to twelve photographers each, making up the 164th Signal Photo Company. The job was to take pictures of captured enemy equipment and personnel, of the training of new soldiers for Chiang Kai-shek, of terrain that might be fought over, and of combat if there was combat in the neighborhood. The pictures got flown to India for internal use by the Army: they were not news pictures. "But Barney was terrifically impatient with that Army brass," Passantino says, "and with that GI thing that dawdled and procrastinated. And the Chinese Army didn't move for Barney the way he thought it ought to move. General Stilwell got thrown out of China for the same reason Barney would have been if he'd been big enough. He would tell *anybody* off. I'd say, 'Barney, now, wait a minute. Hold it. You're in the army; it doesn't work that way.'

"Danger didn't faze him," Passantino recalls. "He took the weapons carrier and drove it two hundred miles to Liuchow, over Chinese roads, Japs all around. He wanted to be dropped behind the lines with the OSS people—I told him, 'Barney, we're not *trained* for that.' When we retook Liuchow, the Air Force people were landing and getting right out, the base hadn't been cleared of land mines. Barney had to go in and stay, for the exhilaration of being there. Our photo-reconnaissance jeep got blown sky-high by a land mine, with two men wounded.

"He was far ahead, mentally, of the average guy you would meet in the Army and he was a little dynamo, but with all of that he wasn't *impressive*. He doesn't look you straight in the eye, he's got that nervous laugh, and his voice trails off, you don't hear the end of what he's saying. Just a little while ago we had him and his wife up to dinner with some friends of mine I thought he might want to do some business with. My friends couldn't believe *that* was Barney Rosset, the owner of Grove Press. . . ."

Though in sales volume it ranks around the middle of the list of a hundred or so American book publishers, Barney Rosset's Grove Press is today the most talked-about enterprise of its kind, especially among the literate young. "The kids in college who think they'd like to be in publishing," says William Callahan, who was executive vice-president of Dell Publishing when Dell distributed Rosset's commercially promising paperbacks, "they all want to work for Grove. It has the same sort of standing Alfred Knopf had forty years ago." Knopf, whose publicity concentrates on the Nobel Prize winners his house has published, would not be pleased by the comparison (and neither, for that matter, would Rosset), but Callahan is probably right. Even within the publishing establishment, Rosset does not completely lack admirers. "When the history of publishing is written," says Jason Epstein of Random House, "Barney will have a place in it. He's bright. He takes a lot of risks that look frivolous to many people, but there's a serious radical impulse behind them all. He's altered the climate of publishing to everybody's advantage. Less than ten years ago it would have been inconceivable that anybody could publish Genet in this country, and now *Our Lady of the Flowers* is in Modern Library; and Barney's done it."

The man for whom history will find a place is slight, lean and alert, with sandy hair going gray and long sideburns, wearing very thick, horn-rimmed glasses, carelessly dressed, and obviously on the run even when sitting. The habitats are Greenwich Village and the eastern end of Long Island, always contemporary in décor. The publishing house operates under three logos: hard-cover books in the name Grove Press, bookstore-priced paperbacks in the name Evergreen, and drugstore-priced paperbacks in the name Black Cat. All three lists are a hodgepodge of serious literature, significant books in sociology and psychology, and pornography ranging from squishy to the edge of hard-core. Also under the name Evergreen, the company distributes films, most of them well underground, though some have at least a nostril or two visible on the surface.

Grove first came to prominence before the public and the booksellers in 1959, with the publication of the unexpurgated *Lady Chatterley's Lover,* and the house is probably best known for the indiscriminate mess of Henry Miller, Victorian wet dreams, Genet, *Histoire d'O,* scatological Burroughs, Frank Harris and Marquis de Sade stuff that appears under its imprints—plus the avant-garde poetry, the wide variety of short fiction, the op art and hot photography and sado-masochistic comic strips that make up the monthly magazine

Evergreen Review. But before *Lady Chatterley,* a Grove book had been reviewed on the front page of the *New York Times Book Review*—a first American publication of Giovanni Verga's *The House by the Medlar Tree,* a classic of that Italian *verismo* tradition which has shown greater staying power than either French or American realism. There had been a dozen volumes of contemporary American poetry, a much-admired *Introduction to Japanese Literature,* and a commercially impossible attempt to publish a series of low-priced paperback art books with first-class color plates, presenting the major figures of the American twentieth century.

On the list before *Lady Chatterley* were three volumes of Brecht and two each of Ionesco and of Brendan Behan, and eight of Samuel Beckett, who in the process of publication by Grove became Rosset's friend. ("Barney and I go to the tennis matches," Beckett said not long ago. "We play games, and we talk politics. We don't talk literature. I don't talk literature much with *nobody*. It's bad enough to have to write these books without talking about them, too.") Rosset published *Waiting for Godot* a year before the play opened. Marilynn Meeker, a quiet, serious, incredibly hard-working editor who has been with Grove since 1953 doing every job a publishing house can offer, was miscast as the New York area salesman at the time *Godot* was published, and she remembers wandering the streets with the slim volume in her hand, lonely as a cloud, unable to get anybody interested. "They'd say, 'Who's going to spend five dollars for *that?* '" In its first year, *Godot* sold a grand total of 700 copies; today, the sales in paperback (at $1.75) are approaching half a million.

The first book Rosset ever published was a reprint of Henry James's *The Golden Bowl* in 1952. He had recently purchased from its young founders the three-title inventory of their tiny Grove Press (named for Grove Street in Greenwich Village), and had personally carted all the books to his top-floor apartment in an old brownstone. They were stacked in his living room, and whenever an order came in, he would wrap the books and take them to the post office in a laundry cart. Having become a publisher, he went to Columbia and took a course in publishing, and while there he met Donald Allen, who had got hooked by Japanese literature while a Navy officer. Allen took the apartment next door, and presently became Grove's first editor (he is now Grove's man on the West Coast). "When I bought the rights to *The Golden Bowl* from Scribner's," Rosset recalls, "Whitney Darrow, who was a personage, came up to see who we were. He walked upstairs and came in, and it was quite an experience for him. I didn't think it was so funny then as I do now."

Nobody who knew Rosset really believed he had found his vocation: it seemed much more likely that he had found another toy. In his essay on Dali, George Orwell tells of a friend who liked to say that he knew he was a genius long before he knew what he was a genius *at;* and Rosset was one of those. Born in Chicago in 1922, he was the adored and feared only child of an Irish mother and a Jewish father, a banker who had made his first million before he was twenty-one, lost it, and then made several more. The family photo album, which Rosset cherishes, shows vacations in Hawaii and on the Florida keys, the family participating in the inauguration of Sun Valley and relaxing on Lake Michigan in the yacht Rosset's father gave to the Navy at the outbreak of the war.

Young Barney was sent to Francis Parker, perhaps the farthest-out of the progressive schools of the 1930s; it became, and in many ways still remains, the center of his existence, the source of what Jason Epstein calls "his old-fashioned avant-gardism." Rosset himself says, "You've got to understand that nothing has changed me since I left high school." Rosset's first wife, the painter Joan Mitchell, a handsome, tough-minded lady with a big talent and fierce dedication to it, began going out with him when they were both at Parker. She remembers that "he ran his class. Everybody looked up to him. He had a car before anyone else had a car, but that wasn't it. He was shy and he didn't talk well and he became class president; and he was a little guy and skinny with thick glasses, and he became the football star. That's pretty good, you know." Swarthmore, Chicago and U.C.L.A. in rapid succession took a crack at changing Barney after he left Parker, and all gave up. Then young Rosset, having breathed the last of a fiery pacifism when Hitler attacked Russia, joined the Army, went off the top of the classification test, and saw the world as a Signal Corps officer. As Passantino observed, the Army didn't change him, either. He loved China; but he learned no Chinese.

The war over, Rosset returned to the University of Chicago ("They couldn't keep me out—I'd never failed any courses, I had a complete incomplete, never took any exams"), and bought an airplane. Miss Mitchell remembers going up with him and hearing him say, as they lazily circled the lake shore, "I've forgotten how to land this damned thing." Passantino remembers saying, "Barney, why do you want a plane? He said, 'Oh, it's great—you get up there, you look down on all Chicago.' I said, 'Barney, what the hell good is that?' The next year he told me I'd been right."

Presently, Rosset and Miss Mitchell went off to live together in New York, to the horror of her parents, who were Chicago society; and Rosset decided to make a movie. This was *Strange Victory,* a semi-documentary about race relations in the United States; it opened in 1949, a decade ahead of its time in topic and a decade behind in treatment. ("Think back—was there ever a hope that flared higher than that hope of midsummer 1945? . . . Nobody knows where that victory is: lost, strayed or stolen, it isn't here. . . ." With endless pictures of differently colored babies in hospital nurseries . . . "Whoever you are, we welcome you: You are now part of the human race. . . . But the world is already arranged for you. . . ." Narrated by Alfred Drake, music derived by David Diamond from Virgil Thomson's 1930s scores for Pare Lorenz, produced by Barnet L. Rosset, Jr.) About a quarter of a million dollars of the Rosset family fortune disappeared in this picture. "I lost a hundred percent," Rosset said recently. "More than that, you can't do."

Shortly after the failure of the film, Miss Mitchell, now legally Mrs. Rosset, received a fellowship to work in France, and her husband tagged along. For reasons Rosset could never figure out, they lived a while in Paris in a room without plumbing ("She convinced me we had to save money, I can't remember why"). Then they went south to Provence, where Miss Mitchell painted and Rosset vegetated, in theory trying to write a novel but in fact lounging about meaninglessly, coming alive to do the cooking at night. "He used to drive me nuts, doing nothing all day," Miss Mitchell says. In fact, he was doing something: he was learning about art by watching his wife. Miss Mitchell had come to France basically a representational painter; she left France an abstract expressionist. "Before I'd met Joan," Rosset says, "I'd thought all art had to be socially useful. Down there in Provence, I was actually watching the breakup of the forms. If I have any taste today, or any emotion about art, and if the Grove covers show any consistency, it's all thanks to Joan." Rosset loved France; but he learned no French.

On return to America, the Rossets began summering on eastern Long Island with the DeKoonings and Pollocks and Klines; and Rosset picked up at early '50s prices some paintings he sold a few years ago on the grounds that he was scared to have anything worth that much hanging on his walls. He was still, in effect, doing nothing. He tried to find a place for himself in Truman's Point-Four program, and with the American Association for the United Nations, but it all came out badly. "If you've ever done for a nonprofit organization," says Howard Turner, who had been Rosset's personal assistant (or "gopher") in the days of *Strange Victory* and remained a friend, "you can imagine how frustrated Barney was." Miss Mitchell decided she was going back to Paris, and did so, alone. Rosset likes to say of their divorce that "all she wanted was her own name back—she didn't want anything from me." "That shows you," says Miss Mitchell, "what a gentleman Barney is: the fact of the matter is that *he* divorced *me,* but he wouldn't want to say that."

And then, quite suddenly, because Miss Mitchell knew a young man who had a half-interest in an almost dormant publishing house and was trying to sell it, young Barney was a publisher.

Grove stumbled along slowly for its first three or four years. From his Columbia publishing course and personal observation, Rosset decided there was no future in paperbacks, and he had his inventory bound; three years later, he decided there was no future in anything but paperbacks, and he had the hard covers chopped off. ("We actually sold those books below their cost of production.") The first employee Rosset hired for Grove was a girl on her work term from Bennington, recommended by Wallace Fowlie, with whom Rosset had taken a course at the New School. Rosset and his father (who was, after all, paying the bills) agreed that if you were going to be in publishing you had to have a list of books, so you could allocate overhead to a lot of items, hire salesmen, etc. There was little chance of a new firm picking up any quantity of publishable original material, so Rosset went off to London and Paris to buy American rights. "The British publishers were very nice," Rosset says, "even the big ones—Faber & Faber offered me *Justine* [the first book in Lawrence Durrell's *Alexandria* series, which sold hugely], and I turned it down because I didn't like it."

In Paris Rosset made contact with Jerome Lindon, whose Editions de Minuit, founded as part of the resistance movement, had become the leading house of the *nouvelle vague*. Though they communicate only with difficulty (Lindon, who had an American grandfather, speaks no English; and Rosset can only struggle inventively in French), they became parallel operations. Among the authors Rosset has taken from Lindon are Beckett, Marguerite Duras and Alain Robbe-Grillet. "Grove is the American publisher closest to our views," Lindon said the other day in his little office in an alley off Saint-Germain-des-Près. "And I like Barney because he is a very fine man. I always say, when the Americans are intelligent they are very intelligent. Barney has a sense of liberty which is rare in Europe, he is extraordinarily *young,* and he has a taste for risk—literary risk, risk of good taste, political risk. There is one difference in situation—it seems to me that in the United States erotic publications are more important than they are here. Myself, I have never published a book that has taken me to the Palais de Justice; I am a Puritan." Rosset's Barbarella comic strip (which he advertised as "banned in France") did *not* come from Lindon.

As the Grove list grew, the floors in Rosset's walkup began to buckle under the inventory, and he took office space in a second-floor loft over an established dry goods store at 795 Broadway. He needed a bookkeeper, which is why he hired Marilynn Meeker, whose ambitions were literary though she had been involved with ledgers in a previous job. And he needed somebody to keep an eye on the business, for which purpose, one day at lunch ("Gee, I wish I had you back with me"), he again hired Howard Turner. Joe Passantino managed much of the production and printing work, on a contract, book-by-book basis. Another employee was a German girl (distinctly not a refugee: her father was a successful banker in Essen), who presently became the second Mrs. Rosset. Rosset's son Peter, now thirteen, was born to this marriage, but could not save it.

Two years after Barney became a publisher his father died, and Barney's share of the estate went into Grove Press—most people think all of it went into Grove Press. "Barney has a thing about money," says Jason Epstein. "He doesn't like it." Turner having returned to making films, Rosset in 1956 hired Fred Jordan, a British-educated Viennese refugee a few years younger than himself, to handle sales and promotion and mind the store while the boss went off to Europe. He returned with an enormous publishing program. From a happy family of four employees and a list of about thirty titles in print at the beginning of 1956, Grove went to an office of thirty employees and the publication of a hundred titles a year, nearly all of them in paper under the Evergreen name. Now some of them were originals (as distinguished from reprints or translations); one such was Kerouac's *The Subterraneans*. Rosset and Jordan, whose previous experience had been as the sole employee of a tiny scholarly press, invented ways to advertise and promote (and get reviews for) new paperback novels. There was also an East and West Book Club, mostly East, based on translations from the Japanese.

In 1957 and 1958, mostly by sheer volume of output, Evergreen became the largest-selling paperback name in bookstores other than college bookstores (where the business was and is dominated by books "adopted" as part of reading lists for courses; Evergreen now has some of that gravy, too). This was living more dangerously than Rosset realized—"Four new houses came into the paperback business," says Richard Seaver, who joined Grove as managing editor in 1959, "and you were cut back from ten percent to two percent of the shelf space"—and shortly Grove made the first of several accordion-like returns to more rational size. The book club was sold to George Braziller. And then came *Lady Chatterley*.

"You're not regarded as having arrived in publishing until you've had a best seller," says Fred Jordan. *"Lady Chatterley* was our best seller." It was a lot more than that. The book made Grove a big-time legal client as well as a big-time publisher. Rosset turned it over to an Easthampton tennis companion, Charles Rembar, a darkly handsome literary lawyer who recently turned author himself with an autobiographical tract entitled *The End of Obscenity*. "There had already been rumblings from the Post Office when Barney talked to me," Rembar said the other day. "And then everything happened so fast there was no time to prepare. But we wanted it fast—I felt that if there was a fat federal case going, the local prosecutors would lie back, and they did."

The judicial officer appointed by the Post Office referred the matter up to the Postmaster General without recommendation; but this dignitary was then Mr. Summerfield, the Michigan car dealer, and he had no hesitation about barring *Lady Chatterley* from the mails. "In these cases, traditionally," Rembar says, "the defense is that it isn't really a sexy book. I didn't want to take that position." Expanding some language in a 1957 Supreme Court decision, Rembar developed what later became known as the social value test. "It was," he says, "a chancy way to approach the case, and I had to leave it up to Barney. There's an old saying around the criminal courts that the lawyer always goes home. And you've got to hand it to Rosset. He didn't want to win this case on the grounds that the Post Office Department had violated the Administrative Procedures Act—he wanted to win it on the grounds that the book was worth publishing. And we did."

Lady Chatterley all by herself almost doubled Grove's volume, despite the rash of pirated editions that appeared almost immediately after the Supreme Court had decided the case. But it did Rosset damage, too—it gave him a wholly misleading notion of the costs of defending pornography actions. A year later, sixty separate state and local prosecutions were brought against Grove's edition of Henry Miller's long-banned *Tropic of Cancer* after the Post Office decided to leave it alone, and because publishers normally warrant that they will hold booksellers harmless for selling their wares, Grove had to defend all of them. Coupled with a constant leak of money from the inflated organization—it's one thing to have everybody pitch in at

5:30 or on Saturday and take care of the week's undone tasks when there are four employees, and something quite different when there are thirty in the office and nobody knows what's undone—the costs of defending the booksellers drove Rosset perilously near the wall. (Later, when he published Miller's *Tropic of Capricorn,* he specifically and publicly disavowed all responsibility for defending those who sold it.) He tried to peddle Grove Press all over New York, and couldn't; the banks wouldn't lend him any money; and he remained afloat, finally, only through the doubtful courtesy of the money-lenders. The accumulated losses of this period—about a million dollars—freed Grove from any need to pay federal tax on earnings until 1967.

Rosset took one more crack at avoiding the commercial responsibilities of a publishing house: he brought in Charles Rembar to be president of Grove. "We coordinated fine as lawyer and client," Rembar says today, "but as business partners we were terrible. The theory was that he would concentrate on editing and I would run the business. It just didn't work. He would say, 'Let's publish X book.' I'd say, 'It's going to get us into litigation and we've got enough litigation.' He would say, 'But it's a good book.' And I'd say, 'But it's a lousy book. . . .' My connection with the business was short-term."

Though the house now has nine editors, Rosset still has not relinquished to anybody the actual decision to publish something under a Grove imprint. "What integrity you can discern in the list," says Fred Jordan, "is Rosset's personality." Richard Seaver, who lived in France for a number of years, keeps up with French publishers; Jordan, who was born in Vienna, follows the Germans. (Much of Grove's volume is in foreign authors.) In English-language material, Rosset is his own first reader. "My important talent," he says, "is rejecting things quickly; everyone else gets drawn into reading them. The one bad thing is that if I'm away for a couple of months the telephone calls start arriving—what happened to my manuscript?—and nobody can give an answer." After a recent summer vacation, Rosset, Seaver, Jordan and Marilynn Meeker sat around a conference table and in one morning threw back four hundred manuscripts on the grounds that the first page was no good. If Rosset feels there may be something here, the manuscript goes out for reading, and then comes back to his desk with recommendations, at which time he will examine it more closely. A purchase indicates his personal approval, though that approval is sometimes given on the grounds that a "treasured editor" (a favorite phrase) badly wants to publish the book.

Pornography is on the Grove list because Rosset likes pornography (both for its own sake and because it offends middle-class squares like the parents of his boyhood friends). Sex alone, however, is by no means a sufficient recommendation to sell Grove a book, though many authors think otherwise ("sometimes you look at a manuscript," says Miss Meeker, "and you know the author thought, 'Aha! *They'll* publish this!' "). Jordan remembers finding a lubricous novel called *Beautiful Wilhelmina,* which had been a big best seller in its native Germany (and later did well here under a more respectable imprint than Grove's). Jordan took it to Rosset with the comment that it was terrible but it had commercial possibilities, and Rosset promptly rejected it. "All the controversial books," says Richard Seaver, "do have some merit you can discuss." This statement is probably not true unless Seaver is prepared to argue that a careful translation of *Histoire d'O* (a dreary tale of sexual indignities allegedly related by a French prostitute) gives the book some merit worth discussing; but others have published even drearier smut than Grove's worst.

In any event, Grove is now a going concern, which can count on its share of the publishing luck. When Doubleday decided not to risk the Black Muslim nuisance that might follow publication of the Malcolm X *Autobiography,* Grove was the natural second choice. *Last Exit From Brooklyn,* the you-stink homosexual fantasies of a talented writer, came to Grove because it seemed the right house; *Games People Play,* a set of psychological parlor tricks which stayed on the best-seller lists longer than any nonfiction book in the last decade, was a by-product of Rosset's prior publication of its author's more serious efforts. Grove is the American end of the Formentor International Literary Prize, and while this venture has not yet turned up any author of great interest, the odds are good that some day it will.

Today Rosset has almost 150 employees and an IBM 360-30 computer to bollix the subscription lists of *Evergreen Review* and the billing for the Evergreen ("Join the Underground") Book Club. The company is still something less than a model for business schools— books appear and disappear from lists virtually without warning to salesmen, high-priced people type their own letters while low-priced people manicure their fingernails, and not long ago when Rosset's invaluable secretary-assistant Judith Schmidt went on vacation his outer office was occupied for five long and terrifying weeks by a young lady from Germany who spoke no English (and Rosset speaks no German).

But the days are gone when Rosset tried to distribute his books through a fleet of Volkswagen Microbuses manned by driver-salesmen, like bakery trucks, and required his editors to buy paper, pick type faces, set production schedules and see books through the press because he felt that production managers do not earn their keep. Now Grove has conventional warehousing and a conventional production department. The confusion of the loft at 795 Broadway, with its low partitions and informal "It's-for-YOU-Fred" telephone system, has given way to a neat white five-story building on University Place with different functions on different floors and a garden-variety switchboard. Destiny, having marked young Rosset as a businessman while he was in his cradle, has finally caught up with him at the enlarged and expanded Grove Press. And for six consecutive years, the house has made money.

Indeed, what worries Rosset's friends (and sometimes his employees) is that he may lose interest in Grove now that the house is on its feet. An ominous rumbling from that quarter came when Rosset revived his long-dormant drive toward film producing. "Film," he explained, "is the natural direction in a lot of contemporary writers, and it's just silly to fight it." In 1964 he commissioned full-length scripts from Robbe-Grillet and Marguerite Duras, and one-act scripts from Pinter, Ionesco and Beckett. He actually produced the Beckett script (which had no dialogue), with Buster Keaton in the leading role, and allowed it to be shown in New York in 1965, under the stark title *Film,* as part of the Lincoln Center film festival. But the others, except for the Pinter (which was given to the BBC to be made into a TV show), have been permitted to lie fallow. When the crunch came, and outside backers could not be found for anything so far-out as Rosset's scripts, he decided not to gamble his publishing house by paying big bills for film production.

In 1966, however, Rosset returned to the movie world from another end: as a distributor, using again the name Evergreen. He purchased the large collection of "experimental" films which had been showing on a club basis ("members only") under the name Cinema 16, and undertook to arrange theater bookings for *Titicut Follies,* a documentary (more or less) about the horrors of life in a Massachusetts public insane asylum. The State sued to prohibit showing of the film, and won (mostly on the grounds that the inmates were recognizable, which violated a privacy the institution was bound to protect). "We've been in court thirteen or fourteen times," Rosset says rather grimly, "and we've lost every time. They want us to appeal, but we won't, because we'd lose again." Meanwhile, *Titicut Follies* is being distributed to universities for showings on campus— "Our assumption, which may be false, is that the state won't interfere at universities"—and is gradually paying back some of its costs, though the total receipts to date are still below the legal fees Grove incurred defending the theater bookings.

Evergreen's other feature-length film currently on display is *The Queen,* the tale of a beauty contest among homosexuals in drag, which Rosset helped to finance and produce. Also in the catalogue is a Norman Mailer extravaganza called *Beyond the Law,* and perhaps a Swedish film which was seized by customs as obscene before Rosset could show it. "No sooner do we touch something," Rosset says, "than it's in court." To guarantee a showcase for future films, Rosset has purchased a 154-seat theater on West Eleventh Street in the tourist part of Greenwich Village. The same building also houses The Black Circle, a bar Rosset has had decorated entirely in black, chrome and mirrors. "We've given it the 1930s Warner Brothers look," Rosset says, "very *moderne*. I always," he adds wistfully, "wanted to run a bar. . . ."

At forty-six, in short, Rosset is still doing things simply because he wants to do them: he is, in all senses of an abused word, an amateur. He is undisciplined on purpose. Coupled with his intensely quixotic view of the world (when Cuban exiles threw a grenade through a Grove Press window one weekend in July—to protest the publication of Che Guevara's diary of his trip through Bolivia with gun and comrade—Rosset told the *New York Times* that he was personally a revolutionary but did not approve of people's throwing grenades through windows), Rosset's congenital amateurism should have buried him. That it didn't can be credited to a unique combination of factors—the large margin provided by his father's estate, an intelligence which repeatedly saves him, like the hero in the third reel, from his own worst follies, and the odd circumstance that he is an unusually likable human being. "The rich kid from Chicago," as he was known to his colleagues on the *Strange Victory* project, has been stung a few times—but much less often than normal probabilities would predict, because the people who work for him become friends.

"I always introduce myself as his secretary," says Judith Schmidt. "He always introduces me as his assistant." The fact that nearly all his senior people have been with him more than nine years says a great deal in itself, especially in the light of all the infuriating mistakes that have been made. Rosset gives (and expects) an extraordinary loyalty, which continues: "I know that if I was in India and something happened to me," Joan Mitchell says, "Barney would be there the next day." Rosset bears no grudges. Still fearfully shy, comfortable only in large parties or the closest of personal relationships, he keeps an eagerly youthful hope about the people he meets; and he wouldn't own a house that didn't have at least one guest room.

Rosset's home base at this writing is an elaborated Quonset hut in Easthampton, out toward the end of Long Island a hundred miles from New York. The hut was sunk in two acres of sand by the French architect Pierre Chareau, on commission from the American painter Robert Motherwell, and Miss Mitchell found it for Barney eighteen years ago. The sand has now been landscaped, two outbuildings have been turned into guest quarters for eight people (one of them held about forty people for an exciting weekend last July, when Norman Mailer turned up with his do-it-yourself crew of film-makers), a rather Floridian swimming pool has been added, and there is a tennis court that dries even before the rain stops. Rosset plays a fierce two-handed game, switching the racket to give him a forehand wherever the ball comes. (He remembers going out for tennis as a freshman at Swarthmore, and the coach saying, "Rosset, if you want to learn how to play tennis, I'll teach you; if you're going to play like that, get off the court.") Among the spectators are a four-year-old German shepherd named Suki and her daughter Yaki. Various rich man's toys, from Morgans to the best cameras to a video-tape recorder, are to be found about the property, and are played with sporadically.

Rosset's third wife, Christine—a slight, pretty dancer who was less than half his age when they were married four years ago—fits easily and quietly into his surroundings. Rosset's friends, including Miss Mitchell (whose opinions continue to be very important to him), give her credit for calming him down and giving him some perspective on himself. Still, he continues to get himself into situations which would be quite impossible for other people. The Rossets have no place to live in New York, for example, because Barney for years had admired a vacant loft building across the street from their house, in the lower part of Greenwich Village which votes for Carmine De Sapio. When the birth of his daughter Tansey threatened to deprive the house of its guest room, Rosset bought the old loft building to be reconditioned into a home. Then he sold his house, expecting the alterations in the loft to be quickly and easily accomplished. Instead, he said the other day, "We are still having great trouble getting a design we like which it is possible to pay for."

This is the authentic, vintage Rosset style, and no great talent is necessary to make fun of it, or to demonstrate that Rosset's luxurious life in Easthampton is about the same as the life he would be leading if he had simply put his inheritance into mutual funds. Nevertheless, the fact remains that he has done something to change the world, like it or not, and that he has done it his own way. "You have to remember," says Fred Jordan, "that Barney is a product of the period when kids were very conscious of phoniness. Barney doesn't want to be a phony." Rosset has achieved an unusual number of childhood dreams of glory, ranging from his sex life to the day Rembar got him an injunction against the District Attorney of Nassau County, ordering that worthy not to interfere with the production and distribution of *Evergreen Review*. The achievement that means most to him is that in the process of growing up (more or less), he did not become a phony.

11

The Volatile Business

[While preparing this article for a 1959 issue of *Esquire* I visited class-rooms in Louisville and in Detroit as part of my work toward *The Schools*. I came back from the trip with a riddle: What do a school and a distillery have in common? Answer: You can't smoke in either.

[The last pages of this piece were written in a London hotel room, and the whole thing was retyped *overnight*, at twenty-one cents a page, in English orthography. The admirable Catherine McBride repaired the spelling, but was not authorized to do much more. For obvious reasons, I had accepted the assignment only upon a guarantee of absolute control over changes, and I was three thousand miles away. I have cut the piece about 10 percent for its appearance here. Honest.]

FEW POLITICAL decisions by the people and government of the United States have been so profitable, financially, as that which late in 1933 returned the mantle of legality to the manufacture and sale of alcoholic beverages. Since 1934, the "distilled spirits industry"—now celebrating with commendable if dull sobriety the silver anniversary of Repeal—has paid into federal, state and local coffers more than $40 billion of special taxes, atop the usual corporate income and business taxes to which commercial mankind is prey. In addition, the liquor industry pays salaries to well over half a million employees and proprietors, who in turn pay income taxes; and to tens of thousands of farmers whose grain, otherwise destined for the surplus bins, winds up on the table in bottled form. In 1958 Americans spent about $5 billion, slightly more than $100 per household, on whiskey, gin, vodka, rum, brandy and cordials. Of that total, considerably more than $3 billion found its way, quickly or slowly, into the hands of the tax collectors.

Anyone, of course, would be proud to be one of the main supports of his government, but the liquor industry's pride in the quantity of blood it gives each year is tempered with a certain bitterness. Because more than half the price of a bottle of legal liquor goes for special taxes, the industry's product can be undersold spectacularly by moonshiners and bootleggers, who pay no taxes and who may have captured one-fifth the total American market for spirits. And the sheer amount of revenue from liquor taxes gives governments an irritating selfish interest in the most minute details of the industry's operations—an interest reinforced and excused by patterns of regulation which have survived (as a hangover, so to speak) from the days of the Noble Experiment. Whatever you do and wherever you go in the "licensed-beverage" business, Uncle Sam is watching you.

The strait jacket of regulation, uniquely tight in this industry, is what makes the liquor business so different from all other businesses. "To run a company like this one," says Seagram's Vic Fischel, a rawboned, tough-minded redhead who bosses the biggest liquor-selling operation in the world, "you practically *have* to be a lawyer."

Nobody who works for a liquor company may have the key to the front door of the distillery; only a federal agent from the Alcohol and Tobacco Tax Division of the Treasury Department may open or lock up the plant. In each distillery there is a separate office (usually a separate building) for revenooers, who weigh barrels full and empty to determine how much whiskey was in them, take samples from the bottling line for chemical analysis, check the hydrometers and thermometers to guarantee that everything is aboveboard at the business end of the still, and collect $10.50 for every proof gallon of liquor that goes out of the warehouse.

Distillers do not have control of their own warehouses, which are "bonded" in the manner of customs warehouses. You cannot take dutiable imports out of customs until you pay tariff, and you cannot take whiskey out of bonded warehouses until you pay tax. Because the whiskey cannot be sold until after the barrels are withdrawn from the warehouse, distillers are always in hock to the banks for the cash to pay their taxes. One exception to the general rule is 100-proof straight whiskey, which may be "bottled-in-bond"—i.e., the tax need not be paid until after bottling. As a standard of quality, "bottled-in-bond" is meaningless—the phrase certifies the alcoholic content of the beverage, and that its whiskey must be aged a minimum of four years. "It's about as broad," says Schenley's boss, Lewis Rosenstiel, "as saying, 'I walked across *a* street in the United States.' "

The federal code which governs the manufacture and bottling of liquor is so complicated that Commerce Clearing House publishes a special service for lawyers, called Liquor Control Law Reports. Jack Daniel's, though indubitably by taste and chemistry a bourbon whiskey, cannot be called bourbon because it is filtered through charcoal before barreling, a technique nowhere mentioned in the Code. Vodka, on the other hand, is *supposed* to be filtered through charcoal, and when Seagram wanted to make vodka by a process of fractional distillation, the company had to beg an amendment from the government. The so-called golden gins which are marketed by several companies get their color by aging three months or so in a barrel before bottling—but the fact cannot be mentioned on the label or in the advertising, because the Treasury Department holds that aging does not in any way improve the quality of gin. Liquor is a business of opinions, in which arguments rage on for years; but the opinions of the United States Treasury Department have the force of law.

Restricted in manufacturing, the companies are virtually nailed down when it comes to selling. In one of the United States, you may not sell liquor at all (for purposes of estimating the annual per-capita consumption of liquor, it is assumed that residents of Mississippi drink about as much as residents of neighboring states). Thirty-two states have "local option," which means that counties or cities may decide for themselves whether they wish to be legally wet. Since Repeal, the liquor industry has had to fight each year, on the average, about a thousand such "local-option" elections. (Liquor spokesmen strongly and perhaps correctly suspect that bootleggers finance the election campaigns for the Drys. Tom Donovan, President of Licensed Beverage Industries, the public-relations arm of the industry, recalls visiting a town in which such an election was in progress, and asking a local dignitary what all the fuss was about. "We're voting," said the dignitary solemnly, "on whether we're going to drink red whiskey or white.") The proportion of the state populations living in legally dry areas ranges from two-thirds in Tennessee to one three-hundredth in Pennsylvania. In Kentucky itself—where about eighty percent of all American whiskey is made—more than half the population lives in "dry" communities.

Then there are seventeen states in which liquor may be sold only via the state government, which runs the wholesale establishments or the stores, or both, and makes a neat profit on the operation. (In fact, the state of Michigan makes more each year from its wholesale liquor business than the total net earnings of all the nation's distillers combined.) These "monopoly states" including such big ones as Pennsylvania, Ohio, Washington and Virginia, account for more than one-quarter of all liquor sales, and the governments make tough customers. Before a state will agree to sell any distiller's liquor, the distiller must sign a contract containing a clause called "the Des Moines warranty," a most-favored-nation deal pledging the distiller not to sell to anybody at a lower price than he charges the state.

Individual states license wholesalers and retailers operating within their borders (at annual fees ranging up to $5,000 for wholesalers in Massachusetts, and $2,000 for retailers in Maryland). The licensing laws of some states are so complicated that, according to John E. Bierwirth of National Distillers (who is also Chairman of the Board of the Federal Reserve Bank of New York, and knows all about government regulations), "it is virtually impossible to do business without violating some provision or other."

Each state taxes liquor sales according to its individual schedule, and sets up individual pricing patterns, so that distillers have virtually no control over the prices the public will pay for its liquor. The price listing in the most recent edition of *The Liquor Handbook* shows a fifth of Seagram's 7 Crown ranging from $3.55 in Virginia to $5.25 in Georgia; a fifth of Old Crow from $3.87 in the District of Columbia to $5.50 in South Dakota. The gap between the highest and lowest prices of Old Forester was $1.80; of Haig & Haig Five Star, $1.95; of Coronet Brandy, $1.62. Thus it is utterly impossible for liquor companies to advertise the price of their products in national magazines. Some states, in fact, forbid liquor companies to mention price in their local advertising, while others have set up long lists of objects *verboten* in liquor promotion.

But the greatest and worst influence of government regulation on the liquor industry lies in the memory of the older men, many of whom still walk their daily rounds breathing the rank miasma remaining from Prohibition. They worry frantically about the portrayal of alcoholics in the movies or on television, about meetings of the rag, tag, and bobtail W.C.T.U.; they writhe when someone says the word "booze." Worst of all, they say, they find it especially difficult to recruit able young people into their business, because of this odd inheritance from prior generations.

Liquor company officials, toward the end of a conversation, tend to speak wistfully about visits to England, where, as National's John Bierwirth puts it, "When you ask a young man what he does, he'll say proudly, 'I'm in the liquor business; I work for Lord Dewar.' The leaders of the industry in England are men of rank and title." Bierwirth himself is as close as an American can come to that description: Hotchkiss and Yale, a tall, handsome man in his sixties, his very posture reflecting that casual grace which is a step up from mere dignity. Alone among the heads of the big liquor companies, he has no enemies; the industry sees in him a symbol of what it may be when everyone has forgotten the illegal trade of the 1920s and the roughhouse competition of the 1930s.

"I wonder what it is the vintner buys," said Omar to his friend Fitz, "one-half so precious as the stuff he sells." Well, the vintner buys grapes. The distiller, on the other hand, buys grain—mostly corn. "This," says Edgar Bronfman, the elegant, very young president of Joseph E. Seagram & Sons, "is an agricultural processing business." American distilleries buy about a million tons of grain a year, three-quarters of it corn, with rye, barley malt, sorghum and wheat accounting for nearly all the rest. Corn predominates for a simple reason: it gives more starch to the dollar. The more starch, the more fermentable sugar; the more sugar, the more alcohol.

Corn is thus automatically the basic ingredient behind nearly all "neutral spirits," which may be, by law, "distilled from any material," provided that the end product is at least 95 per cent alcohol by volume (190-proof; proof in the United States is a term of art arrived at by doubling the actual percentage of alcohol). Vodka is nothing but neutral spirits, the more neutral the better, cut down to drinkable potency by the addition of distilled water. Gin is merely neutral spirits redistilled so that the vapor passes over juniper berries and other flavoring herbs and picks up a gin flavor. Sixty to 70 percent of the content of American blended whiskeys is neutral spirits (among the American blends are such best sellers as 7 Crown, Calvert Reserve, Imperial, and Schenley Reserve). All Canadian and Scotch whiskeys are blends, and while they get their characteristic flavors from the use of other grains (in Canadian, rye; in Scotch, barley malt which has been dried over a smoky peat fire), there is more corn in them than anything else. Bourbon whiskey is by legal definition at least 51 percent corn. About the only distilled beverages Americans drink which are *not* mostly corn are rum (from sugar cane), brandy (from fruits) and rye whiskey, a once-popular drink which has now almost disappeared from the market—though people who live in New Jersey, New York and New England persist in calling for "rye" when they want a blended whiskey made primarily from corn.

Corn by itself, however, produces a rather insipid drink. (This is why old-fashioned corn whiskey, which is 80 percent corn, can be drunk cheerfully after only two years of aging in used barrels: it has few rough spots to be smoothed in by time.) The characteristic flavor of good whiskey comes from the "small grains" which are mixed in with the corn and cooked in water to form the "mash" from which the whiskey will be distilled. Some barley malt is always necessary in the mash, because the malt provides the chemical action by which cornstarch is converted to fermentable sugar. Beyond this minimum requirement, each distiller is free to experiment with his own "mash bill," his own recipe for mixing the different grains. In theory, all mash bills are secret, but in fact every distiller knows what every other distiller is doing. He just thinks his own is best.

The distillates from as many as twenty different mash formulae may be mixed together to form a single blended whiskey, which will owe some of its taste to each ingredient. Blenders can change the taste of their product merely by changing the proportions of already distilled whiskeys which they mix into the ultimate beverage—or, though this is less common in the best blends, by adding sherry or caramel to smooth the mixture. Bourbon and rye and corn, however, are beyond the reach of human art and ingenuity once they have passed the still and gone into barrels. So straight whiskey is the romantic part of the liquor business.

"No Chemists Allowed," reads the hand-painted sign on the main building of the Stitzel-Weller distilleries in the *banlieue* of Louisville . . . "traditional Kentucky whiskey is a natural product. . . . This is a Distillery—not a whiskey factory."

Such is, of course, as may be. But Stitzel-Weller is closer to the old times of the business than any other of the major distilleries. (S-W, which makes Old Fitzgerald, Cabin Still, and private-label bourbon for a very exclusive selection of clubs and hotels, produces about 2.5 million gallons of whiskey a year.) It is a family operation, turning out only one product—the various brands are all the same whiskey, aged a different length of time or bottled at a different proof. The S-W mash contains a higher proportion of small grains than is usual in today's bourbon, and the distilled "high wine" is somewhat richer in congeners before it goes into the barrel. (No beverage can be called "whiskey" until it has been aged in a barrel; congeners are by-products of fermentation, which give the stuff its flavor and body.) The result is a heavier whiskey, which requires and can take greater aging than the other "premium" bourbons, and is probably more like the whiskey of twenty-five—or fifty—years ago.

This, at any rate, would be the boast of S-W's proprietor, Julian P. Van Winkle, a sturdy, stubby-legged man with a penetrating gray gaze, who well remembers the whiskey of fifty years ago, when he was a mere lad of thirty-five. Strong and alert, still gifted with a pungency of expression and an individual dislike for routine, Van Winkle is a living testimonial to the medicinal values of good whiskey consumed in moderation. There is some tendency among people who barely know him to regard him as a "character," an eccentric backwoods fellow named "Pappy," which is, reasonably enough, what his son and daughter call him. His friends, however, know him as "Mr. Van," and his competitors feel great respect for his commercial sagacity—one example of which may be the whole "Pappy" nonsense. Van Winkle probably does care more deeply about whiskey than he should—he has never quite forgiven President William Howard Taft for ruling that "compounds," as blended whiskeys are called at Stitzel-Weller, could be labeled "whiskey." But a profound concern for whiskey is natural enough in a man of eighty-five who has been a distiller all his life. Even Prohibition did not interrupt his career, because S-W was one of the few distilleries licensed to continue the production of whiskey "for medicinal purposes."

Because Van Winkle never misses a sales argument, a trip around Stitzel-Weller makes a thorough introduction to the techniques of whiskey-making and the controversies of the trade. Like most distilleries, S-W carries on its work in a number of separated buildings, partly to reduce fire hazards, partly to avoid contamination of delicate yeasts, partly to make sure that there are at least a few places to which the owners, rather than government agents, hold the keys. A railroad siding in the rear holds the freight cars which bring the grains, and roads wind around the buildings for the trucks that will carry away the bottles. Older distilleries almost always sit beside the streams or ponds which provided the necessary water for the original, smaller plant. (Today most of the water comes from deep wells or—we don't like to talk about this—the municipal water system.) The main office is usually in an unprepossessing one- or two-story building, where the executives and clerical staff work in a rather aristocratic atmosphere of wood paneling and open spaces. At S-W, the boss's office is finished on the inside in brick, as a memento of the past; the chairs and couches are leather; and a fire blazes on the hearth.

The arriving grain is inspected for quality (distilleries to which chemists are admitted subject a sample of each carlot to exhaustive analysis), and then sent up into the elevator. Distillers buy only the top grades of grain, because the top grades have the greatest starch content. "I remember some years ago," says Glenmore's Frank B. Thompson, "a distiller advertised 'selected grains.' When asked what he meant by 'selected,' he said, 'I select the cheapest I can find.'"

From the elevators the grain descends to roller mills, where it is usually crushed rather than pulverized. "We don't make our whiskey from *flour*," says an S-W salesman scornfully. A more important reason why distillers grind their grain rather coarsely is the fact that they expect to recover a considerable proportion of it. Distillers use only the starch content of the grain, and after the whiskey has been made they extract the water from the "slop" and sell the residue as Distillers Dried Feeds for farm animals. About one-quarter of the gross weight of the grain used for distilling goes back onto the farms as Distillers Feeds, returning to the distiller about one-sixth the initial cost of his grain. Obviously, the recovery of feeds is easier if the grain is not too finely ground at the beginning.

The corn, then the rye and small grains, finally (at a controlled temperature) the malt are all dumped into a large tub half-filled with water. This water will accompany the grain through the entire whiskey-making process, and will account for one-third of the "high wine" that comes off the final still. Obviously, it is an important part of the beverage. "Three things have made Kentucky whiskey famous," says the S-W sales line. "Water, weather and the sour-mash process."

There is no Kentucky distillery which does not do some bragging about its water—"limestone water, filtered through seven, or ten, or twenty miles of limestone." On the wall in the New York office of Schenley's Paul Lockwood hangs a map of the north-central United States, with a "limestone belt" shaded in, and an impressive list of names of distilleries spotted within the belt. And yet a doubt remains. The water that winds up in the whiskey barrel will have gone through a process of distillation, which must have removed most of its original impurities. A look at the United States Geological Survey for the Louisville area reveals that some distilleries use wells producing water with four, five and six times the mineral content of the water at other distilleries making a very similar product. (The survey also indicates that the wells on which some distilleries draw are vastly insufficient to meet the needs of the plant, so that city water is getting in there somehow.) Edgar Bronfman of Seagram, which does most of its distilling in Kentucky, feels that "the limestone myth" is worse than nonsense. "All the famous old country distilleries," he says, "used pond water—rain water most of it, the softest water imaginable."

"I have probably spent more time on water than on any other ingredient," says Samuel Pollack, Schenley's chief chemist, a stocky, businesslike man wearing horn-rimmed glasses. "I've read volumes and volumes on water. But from a scientific point of view I have not reached a formula—so many grains of hardness, so much magnesium and so forth. Our water is analyzed twice a year, and it varies all over the lot, and I'm damned if I can see a pattern. I wrote a report recently. I said, 'Despite all allegations in writing on the effects of water on the bouquet of whiskey, we must rely on fifty-four years of practical experience. . . . Irrespective of any chemical or bacteriological analysis, there is no effect of water on whiskey.' The only general rule is, if it's good enough for drinking purposes as water, it's good enough for distiller's purposes."

The grain delivered from the mills is now cooked in this significant or unimportant water, breaking the starch loose from the kernels and then, by the enzyme action of the barley malt, converting it to sugar. At Stitzel-Weller this cooking takes place in a large open "pot" agitated by a wooden paddle; elsewhere it is more likely to occur in a pressure cooker or a "flash converter." "They boil the hell out of it," says Van Winkle, "just to squeeze out another drop of alcohol." Others point out that pressure cookers are often preferred to long boiling in an open pot when the purpose is to retain flavor. . . .

What comes out of the pot or the pressure cooker is the "mash," the basic ingredient of the whiskey.

Meanwhile, elsewhere in the distillery, somebody—usually a chemist, outside Stitzel-Weller—has been growing yeast. Every distiller uses his own strain of yeast, usually the descendant of a culture grown originally nearly a century ago. Yeast is a living fungus and, since its cells are light enough to be airborne, it is all around us. Its function in a distillery is to eat the sugar in the mash, converting it to two parts of carbon dioxide and two parts of alcohol.

Anything as sweet as corn mash will ferment after a while without the help of anybody's trained yeast. Distillers introduce yeast into the mash deliberately to speed and to control the process. The "more virile" the yeast, the more exactly the course of fermentation can be predicted, and unless the same yeast is used all the time, identical mashes in the same distillery will produce different whiskeys. So the yeast strain must be kept free from contamination, and strong enough to guarantee that random "secondary fermentation" from interloping yeasts will be held to a minimum. The *real value* of limestone water, according to Hiram Walker's Carleton Healy, is in this area, because hard water makes a good environment for a controlled yeast.

Most distillers take extraordinary precautions with their yeast. The basic culture is kept in a sterile, laboratory room, under refrigeration, and a microscope slide of the stuff is removed for each vat of mash. After its first hour in a suitable culture medium (usually a "malt wort" of barley malts) each yeast cell will bud every twenty minutes. "You put fifty gallons of yeast culture into a tub," says a chemist at Brown-Forman (Old Forester, Early Times), "and if you were to take twenty drops of that culture, ten hours later, you would find *three hundred million* yeast cells in the twenty drops."

The different yeasts for the different Brown-Forman products are kept at the lab in the Old Forester Distillery, and sent to the other B-F distilleries daily. Only five straight-whiskey distilleries are involved in the Brown-Forman operation, so only five strains of yeast need be maintained. Seagram and Hiram Walker, however, with their repertory of blended whiskeys, will use hundreds of different yeast cultures in a single year. Each whiskey formula requires its own yeast. Seagram will send yeast slides daily from its Louisville laboratory to its distilleries all over Kentucky, in Maryland, Indiana and even Canada. The yeasts used by Walker in making Canadian Club are all kept under sterile conditions in a laboratory in Peoria, Illinois, and shipped up to Walkerville, Canada, as needed.

The mash and the yeast now meet in the fermenting vat, where they are joined—in the "sour-mash" process—by a quantity of yesterday's stillage, that part of yesterday's mash which did not become whiskey. Roughly one-third of the liquid in the vat will be stillage, rich with dead yeast but poor in alcohol and sugars. One purpose of "inoculating" the vat with yesterday's stillage—the advertised purpose—is to maintain the continuity of the whiskey, to guarantee that each day's fermentation contains elements of previous batches. A more important purpose is to control the fermentation. The used stillage contains considerable amounts of the yeast enzyme which does the actual work of converting sugar to alcohol, so that the new fermentation gets off to a better start than can be assured if only live yeast and new mash are used. And the stillage diminishes the "sweetness" of the corn mash, making it less inviting to random yeasts in the atmosphere. The sour-mash process makes for a slower but safer fermentation, diminishing the risk of whiskey that will have to be rejected later on. For these reasons, the great bulk of all whiskey made on this continent—in Canada as well as in Kentucky, in blends as well as in bourbons—is produced by a "sour-mash" process.

These fermenting vats are enormous containers, several stories high. Stitzel-Weller has relatively small vats, made of cypress, holding 13,000 gallons at a shot. Most distilleries today have abandoned cypress for metal alloys which are easier to clean (every sour-mash vat must be "sweetened" and left to lie fallow for at least twenty-four hours after each fermentation). At the Canadian Club distillery in Walkerville, across the river from Detroit, cypress vats and new metal vats ran side by side for two whole years, while chemists and quality-control analysts tried to determine whether there was any change in the finished whiskey as the result of the switch in tub lining. When two years of examination failed to turn up any differences whatever, Hiram Walker decided to abandon the cypress tubs and make all its Canadian Club in metal vats. Fred Klayer of Seagram's, which uses both, "suspects" that there is a difference, nonetheless. The biggest vats in the business are Walker vats, in the Peoria distillery which produces Imperial, Corby's, Ten High and Walker's DeLuxe; each metal monster holds 120,000 gallons of mash.

What goes on inside the fermenting vat is the most dramatic sight in whiskey-making. The carbon dioxide released from the grain sugars by the action of the yeast enzyme comes bubbling up to the top of the mash, and breaks the oily surface in large and small, hellish-looking bubbles. The great mass of yellow-brown liquid is—legitimately —in ferment, washing back and forth in the vat, until finally, after three or four days, the yeast has finished its work, agitation ceases, and the particles of small grain rise to the top to ride with the gradually disappearing foam.

The fermenting room is always separate, with an individual, strong, sweet smell of ground corn. The tubs are well-spaced, and the room itself is light and airy, with high ceilings, to make sure that there will be no overpowering concentration of carbon dioxide in the atmosphere. Some distilleries cap the vats, to pump the CO_2 outside. Hiram Walker's Peoria plant, however, knows a trick worth two of that. It captures the CO_2, makes dry ice out of it: a hundred tons a day.

What is left in the vat at the end of the fermenting process is a heavy "beer," not palatable, containing perhaps 7 percent of alcohol by volume. The mash entered at a temperature of 60° (lower if the fermentation was to last more than seventy-two hours), but chemical action has heated it and the beer goes off in the direction of the still at a temperature of about 90°. At this point, even at Stitzel-Weller, nature is abandoned and artifice makes whiskey.

Distillation is one of the oldest and simplest extractive processes known. Alcohol boils at 173.3° Fahrenheit; water at 212°. A mixture of alcohol and water, heated to a temperature between 173.3° and 212°, will separate into component parts, the alcohol rising in the form of vapor while the water remains below. This alcohol vapor can be caught and cooled (condensed) to produce a "distilled spirit." The simplest kind of kettle can be used in the process—indeed, the malt whiskeys in Scotch and Irish have been made in just this manner. A spout rises from a plain copper kettle, bends, and descends again in coils through a tub of cold running water, usually outside the walls of the distillery. Quantities of water and oil get carried into the distillate by this method, which means that continuous inspection and considerable redistillation are necessary before the spirit can be okayed and put away to age.

On the American continent the almost universal device is the "continuous beer still," a cylindrical column anywhere from fifty to one hundred feet high. The beer, prewarmed to a temperature just below the boiling point of alcohol, is fed into the top of the column and drips down through slanting, perforated copper plates. Live steam comes up from the bottom of the still, heating the beer to the point where alcohol vaporizes, escaping through the top of the still to a condensing unit. The higher the column, the higher the proof of the final spirit. Stitzel-Weller's fifty-two-foot columns produce 80-proof "low wines," as distillers call the end result of this first distillation; in Canada the low wines may run as high as 78 percent alcohol, or 156-proof U.S.

Neither the first vapor off the still when the new beer is introduced, nor the last vapor as the final drops trickle out, will make a palatable whiskey, because the oil or acid content is too high. These "heads" and "tails" are therefore discarded into a special tank, to be redistilled into neutral spirits if money is everything, or thrown away if calmer heads prevail. The rest of the low wine moves on to the "doubler," usually a pot still with a bulb in the spout to permit "reflexing" the spirit back and forth for cleaner distillation. (Some very cheap whiskey is made by barreling and then selling the "low wines" without any further cleansing, but virtually all average and premium whiskey goes through a "doubler.") Distillers whose low wines come off the columns at 80- and 90-proof will use the doubler to boost proof, taking the "high-wine" out of the doubler at 110- to 120-proof. Where higher columns have produced a first distillate at 110-proof or more, the doubler serves more to clean out oils, esters and aldehydes, while proof rises only eight or ten points. Legally, the high wines that will become bourbon whiskey may be distilled up to 80 percent alcohol—160-proof—but in practice few distillers go above 130-proof. The higher the proof of the high wine, the lower the proportion of congeners (fusel oil, furfural, etc.) remaining in the product. Congeners have evil-sounding names, and are not, in fact, pleasant chemicals by themselves. (Fusel oil, for example, separately extracted in the distilling process, is sold to paint companies as a solvent.) But, as Stitzel-Weller puts it, "congeners are as important to bourbon as bacteria is to cheese." Bourbon is a flavorful whiskey or it is nothing; congeners supply the flavor.

These high wines, colorless as mountain-spring water, are the original form of bourbon whiskey. They can be drunk as they stand, though not with pleasure. Men who work in distilleries call them "white dog," and say they have "hog tracks" in them. But a master distiller can predict from the taste of the high wines how good his whiskey will be. At most distilleries, the high wines will be subjected to chemical analysis to make sure everything is more or less all right, and at all distilleries men who have lived with bourbon all their lives will take a sip of the stuff, roll it around on their tongues and spit it out, proclaiming the distillate fit for barreling, or fit only for the dump. The big liquor companies send samples of each day's run to home office, so that Seagram's chief blender Fred Klayer, for example, will taste a few drops of virtually every distillate that comes out of a Seagram doubler. "There are as many alcohols as there are numbers," says Edgar Bronfman, "fractions of C's and H's and O's and 2's. Asters and esters and aldehydes. You can't analyze it fine enough. You have to rely on taste."

"In the early days right after Repeal," said Colonel Frank Thompson of Glenmore, "we had people coming in regularly and saying, 'If I can save you a million dollars, will you give me five hundred thousand of it?' I'd say, 'Certainly,' and they'd tell me to store my whiskey in glass tanks instead of wooden barrels, saving the cost of the barrels. I'd explain to them that it was the charred barrel which gave whiskey its color and smoothed out the taste, and they'd tell me to grind up charcoal and put it in the glass tanks. It was hard for them to understand that a barrel is more than a container, it's a porous membrane, operating on the whiskey by osmosis and exmosis."

Thompson is a Kentuckian, but his colonelcy is not. He has fought in two wars as an officer in the United States Army, and been profusely decorated in both. If he put on a uniform today he would pass for a career officer of the highest sort, who had spent considerable time in semitropical stations: a tall, tanned man with fine white hair and faultless posture, who speaks with the exact diction and careful, steely courtesy of a staff C.O. Like Van Winkle, he grew up in the liquor business. His father founded Glenmore, first as a distribution company buying its whiskey from distillers, then—after a fight with the "whiskey trust" which controlled production in Kentucky, before Prohibition—as an independent operation.

The distillery itself was built mostly by Thompson's uncle, Harry

Barton, who is described by Glenmore's Arthur Bondurant as "a Michigan and Columbia graduate, a bachelor whose hobbies were reading books and making fine whiskey." Until Hiram Walker put up its Peoria plant, Glenmore owned the largest distillery in the world. Like Stitzel-Weller and Brown-Forman, it was licensed to continue through Prohibition. Like Stitzel-Weller again, Glenmore makes only one whiskey, which will be bottled as Old Kentucky Tavern or Glenmore, depending on its age, or blended with neutral spirits to be bottled as Old Thompson. The company ranks seventh in size among American distillers, far below the Big Four (Seagram, Schenley, National and Hiram Walker), well under Brown-Forman, but above such "independents" as Beam, Barton and Stitzel-Weller.

Thompson's admiration for the magical properties of the whiskey barrel is shared by almost everyone in the business. "You put *spirits* in a barrel," says Ed Deutsche, head of Louisville Cooperage, Schenley's barrel-making subsidiary. "You take whiskey out of the barrel. Distillers," he added, underestimating the friendliness of his customers, "won't tell you this. But it's true."

The whiskey barrel is the aristocrat of barrels. Obviously, it must be "tight" cooperage—that is, it can't leak. Each stave must be correctly aged and dried: "One green stave," said a man over the executive lunch table at Brown-Forman, "will simply ruin your whiskey." And, finally, the inside of the barrel must be charred to the correct depth. The burnt wood will give the whiskey, colorless at entry, its rich brown color; and the wood sugars brought to the surface by charring, the "caramel layer," will work chemical changes on the rough spirits to produce the smooth texture of fine whiskey.

Only certain strains of white oak, found in seventeen central states, are suitable for whiskey barrels. The oak arrives at the cooperage plant neatly quartered, and is cut stave-shaped along the rays of the grain by a cylindrical saw. Then it ages for a full year in the open air before going into the kiln for final drying. It stays in the kiln for ten to thirty days, until it has dried out, slowly, to a standard 10 percent moisture content.

In the factory the staves are cut to equal length and similar width, then stood on end in a hoop to make a splayed cylinder. "I love to watch them make barrels," says Colonel Thompson. "I've seen a man discard a split stave, then go over to a great stack and, judging entirely *by eye,* pick out a stave of exactly the size he needs." This splayed cylinder now passes through a twenty-minute steam bath to soften the wood fibers, and as it comes out of the steam an ingeniously simple machine—a metal frame shaped like the end of a funnel —clamps down on the top of the cylinder to press the staves together into a barrel shape. A muscular gentleman who does this sort of thing all day long now picks up a forty-pound hoop and drops it over the top to seal the staves into position as a barrel.

"That bend," says Ed Deutsche, "is now permanent. It will never come out of that wood."

The new barrel dries out from the steam bath in less than an hour, and goes off to the furnace, where eight open frames ride a chain belt like the seats on a Snapper at an amusement park. A man drops the new barrel into one of the frames, and it rides over a pilot light which sets the inside aflame. Each barrel blazes for about half a minute, then rides past hoses which put the fire out with a quick dousing. The charred barrel topples off the Snapper frame, ready to be bound with steel bands, capped with charred tops and bottoms, drilled for the bunghole, and shipped off to the distillery. As a final test, a machine shoots a little water and a lot of compressed air into the barrel through the bunghole, and a man inspects the outside to make sure there are no telltale bubbles indicating a leak. Ed Deutsche says, simply, "There are no defects in a whiskey barrel."

Such a barrel costs something more than $20 to make, and sells to an independent distillery like Stitzel-Weller, which buys its barrels from Louisville Cooperage, for about $25. The "high wines" in that barrel cost about $40 to make, for a "premium" bourbon. The Federal tax on what comes out of the barrel will run around $400.

"We don't know nearly enough about what goes on inside a barrel," says Edgar Bronfman. He noted a quizzing look on the face of one of his associates, and continued, "Of course, we at Seagram know more than anybody else, but we don't know enough."

Bourbon whiskeys come off the final still at about 125-proof, but they are cut to 103-proof by the addition of distilled water before they enter the barrel. (By federal law, whiskey cannot be aged at greater than 110-proof.) The barrel holds fifty gallons when first filled, but when the distiller takes out his whiskey four to eight years later he finds only thirty-eight to forty-two gallons left in the barrel. Between one and two gallons are in the wood itself (a new barrel weighs ninety pounds, a used barrel from one hundred two to one hundred four pounds). The rest of the loss is simple "outage," evaporation of whiskey through the pores of the wood.

Contrary to all the laws of basic chemistry, however, the whiskey that comes out of the barrel will have a higher proof—a higher ratio of alcohol to water—than the "high wines" that went in. Alcohol evaporates more readily than water; that fact is the heart of the distillation process. Then how can more water than alcohol evaporate while the whiskey is aged in the wood?

The answer is the molecular structure of white oak. The alcohol molecule is larger than the water molecule, and will not pass so readily through the pores of the wood. Thus more water than alcohol makes contact with the air, and evaporates. Indeed, most men in the whiskey business will say that if proof does *not* go up in the barrel (which can happen, if the barrel is stored in a damp warehouse), the whiskey has not aged properly and will not taste right. Here is the second of Stitzel-Weller's boasts for Kentucky: "water, weather, and the sour-mash process." And Kentucky weather is, in truth, remarkable. The late Irwin S. Cobb of Paducah once remarked that if you didn't like the weather in Kentucky all you had to do was wait around fifteen minutes, and it would change.

So at Stitzel-Weller and at Glenmore and at most of the smaller country distilleries they have wooden warehouses with corrugated-metal facings, usually seven stories high. Each warehouse has about as many windows as a house the same size, and every day it isn't raining men go around at eight in the morning and open the windows to let the weather in. An open warehouse is inevitably warmer at the top than it is at the bottom, so the barrels are moved around several times a year to subject all the whiskey to the same varieties of weather. Since each barrel weighs about five hundred pounds, the open "metal-clad" warehouses give much work to many strong men.

And the big distillers say that the work is unnecessary. Most of them use steam-heated brick warehouses, and avoid the Kentucky weather. (Some of them use warehouses in Indiana or Illinois, and avoid the Kentucky tax on whiskey in barrels.) "If you'll look at the green stamp on the cap of a bottled-in-bond bourbon," says a Brown-Forman spokesman, "you'll notice that it specifies whether the whiskey was bottled in the spring or in the fall. The reason for that is the fact that whiskey doesn't age in an open warehouse during the winter: too cold. So when the federal regulations first were drawn up, it was considered part of the protection of the consumer to tell him whether he was getting the benefit of the full aging period—the summer—on the whiskey he bought. When you use heated warehouses, of course, it doesn't make any difference which season the whiskey was bottled."

This basic disagreement between those who use metal-clads and those who use heated warehouses is further complicated by an argument within the second group. Brown-Forman believes in "cycling" the temperature in its warehouses, to simulate summer and an easy winter, keeping the whiskey expanding and contracting, "working" in the wood. Elsewhere, the opinion is that the purpose of the heated warehouse is to maintain an *even* temperature of about 60°, allowing chemical interaction of wood and whiskey to proceed at an even pace.

How long the whiskey should remain in the barrel is another source of controversy. Those who use open warehouses hold out for seven or even eight years (with five or six for their lesser-priced brands), while Brown-Forman contends that after a whiskey has aged four years in a weather-cycled warehouse it is as good as it ever will be. "Well," says Van Winkle maliciously, "that's probably true of *their* whiskey." National Distillers' Ben Corrado, a small but vigorous man with a mustache, who was a consultant to the industry and publisher of *The Liquor Handbook* before he went to work for a distiller, likes to point out that most of the "premium" bourbons on the market are four-year-olds. "It's the cheap stuff that needs further aging," he says, "to get the harsh taste out of it."

The fact of the matter is, of course, that differences in the original mash bill and in the distillation process will determine how long a whiskey should be aged. The more corn in the mash bill, the fewer congeners in the "high wine," the less time the whiskey *can* stand in the barrel before picking up a tannic-acid, "woody" taste. Van Winkle's heavier whiskey, on the other hand, has not reached maturity after four years. Indeed, Van Winkle himself likes it best after twelve or even fifteen years in the barrel. "Clean as a pin," he said, sampling an over-age barrel his distillery was bottling for a private party's Christmas presents (at 110-proof). "Gets better every year."

"Well," says Wathen Knebelkamp, a broad-shouldered, white-haired, friendly man who until recently ran Schenley's Bernheim distilleries (I.W. Harper and Old Charter), "taste is an individual deal. I don't care if it's peas. You can make good whiskey in lots of different ways, so long as you know what you're doing and you know how to watch it."

Knebelkamp is a second-generation distiller. His father worked for Kentucky Distillers and Warehousers, the old whiskey trust, in the days before the First War, and named the boy after James Wathen, who isolated a virile strain of yeast which became Knebelkamp's most cherished property. "Wathen," the younger Knebelkamp says, "was the most progressive distiller of his time. He combined the old art of sticking your finger in the tub and licking it with the new arts of measuring the corn for moisture and such. He taught my father all he knew."

During Prohibition Knebelkamp's father took his precious yeast up to British Columbia to safeguard it, and then brought it back to Kentucky to work for National Distillers. Knebelkamp got his share of the wonder-working yeast in his father's will.

Straight bourbon is a natural product; both its taste and its quality derive from the grains that go into the mash and the timber from which the barrel is formed. But agricultural produce varies from year to year, crop season to crop season. Are these variations so great that the same distillery using the same formulae and processes must produce a somewhat different whiskey every year? Are there vintage bourbon years, like vintage wine years? With one voice, the bourbon makers deny the very thought. On the other side of the Great Whiskey War, the blenders insist: the only way to maintain the quality of a whiskey from year to year is by blending, changing the proportions to compensate for nature's whimsical proceedings.

There are a few "blends of straights"—different whiskeys married together for bottling to preserve different qualities in each—but outside of Florida and Wisconsin their sales do not amount to a hill of beans. When distillers speak of "blended whiskey," what they mean is a marriage of several whiskeys, plus grain neutral spirits. Usually, the spirits content of the blend runs three-fifths to two-thirds of the total. The taste of the blend reflects primarily the taste of the whiskeys that have gone into it—but the "neutral" spirits are not necessarily as flavorless as the name implies, and in the better blends the spirits as well as the whiskey will be aged in the wood before bottling.

The whiskey blender has the most delicate and mysterious job in the business. Once or twice a year he must review the taste of the whiskey his company is currently bottling and determine the current state of the company's existing stocks. Assuming he still has some warehouses full of the whiskeys in his current blend, he knows that their taste has changed somewhat during the six months or a year of aging they have undergone since the blend was first established. Moreover, he believes firmly that the next year's batch of each whiskey, though made in the same distilleries from the same formulae, will not be the same as what he has been using. So he must reconstruct his blend from scratch, matching his final version against the "standard," the whiskey now appearing under his brand name, which the customers like well enough to buy. He must have an utterly accurate sense of taste, plus a magnificent knowledge of the company's stock, which in the case of Seagram may include as many as nine hundred different whiskeys. While it is sometimes possible to go out on the market and buy just the whiskey you need from an independent distiller, the blend maker is usually tied down to the whiskeys his distilleries produced four, five and six years ago.

At Seagram, which is by far the biggest of the blend houses, this work is done under the direct supervision (and often in the mouth) of a tall, bony, very serious man named Fred W. Klayer. Actual tasting is performed in a laboratory without windows in the heart of the fancy new Seagram Building in New York. Around the walls are filing cabinets full of whiskey in medicine bottles, each little bottle bearing a prescription-like label with its "code." Hung from the walls are gleaming kitchen cabinets containing full-size bottles of Seagram's own and competitive whiskeys, both straight and blend. Since this is a laboratory, there is also a sink, some test tubes and graduates in which the actual blends are tentatively mixed. The feature of the room is three round tables around which the tasters sit while practising their arcane skills.

All whiskey to be tasted is cut down to about 40-proof (20 percent alcohol), so that the sheer strength of the taste will not confuse the senses, and served in tall, tulip-shaped brandy snifters. The table-top turns, so that the taster need not rise from his seat or request anybody to pass him anything. Beside each chair is a spittoon, because you don't swallow whiskey when you taste it professionally, and in the center of the table is a beaker of distilled water to be used as a mouth wash between tastes.

A sample from every lot of "high wines" or "entry whiskeys" that will be used in every Seagram blend (a list including V.O. Canadian, 7 Crown, Calvert Reserve, Carstairs, Lord Calvert, Four Roses, Antique, Hunter, Kessler and others) passes over this table and over the tongues of Klayer and his assistants. As the whiskey ages in the barrel, every six months, a new sample is taken and tasted, to make sure everything is proceeding properly. When the time comes to make up the next blend, Klayer goes through his files and begins mixing cc's in the beaker, tasting, rejecting, mixing again until the new blend is all it ought to be. At each of the distilleries, at similar round tables, the chemists and tasters employed at the plant are going through similar tasting routines, as a means of quality control. But they do not determine the blending formula, which is sent down to the distillery from New York: so much of each whiskey, so much of each of the distillery's many slightly different distillations of neutral spirits.

Under Klayer's direction, Seagram is constantly experimenting with new mash bills, new temperatures at which to add the barley malt, new yeasts, new temperatures in the fermenter, new proofs for distillation, new degrees of char in the barrels that will age the whiskeys (neutral spirits are aged in used barrels: while they are not necessarily as insipid as the name implies, they certainly do not have the strength to fight off the tannic acid in a newly charred barrel). Each experiment is evaluated at its different stages, to the point when experimental blends are sent out into the field for consumer-tasting tests. But it takes a long time to make a new blend of experimental whiskeys. Half a dozen years must elapse between the time you plan your sample and the time you send out the first test bottles to the market research department; and if consumers seem to like it, you need another six years before you can bottle the blend in quantity.

At Seagram's, the advantages of blending are seen mostly in this light: when you blend, you can make improvements in your product. To Edgar Bronfman, the straight-whiskey maker's emphasis on the natural, untouched-by-human-hands aspect of his product represents a retrogressive tendency in manufacturing. "If you can't change your product," he says, "you can't make it better. We make our whiskeys better every year. From year to year, you can't taste the difference, but the other day I sampled some V.O. bottled twenty years ago. You wouldn't recognize it as the same whiskey we bottle today."

In the other big blend operation, Hiram Walker (Canadian Club, Imperial and Corby's), the emphasis is on maintenance rather than on improvement. "If the public likes your product," says Clifford Hatch, a young man with the easy smile and horn-rimmed glasses of an American, plus the peaches-and-cream complexion of an Englishman, "you'd be pretty foolish to tamper with it. I tasted a twenty-year-old bottle of Canadian Club recently, and if you didn't know it went back to the thirties you couldn't have told the difference."

Walker believes firmly that Kentucky straight whiskey has, in fact, been changing with the years. "They've been getting away from that heavy-bodied stuff," says Howard Walton, who came to Walker from the investment banking business right after Repeal, ran the sales organization and then become president. "Today all the Kentucky whiskeys are much lighter than they were before the war. You know, we had the best-selling bourbon in America before the war—Ten High, which was the lightest straight whiskey on the market. We first sold it only three months old, then six, then nine, finally two years old in the thirties, and it was the biggest seller in the country. Because it was light."

This comment was relayed to National Distillers, the biggest bourbon maker in the nation, which was overwhelmingly the biggest in the days right after Repeal. "Well," said a National spokesman, "Ten High was the top seller, all right. It was also the cheapest whiskey on the market. . . ." Clifford Hatch grinned wryly: he does not remember those days, but his father was president of the company then. "It's true," he says, "that we sold it at a very short profit."

Canadian whiskeys are both like and unlike American blends. There is no "grain neutral spirits" in the Canadian product, but the "high spirits" of the Canadian blend are only a point or so in proof below what the United States government defines as neutrality. The lower-proof whiskeys in the blend come off the still at higher proofs than their American cousins, and are aged in used rather than new barrels because they need less chemical interaction with the charcoal. In most Canadian blends exported to the United States, every drop of spirits, low or high, has been aged at least six years. And there tends to be a somewhat higher proportion of rye in the various mashes which wind up as the various whiskeys married in the blend—though Canadian is by no means a "rye" whiskey. It is probably significant that the two organizations most successful in the American blend market —Walker and Seagram's—are both Canadian companies.

The fading white legend can still be read on the high brick smokestack in the Calvert Distillery outside Baltimore: "CALVERT PURE RYE." In the days right after Repeal, when the distillery was built, straight rye whiskey accounted for about one-quarter of all the whiskey Americans drank. Though bourbon likes to assert itself as *the* American drink through history, a look at the folksong literature demonstrates that rye had always outranked it. (*"Rye whiskey, rye whiskey, rye whiskey I cry; if I don't have rye whiskey I surely will die.*") In 1957, according to a report by the United States Tariff Commission, rye accounted for 4.1 percent of the total whiskey production in America—and virtually all of that went into blends. Straight rye whiskey today represents something like one-quarter of one percent of all whiskey sales; you couldn't see it even on a big chart, except in the states of Pennsylvania and Maryland.

Why?

"The great American ice-cream taste," says a spokesman for Heublein's, which still markets and used to make a rye whiskey. Rye is a stronger-tasting beverage than bourbon, as rye bread is stronger than corn bread. Because rye is more expensive than corn per drop of alcohol obtained, and because rye whiskey must be aged longer than bourbon to attain anything like the same smoothness, rye must cost more than bourbon of equivalent quality. Even before the war, consumers were becoming reluctant to pay a premium for rye; since the war, they seem unwilling to buy rye at all.

These fluctuations in public taste provide the heads of the liquor companies with both their nightmares and their pleasant dreams. National Distillers' John Bierwirth feels that the industry will be moving more and more in the direction of the packaged foods field—"whiskey, after all, is a packaged agricultural product"—and most other executives in the industry agree, with reservations. (Howard Walton of Walker thinks the comparison is easily overdrawn, because whiskey costs so much more than packaged foods.) But everything about liquor is more volatile. Liquor tastes shift rapidly, for or against a brand. Because it takes a long time to mature whiskey, a distiller may be unable to make his hay while the sun shines upon him; because inventories are extremely heavy, a distiller whose brand has lost favor can be washed well down the slope by a heavy storm.

"One of the most fascinating stories in the world is taste," says Lewis S. Rosenstiel of Schenley (known to his employees as "LSR" or "the Chairman"). "You've got your nose to the grindstone, and goddam it this taste change sneaks up on you. Sometimes you can spot generic changes, but even then you don't know how it's going to affect the brands."

Rosenstiel is one of the legends of the liquor industry—a big, very strong man now in his late sixties, who worked up from the bottom to controlling ownership of what is now the second-largest liquor operation in America. "I remember Lew," Van Winkle says rather fondly, "when he was a pinhooker"—a man who rolled barrels in a warehouse. Later he was a salesman, a whiskey broker, and an entrepreneur. Intelligent, articulate and extraordinarily aggressive, Rosenstiel seems to care less than most men about the impression he makes on those around him. He slopes in his chair, plays with his tongue as he speaks, and utters his strong opinions with a growl, expressing dislike and contempt for anyone who might disagree. He thinks nothing of calling up an employee at three in the morning to ask him questions about the operation of his department.

A great fighter, Rosenstiel licked what looked like a cold Justice Department anti-trust case after Schenley absorbed Park & Tilford, and won just exactly the revenue-code amendments he wanted from Congress after the rest of the industry had agreed to settle for something less. Like most fighters, Rosenstiel is also a wonderful hater, with a particular hatred for Seagram and its proprietor Samuel Bronfman. The feud between Bronfman and Rosenstiel has been publicly likened to that between Signor Hatfield and Signor McCoy some years ago. Certainly it transcends business competition: either appears willing to sacrifice profit to do the other in the eye. In his annual report to his stockholders, Rosenstiel writes bitterly of "unscrupulous alien competition"—by which he means Canadians, though most Americans would certainly not think of their northern neighbors as "aliens." Bronfman went one up on Rosenstiel last year with the completion of the spectacular new Seagram Building, probably the most lavish office structure built in New York since the war, which makes Rosenstiel's 1930s-style offices in the Empire State Building look just a little shabby in their luxury. But Schenley is essentially a straight-whiskey house (though its best seller is Schenley Reserve, a blend), and Rosenstiel feels himself riding on the wave of history. In 1959, after sixteen years of trailing on the sales charts, bourbons are outselling blends.

Rosenstiel attributes the continuing rise of straight-whiskey sales to the "taste, maturity and smoothness of bourbon whiskey." He is not concerned about possible variations in the whiskey because of differences in agricultural produce from year to year—"there are no two fingerprints alike," he says, "but it's still a hand. The important thing is taste buds. The human animal has 1,200 taste buds between the ages of fifteen to twenty-one. He loses some of them as time goes on, but those that remain become more sensitive. A lot of taste is born in, it's a cultural heritage. Every British sailor got his dram of rum. In Wisconsin, they buy 370,000 cases of brandy a year; in Tennessee, only 2,000 cases. Metropolitan New York drinks more brandy than bourbon. You know the reason: it's the inherited cultural pattern of people who live in Wisconsin and New York. They're used to brandy."

It is almost certainly true that nobody knows how or why tastes change, though any marketing expert can tell you why after the changes have occurred. Before Prohibition, blended whiskeys accounted for about 70 percent of all whiskey sales. Bottled blends in those days were mostly cheap, raw stuff—ethyl alcohol, flavored. Right after Repeal, straights took over three-quarters of the market: people were worried about drinking "neutral spirits," which had tended to be belligerent rather than neutral during the evil days. Blends had increased their share of the whiskey market to almost 40 percent when the United States entered World War II. Shortly thereafter, whiskey production was virtually stopped, to save grain for food purposes, and existing stocks were stretched by blending with spirits. In 1946, blends accounted for 88 percent of all the whiskey bottled in the United States. Three years later, blends still had an 85 percent share, but since 1949 their proportion has been dropping steadily and rather swiftly. Seagram contends that the decline of the blends was arrested in 1958. How low the curve will dip before tastes change again is hard to predict; but Seagram, which did not even make a straight whiskey until Four Roses Antique came on the market last year, has unquestionably felt a pinch.

Edgar Bronfman believes that complacency on the part of the

blend houses has been the main factor. "We had all the business," he says, "so we stopped selling *blends*. We just sold brands. We were fat and lazy. Meanwhile, the straight-whiskey people were selling *bourbon*." In the 1930s, Seagram ran more than 150,000 consumer-preference tests on blends against straights, and found that seven out of ten Americans preferred the taste of blends. These tests are still conducted regularly by Seagram field representatives, and they still produce the same results. In 1952, *Fortune* magazine, heedless of trend lines, reported that blends had 72 percent of the market, and cited the fact as "remarkable confirmation of Seagram's surveys." Now blends have something less than half of the market, and Seagram's surveys look less convincing.

Bronfman *fils* believes that blends must be sold as *blends* to recapture their rightful share of market, as indicated by the surveys. "What I want to see," he says, "is a man going into a bar or a store and saying, 'I want a blend.' " One of Seagram's competitors commented, "What Bronfman wants, or should want, is people going into a bar or a restaurant and saying, 'I want 7 Crown,' the way they do today." (Despite the trend away from blends, Seagram 7 Crown is still the most popular-selling brand of any kind of whiskey in the United States.) National Distillers, which is very much a straights house, claims that most blend buyers believe they are drinking blends of straight whiskeys, and would be horrified at the very idea that the beverage is two-thirds neutral spirits. "Sell blends as blends!" said a National spokesman scornfully. "Oh, boy—'Let us tell you about this alcohol we put in our whiskey!' "

Actually, of course, the argument is artificial. Scotch and Canadian whiskeys are blends, and the average proof of distillation of all the whiskeys in an imported blend is probably higher than the average proof of distillation in any American blend. But Scotch and Canadian have as much prestige as any distiller could want for his product. The shift from blends to straights is not due to people's dislike of "the alcohol we put in our whiskey," but rather to a change in taste. National Distillers' Bev Ohlandt said, replying to the old-time Kentucky distiller's criticisms of National for bottling its famous 100-proof brands at a lighter 86-proof, "We're not in business to please ourselves. We're in business to please the public. If the public prefers 86-proof bourbon, we'll give it to them."

The big surge in bourbon has come since the old-line name brands began making their whiskey available in 86-proof as well as 100-proof strengths. The first brand to take the step was National's Old Crow which, backed by an aggressive advertising campaign, went from 300,-000 to 2,000,000 cases a year in less than half a decade. Old Taylor, another National brand, has tripled its sales since dropping in proof. Glenmore's Old Kentucky Tavern is another such success story. Today only Van Winkle's Old Fitzgerald and Brown-Forman's Old Forester are still offered exclusively as 100-proof, bottled-in-bond whiskeys. To these companies, 86-proof straight bourbon is an abomination. "You lose the true flavor," says Van Winkle, "when you add that much water to it. If people want it milder, I say, let them add their own water." And it has been observed that the 86-proof drives out the 100-proof when the two are offered side by side. Both are the same whiskey behind the same label, but the 86-proof costs about seventy-five cents less per bottle. In bars, the temptation to serve 86-proof but charge the customer for 100-proof often proves irresistible.

Indeed, Glenmore would argue that the lower price of the 86-proof tells the whole story, and the taste question is unimportant. (The lower price is automatic, because Federal tax is calculated on "proof gallons"; the tax on a gallon of 100-proof is $10.50, while that on a gallon of 86-proof is $9.03.) "When you put 100-proof and 86-proof Kentucky Tavern side by side at a convention or a banquet, where somebody else is paying for it," a Glenmore spokesman says, "the 100-proof always disappears first. But when people go into a store they want to save the money."

"People don't like the taste of whiskey," John Martin of Heublein (Smirnoff vodka) once said. "They like the effect. With vodka, they get the effect, but not the taste. I expect to live to see the day when vodka will outsell whiskey in the United States."

Martin is a bear of a man, who conceals a very quick mind and a very tough disposition behind the open extroversion of a born sales-man and the casual bonhomie of a rich man's son. (He is a Scotch drinker himself: picked up the taste for it at Oxford.) Before the advent of Smirnoff, Heublein was basically a food company, living off A-1 Sauce, though it made a certain amount of gin and cordials. Now it is the proprietor of the fifth-largest-selling brand of distilled spirits in America, and a big enough force in the industry to make the Distilled Spirits Institute back down from its long-standing rule against the use of women in liquor ads. Only a few months before, DSI had used all sorts of political pressure in Washington to force the Puerto Rican Development Commission and its agency (Ogilvy, Benson and Mather) to eliminate women from ads for Puerto Rican Rum. Then John Martin told DSI that Heublein was going to use women in Smirnoff Vodka ads, and offered the Institute a choice of expelling Heublein or amending its rules. DSI knuckled under.

National brought Old Crow from 300,000 cases to 2,000,000— but even at 300,000 the brand was a respectable contributor to Na-tional's income. Martin has brought Smirnoff from 4,000 cases the year he bought it (1939) to more than 1,700,000 in 1958. He says that he knew by 1941 how big a potential vodka had, if sold correctly —not as fiery Russian stuff, but as a neutral mixer. The former own-ers of the brand had given up on it and turned to making something they called "Smirnoff whiskey," and when Martin took over the only corks for the bottles were labeled "Smirnoff whiskey." Since the tax stamp covered the corks anyway, Martin decided to use the "whiskey" corks on his first runs of vodka. Ten cases with erroneously printed corks went to a distributor in North Carolina, who told a young salesman to peddle the vodka. When the young man opened a bottle and saw the cork, he knew his sales line. He prepared paper streamers reading "Smirnoff's White Whiskey—No Taste, No Odor." Martin found out about this development when his minuscule market in North Carolina suddenly began to take all the vodka he could send —fifty cases, then five hundred. Since that episode, Heublein has shelled out small fortunes for market surveys about whether people do or do not like the taste of whiskey (one such project, by Stewart Dougall & Associates, turned up a figure of 54 percent of the people who *drank* whiskey didn't like it). But Martin feels that the proof was already in his hands, when he found out why North Carolina was drinking vodka.

Heublein's Hartford distillery—the only source of Smirnoff until recently, when a new plant opened in Menlo Park, California—is unlike any whiskey distillery. There is no mash, no yeast, no fermenting tubs. Smirnoff buys its spirits already distilled, and merely redistills to assure purity and uniform quality. In Heublein's opinion, the key process in vodka-making is the filtration through charcoal, which removes the last vestiges of taste from the spirit. Heublein licenses firms all over the world to make Smirnoff Vodka for their own home markets, permits them to use their own spirits, but ships Hartford charcoal to them to assure that the product will meet the Smirnoff standard.

In charcoal, too, Heublein buys its raw material once-processed, in the form of burnt hardwood chips. Only hardwood will do: white oak, though perfect for whiskey barrels, contains too much tannin. Then the wood goes through the fire once again, in a long cylindrical furnace, tilted to keep the charcoal moving through the fire. The heat inside is 1,600°, and about one-quarter of the charcoal that goes into the furnace burns up before the diminished chips reappear, apparently unchanged but actually purified.

Cooled and treated, the charcoal goes into vertical cylinders about a dozen feet high which stand in rows in a separate room. The purified spirits from the stills, cut to 110-proof with distilled water, are now forced *up* through these tanks loosely packed with charcoal. Each drop of vodka passes through nine of these tanks during an eight-hour period, after which it goes directly to the bottling plant.

Ideally, vodka should have absolutely no taste and no odor. One of the standard tests for vodka is to pour some of it into a heated pan, and sniff the vapor: if you smell something, it isn't right. "You can make a very good ice-cream soda with Smirnoff's," says a Heublein spokesman. "If it's a good ice-cream soda, that is." The neutrality of vodka has been Smirnoff's selling line from the beginning; nobody at Smirnoff cares for the old-fashioned type who puts some chopped onion and lemon on some caviar, then downs vodka straight as the drink that one drinks with caviar. "Personally," says John Martin, "I've always felt that you can take the Park Avenue market and shove it. There's no real money there."

Nevertheless, part of the success of vodka, which now accounts for some 9 percent of all the distilled spirits drunk in America, must trace to the air of class with which Heublein has surrounded its product. "That was the mistake the gin people made," Martin says. "From the very beginning, right after Repeal, they sold gin as a cheap drink." Smirnoff is a premium-priced brand, but it dominates vodka as no other brand dominates any generic type of spirits. Roughly one-third of all the vodka sold in America is Smirnoff—though all the giants have put out their own brands in competition. Martin, it is reported, was delighted when he learned from Rosenstiel that Schenley was planning to enter the vodka market, nearly eight years after Smirnoff had proved that considerable money could be made in the field. "Lew," he said at a dinner party, "I just want to warn you that it will take five years, twenty-five million dollars and the grace of God to build a vodka brand that could compete with Smirnoff." So far, nobody has put together the three factors, and Smirnoff stands alone.

With the ingenuity that Martin has displayed in selling Smirnoff, he should have been able to build a successful brand of whiskey, too—but twenty years of trying left him barely ahead of where he started. Recently he sold his whiskey distillery in Maryland. "We have proclaimed to the trade," says Martin grandly, soothing the wounds of two decades, "that we are no longer interested in whiskey. We don't think it has any future."

"Marketing," said Samuel Bronfman casually, relaxing in an employee's office in his beautiful new Seagram Building, "is the problem in all business. If you don't sell you don't have anything to make. I'm a member of the McGill University advisory council, and recently the sixteen of us were talking about the biggest factor in our businesses. We all agreed it was selling—even the man from a cement company, where I was sure it would be something else. How do you measure prosperity, these days? By the volume of retail sales."

Generally speaking, distilling is the gentleman's part of the liquor industry; selling is rougher. Seagram has its offices in a soaring monolith of bronze and glass, designed by Philip Johnson and Miës van der Rohe, with interior doors and windows fitted floor-to-ceiling without the economy of standard frames. (The Seagram offices are loaded with wood-paneling and original etchings, lithographs and even oils by prominent artists. In the reception rooms stand collections of van der Rohe's Barcelona chairs, handsome steel-*cum*-leather concoctions which retail at a mere $900 each.)

Seagram's customers, the distributors, usually have their executive offices in the front rooms of warehouses. Though Hiram Walker and Heublein own a few of their own wholesalers, most distributors are at least allegedly independent. Theirs is very much a volume business, depending on fast turnover of the inventory of cheaper liquors to pay the basic bills; profits come out of the somewhat slower-moving premium items, which cost no more to sell but produce a greater unit profit. Wholesalers rarely have much money for frills.

The wholesalers' customers, the bars and liquor stores, may exist in a luxurious or frowsy environment, but they all have problems other retailers do not know. The industry as a whole speaks with horror about the alcoholic, whose antics endanger the good name of the distillers; but the bar and the liquor store must deal with the drunk in the flesh. Moreover, bars and liquor stores are open late, take in considerable cash money at night, and make logical targets for stick-up artists and the like. It is easy to feel too sorry for bars and liquor retailers, who are in most states protected from serious business competition by licensing and price-fixing laws; but obviously, this is no business for a sissy.

Most men in the liquor business regard the bars—which account for about one-third of all liquor sales—as the sore spot of the industry. In most bars, people do not ask for liquor by brand name; they ask for a bourbon sour or a rye-and-ginger or a Manhattan—and in the Northeast will receive the same spirit blend in all three. The "bar bourbon" which receives the "automatic pouring" will be a big item for the distributor who convinces the bartender or his boss that his is the brand to carry, and the opportunity for jiggery-pokery in the sale is virtually unlimited, state laws or no state laws, fixed prices or no fixed prices.

Selling to stores, despite the importance of the wholesaler on the organization chart, is in large part the responsibility of the manufacturer. He pays for the advertising, which runs about $60 million a year—or six cents per fifth of liquor—and which makes customers brand-conscious. Manufacturers provide the displays which dealers have in their windows. Manufacturers also, obviously, design and buy the decanters in which premium whiskeys may be offered before Christmas.

National's selling operation is unified—one sales force, broken into small responsible regional groups, sells all National liquor. The others of the Big Four try to "work like Procter & Gamble"—each brand has its own salesmen who compete with the salesmen for other brands made by the same company. This competition is real and earnest, because the local Corby's manager knows that if his sales do *not* go up, and Imperial's sales *do* go up in the same district, he is likely to be regarded as a poor fellow by the Hiram Walker home office. The national sales manager of the Calvert division complained to his bosses recently that Seagram seemed to be serving more 7 Crown than Lord Calvert at company parties. He demanded parity for his brands at all official Seagram functions—and got it.

The missionary salesman's first job it to ingratiate himself and his brand with the retailer. He brings in trade gossip and good stories, plus helpful commercial hints if he can find them. Should the store be busy when he arrives, he fills in behind the counter, waiting on the dealer's customers himself. He is not too proud to set up displays within the store, or to clean a shelf that looks dirty. Union rules in the organized parts of the business forbid him to write orders (a remarkable restriction), and if he is free to sell he must do so for the account of the wholesaler: liquor companies may not by law sell directly to dealers. Basically, the salesman's job is to see that each dealer is well-stocked with his brand, and displays it prominently. If the achievement of this goal requires him to run down the reputation of rival brands, he is not always scrupulous in his behavior.

"Of all the things that people consume," says Bev Ohlandt, "of all the things that pass their gullets, they know least about alcoholic beverages." This general ignorance, combined with the vigorous competition between companies and salesmen, stimulates one of the world's biggest rumor mills. What might be called "negative word-of-mouth" is a real factor in selling liquor. Thus one hears about the damage that can be done by the "pure alcohol" in spirit blends, or the congeners in straight whiskey; people talk about vodka as "potato likker"; bourbon producers pronounce solemnly that Scotch whiskeys are made from "cereals" rather than "grains"—as though there were actually more than a hairbreadth of definition between the two. One of the most spectacular and specific of these rumors ruined the sale of a brand on the South Side of Chicago, where it had been among the best sellers: "They put something in that there whiskey," the word went, "it makes you impotent."

Promoting your brand by derogating its rivals is a characteristic selling procedure when the market for this *sort* of product is shrinking or stable. Similar though less widely credited rumors abound in beer, white bread, and women's clothing (where salesmen work with vicious stories about the relative demerits of the various synthetic and natural fabrics). Obviously, if the market as a whole resists selling pressures, a salesman is most likely to succeed in increasing his own sales when he can pry competitors' customers loose from their loyalties.

In the decade since the end of the first postwar binge, liquor sales to consumers have held to a level at about two hundred million gallons a year. This steady rate of national consumption—which implies a drop in average per-person consumption, since the population is growing—has contributed heavily to the industry's internecine warfare and the spread of preposterous rumors about different types and brands of liquors. But otherwise, as the more thoughtful leaders recognize, it probably represents a long-term benefit to the industry as a whole.

A benefit to the industry is almost certain if, as seems likely, the drop in per-head consumption reflects a decline in heavy drinking by the minority rather than a drop in casual drinking by the majority. The pre-Prohibition working-class society drank noisily at bars; our new middle-class society drinks quietly at home. The agitation for Prohibition was not purely the creation of religious propaganda; it grew also from observation of the brutalizing effects of liquor on depressed elements in the population. "The steelworker at the turn of the century," says National's John Bierwirth, "worked seventy hours a week, and lived with his wife and children in one room of a boardinghouse. The conditions of his life *drove* him to the bars to get drunk. All that has gone, today."

Gone, too, is the guilt-impelled boozing which was one of the most distressing aspects of what Max Weber called "the Protestant Ethic." Antiquated state laws still force schools to teach "the evils of alcohol," but nobody takes it very seriously any more. Most school children today see their parents absorb an occasional drink and know that no harm comes of it. A psychologist, speaking before the American Association for the Advancement of Science (of all bodies!) recently, advanced the theory that vodka had succeeded so brilliantly because Americans had been warned almost from birth against the effects of whiskey, gin and rum—but no parent had ever mentioned vodka, because nobody had known of its existence. There is an odd smidgen of truth in this argument, because vodka got its start in California and was doubtless helped by the fact that the Los Angeles *Times* did not then accept liquor advertising but did run ads for "cordials," into which category vodka was placed. Otherwise, however, it is the usual piffle of psychologists whose reading speed far exceeds their powers of observation. Most vodka drinkers are relatively young (which is why John Martin of Heublein thinks he will live to see the day when vodka outsells whiskey). And today's young is the first American generation which does not feel guilty when it drinks.

There can be no doubt that a relation exists between the decline in per-capita consumption and the easing of emotional attitudes toward liquor. And most leaders of the industry would rather take the lower consumption (though it means lower profits) if they can gain thereby some release from politico-religious pressures. On this twenty-fifth anniversary of Repeal, the only reasonable forecast is for calmer seas. The passage of years will make Prohibition merely an episode in the history books for both consumers and producers, and will bring stability to the volatile business of alcohol.

12

Two Ambassadors to the United Nations

[A teacher at a private school where I was chairman of the board came up to me at a reception not long after the first of these two pieces appeared, and said, I thought with some courage, that he was a follower of Adlai Stevenson, had read almost everything ever written about him, and thought my article was "not up to your usual standard." I see his point and sympathize. But the piece delivered what the *New York Times Magazine* wanted, which was all I was competent to offer—a feuilleton on a personality at work in an interesting job. Provided it is done unpretentiously, I think there is value in this sort of thing—a value which, oddly, benefits from aging. The first of these pieces was published in February, 1965. The second of them, on Arthur J. Goldberg, was commissioned by the same editors and published, alas!, exactly fifty-two weeks later.]

"The Governor" at Work at the United Nations

EARLY one morning a few weeks ago, a visitor got off the elevator on the top floor of the Waldorf Towers and rang the bell beside the door marked with the big shield: Embassy of the United States. The door was opened, not by the expected butler but by a familiar figure. "Good morning; come in," said Ambassador Adlai Ewing Stevenson. "I'm making your egg. Don't look so frightened—I can cook an egg."

So he can; he can also make orange juice, toast and coffee, and set a table, though he tends to be careless about matching place mats or silverware. The embassy has a cook (Stevenson's own, paid for out of his pocket), but cooks, unlike Security Council representatives, get days off and vacations; and then a bachelor Ambassador with no patience for hotel service has to take care of himself.

To a great extent, Governor Stevenson ("Governor" to everyone in his entourage and to all who are *au courant* at the United Nations) has to take care of himself all day long. He has a large and capable group of assistants behind him at the United States Mission to the United Nations and in the International Office of the State Department in Washington. Both are largely staffed on the senior level with people he chose for their jobs. But his position is unique and highly personal, both at the United Nations and in his own Government. Stevenson is the only Ambassador to the United Nations who is also a member of his country's Cabinet. "And quite apart from that," says a delegate from a friendly nation, "quite apart from the fact that he represents the most powerful nation on earth, he is a *personality* in his own right."

What Stevenson says and does means more than what other Ambassadors say and do in the glass slab by the East River. No diplomat can be more than controlledly indiscreet; the Governor must be more careful than anyone else. As candidate for President, he acquired a loyal following both at home and abroad, and it has stayed with him. "It's an odd thing to say," Stevenson commented recently, "but everybody who has served at the United Nations has known me, personally or by my writings or travel. And they were about 98 percent pro-Democratic during my campaigns. I've often said it was a damned shame I ran for President of the wrong country."

Visitors from any country are more likely to recognize Adlai Stevenson than anyone else sitting about the sunken ring in the Security Council chambers. There is a radiance about the man, an extrusion of cheerful energy toward the others in the room. He seems to be listening more carefully than anyone else to the translation that comes to his right ear through a wire and a pink plug; certainly, he is more likely to react—he has no part of a poker face. He confers more earnestly and enthusiastically during the long successive translations over the loudspeaker, or stumps off to the lounge with his arms moving, his attaché case swinging.

He stands out sartorially, too. The man who ran for President behind the symbol of a shoe with a hole in it cannot be metamorphosed into a striped-pants diplomat. On one recent occasion, during the Security Council debates on the Congo, there were fifty or sixty men on the floor of the chamber, Stevenson in a brown suit, all the others in black or navy blue.

Stevenson probably stands out more than he and President Kennedy had hoped when he accepted the job in 1961. His assignment to the United Nations was a gift with a purpose, to upgrade the importance of the post in the domestic politics of other nations. The chance that others would follow the American lead was destroyed, together with other chances, in the fiasco at the Bay of Pigs. During the Security Council debates on the Cuban invasion, it rapidly became apparent that whatever Stevenson's titular position in his Government, Kennedy had not troubled to tell him the truth about Cuba.

Members of the Secretariat believe that the greatest of all tributes to Stevenson's ability and popularity is the fact that he was able to recover from the extreme embarrassment of those debates and to reassert his credit in the organization. But the incident demonstrated conclusively the limits on the influence of even the most significant United Nations Ambassador. The continuing fallout poisons the comment of an African delegate: "Why do you send him here? He is too good for this job."

Between July 1 and December 31, 1964, the United States Mission received 9,730 telegrams from the State Department in Washington. "United States Government foreign policy runs entirely by telegram," says Francis Plimpton, a former Wall Street lawyer who is one of Stevenson's four assistants with the rank of Ambassador assigned to the various organs of the United Nations. Stevenson has personal contacts, too: he averages a day a week in Washington, dines occasionally with the President and attends as many Cabinet and National Security Council meetings as his duties in New York permit. Ultimately, however, he is at the end of a wire from Washington. He and the United Nations staff take their orders from Washington for the same reason all embassies and other missions do—there is and can be only one originating source for foreign policy. That source in the United States is the President, and his principal operating officer is the Secretary of State. There cannot be two Secretaries of State. Therefore, though Stevenson has Cabinet rank (as did Lodge before him), and would appear to be a co-equal of Rusk, he is necessarily Rusk's deputy at the United Nations. "It's mostly an executive job," he says wryly. "What freedom I have is the result of my own seniority and status."

Even this degree of freedom cannot be extended to the others at the mission who report basically to bureau chiefs at the other end of the line and not to Stevenson. Perhaps the most personal of Stevenson's recommendations for appointment was that of Marietta Tree as United States Representative on the Trusteeship Committee, which deals generally with the problems of the nonself-governing territories.

Mrs. Tree has been a friend for eighteen years, and she and her husband were Stevenson's hosts in Barbados in the difficult weeks after the 1952 election. ("He and the Edison Dicks and the Finletters came down," she recalls. "The rest of us drank rum punches before lunch and napped afterwards; he disappeared into the study every morning and afternoon, and in three weeks he produced a book.") Mrs. Tree believes she has been in Stevenson's office on the eleventh floor of the mission exactly ten times in four years, and she sees him outside the office "only in swirling crowds"—but she is in daily contact with Washington.

Everything a man can bring to the job of United Nations Ambassador, Stevenson has. He was trained as a lawyer and, says Plimpton, "anybody who is a lawyer has an advantage at the United Nations; in many ways this is like a perpetual lawsuit with 115 different parties. You also get into terrific arguments over shades of meaning, terribly reminiscent of arguments you get into when drafting contracts. It matters whether you say 'deplore' or 'regret'—'condemn,' of course, is very far out. It even matters whether you say 'noting' or 'reaffirming' a past resolution. You have to maintain patience or you'd go insane, and you need the sheer argumentative ability to be persuasive in negotiation."

When the lawyerlike attitude looks unprofitable, Stevenson can also call upon an ex-Governor's disdain for pettifoggery. An officer of the Secretariat says admiringly that "Adlai doesn't like to get fouled up with semantics. He has a very helpful impatience with petty things, and he likes to go to the heart of the matter, which isn't true of everybody here. These bureaucracies are all alike; but Adlai isn't a bureaucrat."

In moving about the building, Stevenson has the advantage of a deep and long-standing commitment to the United Nations, and of involvement in its history. He was one of Edward Stettinius' advisers at the original San Francisco meeting, and headed the United States delegation to the second session of the Planning Commission, in London in 1945. In 1946 and 1947, he was a member of the American mission at Lake Success, resigning only to run for Governor of Illinois.

"I've had great faith and great hopes in this organization as an instrument for peace," Stevenson says. "The rationale that civil societies have is self-protection against disorder and anarchy and violence. That which city-states and nation-states have had is now, internationally, not a desideratum but a necessity. Some organization has to be contrived and expanded, so it can withstand blows like the Japanese and Italian withdrawals from the League of Nations. I have always tried to steer the United States along this path, so we can never be charged with using this instrumentality simply for goals of our own." The most fervent internationalist in the Secretariat could not improve on this statement, and nobody has ever questioned Stevenson's honesty. If anything is to be given to the United States as a gesture to its representative, the Governor will get it.

He will get it, too, because people like him—by no means a minor asset in a small body like the Security Council, which meets one hundred times a year. Much of Stevenson's public career has been made by the affection felt for him by those in positions to do him a good turn, from Jake Arvey to Harry Truman to Eleanor Roosevelt. He is unfailingly courteous and immensely charming, a continuing credit to his prep schools and to Princeton. An intent listener, he flatters the people he is with by the careful attention he gives them. When he comes to speak, he pays his auditors the final compliment of choosing his words with great care, giving a cliché a personal phrasing so as never to convey even a hint that he has brushed off what was said to him. A fellow Ambassador likes to talk about "the tremendous humanity of the man."

Some of this care in conversation, of course, reflects a shy pride, an insistence on putting a personal stamp on the common currency, and not everyone approves it. During his election campaigns, Stevenson's aides were furious with him for taking endless hours to polish his speeches when he could have been out shaking hands at supermarkets. Not everyone is enchanted by Stevenson's friendliness, either. Some observers of the United Nations feel that he has been less effective than he might be because he is never willingly offensive to anyone, even to people who have behaved offensively to him or to his country. He is hurt, and shows it; but he rarely strikes back.

Henry Cabot Lodge in similar situations would bull his way into the opposition (and, as Robert Murphy recently recalled in his autobiography, through State Department rules as well), creating the impression that he had greater independent authority. Most observers believe, however, that Stevenson, if anything, has a touch more freedom than Lodge had—"the difference," one of them says, "between being able to call right through to Dulles and being able to call right through to Johnson." He merely chooses to be quiet.

Besides the gentility and the gentleness, Stevenson is an entertaining companion, who likes to be quick on his feet and stimulates others to be the same. He is in demand for parties not only because he represents the United States and gives the event a social tone, but also because he livens things up. Stevenson spends almost all his official working day in conferences, but he then goes on to an appalling number of these parties—several hundred a year, for each of 115 national holidays, visits of foreign ministers, local occasions, etc.

By universal agreement, United Nations parties are work. "I'm a hard-boiled Wall Street lawyer," says Plimpton, "and I'm used to extremely hard work. The difference here is that instead of sweating blood several nights a week at the office, you have to go to several receptions and dinners. You may get a whiskey-and-soda out of it, but somebody wants to collar you and you want to collar him, and it's seldom you go to a party without picking up two or three things you want to send a telegram to Washington about. The working day is 8:45 A.M. to midnight."

Stevenson's working day tends to be even longer, because his breakfast appointments are for 8:15, and when he returns from a party he often has to touch up a memo or a talk.

A great deal of that day is, simply, wasted. For the newer nations, it constitutes recognition to have an appointment with the Governor —and an insult to have to deal with the member of the United States Mission who actually knows the situation to be discussed. Stevenson is therefore obliged every month to keep numerous appointments at which his prime function is to be gracious. The higgle-haggle of the delegates' lounge is doubtless of great significance inside the United Nations, but its values in the colder world outside are considerably less. The portrait of Stevenson at work would typically show a man waiting—waiting before a delayed meeting of the Security Council for ambitious delegates from small countries to hammer out a compromise that will be vetoed anyway, waiting at a conference for someone to say something that directly touches the practical interests of the United States, waiting for an answer to a cable. But that is the nature of the job.

In addition to his United Nations responsibilities, Stevenson serves as chairman of the Field Foundation and the Eleanor Roosevelt Cancer Fund. "Then there are the social engagements," he said the other day at the Waldorf. "You're honorary chairman and patron of every darned thing that happens. The theater benefits. The opening of that bridge I'm looking at," he said, waving at the Verrazano-Narrows Bridge visible in the distance from his dining room. "The World's Fair. The speeches before some organization. And there's been this development of the Award System; they grant awards to people these days for all manner of things. Somebody has to make a speech at the awards dinner, and eight or ten old friends beat hell out of you until you say you'll do it, and then the speech has to be prepared."

Apart from everything else, Stevenson is a celebrity—a term beautifully defined by Daniel Boorstin as "a person who is known for his well-knownness." His appearance causes a stir, his capture by a non-United Nations hostess will be worth much talk under the hairdriers. He is inevitably the most desired escort for an unattached lady at any occasion, and the newspapers carry the story.

"Over Christmas," he said with some distaste, "I read a story about my glamorous social life. I was squiring Mrs. Kennedy, Ava Gardner,

Lauren Bacall and some gorgeous dame I've never even met."

Stevenson has always enjoyed the company of a pretty girl or a high spirited woman (men who call him are normally under orders to send their wives' regards, including a specific comment), and as long as people gossip about wealthy marriageable males he will be in the social columns. But the pages of his social calendar, which he keeps himself, are packed with business-gatherings and duty-gatherings; the time available for genuinely private social life is drastically restricted. Every so often, he sneaks off for a country-house weekend or plays a little wild, enthusiastic tennis at the River Club.

Though Stevenson was the American delegate to the committee that chose New York as a site for the United Nations, and agreed with the European diplomats on the importance of a city with varied cultural attractions, he takes little advantage of the city's artistic resources. From the appearance of the Embassy apartment (standard Waldorf antique) and the office at the mission (standard State Department bulky green leather, awkwardly arranged), he has little interest in his visual surroundings. He likes music and wishes he could go more often to concerts and the opera, but the fact is that he doesn't get there much.

By living in a hotel suite rather than acquiring a home of his own, he emphasizes the point that he is not a New Yorker. "My voting residence is in Illinois," he says, "and I try to keep my Illinois roots. My business interests are there. My family has lived there almost 140 years."

When Stevenson talks about his United Nations work these days, he often falls into the past tense, or gives his voice an elegiac tone.

"This job has been a terrible drill," he said recently. "In my own life I've been accustomed to making policy. I've sometimes been a little restless in this role of executing and articulating the policies of others. There is a disadvantage in being anywhere other than the seat of power. And every issue that comes to the United Nations has its antecedents before it gets here. The State Department has been involved in the negotiations, and now the situation has become insoluble, so it gets dumped onto us. If you could follow these things from their genesis, it would be helpful when they got here—but you can't be in two places at the same time.

"Besides, I can't help but believe that you can wear out on a job like this. You become such an old and familiar face. You take on the coloration of your country, your country's face, and you become predictable. You lose some of the rosy glow you brought with you. Apart from my taste for more creative aspects, the time comes when you should bring in a fresh face and outlook."

None of this means that Stevenson has decided to leave his post; the answer to that question will be given elsewhere. "My decisions," he said somewhat ruefully, "have always come about more by circumstances and events than by my conscious calculation."

He turned down the Democratic nominations for Senator from Illinois in 1962 and from New York in 1964 ("very flattering to be asked to run for the Senate from two states"), mostly because the United Nations was involved in a crisis from which he felt he should not flee. The crisis today is perhaps the severest of all, and Stevenson certainly wishes to see the organization through the settlement of the Article 19 problem (the removal of a vote in the General Assembly from any nation more than two years behind in dues and assessments) and its twin problem of the unfortunate "Uniting for Peace" resolution under which the assessments were laid.

Thereafter, nobody knows. Stevenson is much closer to Johnson than he was to Kennedy. The two men have known each other since 1933, when Stevenson was a young lawyer in the first Agricultural Adjustment Administration and Johnson was secretary to Congressman Richard Kleberg, who wanted some help for his district from the A.A.A.

At sixty-five, Stevenson is not a political threat to a President just beginning a term to which he was elected in a landslide. The hard-nosed lads around Kennedy, who liked to tell stories about "Adlai wanting a Munich," are being replaced by a less austere group who are attracted rather than troubled by Stevenson's rather self-deprecatory grace. One can without difficulty imagine Stevenson full-time in Washington rather than visiting once a week.

But he could also continue indefinitely at the United Nations, wrestling with the old crises in the Congo and Cuba, Kashmir, Cyprus, Angola, Israel and the Arab nations, Malaysia-Indonesia and whatever new crisis the wit of man devises in the coming months. He would not necessarily be unhappy. "It's easy," he says in the familiar involuted manner, "to reconcile a sense of duty with this job."

Goldberg Represents Johnson

UNITED NATIONS, N.Y.

PEOPLE who work behind the eleven stories of stone grillwork at the United States Mission to the United Nations still speak of "the Governor," then shake their heads and grin and correct it to "the Justice." Arthur J. Goldberg has been the American Ambassador to the United Nations for six months now, but in many small ways it is still Adlai Stevenson's Mission. Goldberg is not displeased: his presence by the East River is itself a tribute to Stevenson. "When the President first spoke to me," he said recently, "I thought it was an impossible situation. But, as he very frankly said, there were the difficulties of finding a replacement for Adlai Stevenson. . . ."

The office is still the corner suite on the eleventh floor, furnished in characterless, government-issue mahogany and green leather. Stevenson had his back to the window, while Goldberg keeps the big desk at the other end of the long room, avoiding the possible distraction the view might make for his guests. Stevenson smoked cigarettes and drank coffee, while Goldberg is a nonsmoker and enamored of a colorless dietetic beverage called Like, which the chauffeur carries up in six-packs all day long, and which is offered rather ceremoniously (choice of paper cup or glass) to visitors.

Stevenson was on his feet a good deal, greeting people or showing them out, communicating through the door to his secretaries, or simply spending that nervous energy which was, in an odd way, one of his charms. Goldberg, more neatly dressed, the gray hair in a stiff brush over the wide forehead, remains in his seat; he is a rather small man of no special physical grace and he feels more comfortable when everyone is sitting.

Stevenson loved to tell or hear a story, and his conversation was punctuated with odd observations that might or might not strike a spark in a companion's mind, depending on the companion's education, experience or acquaintance. "To hear him speak, when he was in form," says a European ambassador, "was sheer bliss." Answering questions, he was a master of the pause that tells the questioner, perhaps inaccurately, that he is receiving the courtesy of careful consideration. Goldberg does not much care for stories, and his asides are opinions on legal or social matters; he answers questions quickly and in a straightforward manner, as though there could be no confusion about what is and what is not information.

In the sunken gallery of the Security Council, Goldberg's face is normally immobile and inexpressive, while Stevenson's was at best composed and often reflected a byplay of passing thoughts. Stevenson's calendar was a messy little book he carried around with him; Goldberg's is the leather-bound Economist Diary ($12.50 at Brooks Brothers), which is a compendium of world statistics and maps with space for writing appointments.

Though he says he does not like to talk about himself, Goldberg does so more often than Stevenson did, and considerably more deeply: why he does what he does is significant to Goldberg. "Stevenson," says a man who has worked closely with both, "was always being self-deprecatory, and you had to know him well before you were really sure he didn't mean it. There isn't a self-deprecatory bone in Goldberg's body." What Stevenson was saying, to those who listened thoughtfully and sympathetically, might be of wide importance; what Goldberg is saying is that he is in control of his job. That fact is important, too.

"With ability, courage, industry *and* luck," a permanent representative to the United Nations said the other day, talking of Goldberg, "a man can accomplish something in this organization. And in Goldberg's case, of course, it is also believed—we have no way of knowing—that he has access to the President. . . ."

This belief is the prime source of Goldberg's surprising strength at the United Nations. "When Goldberg speaks, you know," says a staff member of one of the delegations, "you feel you are hearing something." Stevenson, though enormously admired by his colleagues, was merely the representative of the United States; Arthur Goldberg is the representative of Lyndon Johnson. Virtually nobody at the United Nations has any comprehension of the position as Supreme Court Justice that Goldberg gave up to become Ambassador ("There have been some jokes," a European says, "about the man who left such a comfortable lifetime appointment for this risky post") but it is understood that Johnson's vanity is somehow committed to Goldberg's success. And almost everybody at the United Nations understands the nature of personal government—understands it better, perhaps, than any American can.

But as his colleague said, Goldberg has also demonstrated ability, courage, industry and luck—and goodwill, too. As the new Ambassador he had, in effect, one favor he could ask the Congress and the country: he chose a peaceable abandonment of the Article 19 squabble, the fight to make Russia and France (and others) pay assessments toward the cost of peacekeeping operations or lose their votes in the General Assembly. Goldberg himself credits the remarkable calm which followed this announcement to a "lucky thought" he had, which was to consult with President Eisenhower, and win his support, before the decision was made public. (This was a good deal easier for Goldberg than it would have been for Stevenson.)

A cynical ambassador believes that the American retreat on Article 19 could have been accomplished quietly in August, "when nobody was paying attention." Still, people at the United Nations read what the American press says about the United Nations (if nothing else), and they were highly conscious of the storm that might descend on the organization when a Democratic Administration abandoned an oft-proclaimed "principle" to satisfy the Russians and de Gaulle. They believe that Goldberg drew heavily on his personal credit, particularly with Congress, to prevent that storm, and they are grateful. Informed of this attitude, Goldberg says, "I haven't exhausted my credit; I hope to continue to have good relations with the Congress."

The adjective Goldberg's name invariably inspires at the United

Nations is "confident." The American turn in the rotating presidency of the Security Council came only a month after his arrival, and the new boy found on the president's table the war between India and Pakistan. First reaction in Washington had been of the my-God-we-must-*do*-something variety; Goldberg let it be known, firmly, that he thought this was the United Nations' job, not Washington's, a position accepted, first skeptically, then gleefully, after it began to appear that Goldberg knew what he was talking about.

He moved through the incredible procedural and substantive tangle on the East River without ever putting a foot in wrong (the Russians challenged him, just for kicks, on his procedure in calling a Council meeting, and without pausing to consult anyone, he demonstrated he had stayed within the rules). The Council under Goldberg's presidency produced three unanimous resolutions, none of them really easy to obtain even though everybody wanted the same result. "This was the first time in a decade," says a faithful observer of the United Nations, "that the permanent members had taken the lead in the Security Council; up to Kashmir, they had all relied on the smaller powers to find the acceptable solution. It was very remarkable that Goldberg could do it—and even more remarkable, perhaps, that he believed he could do it."

Everyone is impressed with Goldberg's ability to speak to the circumstances and history of an issue. "With Stevenson," an ambassador says, "one sometimes felt he was like one of your astronauts—he saw the problem from a great height. With Goldberg you always have the feeling you are on the ground. You have the facts and figures. You are dealing with a friendly lawyer who knows the dossier."

In the Kashmir matter, Goldberg was undoubtedly helped by the fact that he had been on the scene only a year before, while lecturing on law in India. But, generally, says an old associate from Washington days, "he's a master of knowing *just* enough. He always seems beautifully prepared, but he doesn't clutter his head with needless information; he has an invaluable instinct for what he doesn't have to know."

Musicians and actors say that someone who can learn a part overnight is a "quick study"; Goldberg was trained to that art as a trial lawyer and has never lost it. He absorbs from books ("he reads tremendously and he's one of these photographic guys," says a State Department officer) but mostly from people; he has leaned more heavily on his staff than Stevenson ever did. Throughout the General Assembly session, he met four mornings a week with the entire United States delegation and the fifth with the Mission's staff.

"You know, there are seven committees of the whole," says someone who was at the meetings, "and he wanted to keep up with all of them. But he also wanted to hear from you—it wasn't only that he wanted to know former Attorney General Rogers' problems with some technical legal issue on the Sixth Committee, he also wanted to hear anything Rogers might have to say about Kashmir. He knows how to use a staff; and our tendency now is to involve him, because we know he wants to be involved."

Goldberg is pleased but not surprised by his staff's attitude. Recalling the days when he was general counsel for the Congress of Industrial Organizations during the presidency of Philip Murray, he said: "You know, Phil Murray used to get sick a lot, and I had a lot to do with running the C.I.O. I got relaxed about administration. I am not unacquainted with the problem of keeping twenty things going with a special eye on one."

Stevenson was impatient with the unbelievable minutiae that clutter any international conference, temporary or permanent; Goldberg, who gave the formative years of his maturity to trade-union negotiations, is more willing to suffer both trivia and fools. Also, one of his aides points out, "he has the kind of mind that divides things up into fine points, privately as well as publicly, so he doesn't mind fine points." An assistant from his Washington days says that "he's always assumed that great things come from small things. At a meeting, for example, he would take an interest in where Sorensen sat; he would want to be sure everybody was sitting where he thought they ought to sit."

Such talents are probably applicable to all situations at the United Nations—"The only way you ever get agreements around here is the trade-union way," says a veteran of the Secretariat—but the India-

Pakistan dispute was especially susceptible to their exercise. Everyone seems to agree that Goldberg had fantastic luck in the first issue on which he had to work.

"In many of our questions here," says a senior European delegate, "we're negotiating *away* from the problem, because a solution might be worse than the status quo. Kashmir was a place where, in fact, the Great Powers wanted a solution. It was, therefore, much more amenable to the tactics of labor negotiations, where both sides know there must be a settlement."

Goldberg's performance was enhanced, moreover, by the wild backlighting of potential catastrophe. "It wasn't only the peace of the world," he said recently, thinking back, "but also the future of the United Nations. After a disastrous year, if the United Nations fell apart again . . ." And he could think of nothing sufficiently drastic to complete the sentence.

Agreement on what to do about this bloody little war seemed inevitable from the outside, but on the inside nobody was sure of the outcome until the ink was on the paper. The first night of the war, the deputies of the Big Four had met and agreed on a draft resolution; but the next night, when the ambassadors themselves were meeting, the agreement fell apart. The draft resolution had contained no mention of Kashmir itself, and the French believed, on good authority, that without some such mention the Pakistanis were prepared to renounce the United Nations—Indonesia, after all, had recently quit the organization for much less reason.

Neither the United States nor the Russian Ambassador had come to the meeting ready for a resolution which would mention Kashmir, but Goldberg saw immediately that the French were serious in their position and were not to be moved. The Western powers generally were concerned (perhaps without reason) that if a resolution were not agreed upon that night, the Indian Government would convert the Soviet Union at least to delaying tactics. Goldberg took a quick adjournment and exited with his hand on the arm of Nikolai Fedorenko, the Russian Ambassador. When the two returned half an hour later, a resolution based on the French draft was quickly approved.

Meanwhile, in an episode which delighted the United States delegation, standing around the Security Council chamber with great concern, Goldberg undertook to placate the representatives of the smaller nations, who had not yet been consulted. While the Big Four were meeting, they had drafted a formal note of protest against their exclusion, addressed to Goldberg as Security Council president.

As Goldberg emerged from the private room of the Secretary General, Ambassador Arsène Usher of the Ivory Coast came at him menacingly with a piece of paper. Sensing the significance of the paper, Goldberg started the conversation himself, and said, as those present reconstruct it: "Now that we have finished the meeting of the permanent members, I want to meet with the elected members, and we shall not let the big powers attend *our* meeting." In a few minutes the ruffled feathers were smoothed, and the Security Council unanimously resolved that the Indians and Pakistanis should stop shooting at each other. "It wasn't just Goldberg," says a member of another delegation. "All the Council members deserve a bouquet." But Goldberg had held the center of the stage and had earned his applause.

Center stage has been a new position for Arthur Goldberg, and in many ways not an easy one: he made his reputation, and is undoubtedly still most at ease, in the prompter's box. His worst moment as Ambassador came on the occasion of his maiden speech to the General Assembly. "I didn't make a good speech, and I know it," he says. "To begin with, it was four times too long for the reason that, in the old saw, I didn't have time to write a short one—I was too busy with Kashmir."

Eloquence is not Goldberg's province: his voice is flat and sounds a little hoarse; he has always relied upon information to persuade and upon language only to express agreements. Some ambassadors from the newer nations have felt that Goldberg's interventions in debate, with their almost invariable matter-of-fact tone, show insufficient desire to please. "He has the habit of the lawyer who speaks to the jury," one of them says. "It is not quite like teaching a lesson, but it is a way of talking to people who still have to learn. It does not bother me, but some of my brothers feel he is treating them as though they were not quite mature, and they can be very sensitive."

What negative comment there was on Goldberg's appointment has faded almost entirely. Arab delegates will not speak to the press about the fact that Goldberg is Jewish, but they have not forgotten his Zionist speeches from the old days. He has not forgotten them (or disowned them) either; but he has argued successfully that when he speaks at the United Nations it is as the representative of the United States, not as a Jew or a Zionist or a private person. "Our people here," says an employee of the Arab League, speaking carefully, "are mostly sophisticated people. When they thought about it, they realized that Johnson is not lacking in people who will give him Zionist advice; if anything, Goldberg might be more reluctant than others to give such advice." All normal diplomatic courtesies have been maintained—Goldberg goes to functions of the Arab delegations and they come to his. "When he first came," an African ambassador says, "they complained; they said it was a slap in the face. But now nobody is complaining."

Worries about Goldberg's lack of experience in foreign affairs turned out to be much exaggerated. International relations had been one of Goldberg's concerns for years. "I drew up all the C.I.O. foreign-policy resolutions," he recalls, "after we threw the Communists out. You can tell when that happened because there was a great change in the resolutions."

Goldberg had gone abroad for his clients on business of the International Confederation of Trade Unions and knew leading unionists and Socialists in much of Europe and Latin America. Feelings (or at least professions) of international solidarity have always been central to labor organizations outside the United States; and when Goldberg came to the United Nations important Social Democratic leaders were able to assure their own ambassadors that, as one of them put it, "you will find him very efficient and practical."

Liaison between the Mission and the State Department is closer under Goldberg than it has ever been before. "Rusk was a Cabinet colleague," Goldberg says, "and it's an old relationship, including our wives. It's an easy relationship. He knows I have no ambition to be Secretary of State, despite what the newspaper columnists say."

Perhaps even more important has been Goldberg's cultivation of the Assistant Secretaries of State, and the replacement of Stevenson's friend Harlan Cleveland by the career diplomat Joseph Sisco, as Assistant Secretary for International Organization Affairs. Goldberg and Sisco had never met before but they took to each other immediately. Goldberg has inaugurated a series of lunches, one for each Assistant Secretary in charge of a region, which bring people up from Washington to meet the new Ambassador and spend a few social hours with the United Nations representatives from the areas of their special concern.

The one area where Goldberg feels his performance has been deficient is press relations. He shares some of President Johnson's hypersensitivity to criticism in the newspapers, and he feels he has been unfairly asked to leak details of what he said to the President and the President said to him. "I didn't do that when I was working for Phil Murray," he says, "and I won't do it when I'm working for Johnson."

What irritates him most, one suspects, is that in the past he has been a master at using the press—he was a prime source of stories for selected correspondents while at the C.I.O., and employed "background" interviews with great effect in his conciliation work while Secretary of Labor—but has not yet found the technique that threads the needle at the United Nations. Since so much of his pleasure in the new post has been in his success, the one failure nags him.

Much of the United Nations Ambassador's job is the same, whether the incumbent is a Lodge or a Stevenson or a Goldberg. There are the same demands on time for luncheons and dinners, the same ambassadors from more than a hundred countries to cultivate and when necessary soothe, the same demands from Washington for reports, the same Senators to see and banquets to address, all the various labors needed to justify God's ways to other gods. When the Assembly is in session, which is three months of the year, the job takes seven days and seven nights a week. In any event, Goldberg at present has no escape from the official residence atop the Waldorf Towers (while on the bench he purchased "an old broken-down farm on what was once part of John Marshall's estate in Virginia," but that is a long way from New York and the house doesn't have heat yet).

The social life of the United Nations distresses Goldberg as it did his predecessors (and does his colleagues), but his objections are a little different. "You'd like to get to know some of these people," he says, "but the way you meet them, at dinners and parties, you never do. Fedorenko, for example, is an expert on Chinese literature; there's somebody else on the Security Council, I've been told, who's a poet. Then there's this ambassador who was one of the leaders in his country's revolt, looks like such a young fellow, you'd like to know something about it. But the sheer quantity prevents you from digging."

Both in his work and in his off-duty hours Goldberg prefers the intimate group, the tête-à-tête; and he has a wife (who keeps an office at the Mission) to remind him they both dislike large gatherings and to help him control the number of party or public-affair invitations he accepts.

Goldberg's curiosity about his colleagues has won him less affection than Adlai Stevenson gained merely by his extraordinarily good manners: people sense a clinical as well as a human interest in Goldberg's attitude. By the same token, however, Stevenson could be hurt by an attack aimed at something he had just said, while Goldberg shakes it off easily. "Soviet delegates," he commented the other day, "are inclined to argue *ad hominem*—but that's a very Russian characteristic; if you read Russian novels you find it there."

Goldberg has startlingly high ambitions for the United Nations. "Unlike most people here," a European ambassador's deputy says, "he regards the Charter as a serious and basic document; he thinks that whenever there's a problem, the Charter ought to provide a clue to the answer."

Goldberg agrees: "My attitude toward the Charter is that I think it is a constitutional document, like our own—the more perfect union, the common defense when there was no common defense, the general welfare at a time when the phrase was scarcely known. Sometimes, just because the United Nations is such a great concept, we forget that the Charter is also a legal document, a treaty, and we're bound by it—we have treaty obligations. I have a great feeling that like the Constitution the Charter is a developing document; I've always been mindful that it's a *Charter* we're expounding. My Soviet colleagues look to the document, the words; I look for a way to give this document the same attention the Supreme Court gave the Constitution. I remember one evening I got into an argument with the Soviets about the powers of the Secretary General, and the Jordanian Ambassador supported me with an argument which was right out of John Marshall, though I don't think he knew it. That's the direction in which we have to move."

When Goldberg accepted the job, he received a pledge that he would have "a voice—a coordinate voice, not a subordinate voice—in the making of American policy." In his press conference at the end of the General Assembly, Goldberg said, "That commitment has been honored by the President of the United States." (But Goldberg also knows that, as a veteran of the Kennedy Administration recently put it, "no President's word is ever binding.")

Since Eisenhower exalted it to Cabinet rank, nobody has ever been able to describe with any confidence the job of United States Ambassador to the United Nations. Stevenson's appointment was an emotional commitment, but also, obviously, a way of sidelining someone with an independent power base who could otherwise have been embarrassing to his government on the domestic scene. Goldberg's appointment and his first six months in office have said something more about the job itself: they are, at the least, strong circumstantial evidence that both Goldberg and Johnson consider it a big job, indeed. The United Nations likes that.

13

Computers and the Man Problem

[Intellectually the most difficult job I have ever done for a magazine, this article grew from a cocktail conversation between an editor of *Esquire* and a middle-management type at IBM. At least one of them must have been drunk, because the word came back to Harold Hayes that IBM was taking bus drivers from buses and drop-out children from play and old men from chimney corners, and turning them into original and significant programers for the computer. Hayes suggested that this would make a story, as indeed it would; but of course it isn't true. I dutifully ate IBM's bread at a lunch, and reported back that the story wouldn't stand up; and Hayes said, Well, nobody knows who these computer fellows are, the important ones, and there's a story in that.

[To understand what these men have done, of course, it is necessary to understand a fair amount about computers. I was three months late in delivering this piece in 1968. I handed it in with the words, "I worked like a dog on this damned thing, and the reader can do some work, too."]

WHEN the balloon went up—well, just a little way up—at Columbia University last spring, one of the things the experts on balloons noticed was that the engineering students barely participated in the ascension, even as observers, and that the electrical engineering types around the computer lab were the least interested of all. In our odd era, the revolt of the intellectuals—well, *almost* intellectuals—has been essentially Luddite, against the machines, the divisions of labor, the organizations which sustain the functioning of a world grown too complicated to be understood. And of all the machines, the most threatening is the computer, with its Myrmidons of stiff cardboard; but its proprietors, of course, don't feel threatened.

Like sex drives, card tricks and the weather, computers tend to be discussed in terms of results rather than processes, which by definition makes them scary. Historically, after all, man has prided himself on his unique capacity to create and manipulate symbols, and now there are these machines which somehow, incomprehensibly, manipulate symbols. To say that the computer can do only what it is programed to do begs the question. In rough translation, after all, this is what we mean when we use the word "culture" with reference to human society (if the big hand came down and picked you out of your chair and set you on the ground naked in the Amazonian rain forest you would quickly find that there are lots of things you aren't programed to do). Moreover, the programs now being fed into the memory cores of our largest computers are themselves so complicated that the programmers have only a rough notion of the limits on what the machine will be able to do after it has ingested them. This is probably why so many of the new systems don't work; but they will, and soon.

The new "time-sharing" schemes, by which people carry on dialogues with the machine, permit both parties to the conversation to hone their intellectual skills. Whatever this capability may do to the human participants in the dialogue (Robert M. Fano, who runs M.I.T.'s Project MAC, proprietor of the earliest "Multiple Access Computer," says it turns some researchers into "computer bums, like tennis bums"), it is highly educational for the machine. And what the computer learns, barring deliberate erasure, it does not forget.

Still, the people who work with the machine aren't scared, partly because it is their toy—the brightest and shiniest and busiest toy since the giants threw Valhalla together for Wotan—and partly because they know it was made by men, with identities and origins and endings. A little better understanding of who these men are and what they have done might enable even the almost-intellectual rebels to approach their fears in a more mentally healthy state. Everybody ready, now? Gung ho:

The basic machine is the offspring of an unexpected marriage between electrical engineering and a rather separate branch of mathematics called numerical analysis. Mathematicians with an interest in numbers had been developing computing machines for a long time —Pascal in the seventeenth century invented an adding machine which is still mass-produced for sale to children by mail order, and in early Victorian times a brilliant nut named Charles Babbage, with financial help from the British Treasury and some additional input of brainpower from Lord Byron's daughter, came very close to a mechanical universal calculator. And ever since the installation of the first, apparently miraculous pendulum clocks in the church towers of medieval Europe, the Christian world has been fascinated by the idea of the soulless automaton. Perhaps the scariest of them to the romantic temperament was E. T. A. Hoffmann's Talking Turk, who knew your secrets, just like the modern data bank.

At first, electricity was applied to the calculating problem only as a way of powering a mechanism. Mechanical switches, in fact, were at the heart of the device usually considered the first real computer —Howard H. Aiken's Mark I, which was put in service in 1943 along the walls of the basement of Harvard's Memorial Hall, where now (*autres temps, autres moeurs*) psychologist B. F. Skinner keeps his pigeons. But even as Aiken's machine ground out ballistics trajectories for the Navy, J. Presper Eckert and John W. Mauchly of the University of Pennsylvania put together the 20,000 tubes and associated circuitry of an electronic computer, which counted by means of pulsing electric signals rather than by the positioning of switches.

Operating either of these machines, however, was an incredibly tedious business, because exact instructions for each computational step had to be fed separately into the computer. Both machines included a minimal memory, to store the partial products of calculations. John von Neumann, a Hungarian mathematician with the style of a meteor, temporarily housed in Princeton, saw that what was needed was a larger and more useful memory, which could store prearranged sequences of computational steps—"programs"—for use by the machine at specified intervals. Von Neumann was also an automaton hobbyist, and he first thought of these memories as monstrous mechanical relays. Then somebody introduced him to Jan Rajchman at RCA labs.

For Rajchman, a blunt and cost-minded Swiss who came to the United States as an electrical engineering student in the 1930s and has been with RCA all his working life, von Neumann's problem was simply one of controlling the passage of electric currents from place to place. As a radio man, he saw ways to handle that problem through the device of a vacuum tube, and presently he produced a tube the size of a man's two fists, one on top of the other. The tube contained a charged matrix grid which "remembered" windows through which a current could flow and walls through which it could not. This horrifically expensive device was used by the Rand Corporation in its first computer, but not, as it turned out, by von Neumann, who went instead for a memory unit which used a deflected electron beam in a different kind of tube, rather like a TV picture tube. "Much cheaper," Rajchman says censoriously, "and much less reliable."

During the course of his work for von Neumann, Rajchman developed two principles to which he has clung for more than twenty years. The first was that any memory unit for scientific work had to offer "random access"—that is, every piece of the memory should be as easy and quick to reach as every other piece: "Universality and generality are the key words, unless you want your device to impose a format on your program." The second was that the one sure way to get usable random access memory was through wires: "If you make something for every point and run wires to it, then when you put electricity in you know you will get to it." The only way to meet these principles at anything like feasible cost was to make each bit of memory a little magnetic field which could control a little electric current—and Rajchman invented a "magnetic core" memory. (So did M.I.T.'s Jay Forrester, working quite separately; the dispute on who deserves what patent still rages.) Today's RCA memory units offer tens of millions of these cores, each separately wired to form fantastically elaborate miniature baskets.

All the early computers suffered bouts of inaccuracy, which would shut them down for days while people struggled to find out what was going wrong. Indeed, it was by no means easy to find out that something *had* gone wrong, and to keep tabs on the operations the early computers ran problems through twice, on different programs, with the thought that any discrepancy of result would tip off machine error. Quite apart from the wastage of half the capacity of the machine, this procedure gave the operators little clue to *where* in the machine the error was occurring. Mauchly and Eckert's ENIAC spent as much time at the psychiatrist's, having its logical processes dissected, as it did on the job. There were technical reasons why many mistakes would repeatedly pass undetected—and, as Richard W. Hamming of Bell Labs liked to point out, the idea that the programmers produced really independent programs for checking purposes could be entertained only by supervisors who forgot that their programmers lunched together.

Hamming is a man in his fifties with a long head and a narrow, innocent gaze, easily but incorrectly envisaged singing songs at Rotary. He got picked up from an instructor's job at the University of Louisville when the Manhattan Project needed somebody to do the pure math associated with the atom bomb, and he made the predictions of how big the test bomb would be at Los Alamos. "I stayed home when the others went off to the test site," he recalls; "I figured my math was probably wrong and I'd better start again. Turned out the calculations were very close, which was a good thing—if the bomb had been ten times as big, none of them would have come back."

Somebody from AT&T convinced Hamming that he could do numerical analysis just as comfortably at Bell Labs as at a university —teaching in his spare time as he wished—and Hamming came to the enormous research installation at Murray Hill, New Jersey. The Bell System was heavily engaged in installing automatic switchboards all over the country, and the mathematics of doing this economically and accurately was a matter of the greatest interest to top management. The relationship between the computer and the telephone switchboard is closer than you might think; and Hamming was interested in computers. He developed a "checking code" by which a machine could keep track of its own accuracy, step by step, with a minimal extra input from the program.

Hamming's code, which relies essentially on the distinction between odd and even numbers of pulses in each sequence of the matrix, is one of the few inventions in the field which provokes pure, green envy from the younger men, who like to say that many people were working in this direction and it was just accident that Hamming found it. The reason for the envy is the code's extreme simplicity; Hamming likes to say that the paper in which he first proposed his code, in 1950, "can be read and understood by anybody with high-school mathematics. Do you know Klein's book *Elementary Mathematics from an Advanced Standpoint?* Well, I'm interested in the opposite—advanced mathematics from an elementary standpoint."

Hamming says he has "turned my back on checking codes, so as not to spend the rest of my life on one thing, like Einstein on relativity. I'm really a philosopher. I've solved a lot of problems in my life, only to find they were the wrong problems, so now I'm looking for problems." He is the head of a division at Bell Labs, but the division is empty, because he refuses to have anybody working for him. Something based on Hamming's code is built so deeply into the hardware of all computers that only the old-timers are still conscious that somebody once invented it.

In the early 1950s most computers were handmade at universities or research centers, but Sperry-Rand had begun commercial production of its UNIVAC, and IBM salesmen were out in the field renting the Model 701. There was some skepticism about the future usefulness of the gadget. There are a limited number of problems, like ballistic trajectories, where it is useful to solve a single set of equations for an enormous range of variables, and programing a machine to handle new sets of equations was for many applications as time-consuming as solving them by hand. "A computer's conversation mode," says Irving Ziller of IBM, "is binary notation"—i.e., a number system with only two possible integers, 0 and 1. (What we call 2 is written 10; what we call 4—2^2—is written 100; what we call 8—2^3—is written 1000; what we call 256—2^8—is written 100-000000.) "That's a very tedious way to communicate."

Ziller, who came out of Brooklyn College with a math degree in 1952, joined John Backus at IBM in a search for a more economical way to communicate with the computer. Backus at twenty-seven was already a senior citizen of the computer world. The need was for a "language" which could be translated, by the computer itself, into the binary notation which was its "machine language." The result would be the reduction of new programs from the then-required tens of thousands of cards or miles of punched tape to a few dozen cards which would contain all the necessary information. A permanent program—a "compiler"—could then be implanted in the memory unit to do the translations.

"There had been efforts to build pseudo-languages," Ziller recalls, "but the result was always degradation of the performance of the machine. Our challenge was to demonstrate that one could set up a higher language, expressing usual mathematical notations—variables, subscripts, iterations—which was easily translatable by the machine. The problem was to pick the right level of language." Backus and Ziller called their language FORTRAN, for Formula Translator; its development required three back-breaking years. "I don't know why it worked," says Ziller. "We were lucky; we guessed the right level." The first FORTRAN was still fairly clumsy—Ziller's friend Paul Herwitz, who helped put together the Defense Department's computer system for the Distant Early Warning line, says that "the first wheel was probably octagonal." But it was thousands of times more convenient to use than machine language (as an elementary illustration of its advantages, it allowed programmers to write numbers in their accustomed decimal notation); and it proved capable of great refinement and sophistication. Other "high-level languages" followed.

Not long after the introduction of FORTRAN the engineering of computers changed out of all recognition, and the cost per usable unit of work or memory was reduced by several orders of magnitude, through the development of semiconductor diodes and transistors to replace the old hot and fragile tubes and by the invention of new ferrites to be magnetized in the computer memories. Microminiaturization required by the space program accelerated the invention of integrated circuits to be painted or etched onto bits of board, which could do the processing previously requiring many sockets and tubes and resistors and yard upon yard of spaghetti wiring. As the machines got bigger and faster, even the development of higher order languages became clearly inadequate as an answer to getting the most from a device which could process problems so much more quickly than they could be presented. A typist instructing a computer at the rate of one hundred English words per minute would feel he was flying—but on the time scale of the modern computer a hundred words a minute is, to use a common if not quite true analogy, like receiving a telegram at the rate of one character a day.

This difference in speed between mechanical input and electronic operation was initially managed by "batch processing." Programs were prepared on punch cards because that's what everybody had, and then coded onto magnetic tape, which could present instructions to the computer much more rapidly. The programmer received his results a few hours after he had delivered the cards to the computer room—and not infrequently the print-out informed him that he had committed a "format error" which had caused the machine to reject his program. He could then "debug it" and learn that he had left off a comma after a parenthesis in a FORTRAN statement.

But even the spinning reel of magnetic tape, it turned out, could not keep the machine fully employed. New devices were developed to permit several reels of tape to do their thing simultaneously, with the machine responding to all of them. Now several people, most notably M.I.T.'s John McCarthy (now at Stanford) and Fernando Corbató, decided that if "time-sharing" could be made to work with a few reels of tape, it could also be made to work with a much larger number of much slower inputs.

The new time-sharing, which purists call "interactive computing" to distinguish it from the kind of time-sharing that goes on with several reels of tape, provides a number of "access terminals" plugged into a single computer, allowing a number of users to work simultaneously on a single machine. The access terminals are usually electric typewriters. The simultaneity is from the users' point of view alone, of course: the machine is processing their programs one at a time, but simply switching its attention around the group at electronic speeds. The switching is accomplished, naturally, by a separate program built into the guts of an associated separate computer.

Time-sharing has created an entirely new mode of interaction with the machine. The user can now be "on line in real time." The computer can tell him when he is wrong (which makes possible "computer assisted instruction," today just a trivial way of drilling students but tomorrow maybe something more); and he can tell the computer when it is wrong (which makes possible the growth of "heuristic" programs and "artificial intelligence" by giving the computer a constantly available real world—the programmer—against which to test successive approximations).

The idea of time-sharing is not really strange—it is comparable to a chess master playing fifty "simultaneous" games, but moving around the room very quickly. The guiding principle of the program is the allocation of priorities to things which can be done very quickly —that is, to things which do not involve extensive and repeated searches of the memory cores. But the writing of a program to allocate time and (especially) memory is an enormous challenge. M.I.T.'s Project MAC is in process of moving from a system which permits about thirty access terminals to be used at once to a system which will have place for about fifty. "Its complexity," says Robert M. Fano, the project's director, hitting his forehead with the palm of his hand, "is at the very limit of human understanding." Part of this complexity, incidentally, is required by the need to maintain the security and privacy of each user's programs. "Experience has shown," Fano wrote grimly in a recent issue of the *Journal of Engineering Education,* "that vandalism within a time-sharing system and the forging of user accounts are to be expected in universities as well as elsewhere."

Fano is Italian by birth, a small, round, dark man of deceptively sloppy appearance who came to M.I.T. as a graduate student in electrical engineering shortly before the war. Both in hardware and in concept, he is with John McCarthy the pioneer of the idea of the "computer utility" to "raise very substantially," as he told a meeting at Dartmouth, "the level of complexity which the human mind may successfully comprehend and contend with." Fano likes to say that "when you put an electric drill in a man's hand he can drill not only faster but better, because he can concentrate on keeping it straight." He looks for a future in which people will communicate *with each other* through computers, "because intellectual activities are primarily cooperative in nature."

At the end of a recent interview, a reporter congratulated Fano on his extraordinary power in the use of English, which is not, after all, his language. He disowned the compliment. "My English is not so good," he said. "But I think very clearly. . . ."

All right, now. So why are you confused?

Because, unfortunately, the computer is for the normal human animal an inevitably confusing device. Even scientists and mathematicians have their troubles with it. But different people are differently victimized.

The worst off are the non-hams, the people who have never played around with electrical equipment of any sort and do not realize that an electric signal can be split and used simultaneously in different operations. As all the "logic" circuits of a computer involve subjecting inputs to different kinds of combination and then comparing and combining the results, the man who has never read an elementary wiring diagram gets lost at the start. This is not necessarily any more disabling than getting lost later.

Another inevitable victim of confusion is the non-spy, who has never paid any attention to cryptography, for whom a number is a number. Computers use numbers most of the time as parts of a code, normally with a "word" which consists of seven "bits," arrayed to provide 128 possible different combinations of Yes-or-No. (The number zero, which might stand for A, could be No-No-No-No-No-No-No; the number 13, which might stand for M, would be No-No-No-Yes-Yes-No-Yes; the number 57, which might stand for dx/dy, would be No-Yes-Yes-Yes-No-No-Yes, etc.) And a computer's code is not restricted to the expression of written symbols. Because we are dealing with electric signals rather than with inert letters or numbers, we can use the code to identify all sorts of desired output, like brightening a dot on a TV picture tube or oscilloscope, or lowering a drill punch to a predetermined depth in an engine block.

But even people who can follow the logic circuit easily, and can understand the recognition function of the code, grow totally confused by the contrast between the simple processes they understand and the computer print-out, which belches forth from the plugged-in typewriter at the rate of 120 lines a minute (so that this article could be typed—or for that matter set in justified lines of type—in something less than five minutes, using only a fraction of the capacity of the computer). These people are the nonphilosophers, and their difficulty is conceptual. Man's mind is not built to comprehend operations which occur at rates up to several million per second. Hamming, with his belief in the elementary standpoint, once explained the significance of these speeds to a symposium on applied mathematics: "Imagine two situations: First you have only one dollar, and second you have a million dollars. You can readily see that this difference is not trifling but rather it can affect your whole outlook."

Nobody does in fact live with these speeds. "I have no gut feeling for what it means to have something happen in a nanosecond," says Anthony Oettinger, who heads a computer science section at Harvard (and is president of the Association for Computing Machinery, which combines the function of professional and trade association). A nanosecond, in words, is a billionth of a second; the biggest new computers provide information retrieval at the rate of a few nanoseconds per bit. "But there's nothing in my daily work for which the absence of this intuition makes any practical difference. We have an operation now that takes eleven seconds, which is too damned long. We think there are repetitions in the program which could be eliminated and would save forty percent, and that's what we're working on."

Most imaginative programing is still done on a wholly pragmatic (Fano says "phenomenological") basis—we make this change, and we see what happens. The attitude, very difficult for people without training in physical science, is that of the man confronting the "black box"—he knows his inputs, he knows his outputs, and in one sense what happens in between is irrelevant, provided he can accurately predict the results. Especially in working with the big new scientific computers, with their masses of modular microcircuits, even the most sophisticated programmers have only a fairly vague notion of how the machine secures some of its results.

The central distinction between different kinds of black boxes is whether they are primarily memory ("storage and retrieval") systems, which is what business needs, or primarily computational systems for research use. The computer which prepares the payroll simply churns forward through lists of names, slotting in as needed appropriate changes in salary data, hours worked, percentages for deduction, etc. Though the memory function is vital, the memory device can conveniently be a simple reel of magnetic tape, which gives a predetermined sequential access rather than random access, because the payroll is processed from Joe Aadvark to Harry Zilch, or by division of the company, and not in an unpredictable order. Sequential memories are also suitable for activities like listing the contents of the warehouse, or for calculating the status of insurance policy holders or owners of mutual fund shares, or for continuously computing interest on savings bank deposits or printing out people's bank balances.

Other activities need the computer as a kind of superfiling system, so decisions can be made on the basis of full information. A fine example is the scheduling of examinations at, say, a college with 10,-000 students who among them take 1,100 courses, all of which must be examined in 150 rooms over nine days. If the aim is to assure that no student is scheduled for two exams at the same time, the job is beyond the abilities of any person, because nobody can keep that much information in his head. Properly programed, however, the computer can assign each course to a room of the right size at a time which guarantees the elimination of conflicts. (The student who dislikes being in a world where he may not fold, spindle or mutilate might pause for a moment and consider how much more he would dislike being kept in an exam room for nine hours straight, with a proctor bringing him a ham sandwich, because human incapacity produced a faulty schedule.) For this purpose, a memory on reels of magnetic tape is inadequate, because the machine must do considerable checking back on already processed data. But the electronic speeds of Rajchman's magnetic cores are not required: a mechanical whirling drum or disc with magnetic coatings will be sufficiently random and sufficiently fast. Note, incidentally, that the computer is not computing when it does this sort of job—all the math is in the design of a program to optimize the sequence of the processing operations.

Finally, a very different black box is required if the machine is to be used for immensely rapid computation of immense numbers of variables—to control a rocket, or to guide an airplane into a socked-in airport, considering constantly all factors of height, speed, distance, engine thrust, wing design, temperature, humidity, etc. Such computers can simulate scientific experiments, changing patterns of DNA molecules, for example, or analyzing the flow of liquid through a bent pipe. This system demands an enormous random-access memory delivering its information at maximum speed, because so many possible different programs must be available for processing depending on the results of prior computation. Indeed, the programmers for the big scientific computers are now demanding memories far beyond the state of the manufacturer's art. "A billion-bit memory would be very useful," says RCA's Rajchman. "But if you had a machine which turned out a wired core every second, it would need thirty years of continuous full-time operation to produce a billion-bit memory." So the makers of memories are seeking to cut deeper, to the superconductivity of metals at the temperature of liquid helium, the vast stores of information that can be etched on a photographic plate using the coherent light of a laser beam, devices to be used by many and understood by very few.

Very large computers with very large memory units are beginning to force changes in human thought processes; and this in itself has become a special function of the machine. "When one attempts to put many of the well-known processes of mathematics on a computing machine," Hamming told a meeting of the American Association for the Advancement of Science, "one finds that there is a great vagueness, and waving of hands, and occasional shouting of 'Any fool knows!' and that in the long run a much more careful examination of the basic ideas and processes must be made before one can make much progress. I have been repeatedly shocked to find out how often I thought I knew what I was talking about, but that in the acid test of describing explicitly to a machine what was going on I was revealed to have been both ignorant and extremely superficial."

Man's intelligence as improved by evolution bottoms on the search for equilibrium, and the computer makes contact with a world of endless flux. "There are problems," says Fano at M.I.T., "which you cannot deal with in English or mathematics because you need a flow chart. And without the computer you cannot keep track of what you are doing in the flow chart." As Joyce's Finnegan saw, toward the very end, it is all part of Tobecontinued's tale. This is a newer world than America or the moon, or perhaps even the inside of the atom, and it would be presumptuous (not to say silly) to predict what will be discovered there.

To this point we have been considering the machine itself, and some of those who have made it what it is today. But the stock market says IBM is worth more than General Motors because of the people who have given the machine practical things to do. Let us take a quick look at that, and at them.

For example, Alex Bernstein, a round-faced man rather quiet behind horn-rimmed glasses, came out of New York's City College in 1951 with a degree in mathematics and went on to Columbia to study medieval literature, paying his bills by solving cubic equations for Columbia's department of civil engineering. He was drafted in 1953, and the Army a year later put him to work at IBM, in civilian clothes, to help simulate on computers the effectiveness of varying air defense systems. Later he sold IBM the idea of a chess-playing program, which he refined to the point where it could beat most pretty good players but not masters. (This program caused internal uproar at IBM. Stefan Bauer-Mengleberg, formerly a philosophy teacher at New York University, then part-time conductor of the St. Louis Philharmonic, now president of New York's Mannes School of Music, also teaches the theory of mathematical theories at IBM's in-house university. He remembers a time "when all programing at IBM came to a halt, because everybody was playing chess and claiming he was working for Alex Bernstein.")

When the chess games stopped, Bernstein proceeded to simulate on the computer the process of manufacture in a large job shop— that is, a factory where orders are produced individually, as in a turbine generator plant (GE had commissioned the original study) or at a heavy machine tool maker. "It's a problem of n work groups and m machines," Bernstein said the other day. "You make your own mix. We came up with 125 variables which define your factory. You have the problem of a moving bottleneck—you buy a new machine for the job that seems to be holding you up, and it changes nothing. Sometimes you can make it work by changing the dispatching rules, which order gets done first. In any machine shop there's a tremendous bunching of orders completed at twelve and at four-thirty: people time their work so they get something done just before they leave the bench. Then, companies have their own criteria. GE has a union, and they can lay people off, so their target is to minimize labor costs. IBM never lays anybody off, isn't interested in using fewer employees, wants a big backlog. You have to put all these variables into the computer. Any change a company wants to make, it's only intelligent to try it out first on the computer. When I left IBM, there were eighty companies and the Harvard Business School using the program."

From IBM Bernstein proceeded to a social-science research operation called Simulmatics, where he drew up a program which simulated the 1960 election for John F. Kennedy, using census data and past and current public opinion polls. Comparing the simulation with the current polls, Simulmatics advised Kennedy that he had already lost all the votes he would lose on the religious issue but had not yet won all the votes he could win—and The Family invested heavily in spot commercials for televising in predominantly Catholic areas, showing the candidate's confrontation with the Protestant ministers in Houston. Among Bernstein's last jobs at Simulmatics, before he was seduced back into the business world in January, was a program for the Riot Commission, which provided a way to index and tabulate under appropriate headings all the newspaper stories and broadcast coverage of the Civil Disorders of 1967, as they were reported in twenty-three cities.

Bernstein's work has been at one extreme of the art of applying computers to problems, in that he has been controlled at all times by the information available to him. At the other extreme is Paul Gilmore, who is interested exclusively in theory, and who teamed with Ralph Gomory to create a computer program for "linear programing," perhaps the most famous single piece of work in the field. A Canadian who came to IBM in 1958 after teaching math at Penn State and Toronto, Gilmore began his career in commerce with the most abstruse imaginable question, trying to find out whether computers could generate mathematical proofs. (The answer is maybe but not yet.) Then he ran into somebody at a cocktail party who talked about an optimization problem and said it was like something Gilmore was working on. "It wasn't," Gilmore says, "but I got interested."

The problem was to tell a dress manufacturer how to cut the patterns from his cloth in the one way that would waste the least cloth. The approach was through a matrix which listed activities down the columns and goals along the rows, but a matrix listing all the possibilities would be too big to manage. Gilmore and Gomory worked out a solution by which a piece of the matrix was kept in the computer and the rest was generated and substituted as needed. Paper manufacturers immediately appropriated the program to tell them how to cut huge rolls of newsprint to meet orders from newspapers, and more recently it has been adapted for use by the manufacturers of enriched chicken feed and sausages.

Gilmore himself moved on to simpler things, and is now working on the foundations of set theory. Though his offices are at the IBM research lab—a Dark Tower curved and sheathed in black glass in the quiet hills of northern Westchester—Gilmore has no terminal from the computer in his room. "I haven't been near the beast," he said recently, "in two years."

Somewhere between Bernstein and Gilmore in the degree of his interest in information is an apparently casual young man named David Fox, now thirty-two, who had his own consulting company half a dozen years ago, and last year sold out at a stiff price which brought the purchaser nothing but a few personal service contracts. "When I had my own business and I had to be a salesman," Fox said, "I described myself as a system understander."

The son of the head of the nuclear reactor at Brookhaven Laboratory, Fox abandoned physics for math ("because I realized I didn't like physics") and while at N.Y.U. in 1956 he got a part-time job to do the donkey work on batch processing of tapes sent down daily from Brookhaven to New York. "I couldn't get any studying done," he recalls, "because I had to jump up every three minutes and change tapes. FORTRAN was just coming in. I said, God damn it, I'm doing things the computer could do itself. I had to design a way to stack tapes so I could study. It's only now when I think about it that I realize I was twenty years old and tearing apart the most powerful and complicated machine then in existence. But I got it to work, and after that I would just sit cross-legged on the console, four hours at a time."

Fox's biggest customer when he had his own business was IBM, for which he simulated the performance and marketing of possible future computers still on the drawing boards; the project was called Early Objective Product Evaluation. He also did a fair amount of war gaming for the Defense Department, but found the work distasteful—especially after his simulation of the performance of an aircraft carrier in time of nuclear war indicated that the carrier was sure to be sunk, and an admiral rejected the study with the comment, "Aircraft carriers don't sink." A project of which he is especially proud made a start toward the retrieval of case citations for lawyers. At one point, Fox claims (others are skeptical), the program was sufficiently refined that a question on the phrase "did violence to the law" produced from the computer a case with the phrase "made a mockery of justice."

As head of an R&D division at Leasco (which does much of the computer work for the National Aeronautics and Space Administration), Fox is working particularly on problems of "natural language. Decision makers shouldn't have to rely on me to turn their questions into programs," he says. "That's why computers should speak English. Anyway, I've promised my wife she will have a computer to do the housework. That computer is going to have to understand spoken English [actually, in the case of Mrs. Fox, spoken Swedish will do as well], and it's going to have to *see*."

None of the pieces of Fox's vision, incidentally, is wholly implausible. The handling of natural language, in problems like translation by computer, has proved to be much more difficult than was realized by programmers or linguists (even at their own low standards for written English), but the sort of ultra-large memory Rajchman is talking about will eventually produce the resources for the necessary subtlety. "Voice recognition" is already in the works, though at present only for the dull purpose of building systems by which the facilities of the telephone company can be used for automated ordering of merchandise and paying of bills. And machines that "see" have been built at the Stanford Research Institute (where a computer on wheels finds its way around its home of children's blocks) and by Marvin Minsky at M.I.T. (whose machine has a working artificial hand, "understands" gravity and builds towers of blocks). If computer intelligence is indeed like human intelligence, Albert J. Caron's recent experiments with very young children would argue that getting from squared-off blocks to curved shapes is going to be a hell of a job; but only a very brave man would wish to commit himself to an inevitable maximum value on the learning curve of future computers.

It is hard to predict what future programmers are going to be like, too. The men who have brought the computer to its present competence do not have much in common; indeed, though the most important contributions have been made by men whose background was in math or the "hard" sciences, the field has had significant input from psychologists, linguists, philosophers, even business-school scholars of industrial management. Anthony Oettinger got authorization this winter for two new tenure professorships in his computer science wing of Harvard's Department of Engineering and Applied Science; one of his new professors came originally from medicine and biology, the other out of linguistics. "The Association for Computing Machinery has been around twenty years," Oettinger says, "and I'm the first president of it who didn't grow up somewhere else. Anybody in the second generation—who studied computer science at college—has to be under forty."

IBM's David Mayer, who has been studying computer personnel for the Association of Computing Machinery, says that the attribute which correlates best with success in programming is "general intelligence—which also correlates with good lawyers, good doctors and so forth. That means anybody can program. Vocabulary is a good indicator of both intelligence and programing potential." Donald Madden, director of A.C.M., looks for "the brightest guy I can find. That's the only thing that stands up."

Bell Labs' Hamming is not so sure. "Once you get beyond 120–130 IQ," he says, "it doesn't do much good to be more intelligent. You need drive, of course, energy. But you see lots of men with energy running around aimlessly. The most important thing is a sense of how and when to do the job—a sense of *taste*."

One psychological test seems to predict performance as a programmer: the Strong Vocational Interest Blank, which lists kinds of people, activities and subjects and asks whether the person taking the test "likes," "dislikes" or is "indifferent" to them. At the bottom of the like list among programmers is "energetic people," who are liked by only 14 percent; and only 22 percent like "observing birds" or "giving first aid." "Algebra" and "mathematics" inevitably top the list with 90 percent on the like side, but right after them comes "conservative people," who are liked by 84 percent of programmers (only one percent dislike them). THINK.

David Fox feels that the key to whether or not a man will make a first-class programmer is his "affinity for a foreign language. He enjoyed Latin grammar, French grammar. It's an ability to use symbols that are not ingrained in you." M.I.T.'s Fano, remembering his struggles with English, has little affection for this proposition, and believes that at the present time the closest correlation is still with the sort of detail work involved in masculine mechanical hobbies: "The kids at M.I.T. who are wizards at writing programs were big members of the model railroading club. Putting together that sort of thing takes the same talents as putting together the usual program. But all this is changing.

"At the very beginning," Fano continues, "you get artistic types, who contribute pure imagination. In radio, people like Marconi were artists: they didn't know what they were doing. Then comes the more systematic, introspective—let me say, scientific—person. In a lot of the work, even today, raw native intelligence is still worth more than a lot of experience. But we are coming to a time when the computer will be used to develop and draw consequences from models much more complicated than the human mind can handle. Then we will need the scientifically trained mind, because to do such work you have to understand what it means to make a model and test it."

After a decade of ducking the issue—apparently for fear that somebody could accuse them of doing something useful, which violates the liberal arts tradition—the universities are now beginning to train people to work in and with computers. (The burning question of academic politics, whether this training should be done by the math department or the engineers, is being resolved on most campuses in favor of the engineers, because the mathematicians snobbishly don't want the job.) To this new breed there will be nothing at all unusual about aspects of the machine that are still highly exotic to people like David Fox—who found recently to his horror that a problem he had solved for a fat fee after months of work only five years ago has become a routine examination question in an *undergraduate* course. And Fano must be right in his feeling that the newcomers will see new worlds in a new way. Man, who knew he was a tiny speck in the universe before he knew anything else, has learned (not always painlessly) to live with notions just as uncomfortable as the discovery that brains need not be made of meat. Meanwhile, it is comforting—at least to the computer science students—to know that the new generation of programmers will count for much more than the new generation of machines.

14

The Man Who Put the Rhinestones on Miami: Morris Lapidus

[The assignment to write this article grew out of an *Esquire* editorial meeting in 1962, and it was the brainchild of Byron Dobell. Esky was very pleased with the piece and bought it, but for personal reasons unknown at the time of the assignment, could not run it. So it wound up, cheerfully, at *Harper's,* where Russell Lynes helped rid it of three rather pompous introductory pages. Larry Tisch has since gone on to buy cigarette companies and such, and has put together one of the nation's larger conglomerate corporations.]

THE PEOPLE who invest their money in buildings have gone to Florida again, as they do every winter, and between massages they are looking around them; and in the North, architects and designers are getting braced to greet the new wave of kitsch that annually accompanies the returning travelers. For Florida has become the home of a kind of gaudy, frantic, highly temporary luxury, and its influence is now felt through the country in hotels and motels, restaurants and cocktail lounges, even in the lobbies of new office buildings and apartment houses. The décor provokes rage among people who take pride in their visual taste: when the American Institute of Architects held its annual convention at the Americana–Bal Harbour in 1963, one of the speakers opened his remarks by denouncing "this vulgar building" and its "thin, cheap, improbable materials." His audience echoed him, and was only slightly abashed when Morris Lapidus, the architect of the Americana, rose to defend his work as "a place where people can have fun."

Colleagues, professional critics, and assorted intellectuals have had lots of fun with Morris Lapidus, making cracks about his buildings and tarring him with all the fancy feathers of the spreading Florida style. It can be argued that they are right. A conventionally handsome, gray-haired, soft-spoken man who never designed a building until he was over fifty, Lapidus (pronounced *"lapp-*idus") has been the premier provider of jewels for the paste diadem of Miami Beach, and he was the first to carry the style north, with a green hotel called The Summit that opened on New York's Lexington Avenue in 1961. But the explosion of sniggers that greeted The Summit ("a very *nice* hotel, but a little far from the beach") rose also from the fact that Lapidus was safe to attack. His other New York hotels, especially the Americana atop the theater district, made the attacks even safer. Angry at the packing crates that their architects were planting up and down their avenues, but taught to value plainness for its own sake, New Yorkers had been looking for a target. Like the carny at whom the rustics throw baseballs at the county fair, Lapidus had been paid to provide one.

The attacks have not hurt him professionally. He has recently designed or is working on flocks of apartment houses in New York, Washington, Miami, and Puerto Rico; he is the architect for what will be the largest privately owned office building in Washington; he is architect-in-ordinary to the national chain of "Quality Courts," with a number of motels on the drawing boards for them and others— and he is about to extend his influence abroad, to luxury restaurants being built by England's Lyons Group (formerly renowned for its one-arm "Corner Houses").

Personally, however, Lapidus has suffered. An architect who has known him for years finds a modern tragedy in intellectual New York's reaction to his friend's work: "You know, he's never built anything so hideous as the Coliseum, or so depressing as that junk up at Columbia, or so totally undistinguished as those Emery Roth boxes on Park Avenue. The one thing you must say about Morris, whatever his problems, he has always thought of himself as somebody who works to make people happy."

Actually, Lapidus does not come from Miami Beach at all, though he and his wife live there now, in five rather small, overfurnished rooms on the second and third floors of a modest FHA-financed apartment house he designed himself. He was born in Russia and raised in the Williamsburg ghetto of Brooklyn, and he lived in Brooklyn until 1959. "The Fontainebleau and the Eden Roc," he says, "were designed while I was hanging on a strap on the BMT subway. When I moved to Miami I used to joke that I didn't know when I'd find time to get ideas, without the subway ride."

As a boy, Lapidus had exactly one talent—he could draw. (He still can: he makes his own renderings, and the walls in his home and his New York and Miami offices are covered with watercolors and oils he has done in a significant mixture of styles, now Manet, now Redon, now Turner, now blue-period Picasso.) He was "left back" twice in elementary school, "mostly because I was so shy my teacher didn't know I was there." At Boys' High he found the love of his life: the theater. When he went on to N.Y.U., it was as a drama student.

"You must keep in mind about Morris," says Charles Spector of A. S. Beck, who commissioned a number of store designs from him in the old days and introduced him to his first Florida hotel types, "that he's a frustrated actor. If we still had a Beaux Arts ball in this city, and somebody asked Morris to do the sets for it, he'd drop everything else he was doing, even if it was the biggest hotel or office building in the world, and design the sets." He recently did just about that, writing a revue (complete with monologue for himself, attacking contemporary architecture) for a party at the Lambs Club.

"I was in college," Lapidus recalls, "in the days of the Little Theater movement, and if you wanted to get in you did everything— painted scenery, made costumes. I used to get parts by blackmailing them, telling them I wouldn't paint the scenery unless I had a part. Then I was a standby in one of the first Theater Guild productions, sitting around every night backstage, in case somebody couldn't go on. I decided it was dull, hanging around waiting for cues. All my life I'd lived with the fact that I could draw, and with the question, 'What am I going to do with it?' I decided I'd be a scene designer. But to be a scene designer, you had to be an architect."

Lapidus went to the Columbia School of Architecture. "He must have been the kind of student that annoyed me most," says his son Alan, who won the school's gold medal in the Class of '63 (even though he had led a picket line in 1962 to protest the new "uglies" on the Columbia campus) and who now works in Lapidus' office.

"He always did beautiful renderings of his projects, and he always got them in ahead of time." There were other and nastier reasons why Lapidus would be unpopular. Neither the architecture profession nor Nicholas Murray Butler's Columbia was then highly hospitable to Jews, and some years were still to pass before Lapidus could shake the manner and accent of Williamsburg. Most of Lapidus' friends believe that the scars of his years at architecture school have never healed—that his inability to form partnerships with other architects unless he believes he trained them himself, his recurrent feuding with the American Institute of Architects, which once expelled him, are the result of his three lonely years at Columbia.

When Lapidus emerged from architecture school, nobody needed a new scene designer: "They all said, 'You're an architect—go work for an architect.'" After his internship, Lapidus found a job with Ross-Frankel, Inc., a construction firm, and for sixteen years he designed for jobs on which Ross-Frankel wished to bid. In the Depression, the only work around was modernization—and it was mostly the low-priced stores that could afford to modernize.

Some Lapidus store designs of the 1930s are still visible in New York, and are acquiring an antique charm, like Herberts ("Home of Blue White Diamonds") in Harlem, the elevator lobbies in the RCA building, Sachs Furniture, the Beck shoe store at Fifth Avenue and Thirty-seventh, Regal shoe stores scattered about the city. Other examples of vintage Lapidus have disappeared in a further wave of modernization by more fashion-conscious businesses like Doubleday and Wallachs. Much of this work was in the open, clean style of the German *Modernismus* of the twenties, which was emphatically *not* what Lapidus had been taught at Columbia, the last of American architecture schools to abandon Chicago's Columbian Exposition and the French Second Empire. Lapidus' fanciest interior involved the construction of elaborate wood paneling for the executive offices of Seagram, a firm which was later to reverse field entirely, moving up from the Lapidus version of the English eighteenth century to the even more expensive austerities of Miës van der Rohe and Philip Johnson in its new Park Avenue building.

In 1943, urged on by his wife, a former Brooklyn schoolteacher very proud of and ambitious for her husband and their two sons, Lapidus left Ross-Frankel and set up shop on his own. ("You're a coward," she said. "If you're going to go on working for somebody else all your life, I can't respect you.") Presently he bought a brownstone in Manhattan's East Forties, remodeled it to look rather like a store, and moved in with a partner, associates, and staff.

With the postwar boom, the jobs got bigger. Lapidus designed windows and interiors for Bond clothing stores all over the country (including the seven floors below the hotel in Cincinnati's Terrace Plaza), shoe stores, department stores, showrooms. He worked in a bewildering variety of styles, from the severely rectangular John Forsythe shop on Madison Avenue to the mishmash embroidery of Martin's on Long Island, but the aim was always the same: to sell. Though some of his work was pleasing even to severe tastes, Lapidus rested his case as a store architect less on the aesthetics than on the efficiency of his designs—they worked as stores, and they pulled people through the doors.

"I might as well admit it," Lapidus says. "I'm still selling like mad. Schools, hotels, offices, apartment houses—they're the broad form of merchandising. Everybody does it. The lawyer makes an argument, his opponent says, 'I'll buy that.' No one yells at Madison Avenue for ballyhooing—why do they yell at the architect?"

It was Lapidus' talent for ballyhoo that was in Charles Spector's mind when his friend Ben Novack called from Florida in 1949 and asked whether Spector knew anybody who might "add some flairs" to his new Sans Souci hotel, which was already half built. Harry Mufson, then Novack's partner, came up to New York and had dinner with Lapidus, who looked over the plans for the hotel and began making suggestions for grand entrance, façade treatment, lobby arrangements, restaurant decor. Mufson got excited, and asked how he and Novack could buy Lapidus' designs.

"If you like my ideas," Lapidus said, "I'll present them to your architect."

Mufson wanted to know how much. Lapidus, who has somehow managed to avoid becoming rich, quoted "a ridiculous fee—fifteen thousand dollars." Mufson was not used to professional fees; he shook his head sadly and said, "Too much," and dinner ended with expressions of mutual esteem.

On his return to Miami Beach, Mufson described Lapidus' ideas to his partner. "If he has what we want," said Ben Novack, who by shrewd prodigality had managed to become exceedingly rich, "that's not too much."

The Sans Souci, finished by Morris Lapidus, opened lavish and gay and more than a little exotic. Many architects who saw it when new thought it was flashy to the edge—but not over the edge—of outrage. One of them says that it met rather tastefully the special needs of Miami Beach décor: "To convince the sucker who's spending fifty bucks a day that he's really spending a hundred bucks a day." Lapidus found to his delight that a hotel gave him a chance to exercise his theatrical tastes to the full—he could design not only the night-club and ballroom stage, and the sets, but also the costumes for waiters and waitresses, busboys, chambermaids, etc.

The triumph of the Sans Souci brought Lapidus half a dozen other Miami Beach commissions "to doctor other people's hotels." He also decorated public areas for Executive House in Chicago, the Ambassador in Los Angeles, the Concord and Grossinger's in the Catskills. Indirectly, the Sans Souci also brought Lapidus into the housing field, which now accounts for most of his work. A Brooklyn builder named Fred Trump called him and asked him to decorate the lobby in a new apartment house Trump was finishing in Queens. "I told him, 'I don't do lobbies.' He said, 'You did one at Sans Souci.' So then I designed Trump Village, thirty-eight hundred apartments at Coney Island."

"On those first Florida hotels," Lapidus recalls with some distaste, "I was the pastry chef. But I learned a lot. Then one day I picked up the paper and saw that Novack had bought the Firestone estate, and was going to put up a big hotel to be called the Fontainebleau, and I was going to be the architect. I had to call him up to see if it was true."

"Morris," said Ben Novack the other day, leaning back in his chair in his office at the Fontainebleau and eying his interlocutor coldly, "was a storefront architect for Bond and A. S. Beck. Morris had talent as a decorator, not much as an architect. You must understand, Morris and I are not friends. When I added the new wing to the Fon-tan-blue, I didn't go to Morris. I'm not here to praise Caesar, if you understand what I mean, I'm here to bury him.

"Anyway, in 1949 I was putting up the Sans Souci [Mufson's name does not cross Novack's lips; they had a fight], and I wanted a little more décor just before the final building was completely finished. I brought Morris in at a very small price to help me booster up the finished detail of the Sans Souci. And the little flairs he gave it, I was satisfied.

"Now, many people on this island look to me. If I make a mistake, they'll copy me. Other people hired Morris for the same purpose —Algiers, Lido, Nautilus, Biltmore Terrace. Then I was going to do Fon-tan-blue, and I had every architect in the country chasing me. Morris read in the paper he was going to be the architect of the fabulous 560-room Fon-tan-blue. He called me up, he said, 'Ben, how about I fly right down?' I said, 'No, Morris, let me send you a plot plan. You do some rough sketches, very inexpensive, then come down.'

"He came down with twenty-six sketches. I said, 'These for me?' He said, 'Yes.' I said, 'May I do anything I want with them?' He said, 'Yes.' I tore them up and threw them in the wastebasket. I designed what I wanted. I said, 'Morris, all I want you to do is paint up a rendering of this so I can use it to get mortgages. . . .' "

A gamecock of a man with a grating voice and a need for adulation ("The reason these people want to own hotels," says Lapidus' wife, "is that when a man walks into his own hotel, everybody falls down dead"), Novack was not an easy client. But he had grown up at his parents' hotel in New Jersey and spent his entire adult life in the business: he knew it backstairs, upstairs, and downstairs, and introduced Lapidus to many mysteries. And he was the only client Lapidus has ever had who was willing to spend whatever it cost to buy the best in materials and supplies. ("I insisted on gran-doar," Novack says. "When I went for plumbing, I went to Crane De Luxe

—then you get something. I am probably responsible for the rejuvenation of marble in this country.") The many changes Novack has made in the Fontainebleau since he broke with Lapidus are wrongheaded—the mausoleum added to the south end to increase seating capacity in the night club, the huge north wing with another four hundred rooms, the further flairs in an already perilously fancy lobby —and it is hard to take too seriously Novack's claim to credit for the features that made the original Fontainebleau pleasant to look upon. But it is also true that, with the possible exception of the stark one-story laboratory for the Variety Children's Hospital in Miami, Lapidus has never built anything else of the aesthetic quality of the Fontainebleau façade and public areas, the simple quarter-circle of a building embracing the formal gardens and the ocean, the same curve expressed in the lobby less by the walls than by the parallel lines of the marble-covered steelwork. (Lapidus' later attempts to set "curved" lobby areas into essentially rectangular spaces, by the use of circular rugs and furniture arrangements in the Aruba Hotel and in Washington's new International Inn, are inevitably far less successful.) "The Fontainebleau," says Lapidus simply, in his most self-deprecatory manner, "is the building Frank Lloyd Wright almost complimented me on, when I met him."

After Fontainebleau, Lapidus did an office building in Miami ("the first time I ever had to design steelwork; I walked past that building every day, expecting it to fall down"), and the ornaments and landscape architecture for the stagy but charming pedestrian mall at Lincoln Road, the prime shopping street of Miami Beach. This design provided the only occasion when anyone ever accused Lapidus of a lack of interest in selling. His first plan had included benches along the walks, and the Lincoln Road merchants insisted he take them away, because people would sit on them when they could be shopping. In the absence of benches, people sit on the big concrete flowerpots that dot the center of the mall. While Lapidus had his office on Lincoln Road, he had to enter the building from the rear—if he walked down the mall the storekeepers would run out, grab him by the lapels, spin him around to the offending places, and say accusingly, "Look! They're sitting!"

The success of the Fontainebleau made Lapidus the hot architect for people planning resort hotels. He built on the Florida Keys, on the Gulf Coast, in Jamaica, and in the Netherlands Antilles. And he built more on Miami Beach, first the Eden Roc, just north of the Fontainebleau, for Novack's old partner Mufson; then, farther north on the atoll, at Bal Harbour, the first of several Americanas he was to design for the Tisch brothers, proprietors of Loew's Hotels and Loew's Theaters. This original Americana remains the *locus classicus* of what people dislike in Lapidus' work. Its senseless lobby area, centered around a huge glass funnel which drops through the floor and contains an assortment of apparently man-eating plants, conveys the you-can't-sit-here feeling the merchants miss in the Lincoln Road mall; and the windows of the rooms, angled out from the building in a sawtoothed pattern, offer a continuously nervewracking vista of randomly juxtaposed corners. The Tisch brothers, who have a very sensitive eye for figures on a ledger, thought it was beautiful. "And today," says Larry Tisch triumphantly, "ninety-five per cent of the public agrees with me."

Laurence Alan Tisch (about forty and almost bald, the financial wizard of the pair) and Preston Robert Tisch (a few years younger, the construction and operations expert) had warmed up for their building ventures by leasing New York's Belmont Plaza for three years, and when the Americana–Bar Harbour opened, they were ready to return to New York. "You can't have anything good in America," says Larry Tisch, "without being good in New York." Between the summer of 1961 and the end of 1963, the Tisches opened six new hotels in Manhattan, four of them (The Summit, Howard Johnson's Motor Lodge, the Americana–New York, and Loew's Motor Inn) by Lapidus.

The first question about The Summit was why Lapidus—or any architect—would attempt it. The problem was not capable of solution on any terms. Nobody could build a convincing "luxury hotel" with only seventy feet of frontage on Lexington Avenue, where the entrance had to be. Lapidus' solution was to leave the Lexington façade, which could never look like much anyway, a wall of blank marble, and to stress the length of the plot by giving the 51st Street façade a curve out, then in again. (Lapidus says, somewhat to the surprise of his fellow architects, that the curve also gave him space for an additional six rooms per floor.) On the standard New York gridiron block, its curve oppressed by the flat façade of the urine-colored Grolier Building across the way, Lapidus' green Summit was simply a freak.

The lobby was remarkable. On the seventy-foot frontage there had to be a coffee shop and a restaurant as well as the hotel entrance, leaving room for a lobby not much larger than an old-fashioned living room. To conceal the tiny size of the lobby, Lapidus covered the walls (one of which had to be a mere partition less than ceiling height, to meet fire laws) with what can be described only as a tropical garden of Lapidoid shapes, based apparently on traceries of a duck waddle. As a final complication, the hotel was given the suggestive name of Summit (it had originally been called the Americana East), and the advertising people trumpeted it dramatically as "New York's first hotel since the Waldorf" in incessant commercials over radio station WMGM, which the Tisch brothers then owned. In one sense, the ballyhoo was successful—nobody pointed out that The Summit was just an unimportant middling sort of commercial hotel. Instead, everyone screamed about how ugly it was.

For both the Tisch brothers and Lapidus, public reaction to The Summit was a thunderclap from a blue sky. They lost a little confidence in each other, and in themselves. The lobby décor was considerably softened, though Lapidus still thinks it was about right as it started and the Tisch brothers feel much too much fuss was made about it. "If we have to credit everything in modern design and gaiety to Florida," Larry Tisch says, "it's quite a tribute to Florida."

The Americana–New York was already in construction on the full blockfront from Fifty-second to Fifty-third Streets on Seventh Avenue, above Times Square. Lapidus, after the opening of The Summit, became more amenable to suggestions from Diesel Construction about ways to cut costs (and he had always been highly amenable: "For a professional man," says Robert Tisch, "he's very easy to work with"). The Tisch brothers, who work intimately with their buildings, breathing the dirt at the construction site, hired Jay Aronson, semi-retired architect and decorator, as "counsel to management" on questions of décor. Aronson's job turned out to be mostly a matter of taking ornaments off the walls and out of the elevators, cutting ferrules off the furniture, eliminating murals, and generally throwing out what both the theatrical and design fields might call bits of business.

Lapidus sat still for all changes, but the week before the Americana opened was one of the gloomiest in his life. The Americana that Loew's launched in September, 1962, was in many ways not the hotel Lapidus had designed. Only the fifty-story slab that holds most of the two thousand guest rooms was unchanged from his original design, and was still a technical if not a visual triumph. (The Americana is not the tallest hotel in the world, as advertised, but it is certainly the tallest hotel of reinforced concrete, which was used instead of steel because it is cheaper and because the chance to run ducts through the concrete allows the architect to squeeze fifty stories into a height that would accommodate only forty-two or forty-three stories of steel construction.) It is not really a criticism of this slab to say, as some critics did, that "the thing looks like a bent piece of cardboard," because it was supposed to look like a bent piece of cardboard. "If one tries to stand a playing card on end," Lapidus wrote in his own explanation of the new hotel, "he will obviously have difficulty, since the surface on which the card rests is too thin and will not afford proper balance. If, however, one bends the playing card first, the card will stand quite firmly by itself and will even, if pushed lightly, resist falling over." Because of the bend in the thin slab, Lapidus was able to dispense with special wind bracing, which he believes had added more than a million and a half dollars to the cost of the new Hilton hotel built in a purely rectangular slab on the next block.

Lapidus had intended, however, to house the equipment atop the building in something more attractive than the gray shed that now offends the skyline. He had designed the Seventh Avenue façade in an S-curve, with a driveway bending in to the main entrance and explaining the glass rotunda at the Fifty-second Street corner; but the driveway was abandoned, a straight-line façade was pushed out to make room for more rentable stores, and the rotunda was left as an unexplained pimple.

Inside, skimping on décor items gave a pervasive air of shoddy to what had to be luxurious. The purchasing department cut the thickness of the brass in the scalloped lamps which light all the corridors, leaving them with the appearance of dime-store goods (and then all the savings were lost because somebody ordered several hundred lamps too many). In the Royal Ballroom, aesthetically and acoustically too long and narrow with too low a ceiling, the effect was to be made by luxurious red velvet drapes, but the material used is cheap and nasty and the least expensive fasteners tie it to the walls. Following the lead of the Seagram building, and trying to disguise the low ceilings, Lapidus had designed floor-to-ceiling doors; but the quality of construction left irregularly shaped and ugly strips of plaster between the frames and the ceilings.

The man most disturbed by the texture of the final building was Claudius C. Philippe, who had formerly managed the banquet department at the Waldorf and was going to get even with those so-and-sos at the Waldorf by taking their business to the Americana. ("Like the Waldorf," he said, crossing himself, "we are only two blocks from Fifth Avenue.") Philippe blew up when shown the grand ballroom, with its impossibly low ceiling and its substitution of gilding for gold. "Maurice!" he screamed (he never called Lapidus anything but "Maurice"). "This is *not* a crystal chandelier!" But Lapidus already knew it. Throughout the public areas, every gamble he had taken, whether well-thought-out or not, had been doomed to lose simply because nobody had bought the tickets.

The Tisch brothers, of course, get the buildings they order. The question of Lapidus himself is far more interesting. As a man, he commands both sympathy and curiosity—blending a deep insecurity with flashes of real arrogance, a fanatical devotion to the drawing board ("I've seen him work," says his son, "in a kind of fury") with a curious willingness to see his designs cheapened by builders, a fierce intelligence with little intellectual interest or sophistication. The names he gives to the public rooms of the hotels are straight out of the worst traditions of Hollywood. His understanding of other people's "wants" and "needs" is rarely complicated by thoughts about the human condition. Speaking the other day about "a large apartment house for senior citizens" which he is designing for Miami Beach, Lapidus said, "With six hundred families, we can have a movie theater, hobby rooms, card rooms, social rooms. There can be doctors' offices right in the building. These people can really live the good life."

As an architect, Lapidus deserves credit for the attempt to break with the habit of mind which sees buildings as merely repeated successions of modules, to fight for the human function of enclosed space, to lavish love on the details and decorations that make a building something more than "a machine for living." One of the marks of the Lapidus hotel, for example, is the total absence of long, institutional corridors down which the visitor walks in a Kafka-esque dream. All Lapidus' halls are broken up, sometimes most ingeniously, to avoid this oppression of parallel lines. Only in Lapidus-designed buildings does one consistently find more booths in the ladies' rooms than in the men's rooms, to adjust for well-known physiological differences. The new hospital Lapidus is designing in Miami will have a unique room, off the operating theater, where the surgeon can take a stretch, snooze, or smoke between jobs. In the middle-income housing he and Harold Liebman designed for Cadman Plaza in Brooklyn, different lines of four-room apartments will be really different, to meet the varying needs of families with different living habits—an unheard-of notion in modern apartment building.

Lapidus is fascinated by the many uses of space in a complicated building like a hotel. "We employ," he said of the Americana, the week before it opened, "two thousand people. We are dealing with the most expensive commodities, labor and service. We have to get two thousand people to their dressing rooms, feed them, get them to stations, without wasting a minute, because they're paid from the moment they check in.

"We have to handle a great deal of food. Any leak is terribly expensive. There must be controls, check-in and check-out procedures. We have a sociological problem, because this is a community. Busboys don't mix with bellboys. Waiters don't mix with captains. Waitresses don't mix with hostesses. We have to have separate bathrooms.

"The housekeeper has to make four thousand beds every day. We handle enormous quantities of linen. We have a bigger production line than Ford—and all this the public never sees.

"And from the moment the public walks in, you have to be Madison Avenue, selling him. You have to convince him he's Mr. Big. As he walks down the corridor, does he think, 'They're charging me twenty-four dollars a day; is it worth it?' The room opens from the door; does he say, '*This* is twenty-four dollars?' Or does he say, 'This is nice'?

"The last thing I think about is the man on the street looking at the package. I feel most architects have lost touch with what they want to do. They've been designing what people look at, the package, the box, rather than what's inside it."

Lapidus paused, and shrugged his shoulders. "Am I saying all this," he asked rhetorically, "because I believe it, or because I'm trying to justify myself? I don't know."

Careful, loving attention to human detail—which is what Lapidus claims for himself as against most of his fellow architects—implies extra expenditure both of money and of time, neither of which has been available to Lapidus in large dollops. ("It's one thing," he says rather bitterly, "to work for clients who want nothing but the best; it's something very different to work for clients who of course want nothing but the best—at a price.") To design what was probably the last successful neo-Baroque building, Charles Garnier worked thirteen years on the Paris Opéra. Lapidus, seeking to achieve a modern Baroque, has designed in a decade literally scores of new buildings larger than the Paris Opéra.

He might have missed his targets with all the time and money in the world. Painting, stage design, and store construction are all poor preparation for a career as an architect. Nowhere, not even in the Fontainebleau, does Lapidus show much feeling for a building as a three-dimensional object that can be seen from many angles—and that will also serve as a set of vantage points for the people in the building, looking out. Charles Spector remembers that even in the store-design days, Lapidus "had a fear of a blank wall." Expressed in busy patterns which distract from real shape, or in such incredibly disjointed décor as that for the original lobby of the office building at 555 Madison Avenue (now calmed down at the insistence of the tenants), this fear inevitably creates vulgarity. And the vulgarity is then compounded by Lapidus' apparently inborn tendency to equate the selling function of any building with the selling function of a store.

Lapidus' career as an architect—from "flairs" ten years ago to a position among the nation's twenty largest today—has grown through his ability to design buildings that are relatively inexpensive to put up but look (to the untutored eye) like something rather luxurious. His future as an artist, if he has one, lies in his ability to blend his own ambition, technical skill, and sense of function with the talents of associates less fearful of the aesthetics of architecture. The design to judge him on may be the housing to be built at Cadman Plaza in downtown Brooklyn. New York's desire "to show what a city can do," as Lapidus puts it, has given him a little better budget than these jobs usually command, while the procrastination of the Board of Estimate has provided time for the design to be worked over and over again.

Whether Lapidus can collaborate with anybody is still most uncertain. He no longer has partners: "Some day," he says with great bitterness, "I'd like to write a book on the modern young man in the professional world. They're all hungry for the fast buck." Asked how many architects work for him, he says, "I have forty-four *draftsmen*. I have to do all the design myself." In fact, some of the young men are highly talented. Lapidus never saw the design that won his office its greatest honor—first prize in the architects' competitions for the parcels in Washington's South-West Urban Renewal Area—until the work was ready for a final rendering. As a result, he doesn't talk about it often and, when he does, he gives no credits.

But there are also moments, usually moments of depression, when he faces other facts. His son, his friends, his doctor, and his own eyes tell him that he cannot by himself design the structure, façade, services, interiors, décor for a dozen different buildings every year.

"Gropius was right," Lapidus said sadly the week the Americana opened. "Modern architecture has to be a collaboration—no one man can do it all. The day of the master is over."

Still, as the hotels keep struggling to say, why be sad, when with a big effort you might be gay. . . .

15

Reiner's Orchestra

[Fritz Reiner's death has I think released for publication the great story from the work on this article. The setting is Reiner's home in Weston, Connecticut, where my wife and I spent a summer's afternoon, my wife in the Reiners' swimming pool, myself in the maestro's study. When the long interview was over, and Mrs. Reiner had come home from shopping, the four of us sat in the study sipping gin-and-tonics. This was the week Bernstein and the New York Philharmonic were in Leningrad on the tour Reiner and his orchestra had been supposed to take, and the front page of that morning's *Times* had featured a photograph of Bernstein and Pasternak embracing. "You know," Reiner said suddenly, not referring to the photograph, "Lenny was a pupil of mine." I knew. "At Curtis," Reiner continued. "One day Lenny came to me and said he was going to spend the summer at Tanglewood. I said, 'By all means go to Tanglewood. It's near your home. But don't come back here—the two styles [Reiner's and Koussevitzky's] don't mix.' He cried. He wrote me a letter six pages long on blue paper, I show you the tear stains. Also he wrote Mrs. Bok. So I agreed I would take him back for one year, but then he would have to go." Reiner sipped his drink. "He was *very* talented. Of all my pupils—and many of them have very good jobs today—of all my pupils, Lenny . . . was . . . the *most* . . . talented." Reiner nodded with pleasure and sipped the drink again. He put the glass down and shook his head briskly. "But not," he said, "not for conducting. . . ."

[This article, which appeared in *High Fidelity* in 1960, was written for people who knew Reiner's work better than it is likely to be known by readers who come upon the piece in less musical surroundings and after Reiner's death. Though I found him less interesting than others thought him in the work of the early romantic Viennese (to describe Haydn or Mozart, let alone Beethoven, as "classical" strikes me as dangerous distortion), there can be little question of his primacy in the Germanic and Eastern European music of the period, say, 1890–1930. Even when he played Mahler, whose music he came to admire rather late in life, his performances were exquisitely accurate and powerful. And he was by universal consent the greatest technician of the baton in our century.

[Several of those mentioned in this article are no longer associated with the Chicago Orchestra. Hendl has gone on to be head of the Eastman

269

School of Music in Rochester, and the orchestra is now on its third manager since Kuyper. The hall has been acoustically reconditioned for $3 million; the annual deficit beyond contributions has risen alarmingly to $800,000 from unrestricted funds, and an endowment drive is afoot. The minimum salary figure of $170 for twenty-eight weeks ($4,760) will by 1970 have gone to $245 a week for fifty-two weeks ($12,740). The year before his death, Reiner made peace with Rudolph Bing, and he was readying himself for rehearsal of *Götterdämmerung* when the final illness struck.

[Reiner did not like the article.]

REINER walks onto the stage for rehearsals in a rather preoccupied way, nodding distantly to the members of the Chicago Symphony Orchestra, a large but meaningless smile fixed on his round face. He wears rimless bifocals to help him read the score, his shirt is open at the neck, and he buttons only the bottom button of his single-breasted jacket. There is nothing imposing about his presence, the dumpiness of his figure accentuated by the informality of his entrance. At the podium, he may exchange a word with his assistant conductor, Walter Hendl, a blond, square-shouldered, businesslike musician, young and American and serious behind black-rimmed glasses. Or he may comment on something to Sidney Harth, his concertmaster, a very large, stout young man in a smoking jacket, who does not interrupt his tuning and flexing while chatting with the maestro. Then Reiner mounts—and mounts is the operative word—the very high chair which has been the conductor's rehearsal chair in Chicago since the days of Frederick Stock. He opens his score, glances again at Harth, who has resumed his seat, and coughs lightly.

The period of informality has ended, and the orchestra focuses on its conductor with nervous attention.

"*Pini di Roma*," Reiner says. The smile takes on meaning, the wrist flicks, the tip of the white baton descends—and the orchestra attacks.

The chair on which Reiner perches is absurdly too tall for him—so tall, in fact, that local rumor says (incorrectly) it was designed for Klemperer. The long iron legs are made rigid by crossbars, and Reiner, after climbing up them, rests the balls of his feet on the bars. He does not so much sit as settle on the round, brown leather seat, and he treats it as a stool: his back never makes contact with the back of the chair, and his arms ignore the arm rests. Everything about him pushes forward toward the orchestra: knees, stomach, shoulders, chin, baton. From the rear he seems a slumped, resting gnome, but from the front his appearance is very different. The bright, sharp eyes dart everywhere in the orchestra; the skin is taut on the forehead as though to help the ears pull in the sound; the right arm, elbow suspended just above the arm rest, never making contact with it, beats precisely, economically, with the smallest visible gestures. Reiner's famous "vest-pocket beat" is not something he reserves for concerts. Its purpose is to make sure the men are paying attention, watching the conductor rather than counting their own measures, and Reiner wants his men to watch the conductor at rehearsal, too. When attention seems well fixed, the beat expands to normal patterns.

If Reiner hears something he does not like, he halts the orchestra by stopping his beat and shaking his head. He scorns the usual practice of rapping the baton on the music stand, with its clear implication that the men would not know the conductor had stopped unless they *heard* something from the podium. The head-shaking continues until the music has ceased, which may take a few seconds, and then Reiner peers at the offending spot, visibly impatient, trying to control his irritation before phrasing his objection. As the head stops wagging, the left foot begins, the heel shaking rapidly back and forth until the music resumes.

"At F, there must be *complete* silence," Reiner says in a rather soft voice to the percussion section, which was unable to get everything quiet at once the first time around.

"I want six bars," calls a voice from the percussion, as Reiner raises his baton again.

"Take nine," Reiner calls back, and almost immediately the downbeat is upon the men—but they are ready. After six years with Reiner, the Chicago is ready for almost anything.

F arrived again, and the echo of the triangle died away in the hall. Reiner moved on to the next section, and called over the fiddles to the percussion, "Good. That was very good."

Reiner wastes no time. If an instrument makes a wrong entry or plays a wrong note, he makes a mental jotting of the matter and keeps going: such routine mechanical errors are not serious enough to stop the work. Despite his apparently authoritarian attitude, he delegates more responsibility than most conductors would consider safe. First-desk men in Chicago are supposed to be more than soloists: they are also "section men," held accountable for the work of the musicians who play behind them. After a rehearsal, Reiner may call one of them aside and tell him that a man in his section played an A rather than an A-flat; could he find out which man it was, and make certain that the score is correct. The members of the orchestra respect this approach, and admire the section men who can handle the extra work involved. A cellist speaks rhapsodically of Frank Miller, who took over as principal cello in Chicago this year, after a career as first cellist for the NBC Symphony and conductor of the Florida Symphony in Orlando. "That man," says the cellist, "has eyes in the back of his head; he knows just who is doing what."

Technical discussions of performance or of music itself are time-consumers Reiner saves for social evenings. His language with the orchestra is ordinary (slightly accented) English, with no interpolations about bowings or tonguings. Despite his impatience, he has enormous confidence in his men, and will illustrate what he wants in the line of phrasing by singing the notes once, with remarkably good pitch, then plunging into the full orchestration. His direction of complicated rhythms, of course, is a legend in the trade: nobody subdivides a beat so easily or so efficiently. Occasionally, in really complicated passages, he will bring the left hand into play—but as an ordinary matter, even in so tricky a score for the conductor as Stravinsky's *Mavra,* a joining of independent motions by right elbow, right wrist, left shoulder and chin is sufficient to make his desires completely clear. Sometimes, when he is really concerned about a soloist's phrasing, he will point the baton at the man and twist it as the solo proceeds—but the loving, crowd-pleasing shaping of a phrase with a graceful gesture of the hand is a conducting technique he regards as below his personal dignity, and that of his orchestra.

Chicago's Orchestra Hall is by no means an easy place in which to prepare a program. It has the most shallow stage of any major hall in America, which means that Reiner must spread out his 106 men across a great stretch of space. The different choirs cannot hear each other; men who are to play solos together must rely more heavily on their conductor, and on their own advance planning. Indeed, it was not until the orchestra went on tour in 1958 that anybody knew for sure how good they were. After the first rehearsal in Boston's Symphony Hall, Reiner came backstage with his eyes shining, and marveled at what God had wrought. Today, Reiner, part of whose patent is infallibility, tends to say that he had known all along what a superlative orchestra the Chicago was—"but the men," he says, "the *men* never really heard themselves until Boston."

It is widely believed, even among members of the orchestra (who should know better), that Reiner has improved the Chicago by means of wholesale replacements of personnel. The more interesting fact is that today's orchestra is largely the same group Reiner inherited from Kubelik more than six years ago. During Reiner's reign to date there have been only thirty-six replacements—fewer than the union contract would allow, and little if any more than normal turnover in any large musical group. Of the orchestra's fifteen principals, responsible for solos and the conduct of sections, only six are Reiner's appointments: of the four first-desk men in the brass section, which is the orchestra's particular glory, three were in their places when Reiner arrived. Reiner can be unceremonious to the point of cruelty when he does fire people (last year's one-season first cellist learned his fate when Reiner called him in and told him that he would not be playing the solos in a performance of the Strauss *Don Quixote,* "since you're not coming back next year anyway"). But he has brought the Chicago to its present pitch by stimulating and controlling the existing personnel, not by importing a classroom full of teacher's pets.

Reiner does not have pets, anyway. He is not the sort of conductor who takes (or pretends to take) an interest in the private lives of his men. Musicians who have troubles are more likely to take them to the management of the orchestra than to Reiner. On occasion, a few Hungarians in the orchestra have tried to appeal to Reiner's recollections of his childhood by speaking to him privately in his native tongue, but he does not like it. "You are in America, now," is his usual reply. "Speak English." Reiner and his orchestra do not seem to feel much warmth for each other—but the coolness of the relationship is easily counterbalanced by a deep and very genuine respect on both sides.

One of the oldest saws in the concert business holds that there are no bad orchestras—only bad conductors. In a sense, every orchestra is the property of its permanent director, and picks up his qualities and defects. The dominance of the conductor has probably been stronger in Chicago, however, than anywhere else. No other resident orchestra in America ever took a conductor's name for its own, as Chicago once did to honor Theodore Thomas; and no conductor anywhere has ever duplicated Frederick Stock's thirty-eight-year tenure as music director of the Chicago.

Thomas founded the orchestra in 1891, when there were only three such resident organizations in America—two in New York, and one in Boston. His connection with Chicago was firm. He had first visited there in 1854, as a nineteen-year-old violinist in a traveling concert package, and he had made the city the western terminus of his own orchestra's ambitious tour in 1869. His affection for the place was demonstrated in several subsequent tours, and reinforced by marriage to a well-connected Chicagoan in 1890. Shortly thereafter, he quit his post as music director of the New York Philharmonic to break ground in Chicago, and so far as is known he never regretted it.

He lived long enough to see the Chicago Orchestra established in its own building, and to conduct the first three concerts in the new hall. When he died in 1905 he deeded his position to his assistant, Frederick Stock—like Thomas, a German by birth. Under Stock, the orchestra formed the pattern of activities which still continues. In 1916, while on a visit to New York, the Chicago played for the first recordings ever made by an orchestra under its permanent conductor.

Stock put the Saturday-night Popular Concerts on a regular basis, and started the first subscription series of children's concerts to build future audiences for the orchestra. Perhaps his most spectacular innovation was the Chicago Civic Orchestra, a permanent training ensemble for students looking toward a symphonic career, which Stock founded in 1919, after his largely German orchestra had been riddled by the enthusiasm and bigotry of the First World War. Today, about half the members of the Chicago Symphony are Civic graduates— and, says George Kuyper, the Chicago's manager, "there isn't a prominent orchestra in America without at least one Civic alumnus. Conductors come through here every spring, to audition Civic talent."

The structure Stock left behind him was solid enough to survive a confused decade after his death in 1942. For a season the orchestra worked with a succession of guest conductors, and then Desiré De-fauw took it over for three difficult years. Thereupon followed a dazzling and demoralizing season with Arthur Rodzinski, whose farewell gesture at the end of his one-year tenure was to bring his little son out on the stage before the embarrassed but cheering audience, to show him that "the people really love me in Chicago." Two more years of guest conducting kept the orchestra playing in public before the management engaged Rafael Kubelik, whose three years as music director were marred, to say the least, by the unwavering disapproval of Claudia Cassidy, the critic of the Chicago *Tribune*. The orchestra Reiner inherited from Kubelik was unquestionably on the way up once again (among the reasons Reiner had to make so few personnel changes was the quantity and quality of the men Kubelik brought it). But RCA Victor's Richard Mohr, who has been the director for most of the Chicago's recordings under Reiner, testifies to a continuing tonal improvement throughout the six years of Reiner's supervision.

A post in the Chicago is one of the half dozen most desirable ensemble jobs in America. Union scale minimum is $170 a week, and something like half the orchestra is paid more than the minimum. The season is twenty-eight weeks long, with a maximum of four concerts and five 2½-hour rehearsals a week. The men are paid extra for the year's dozen or so recording sessions, and for the Sunday-night television concerts over WGN. (*"Color* television, if you please," Reiner observes, shrugging his shoulders.) Every so often, the season is extended by a fall or spring tour, and every summer most of the men play the six-week outdoor festival at Ravinia, north of the city. Like orchestral musicians everywhere, they give private lessons in what little time remains; and the first-desk men give section lessons to the aspiring talent of the Civic Orchestra. A man who plays in the Chicago can probably expect an annual income of $8,000 to $11,000 a year—not munificent, but well above average as America rewards its musicians. And a first-class card player can augment that income considerably by participating in the high-stake four-handed cribbage game which assembles in a small room off the stage during every break in a rehearsal or a recording session.

Orchestra Hall, the fruit of Theodore Thomas' labors on the civic initiative of Chicago nearly sixty years ago, sits on South Michigan Avenue, overlooking Grant Park, Lake Michigan, and the Fine Arts Museum. Its carved brown façade, doubtless impressive when new, lacks grandeur by comparison with the two large office buildings that squeeze it onto its rather small plot in the middle of the block. (The hall had to be closed down for some months while the new Borg-Warner building was going up beside it, because an overenthusiastic construction gang pumped sand and mud out from under Orchestra Hall's foundations as well as their own.) Inside, the building offers a rather impressive marble lobby, and a wide, shallow auditorium to match the wide, shallow stage. The wall behind the stage is a shell-shaped reflector—Wedgwood blue with Wedgwood-type white decorations—rising from a wooden chorus stand up to the ceiling.

Acoustically the hall is adequate, though there are dead spots on the stage and in the audience. When Reiner plays a work with vocal soloists, he has them stand on a high platform at the rear of center stage. ("Singers don't like it," says a man who works with the Chicago, "but Reiner's Reiner. And it's true that voices carry better in this hall from that location.") Get the people out of it, however, as the engineers say, and Orchestra Hall makes a fine recording studio, especially for stereo. Reiner says that he would rather record in Orchestra Hall than anywhere else in the world.

The side walls of the auditorium are the walls of the building, and space behind the stage is restricted to a narrow runway and a few small rooms. Downstairs in the basement there is a large dressing room with green metal lockers for the musicians, plus a trunk room (which is emptied of trunks and turned into a makeshift control room when Victor comes to record), and a modest but rather pleasant rectangular "recreation room" featuring card tables, Morris chairs, and a machine which sells hot soup. Most of the men spend their rehearsal breaks in the dressing room, however, playing bridge on the piano, upended trunks and folding tables. Upstairs, above the hall, reached by an elevator with wrought-iron gates, are half a dozen floors of offices. The orchestra owns the lot, and the rental of the office space, plus recitals and religious meetings in the auditorium itself, about pays the cost of maintaining the building.

Nevertheless, despite an average 90+ percent sellout of the hall's 2,580 seats, the Chicago's deficit is very large. In the 1958–59 season, music-making cost the orchestra about $450,000 more than its receipts. (The Philadelphia, by comparison, lost only $234,000; no orchestra made money.) Chicago has a good endowment—$8,200,-000, at conservative valuation, exclusive of the value of the building —but a chunk of the total is restricted to the pension fund or to educational uses, among them the operation of the Civic Orchestra, which charges no tuition. Income from the endowment fund, applicable to the operating loss, came to about $220,000 in 1958–59, and another $165,000 was raised from current contributions—leaving about $60,000 to be extracted from capital and paid to creditors.

Wrestling with these problems is the task of a fifteen-member Board of Trustees and of George Kuyper, the orchestra's manager. President of the Board is Dr. Eric Oldberg, a rather small, white-haired, socially prominent Chicago surgeon whose father was professor of music at Northwestern, and whose wife is a pianist good enough to have studied with Schnabel and played with the Chicago Symphony (before Oldberg was its president, of course). Kuyper, who came from Boston toward the end of the Stock regime, is a tall, large-boned, rather Lincolnesque man with a mane of white hair and a solid grasp on the two first requisites of a successful manager—a calm temperament and a matured sense of humor. It is a measure of Kuyper's diplomatic skills that John Weicher, who had been concertmaster of the Chicago from 1937 to this season, consented to remain with the orchestra as principal second violinist after Reiner decided that he wanted Louisville's Sidney Harth as concertmaster.

Chicago musicians credit Kuyper with holding the orchestra together during the long interregnum separating Stock and Reiner. Kuyper is at least as proud of the orchestra as Reiner is, and gets even more chance to show his pride, because Reiner takes no interest in what is done at Ravinia or by the guest conductors. Most conductors are appalled by the need to cram all preparation for a Ravinia concert into one three-hour rehearsal, and react skeptically to Kuyper's assurance that the Chicago is one big fast study. They apologize later for their skepticism. Aaron Copland, who came to Ravinia not long ago for a program of his own works, made his apology public. He opened the rehearsal by telling the orchestra that he didn't think they could master the pieces on the program in three hours, "but Kuyper says you can do it." He wound up dismissing the orchestra half an hour early with the words, "Kuyper was right."

On musical matters, of course, Reiner's word is law. "When the Association appoints a Music Director," Kuyper said, "it delegates all musical authority to him." Reiner is basically antagonistic to serial composition: "I do not believe," he says, "in using musical expression to experiment with mathematical formulas." He has programed Stravinsky's *Agon* and the Webern *Six Pieces* ("which made a great failure," he observes; "and they were very well played, too"). Reiner continues, however, to play a great deal of the music of twenty and thirty years ago—music by Bartok, Hindemith, Prokofiev and Stravinsky, much of which he was responsible for introducing to America. And such music, as observers have noted all over the world, remains quite radical enough for the ordinary symphony subscriber.

In 1957, Reiner and Margaret Hillis organized the first permanent chorus to be affiliated with the Chicago Symphony, and the last three seasons have seen greater numbers of choral works on the programs. Though it is not likely that RCA Victor or any other force in heaven or earth could dictate Reiner's choice of music to play, the Victor recording contract does influence what will be played during any particular week. One Saturday-night Popular Concert, for example, offered the interesting program of four Rossini Overtures and the Beethoven *Seventh,* because the orchestra was to record those pieces the next day.

Reiner usually stays away from managerial questions as carefully as Kuyper avoids interference with the conductor's managerial prerogatives, but last year the rule was broken with a bang. As is rather widely known, the tour of Russia and adjacent lands on which the New York Philharmonic accompanied Leonard Bernstein last summer was not originally planned for the New York orchestra. It was planned, by George Kuyper, his assistant Philip Hart and a posse of ANTA experts, for the Chicago and Reiner. Visas had been secured, passage purchased, shipping arranged, reservations confirmed, supplies of Chicago bottled water (which Reiner particularly likes) readied for shipping to European *entrepôts*—when Reiner suddenly decided he did not wish to make the tour.

Nobody really knows Reiner's reasons (the explanation he offered the orchestra was that the weather was wretched in Eastern Europe at that time of year; they wouldn't like it), but the effects of the decision were instantaneous. To say that the orchestra was unhappy about losing the trip would understate the situation substantially, and even now the men speak of "what the Philharmonic did on our trip to Russia." For some of the musicians, who had already spent the $2,000 or so they would earn on the trip, Reiner's decision was a personal disaster. It was reported that the orchestra hissed its conductor at the start of the first rehearsal after he had vetoed the tour, but apparently the report was false. What happened was that most of the men had decided to give Reiner the silent treatment, while a few had decided to talk loudly as a sign of displeasure. The majority shushed the minority, creating a sound suspiciously like a hiss. Nevertheless, "Reiner's Reiner"; the men were proud of the quality of their orchestra and knew how much their conductor had done for it; and relations presently returned to normal.

Reiner and his wife live just outside Westport, Connecticut, in a beautiful house, a two-story, L-shaped, white-stucco enlargement of a European farmhouse which they built for themselves in 1928. The property is a large one: a park, formal garden and swimming pool surrounded by acres of woods. The rooms inside the house are large and dark and rather elaborately fitted; the front door, perhaps significantly, is disproportionately small. For the Chicago season, the Reiners maintain an apartment in the Loop, near Orchestra Hall; but it cannot be said that they live in Chicago. Unlike most conductors, Reiner will not go out of his way to cultivate the social leaders of the community which supports his orchestra. He knows few people in Chicago, and apparently does not care to know many more.

The Chicago Symphony is unquestionably Reiner's for as long as he may want it, but his aloof attitude toward the community gives rise to constant rumors that he is about to quit. Such rumors are almost certainly premature. The current season is only the second of a three-year contract, and Reiner is sure to be back for 1960–61. After that, nobody knows—possibly not even Reiner.

In most respects, the Chicago job is as desirable as the American continent offers. The pay is good, the orchestra excellent, the management professional, intelligent, and rich enough to allow great leeway in programing. From Reiner's point of view, however, there may be certain disadvantages. Though his American career has been mostly with orchestras, Reiner is first and foremost an opera man: Chicago got him, in fact, only after he had decided that he could not go along with Rudolf Bing's notions of how to run an opera house. The Chicago season is a long one, and as music director Reiner is committed by contract to nineteen of the twenty-eight weeks (in this season; next season he may be able to ease off a week or two). Reiner is seventy-one, and though his health is excellent he worries about it. He came to prominence as a young man, and most of the conductors he competed against are now dead, which depresses him. He has days when he regards nineteen weeks of three and four concerts a week as a considerable physical burden.

Moreover, Chicago's musical scene displays an unusual degree of political nastiness. Hog-butcher to the world, Sandburg said, and the place still likes a good blood-letting once in a while. Criticism in the Chicago papers tends to be more cutting and more personal than is customary in this country—a situation caused and regularly exacerbated by the extraordinary skill of Claudia Cassidy. At the beginning, Reiner had Miss Cassidy on his side, but this season, perhaps because of incidents just before and just after the collapse of the Russian tour project, Miss Cassidy seems to be chiseling Reiner's name on one of her surplus gravestones. For example, her criticism of Reiner's *Pines of Rome:* "What was missing . . . was the visionary mysticism without which the louder passages sound like a speech by Mussolini." Now, this is a brilliant phrase, pinpointing with graceful economy one of the objections to a meretricious piece of music. The march of the imagined Roman legion *is* a speech by Mussolini. One may doubt, however, whether Miss Cassidy would have blamed it on Reiner in previous years.

Lacking Miss Cassidy's marksmanship with the small bore, her rivals have been virtually forced to use heavy artillery to secure equivalent killings. Moreover, the instability of the years between Stock and Reiner gave almost everyone in Chicago a somewhat exaggerated notion of the function of the newspaper on the musical scene. Robert Charles Marsh of the *Sun-Times* is a first-class reporter as well as a critic; and the Chicago atmosphere has led him to lard his columns with somewhat more greenroom gossip than conventional canons would allow. Like every writer, Marsh comes to believe his own stuff, and once climaxed a campaign for a second permanent director to share the job with Reiner by telling an ambitious visiting conductor that the Board of Trustees was looking for such a man. The visiting conductor, not the phlegmatic type at best, came out of his interview with Marsh on the verge of a nervous breakdown. Even Roger Dettmer of the *American,* who behaves more like a normal critic than either of his peers, became overexcited in print during the fight which split the management of the Chicago Lyric Theater a few years ago.

Reiner claims not to read the critics, and will go to outrageous lengths to support his claim. Not long ago, Marsh's name came up in a casual conversation, which Reiner thereupon interrupted. "Who?" he said querulously.

"Marsh. Robert Charles Marsh."

"I never *heard* of the man," Reiner said with satisfaction, and firmly steered the conversation back where it had been.

All claims aside, Reiner obviously does read what is written about him, and deeply resents unfair criticism—a description which every artist uses to cover a wide spectrum of negative reaction. Reiner's attitude toward his fellow man is one of more or less genial contempt, and like most people who hold such attitudes he feels himself in a relatively isolated and exposed position. Thus, for all his world-renowned mastery of the rude remark and the pointed silence, he suffers from a relatively thin skin—by no means an asset in Chicago.

Nevertheless, even a concerted attack in the press, which is unlikely, could not drive Reiner from Chicago if he wished to stay. Reiner has said so many outrageous things so often that observers tend to forget that he *knows* when he is being outrageous, and enjoys it. Behind his contempt for others lie an unusual intelligence, verbal as well as musical, and a thoroughly if somewhat peculiarly developed sense of humor. Though he cannot take criticism well, he does take a joke, and over the passage of time most criticisms become jokes. At last year's party for the men, Reiner asked the orchestra's mimic to do his imitations of conductors, and then, a touch maliciously, asked for the imitation of Reiner. This act was cleaned up a little—inevitably—but the audience thought it contained several palpable hits. Reiner loved it, and recalls it happily as rougher than it was.

Musicians in Chicago believe that Reiner would now like, oddly enough, the sort of proposal Marsh made a few years ago—a second regular conductor, subordinate to the Music Director, to take a greater share of the seasonal burden. Failing the discovery of someone able to carry the job and yet willing to remain under Reiner—or strong public acceptance of Walter Hendl, Reiner's young assistant, whose work for the American Recording Society a few years back marked him as a major talent in his generation—it is generally believed that Reiner will simply renew existing arrangements. He has built orchestras in this country for Cincinnati, Pittsburgh and now Chicago, and the last of them is not only his best but one of the great ensembles of the world. People who know Reiner well find it hard to believe he would give up this magnificent, flexible, responsive instrument to cast himself into the irritating inefficiencies of guest-conducting other men's orchestras.

16

The Best Fellows at Harvard

[Starting with a luckily unpublished novel in 1949, I have written too often and too much about Harvard—and it always comes out with a kind of awed affection for the place, though I am quite sure that the nation and Harvard and those of us who care about intellectual matters all suffer from excessive concentration on this one, rather small university.

[Wassily Leontief, who figures largely in this piece as the current president of The Society of Fellows, was my tutor when I was an undergraduate—and the young lady who told me that all I knew was facts was the Leontiefs' baby-sitter, so I saw my tutor occasionally at home, too. He changed the whole pattern of my ambitions by a comment he made on a paper I had written, attempting to amend Enrico Baroni's equations on the allocation of resources to make them applicable to conditions of monopolistic competition. Leontief spoke kindly of my efforts, then said, "But you don't *use* mathematics. You decide what you want to say, then find the mathematics to express it." This was absolutely true; and it had never occurred to me before that there were people who used math as anything but a language; and from that moment I knew I was never going to be an economist. We have kept up in the years since, in the rather remote manner of teacher and ex-pupil; and he was, of course, immensely helpful in the work toward this piece, which was commissioned by Byron Dobell of *Esquire* and ran in 1965.

[Carl Kaysen has since moved on to be director of the Institute of Advanced Study at Princeton, and James Watson has carried the Society's idea of good conversation into print with *The Double Helix*.]

On September twenty-fifth, 1933, in Harvard's mock-Colonial Eliot House, in a brand-new oak-paneled room designed to look old, six young scholars sat down to a private dinner with seven of the great men of academic life. There had been sherry first, in an equally private Anglican parlor, and there would be a choice of madeira or cognac at the end; and with dinner there were two wines (or Dutch beer), one of them a Romanée Conti of a great 1920s vintage. Dinner itself had been especially, and carefully, prepared in a private kitchen just behind, and it was ceremoniously served. The young men had never seen anything like it; nor had they dined before with the likes of Alfred North Whitehead, or John Livingston Lowes (author of that masterpiece of literary snooping *The Road to Xanadu*), or A. Lawrence Lowell, the recently retired president of Harvard. But they were to dine together in this company every Monday night in term, joined as a single Society of Fellows in pursuit of the twin evanescences of knowledge and civilization. Indeed, the dinners were to be the young scholars' only formal obligation to Harvard for a three-year term; otherwise they were on their own, being paid to do whatever work seemed necessary to them. Whitehead explained to the younger men the values of scholarship, telling them about an old Scottish lady who had dreamed three times of three groups of three things, had thereupon multiplied three times three times three, put her life's savings on Number 28, and become exceedingly wealthy. . . .

The Society of Fellows still dines together each Monday night in the same rooms, and after some years in which the members ate food from the common Harvard kettles the dinner is again first-class, specially prepared in the kitchen by a French lady whom the new chairman, the economist Wassily Leontief, has borrowed from Boston's Odd Volumes Club. There are now twelve governing "Senior Fellows" and twenty-four young scholars, the "Junior Fellows," in one stage or another of their three-year fellowships. Neither presidents nor past presidents of Harvard are likely to be in attendance, the incumbent and his predecessor having other interests. But there will certainly be guests, and the range during the Society's thirty-two years has been from T. S. Eliot to Nils Bohr, Bernard De Voto to Isaiah Berlin. Because every fellow (or past fellow) has the right to bring a guest to any dinner, nonacademic types show up occasionally, too. "Once," says the historian Crane Brinton, who served as chairman of the Society from 1942 to 1963, "we had the Chief of Police of Teheran—not the real police, the secret police. He was a tough character."

"To be in the Society of Fellows," says Federal Judge Charles Wyzanski, a great polymath who can find a contribution to any conversation and who holds an appointment as the first Honorary Senior

Fellow, "is to be at the center of intelligence of the center of intelligence. It's the best club in the world. If I were offered a choice of the Society of Fellows or the Supreme Court, I'd take the Society of Fellows."

The comparison is certainly just in one sense—of small educational institutions, only the Court, in the persons of the Justices' former law clerks, can show so spectacular an alumni as the Society of Fellows. The first group of six Juniors included the mathematician and physicist Garret Birkhoff, the philosopher of logic William van Orman Quine and the behavioral psychologist and novelist B. F. Skinner, now notorious as the inventor of the teaching machine. In the second batch were Harry Levin, resident proprietor of comparative literature; the sociologist and historian George Homans; the research pathologist George Hass; and the anthropologist Conrad Arensberg, whose classic *The Irish Countryman* was written during his fellowship. Those entering in 1935 included John Bardeen, who was to share a Nobel Prize for his work in solid-state physics; the classical archaeologist George Hanfmann; Paul Ward, historian and now president of Sarah Lawrence; Henry Guerlac, one of the inventors of the history of science as a field of study; and Ivan Getting, who is widely regarded as the perfector of radar. In the fourth year, the Juniors included George Haskins, lawyer, law professor and legal historian; James Fisk, now head of Bell Labs; and William F. Whyte, author of *Street Corner Society*.

Among later alumni are the economist Paul Samuelson and the political economist Carl Kaysen; Walter Jackson Bate, a great Johnsonian whose book on Keats won a Pulitzer; James Baker, whose cameras track the satellites; Thomas Kuhn, author of *The Structure of Scientific Revolutions;* the Pulitzer Prize poet Richard Wilbur; Robert Woodward, who synthesized quinine; Noam Chomsky, perhaps the outstanding figure in contemporary linguistics; John Sawyer, president of Williams College; the art and literary critic Pierre Schneider; the mathematician Creighton Buck; and such political figures as Arthur Schlesinger, Jr. and McGeorge Bundy, the *machina ex deo* of the Johnson administration.

Nearly all the others have done well, too; as Harry Levin, now a

Senior Fellow, puts it, "There are only one or two whose pictures we have turned to the wall." Without exception, they all worked harder for themselves than they could have worked on any formal assignments. The biographies are available in a little book called *The Society of Fellows*, published by the Society itself and only *distributed* by the Harvard University Press. It is known inside as "the red book." "Most of us spend a lot of time reading the red book," says one of the current Juniors, rather wistfully.

Nobody can apply to be a Junior Fellow. Instead, candidates are "recommended," preferably by professors under whom they have been working. It has been firmly in the rules from the beginning that no candidate could be considered who would be more than twenty-eight (at first, twenty-five) upon assuming his fellowship, and it is typical of the Society's attitude toward rules that one of the charter Junior Fellows was B. F. Skinner, who was almost thirty. The founding Seniors, who had had their eye on the British "prize fellows," assumed that all Juniors would be single on appointment, but one of the first batch got married the summer before his fellowship was to start—and Whitehead, who had seen the debilitating effects of imposed celibacy in England, persuaded the outraged Lowell to admit the deviant scholar. Other times, other manners: of those who started their fellowships in the fall of 1964, all but two were married—and one of the exceptions was a Jesuit priest, the Society's first cleric.

About seventy young scholars are recommended each year, half of them from within the Harvard community; and selecting the six to eight winners is the real job of the Senior Fellows. For this back-breaking assignment, and for their time on Monday evenings, the Seniors are paid five hundred dollars a year. Candidates' work is submitted with the recommendations. "It's a very humbling experience," says Levin, "to see how much more these young people know than you do." About twenty-five of the seventy candidates are interviewed every fall, flown to Harvard if necessary, expenses paid. In the early years, their sponsors were interviewed, too, but the burden grew too heavy. Other Harvard professors can be co-opted for interviewing purposes. Wassily Leontief's first contact with the Society, in the mid-thirties, came when Lowell asked him to sit in on an interview with a budding economist. "Lowes used a horn as a hearing aid," Leontief recalls, "and Lowell by then was deaf. We shouted at each other, with the poor candidate in the next room—'WILL NOT DO! WILL NOT DO!' "

Candidates who *will* do now receive $3,500 a year if under twenty-five, $4,000 if older, plus room and board at an undergraduate House (dormitory to the vulgar), and all fees and scholarly expenses. (Harvard professors who wish to attend meetings of learned societies pay their own way unless they are delivering a paper; Junior Fellows can go at the expense of the Society.) Married Juniors get a $1,500 living allowance in lieu of accommodations. The income is all tax-exempt— at least, the Internal Revenue Service has never tried to bleed it— and there are other perks, too, ranging from the squat silver candlestick each Fellow receives as a gift (with a second candlestick as a wedding present) to an eight-month sojourn at a promising dig, say, for an archaeologist.

One current Junior Fellow is a folklorist specializing in prison songs and stories; the Society pays for his travel and for his recording tapes. Another is a composer for whom the Society recently sponsored a concert, on the grounds that public performance of his music was for him what the use of a lab is for a biologist. The Society has purchased electric typewriters for Juniors, and helped publish their books. To accommodate the mathematically inclined, it rents a block of time on the University's computers (which is considerably more than a bookkeeping transaction at Harvard, where "each tub sits on its own bottom"; the Society even pays "tuition" for each of its Juniors).

Perhaps the most startling of recent investments was a trip around the globe to help Joseph Fletcher, a young man studying world history from the inside—that is, from the point of view of the Central Asian tribes. He worked in libraries and archives in Japan, India, Russia, Turkey, Iran and Austria. Crane Brinton remembers with delight this Fellow's interview, conducted by the late Arthur Darby Nock, the beau-ideal of a Senior Fellow. (A profound and persnickety scholar in the history of religion, Nock was also a celibate who enjoyed reciting parodies of his own obituary and who lived his life at Harvard in one of the Houses, much as an eighteenth-century don lived at an Oxford college.) "Nock asked him," Brinton recalls, "whether he had the *languages* for such a job. The boy said, 'Well, my Latin and Greek are good, of course, as good as my French and German and Turkish. My Russian is adequate. My Chinese and Mongolian are all right for reading, though I can't say how well I speak them. Unfortunately, my Tibetan is still weak.' " The Society accepted him despite the weak Tibetan, and sent him off to look for documents.

Fletcher's search took him to Japan and Taiwan, Nepal and Afghanistan, Baghdad, what's left of Babylon, Istanbul and Rome. (There are treasure troves for his purposes in Leningrad, Tashkent and Peking, too, but he hasn't been able to get at them.) His earliest interest was what he describes as "the first conquest of the world," by Genghis Khan. The field is brand new, because, Fletcher says, "really, until my time, it wasn't possible to learn all the languages. For some of them, there were no dictionaries and grammars, and you needed a lifetime to learn any one. Now, thanks in part to work by Russian and Chinese scholars, there are books. The lucky fact that I studied Russian and Chinese as an undergraduate opened them up for me."

This three-year fellowship (which the Society just renewed for another three years) has already produced a major discovery, though a negative one. "It's about the period when Outer Mongolia first became subject to China," Fletcher says, "in the time of the last Chinese dynasty. Everything written about it was based on Chinese sources, translated into French. Then in the nineteenth century there appeared a Mongolian chronicle which seemed to confirm the story, and everybody thought *that* was settled. But when I read the Mongolian chronicle it looked familiar to me. There's a Manchu history, pieces of the text at Columbia and Chicago and the University of Marburg. I looked them up—and the Mongolian chronicle was just a translation. So everything was from the same source, really, Manchu propaganda, and it couldn't be trusted. What I did, of course, was just a lucky accident—running into both sets of documents." It is hard to imagine an "accident" which more neatly fits Pasteur's aphorism about chance favoring the prepared mind.

The project on which a candidate wishes to work is important in his selection, but Fellows are not held to their original plans. Indeed, there is some feeling that the Society has scored a success when a Junior shifts horses in midstream, provided he makes the transfer elegantly and displays panache in the process. John Howard of the Ford Foundation went from chemistry to law while a Junior Fellow, and another moved from classics to the Episcopal ministry. Early on, Henry Guerlac told some of his colleagues at lunch that he was going to have to quit their company because he had signed on as a bio-chemist and had lost interest in the field. Word of this was carried back to Lawrence Henderson, the first chairman of the Society (and himself a professor of biochemistry), who snorted through his red beard. "Nonsense!" Henderson said. "We didn't elect him as a bio-chemist. We elected him as a man."

In the founding of the Society, A. Lawrence Lowell was the in-dispensable begetter. "He was very intelligent," says Wassily Leontief, who does not utter this tribute easily. "And he was a Boston Brahmin not of the revolutionary tradition but of the cotton-mill tradition, which meant he had much more money." His brother was the astron-omer Percival Lowell; his sister, the poetess Amy Lowell (and among his great-nephews, incidentally, is McGeorge Bundy). Though he seems to have gone down in history as the man who told the Gover-nor of Massachusetts that Sacco and Vanzetti had received a fair trial, he was also the president of Harvard who announced that if Harold Laski was forced to resign from the faculty for supporting the Boston police strike he would send in his own resignation with Laski's. Lowell was a political scientist of high quality, whose books are still worth reading (though not many people seem to have read them), and he created at Harvard a pattern of undergraduate educa-tion which made the place the prototype of almost everything that is worth retaining in this wretched business. Graduate education trou-bled him; he hated the labyrinthine machinery that clanked out

Ph.D.'s, and he was sure able men shunned academic life for fear of it. "We have developed," he once wrote, "into a mass production of mediocrity."

For Lowell, the Society of Fellows would be an alternative path to an academic career; the initials "J.F." would come to mean at least as much as "Ph.D." after a man's name. Moreover, such a Society, while it might not be able to "teach young barbarians the whole art of living" (as the first report on its feasibility admitted), could introduce the best of young American scholars to the existence of a civilization outside the libraries and laboratories. Lowell did not imagine that such an institution might be limited to Harvard alone. Moved by what Levin has called his "imperial parochialism," he was sure the idea of "prize fellows," imported by him from England, would sweep the American university scene once Harvard established it. Even the discovery that nobody was willing to foot the bills could not diminish Lowell's confidence; and when he decided to retire as president of Harvard he established the Society himself, with an anonymous gift of a little more than a million dollars (in 1932) from his private fortune. The Lowell endowment, multiplied by bull markets and with income capitalized during the low-expense years of the war, still pays the society's costs of about $200,000 a year.

Two other men were almost as significant as Lowell in starting the Society—Lawrence Henderson and the Boston lawyer and writer Charles P. Curtis. These two had already collaborated on a book which lay outside either's professional field of interest—an introduction to the work of the Italian philosopher-sociologist Vilfredo Pareto. They were both friends of Lowell's, and Curtis was a member of the mysterious, awesome, self-perpetuating Corporation which owns and operates Harvard University. Both were great talkers and formidable intellects, but Curtis had a sense of humor and a common touch that Henderson lacked; later, in addition to his contributions to jurisprudence, he would help to write that oddly charming book *The Practical Cogitator*.

Henderson, as the Society's chairman, dominated its early years; but Curtis' ease and presence kept it alive. Probably the worst crisis the Society has undergone came in 1935, when Curtis was dismissed from the Corporation and the Society after a marital scandal. The Junior Fellows were bitter at his departure, and chipped in to buy him as a farewell offering a first edition of Hobbes' *Leviathan*. This was probably one of the books Curtis was hoping to rescue on the night in 1959 when he plunged back into his burning house, and was killed by fire. Shortly thereafter, in partial amends, the Society acquired a bust of Curtis which sits on the table in the anteroom, where the sherry is poured before dinner.

The other people portrayed in the Society's rooms are Lowell, Brinton and Henderson himself, who glares from a painting like Henry VIII in modern dress. (There used to be a bust of Whitehead, but it disappeared over a football weekend a few years ago; some of the Senior Fellows feel a dire suspicion that a good search of the fraternity houses at Dartmouth would turn it up.) Not every survivor from the Henderson days has the happiest memories of the man. Levin once said, paraphrasing John Bates Clark, that Henderson had "an irrational passion for dispassionate rationality." It came out in an inability to believe that anyone who disagreed with him was rational. "He would occasionally lose his temper," Crane Brinton recalls. "And without actually banging his shoe on the table, he was a little heavy."

Still, he had accomplishments to back his arrogance. A medical doctor turned researcher, he had done the basic work in blood chemistry that backed Walter Cannon's theory of homeostasis, the equilibrium of the bloodstream. A professor at the Harvard Medical School, he became head of the famous Fatigue Laboratory at the Harvard Business School, where his collaborators included Elton Mayo, the pioneer sociologist whose studies for the Western Electric Company revealed the "Hawthorne effect," the tendency for *any* deliberate change in the working conditions of a factory to improve the performance of the people on the job, even if the change made life harder for everybody. Henderson also gave a seminar in Pareto which was a command performance at a time when a number of Harvard professors were known as great actors who could be counted on for a show. He knew enough about the middle ages to hold his own in argument with Henry Osborn Taylor, author of *The Medieval Mind* and a frequent guest at the Society's dinners in the early years. A

Francophile and a great gourmet, Henderson ordered the wine for the Society, and talked learnedly about it. As a sociologist *manqué* and a black Republican, he knew exactly what was wrong with the New Deal, and shared his knowledge.

Lowell's crusade against the Ph.D. was abandoned, regretfully, before the old man's death in 1943. The moment of truth came when a singularly promising Junior Fellow was unable to get a job, mostly because accrediting organizations rate colleges and universities by the proportion of Ph.D.'s on their faculties. "This young gentleman was an odd one," Brinton recalls. "We had at Harvard the three world-famous authorities in his field, and all his time as a Fellow he never spoke to one of them. But he'd written a remarkable book, and had pretty near finished it. Henderson wrote thirty or forty letters for him, trying to find him a job, and the answer kept coming back, 'He has to have a Ph.D. if he wants to be an assistant professor.' Finally, his department, very gallantly—because the Society has never been one-hundred-percent accepted around here—gave him a two-hour exam, accepted his book as a thesis, and granted him his Ph.D." The rules of the Society still forbid any Junior Fellow to take courses for credit, but the man can now be a candidate for a degree, with a dissertation to write.

From Henderson's days remain most of the original furnishings (including the round table at which Oliver Wendell Holmes played Autocrat over breakfast), a custom of wines *mise au chateau,* and a flavor of misogyny. It is totally unthinkable that a female shall ever be a Junior Fellow, and in the entire thirty-two years of the Society there has been only one dinner with ladies in attendance. (The occasion was the annual party the Society gives for the Nieman Fellows, newspapermen who have won a year to study anything they like at Harvard; and a lady Nieman wanted her evening.) Among the other traditions that survive is the annual softball game at which the humanists play the scientists, with the social scientists allowed to choose either side. There used to be frequent dances, too, in rebellion against the monkishness of Monday night, but now these are mostly banished by the new seriousness.

With Henderson's passing and the accession of the gentle Brinton, conversation at the big horseshoe table became more of a free-for-all. At one time and another, the talk has been dominated by arguments about the scientific validity of Freudian psychology, about the difficulties in communication which C. P. Snow was later to label "the two cultures," about existentialism, about linguistics. Politics ebb and flow: last year a single Goldwater Fellow (a Junior in theoretical physics) took a fearful beating. Neither sex nor sports (nor academic politics) has ever been excluded, and there has always been considerable talk about the arts, talk which is not normally inhibited by the presence of artists. In recent years the Society has taken on a few composers, some poets (Donald Hall and John Hollander as well as Richard Wilbur), and a few men who turned out to be journalists (among them, Geoffrey Bush and the world federalist Cord Meyer, Jr.). With Leontief at the helm, there will probably be painters and sculptors, too—Leontief has a deep interest in the visual arts, and arranged the loan of the Mark Rothko murals that decorate the grandiloquent reception rooms atop the three-dimensional IBM card of Holyoke Center, the University's new central headquarters. In any event, the Society will continue its search for eccentrics: "Our selection is not good," Leontief said recently, "unless we have at least a couple of crazy Fellows."

Lunacy, especially in recent years, has been less of a bar than sociology. From the start the Society has been dominated by philosophers, literary scholars, scientists and historians; apart from Lowell and his relative Bundy, Leontief is the only social scientist ever to hold an appointment as a Senior Fellow. (And Leontief, a fiercely unconventional mathematical economist, fits nobody's image of the social scientist; he leaves such matters at the office, travels hugely in search of the cheerfully strange, and enjoys his own wry, almost private wit; his closest friends among the Senior Fellows are the Nobel Prize physicist Edward Purcell and the young midwestern biologist James Watson, who has a similar private smile and an equally intense interest in graphic arts.) Thirteen of the current twenty-four Juniors are in mathematics or science, five in history and literature, four in one or another of the scholarly aspects of the arts, and only two in social science—and even these two cover their bets, one hedging economics with economic history, the other coupling psychology with biology.

Nobody can put a finger on precisely why the social scientists have been relatively scarce. Leontief believes it is because "unlike natural philosophy, belles lettres and art, the social sciences are barely two or three hundred years old." Others feel that it is because social scientists have an almost incorrigible tendency to talk about their work, which is bad form. As in any true interdisciplinary enterprise, the Fellows of the Society tend to make contact best in areas where both parties to the dialogue are amateurs.

But these are inspired amateurs—inspired, at the least, by the clarity and power (not always the speed) of their own minds. One former Junior, replying to an anniversary questionnaire, praised his experience because "it taught (and teaches) badly needed humility." Commenting on this reply, Brinton said that it was not "representative"—but it was certainly reasonable. Conversation today is not pressed in the vise of a Henderson—who once greeted a remark of Skinner's with the announcement, "Skinner, that's the stupidest thing I've ever heard you say." But any weakness in a guest's or a fellow Junior's presentation will be pounced on, probed and blasted open, courteously but explosively. Senior Fellows, though generally in a more protected position (caste is caste), often find it wise to be as careful as they are clever:

"Biometric analysis of population trends is all very new, of course. What sort of mathematics do you use?"

"You'd think we knew everything about how microbes move, but in fact if you want to work on it, you almost have to go to Denmark. To Cambridge [which means England] or to Denmark . . ."

"The problem of the military in Okinawa is that they have two perceptions of their situation. One is that they are surrounded by funny little yellow men who don't speak English; the other is that it is very un-American of the Okinawans to want to be Japanese. Now, in fact, both of these perceptions are correct. If you know the Japanese islands, you know that there's a height gradient, with tall people living on Hokkaido, getting smaller and smaller as you go south, and by the time you get to Okinawa most people are under five feet. And it *is* un-American of the Okinawans to want to be Japanese. So we've got to have policy. . . ."

"There, of course, the musicians and the musicologists don't even recognize each other when they meet in the halls—not that it's much better here, of course. . . ."

"Do they have any more Henry Moore drawings there?"—"Yes, but not as good as mine, at that price. . . ."

"But what are you talking about when you correlate the educational effort and economic growth? Look at England after the Exhibition. Were there any causative elements?"

"He has everything to gain by turning down the Nobel Prize, of course—he can say he keeps his independence, and it puts his price up. . . ."

As Monday evening ends, with smaller and smaller groups coalescing over the wine decanter or the brandy flagon, the talk normally mellows and the rather dim anteroom is shadowed by a half-adolescent, half-elderly sadness. The future, always uncertain, grows larger and more menacing—in part, perhaps, because academic life is so ill-defined at this point in time; in part because a Junior Fellow is so clearly a hero-figure and an assistant professor at a midwest university, which is what he will presently be, looks heroic only to his children. At the end of three years, the man goes (renewals are possible and two were granted this year, but it's unusual). By the fall of his third year, he had better know where he is going. To attend the scholarly meetings over Christmas without a job in hand for next year is considered humiliating—and highly dangerous.

About four-fifths of the two hundred-odd former Junior Fellows have remained in academic life, and about a third of those have stayed at Harvard. ("As a recruiting device," Skinner says, "the Society has saved the University *millions* of dollars.") But few of the Juniors come back to dine with the new company, even occasionally.

The clans have been gathered only once, to toast Crane Brinton on the occasion of his retirement in June, 1963. This was to be a surprise party. The universal respect for the efficiency of Miss Elizabeth Hoxie (the Society's and Brinton's kindly secretary, known to a generation of Fellows as "Miss Moxie") was coupled with Miss Hoxie's confidence in the Juniors who were in charge of the plans, and the Juniors' confidence in the Seniors who they thought were handling Brinton. In the end, the secret was so well protected that Brinton never heard about the party at all, and was driving to his summer home in Vermont while several score of outstanding scholars, many of whom had come hundreds of miles to Harvard for the occasion, stood around and felt their champagne go flat. Still, though some participants in the affair kept seeing Banquo's ghost all night, there was enough joviality to persuade the others that an annual mass meeting of Fellows would add to the gaiety of nations, and the party will probably be resumed.

What worries the Juniors most, inevitably, is the fear that they will not match the records of their predecessors, and it is on all counts an un-neurotic fear. "At the beginning," Leontief says, "being a Junior Fellow was like being collected for Paradise. The income was fabulous and the responsibilities were zero." But the once-luxurious stipend of $1,500 had dropped well below the poverty line before it was raised in 1958, and even today the $5,500 maximum for the married man compares badly against the $9,000 the University of California offers in almost equally free, if less glamorous, fellowships. The added services the Society supplies are somewhat less appealing to the man who must return from the four wines of Monday dinner to give the baby his midnight bottle.

"We think of ourselves as the New York Yankees, or the Boston Celtics," says Brinton. "And it would be silly for us not to know there is competition, especially at Berkeley. And if Texas ever gets into this . . . well . . ." Sometimes the Senior Fellows have been tempted to vary payment by field ("You can get a Greek scholar for a third of what a physicist commands," Brinton says), or to take the natural scientist at a younger age than the others. But the first procedure would violate a commitment to the equality of souls, while the second would, in Levin's words, "negate the whole purpose of the Society" by adding further inhibitions to free interchange among wildly different young men now united only by their common age and status, and uncommon abilities. Clearly, the money in the fellowships will have to increase across the board. Brinton resigned not only because he felt that twenty-one years was enough, but also because "I didn't want to raise money." Leontief is not crazy about fund-raising, but will do it.

For Lowell's notion turns out to have astonishing vitality: people are, somehow, obscurely helped just by steady conversational contact across the lines of their disciplines. "I'm puzzled," Skinner says, looking back over the full history of the Society. "You can't possibly justify their selection techniques—but when you examine the results, they're very good."

[A few weeks after this article was published, I received a letter from Mrs. Hilda Carter of Eau Claire, Wisconsin, which read in part as follows:

[". . . I was secretary to L. J. Henderson and to the Society of Fellows from 1934 to 1941, and I was pleased to find something written in depth about Dr. Henderson, for I have always felt he was a colorful and influential person who, though numbered among the 'greats,' is little known by people in the academic world, outside the Harvard milieu of his day. . . .

["Dr. Henderson was a very kind man. In seven years of association with him, including some time spent at his summer home in Vermont, I do not remember one unkind word. True, he was brusque and somewhat unapproachable. But this was an excellent discipline for anyone who came in contact with him. I have always been immensely grateful for it. I believe the word 'arrogant' to be too strong and misleading. The quality of conversation around the table when he was present could not have been anything but stimulating and worthwhile simply because one would not have allowed oneself to say anything foolish in his presence. Accuracy of expression he insisted upon. . . . He was not all rationality. I sat in on the interviews of prospective Junior Fellows and took notes, and I remember one candidate whom he and I were very enthusiastic about, a charming Irishman whose only interest was in Ireland. When he came back from the meeting at which this man was elected to membership, he expressed his delight, but an immediate reservation as to whether his own vote for him might have been based on admiration for the man's charm. . . . He had a personal life shadowed by tragedy and a chronic illness that caused daily discomfort, yet I never knew him once to yield to complaint. Incidentally, it was thought that he strongly resembled Edward VII and he always wore suits tailored in London. . . .

["I cannot agree that the selection process was 'haphazard.' If so, only in the sense that enormous compilation of test scores, etc., was not part of the process. To my mind, the intuitive judgment of men of this caliber, with certain basic materials on file for each candidate, resulted in a process more valid than methods that are in use in many 'selective' processes today. . . .

["One other rather charming little detail—when I left Cambridge in 1941 to move to the Midwest, Dr. Henderson came in one Tuesday morning with an unwrapped package and said, "Here." It was a sterling silver bowl of the Paul Revere pattern engraved around the base, 'To Hilda Richardson Carter from the Society of Fellows, October 1941.' It was covered with the finger smudges of all Junior and Senior Fellows, who had passed it around the table the night before."]

17

Bernie Cornfeld's First Billion

[The story of the writing of this article is almost as complicated as the tale it tells. I was in and out of Geneva between fall, 1964, and spring, 1967, working on a report on international secondary education for the Twentieth Century Fund (published by the Fund, under the title *Diploma,* in spring, 1968). During one of my last trips, somebody mentioned the name of Edward Cowett, whom I had known as the brother of a friend. I looked Ed up in a spare hour, and he exposed to me some of the wonders of Investors Overseas Services. I said it would make a hell of an article, and Ed agreed, but said, "Not yet. Wait until we get out from under our troubles with the SEC."

[When the SEC settlement was announced, I talked about this story with Otto Friedrich of the *Saturday Evening Post,* and he assigned it to me. But I could see no way in. Cowett had decided I.O.S. should not go after publicity; and Cornfeld's New York lawyers, one of whom was among my closest friends, were very concerned about the information I had begun to receive from the United States Government when I started asking around about I.O.S. Then I ran into Rosser Reeves, former chairman of the board of the Ted Bates agency, who had figured largely (not to say hugely) in *Madison Avenue, U.S.A.,* and for whom I had subsequently written a not-to-be-published, now-destroyed history of Ted Bates & Co. Reeves, it turned out, had gone into the consulting business, and among his clients was Bernie Cornfeld, the Grand Cham of I.O.S. Reeves set up a lunch with Cornfeld in New York, and over the lunch table, at 3:45 in the afternoon, Cornfeld agreed to cooperate. He said he thought I was *heymisch,* and he was *heymisch,* and we would get on.

[And in fact, though neither of us is *heymisch,* we did get on. What probably does not come through in this piece is that I liked Bernie and still do, though I believe he has grown a little weary of me. He did outrageous things on my visit to Geneva in connection with this piece—for example, he took me along with a gaggle of the girls to Ba-Ta-Clan, the lowest strip joint in town, and in my presence propositioned one of the strippers. ("Howard," he said, returning to the table, "I'm having Monique for lunch tomorrow." Howard, a New York lawyer, very savvy, said, "With an apple in her mouth, Bernie?") But such assertions of his own vulnerability, which are often distasteful in the subject of a piece, were in an odd way charming in Cornfeld.

[So I wrote the piece and submitted it to the *Saturday Evening Post,* and Friedrich sent back an almost despairing editor's letter, asking me to remember that I was writing for an audience which did not know what a proprietary fund is and did not care to learn. On consideration, I decided that what he was saying was that the piece was for *Fortune,* not for the *Post.* I called Louis Banks at *Fortune,* whom I had never actually met (we had talked on the telephone a couple of times), and he said, sure, he'd look at the piece, but it was pretty unlikely. I delivered the manuscript at four o'clock Friday afternoon. At eleven o'clock Monday morning Banks called—he wanted it. Friedrich very graciously released the *Post*'s rights. Something *Fortune* had counted on for the March issue had just dropped out, I learned later, and this piece dropped in like manna. To say the least, it made my day.]

"IT'S ONLY about a dozen years since I ran the whole business out of my studio apartment in Paris," said Bernard Cornfeld, a short, sad-eyed, balding, complicated forty-year-old former socialist from Brooklyn turned finance-capitalist from Switzerland. He was taking the afternoon sun of a fine winter's day in the foothills of the Alps, stretched out on the terrace of the thirteenth-century castle he is steadily converting to a forty-room bachelor's pleasure dome at a continuing cost of about $150,000 a year; and he was reminiscing on request. "There was a secretary who would come in in the morning, and we'd have a cup of coffee together and open the mail, and then I'd go to work. Now it takes twelve people just to open the mail—in fact, they don't open it; that's done by machine. I need twelve people every day full-time just to *sort* the mail."

In addition to the mail sorters, Confeld's business now employs fourteen thousand people and three computers to sell the mutual-fund programs and life-insurance policies which are his stock in trade and to process the paperwork. For Investors Overseas Services, which Cornfeld founded in Paris in 1956 and moved to Geneva in 1958, is today by far the world's largest financial sales organization and one of its largest private financial institutions. From door-to-door selling in the PX community of NATO a dozen years ago, Bernie Cornfeld, mostly by his own intuition, energy and intelligence, has achieved the control of more than a billion dollars in investment funds.

It has been an inventive if not a peaceful progress, on a path paved with new ideas—among them, for example, the Fund of Funds, an investment company to invest in other investment companies; an effective plan for compensating salesmen by stock options even in the absence of any public market for I.O.S. stock; and all sorts of labyrinthine ways around the currency and citizenship regulations of a number of countries. The driving force of the operation, however, has been a single original insight: that investments in American securities could be sold to great numbers of middle-class Europeans (and Asians and Latin Americans) who had never before put their money into anything but bank accounts and land.

I.O.S. today has branch offices of some size in fifty countries, and its quarter of a million shareholders, policyholders, and other "clients" include citizens of every United Nations member nation (including all the Communist nations). One I.O.S. rep remembers affectionately selling all but one of the German nationals in a whole country on a single trip—four, that is, of the five Germans in Nepal; the fifth overslept and missed his appointment. Another salesman recalls a one-month organized tour behind the Iron Curtain during which he broke away from the guides long enough to sell $3,500,000 of investment programs to government, press, and diplomatic personnel who had access to convertible currencies. In the Port of Rotterdam, delegates from the local I.O.S. office—they include Greeks, Norwegians, Italians, and Germans—race around the harbor to greet the incoming ships and sponge up with mutual-fund shares whatever loose money may be lying around on board.

Despite the opposition of the Securities and Exchange Commission, which no longer allows Cornfeld to sell his shares and investment programs to Americans, I.O.S. is growing steadily. At the turn of the year, new money was pouring into the Cornfeld mutual funds, insurance companies, and banks at a rate of more than $2.5 million a day. On some days I.O.S. purchases and sales of securities on American markets equal 4 percent of all the trading on the New York Stock Exchange.

Because this money comes from non-Americans, and the great bulk of it is put to work on Wall Street, Cornfeld all by himself is a significant factor in the American balance-of-payments equation. In 1966, I.O.S. contributed about $324 million to the strength of the dollar on the international money markets; this year the forecast is for an inflow of about $500 million.

Cornfeld was born in Istanbul to a Rumanian father and a Russian mother; they brought him to the United States when he was four years old, at the bottom of the Depression. He worked his way through tuition-free Brooklyn College, where, despite an almost disabling stutter (which he has since lost), he became president of the nation's largest chapter of the Congress of Racial Equality and in 1948 set a world record in number of signatures gathered on Norman Thomas-for-President petitions. Not until after he had served a year as a social worker in Philadelphia did Cornfeld become a full-time salesman of mutual funds—and he was no great shakes at it even then. "He made nice sales," says Walter Benedick, president of Investors Planning Corporation, who gave Cornfeld his first selling job. "But nothing outstanding."

In 1955, Cornfeld took a vacation trip to Europe and decided he wanted to stay there. The obvious way for him to support himself was by selling mutual funds to the large expatriate and military colonies in and around Paris. I.P.C. was willing enough to take the sales he made and pay him 3.8 percent of whatever the customer signed up for; but it was not prepared to finance a branch office for him, and Cornfeld on consideration grew dubious about the European sales potential of the fund he'd been selling. What he really wanted to sell was Dreyfus Fund, the first of the "growth funds."

While still working for I.P.C. in New York, Cornfeld had gone calling on Jack Dreyfus, suggesting that the fund would grow more rapidly if it switched from a policy of selling shares only on a straight pay-now basis to a policy of selling ten-year automatic reinvestment programs. Now he wrote a "Remember me?" note from Paris and made the suggestion again. This time Dreyfus was ready to move; Cornfeld left I.P.C. and became a Dreyfus dealer. His instinct was right: on the basis of the new Dreyfus prospectus, the fund's sales rose sharply; and Investors Overseas Services, as Cornfeld called his new selling organization, became its largest dealer. In 1962, I.O.S. sold almost $64 million of "systematic accumulation programs" in Dreyfus Fund, plus another $10 million of fully paid programs. By then Cornfeld had expanded I.O.S. well beyond Paris and beyond the expatriate American colonies elsewhere; rapidly rising proportions of his sales and of his sales force were European.

Cornfeld brought to Europe an almost messianic insistence that mutual-fund buying is good for the customer. Where possible, salesmen are recruited from the ranks of customers, who have demonstrated with their own money their high opinion of what they are about to sell. The sales pitch they are taught, while familiar to many Americans, is new and powerful in Europe. What the "client" buys from I.O.S. is not a piece of paper of indeterminate future value but "retirement with dignity, education for your children, a home of your own. . . ." There is nothing that the recipient of the call can say which the sales rep is not glad to hear—if "Mr. Prospect" (as the salesmen's instruction booklet calls him) already owns mutual funds, the rep is pleased at the chance to discuss the I.O.S. program with somebody who understands; if Mr. Prospect has no money, no matter because the rep wants to talk about *him,* not about money; if Mr. Prospect would rather have the literature arrive by mail to avoid wasting the rep's time, he is a thoughtful man indeed, but as it happens the rep is going to be in his neighborhood anyway. "Would Tuesday at seven or Wednesday at eight-thirty be better for you?"

The rep's belief in the value of what he is selling is further enhanced by Cornfeld's compensation schedules. Everyone in the field works entirely on commission, with a sliding scale that awards higher commission rates as volume increases. When a man sells more than $500,000 worth of investment programs, he gets an option to buy I.O.S. stock, at its present price, over a period of time in the future. The price is determined by a complicated formula based on book value, assets under management, and number of salesmen at work. The formula virtually guarantees a steady increase in the price, and thereby assures that the most effective members of the sales staff will stay cheerful, and their sales pitch will stay high-keyed. Too many sales to customers who fail to meet their payments, however, reduces both commission income and opportunities to buy stock. Thus the compensation system also works, Cornfeld believes, to police the "quality" of I.O.S. sales.

Cornfeld's evangelistic sales drives and "American methods" made him an irritant and then a nuisance in the strait-laced world of European finance, and his casual manner doesn't help either. Nobody who has ever met him—not even the receptionists at the office or the domestic help at the castle—ever calls him anything but "Bernie." The I.O.S. offices look like a branch of the Playboy Club, with a splendid multinational collection of mini-skirted girls. Invited to address a group of conservative and hostile Swiss bankers at a luncheon meeting a few months ago, Cornfeld turned up wearing a sports jacket with a blonde on his arm. It was a very good sports jacket, tailored (like all his clothing, including his shirts and his socks) by Pierre Cardin, who came to prominence as Jacqueline Kennedy's favorite couturier. And it was also, as always, a very good blonde. But it was no way to make friends with the gnomes of Zurich.

The Swiss bankers would not have cared much what Cornfeld looked like if he had remained merely a dealer in SEC-registered American mutual funds. Whatever its attractions, Dreyfus Fund had certain disadvantages for Europeans: when the investor went to cash in, his proceeds were subject to American capital-gains taxes—and Europeans are not used to capital-gains taxes. If the sale was part of an estate liquidation there might also be American inheritance taxes, and these might take years to process; meanwhile, the entire proceeds of the liquidation had to stay in the United States. Moreover, any American fund is required by law to keep complete records of its shareholders; and lots of Europeans, for good reasons or bad, want to make their investments secretly. To hunt a lot of European business, Cornfeld would have to ride vehicles that were not subject to United States taxes or regulation; and he began inventing such vehicles in 1962.

Nothing in Cornfeld's background, of course, equipped him to manage the investment of other people's money. Starting his first fund, IIT (an international investment trust), he asked a Swiss banker in Zurich to make his investment decisions. Shortly thereafter, Cornfeld's organization latched onto C. Henry Buhl III, an amiable jet-setter, grandson of a man who had backed the Fisher brothers in their little flyer in automobiles and wound up one of the largest stock-holders in General Motors. Buhl, who was still in his early thirties, had been working for the Wall Street house of McDonnell & Co. and had got bored with it. He had come to Geneva looking for something amusing to do. One night a girl referred him to Bernie Cornfeld, who seemed very amusing. Cornfeld hired Buhl, whose social position would gain him access everywhere (when Buhl got married a few years ago, the late Francis Cardinal Spellman flew the Atlantic to officiate at the wedding), to persuade European banks and dealers to sell IIT.

Buhl's efforts to wholesale IIT were relatively unsuccessful, in part because the fund itself was unsuccessful: the Swiss management was inadequate to the job. "The Swiss philosophy," Buhl says, "is protec-tion of capital, not making capital grow. Our little fund had $2 mil-lion and it was in 125 different issues." Buhl took over the manage-ment himself. He had never managed other people's money either; however, his wide acquaintance came in handy, for he had no diffi-culty arranging with half a dozen major banking firms—in England, Holland, Germany, France, and Switzerland—to advise him, for a fee, on investment decisions. Since Buhl took control in late 1962, IIT's price per share has more than doubled, and the fund now has about $200 million in assets—all of it invested in only about forty issues.

Meanwhile, Cornfeld had found another way around the problem of his lack of expertise in the market—a "fund of funds," which instead of investing in the shares of individual enterprises would in-vest in the shares of American mutual funds. This notion was a true stroke of genius: it gave I.O.S. a product which could be sold to the strains of "Star-Spangled Banner," under an incomparable brand name. "Fund of Funds," says Walter Benedick of I.P.C. admiringly. "It has such a marvelous *sound,* like King of Kings." Performance has been salable too: Fund of Funds has consistently, in good years and bad, outperformed the great majority of publicly held American mutual funds. It is the heart of the Cornfeld empire, with more than $600 million in assets as of the close of 1967 and almost $2 billion more scheduled to be purchased under existing contractual programs.

I.O.S. itself is a limited-liability company incorporated in Panama in 1960. Bernard Cornfeld was originally the sole stockholder, but over the years he has given away to his employees as bonuses, or sold to them under various stock-option plans, about five sixths of his shares in the company. He still controls it, of course; employees own their stock only so long as they are employees, and they may not sell it without offering it first to I.O.S. for repurchase at the formula price. Eventually, Cornfeld and his associates hope to reap the benefits of going public, and a partial harvest will be attempted this month, with a public offering of shares in the Canadian corporate subsidiary that gets the management fees for IIT and Fund of Funds. The possibilities of a piecemeal sale of the business are immense. Cornfeld's one sixth holding of I.O.S. today is worth about $20 million under his stock-evaluation formula; beyond that, there are many subsidiary corporations wholly or partially owned by the parent company and by each other. The most important of the subsidiaries are:

■ The I.O.S. sales and management corporations.
■ The mutual funds (especially Fund of Funds, Ltd., a nonresident Canadian corporation, and the IIT fund, a Luxembourg corporation).
■ I.O.S. Bank Holding Co. (U.K.), controlling, among others, Investors Overseas Bank, a Bahaman corporation, and Overseas Development Bank, a Swiss corporation.
■ International Life Insurance Co., S.A., a Luxembourg corporation controlling I.L.I. (U.K.) in Britain and other insurance companies, including Pension Life Insurance in the United States.
■ INDEVCO, a real-estate company currently engaged in building many apartment houses on Spain's Costa del Sol, with plans to build in Mexico and in Miami Beach.

The unlikely-sounding home bases for the corporations were chosen mostly for tax reasons. They were obviously chosen well: in 1966 I.O.S. paid only about $375,000 in total taxes on profits of $6 million.

These various operations mesh together nicely. Cornfeld's standard package for the mutual-fund customer includes an insurance policy that guarantees the completion of the customer's purchase program if he dies; the insurance is written by I.L.I. If a customer wants to finance a large mutual-fund purchase, he can borrow from O.D.B. Venture capital for the real-estate company can be supplied by the mutual funds, and mortgage money can be supplied by the banks. And when the time comes to sell the cooperative apartments, what more likely customers could there be—Cornfeld asks himself—than the owners of shares in Fund of Funds?

All the other I.O.S. enterprises are minor, of course, next to the selling effort. In 1966 the parent company and its major subsidiaries together had a gross operating income of about $60 million, of which about $50 million represented the proceeds of selling the funds and insurance. The biggest seller is a long-term (ten- or fifteen-year) program for the purchase of mutual-fund shares through monthly payments. The minimum plan is $3,000, paid in monthly installments of $25 each over a period of ten years. Most plans run about $50 a month.

What makes it possible to support a big sales organization on such small monthly amounts is the fairly steep commission charge on mutual-fund sales, and the "front-end load," which assigns about half the total commission for a ten-year program to the purchaser's payments during the first year. Counting both commission and a monthly "administration" charge, $659.99 of a $6,000 plan—one penny short of eleven percent—will be deducted from the customer's total payments before the investment of his money; but $312.10, or 52 percent, will be taken out of his first $600. (Insurance, if any, is extra.) Front-end loads are in no way special to I.O.S.—they are a familiar feature of the American mutual-fund business, although the Securities and Exchange Commission doesn't like them and has promoted legislation to end them.

With few exceptions, I.O.S. plans are sold in dollars, and it is up to the customer to convert his local currency into dollars; I.O.S. assumes that he does it legally, and prays that its eager salesmen do not help him do it illegally. In fact, of course, a salesman working on a straight commission basis has considerable incentive to remove any technical barriers that may keep the customer from buying his product, and to stress the anonymity for tax purposes that I.O.S. by virtue of its Swiss base has been able to offer. One or the other (or both) of these appeals to customer cupidity has got I.O.S. in more or less publicized trouble in a number of countries—most notably in Brazil, where the military government broke the anonymity of the Swiss numbered accounts by the simple expedient of opening mail and searching homes.

An organization with a billion dollars in assets under management cannot afford scandals of this kind, especially when the countries losing the money are poor. In the fall of 1966, Cornfeld hired James Roosevelt in an effort to boost sales in countries where the export of capital was frowned on. Roosevelt resigned as Number 2 man in the United States Mission to the United Nations to become president of the I.O.S. Management Co. He has widened Cornfeld's perspectives in several directions. "Recently, we had some trouble in Iran," Cornfeld recalls gratefully. "Jim telephoned the Shah, and we went up to St. Moritz and the three of us began working it out up there. . . ."

Roosevelt's particular baby is the creation of "national funds," I.O.S. subsidiaries separately tailored to the laws and resources of each country and available for sale in the local currency (thus reducing the hostility of the local banks, which receive commissions when the currency is converted into dollars). The first such funds have already been launched, as Fonditalia in Italy and Investors Fonds in Germany, both of which are expected to invest about half their money in domestic industry. The prestige of the I.O.S. German operation (which continues to sell Fund of Funds and IIT) has been greatly boosted at home by the appointment of Erich Mende, former Vice Chancellor of Germany, as its president.

Roosevelt has also been traveling around South America and Asia, visiting with presidents and prime ministers to lay the groundwork for national funds in developing countries; and by means of what are in effect private treaties between the governments of these countries and I.O.S., special funds and insurance plans will presently go on sale in the Philippines, probably Venezuela, and maybe Chile. Mexico, from which I.O.S. was chased five years ago for failure to register under Mexican law, returned to the fold in January, following extended negotiations climaxed by a two-day visit by Ambassador Roosevelt. Under Roosevelt's arrangements, I.O.S. guarantees that some of the money people pay for their I.O.S. certificates will remain in the country, either through fund investments in local companies or through reciprocal arrangements providing for I.O.S. to underwrite sales of the country's bonds in European markets.

The argument Roosevelt uses is simple in the extreme. Today, wealthy people in underdeveloped countries smuggle their money out, because there is no home capital market where it can be put to work. I.O.S. will enable such money to move out in an orderly fashion, with the government keeping track of who owns what where; furthermore, I.O.S. local investment of part of the receipts will help create local capital markets. "I'm not such an optimist as to believe we can get more than perhaps twenty percent of what now goes out as black-market money," Roosevelt says. "But even twenty percent would be meaningful."

Cornfeld's difficulties in 1966, when Roosevelt came aboard, were by no means restricted to the problems that stimulated the idea of the national funds; in fact, he was in trouble all over the world. The cause of his trouble is best explained, perhaps, by a personal policy statement from the executive vice president and general counsel, Edward Cowett: "Everywhere we go we comply with the local law— no more and no less." Governments naturally tend to be annoyed by the I.O.S. policy of looking to the letter rather than the intent of the law.

In England, for example, exchange controls did not permit British nationals to convert their pounds into dollars for the purpose of buying Fund of Funds without payment of an exchange premium that often ran as high as 30 percent. But there was a way around this requirement. London has always been the world center of the insurance business, and to maintain that profitable position the Bank of England has always permitted British insurance companies to lay off their risks—to "reinsure"—anywhere in the world, and to convert pounds freely in the process. I.O.S. already had its Luxembourg insurance company, formed to handle the insurance on the I.O.S. programs. In 1963, I.O.S. organized a subsidiary of this company, calling it International Life Insurance (U.K.). The subsidiary would sell to the British, not the mutual funds, but an original Dover Plan—a name that, as the I.L.I. (U.K.) 1967 annual report explained, is associated with "the White Cliffs of Dover, a symbol of strength and protection for 2,000 years." In a Dover Plan, the customer buys a term life-insurance policy plus a "variable endowment"—that is, a cash value which fluctuates according to the market price for the assets in which the company invests the endowment funds. These assets are, in fact, shares in a mutual fund; but the monthly payment by the customer is legally the premium on a life-insurance policy. The policy can, of course, be "reinsured." I.L.I. (U.K.) cheerfully reinsured its premium income with I.L.I. Luxembourg—which put the money into Fund of Funds. In effect, the English policyholder in I.L.I. was buying the same merchandise as the German purchaser of an I.O.S. insured investment program. The latter would have been illegal in Britain; the former was legal—barely legal. Some bankers who understood what was going on admired the ingenuity of the operation. As one of them put it, "All that I.O.S. did was to get up a little earlier in the morning than the Bank of England. I can't see that there's anything *wrong* with that."

The Bank of England itself disagreed and cracked down on the I.O.S., in effect telling Cornfeld, "Law or no law—you leave our pounds here." Cornfeld said didn't-know-you-cared, sorry-about-that, very blithe and free, and shifted incoming Dover Plan money from the original Fund of Funds to a newly formed Fund of Funds Sterling, which would limit its investments to securities that British subjects could legally buy with pounds. In 1967, the per-share market value of Fund of Funds Sterling rose more than 60 percent, and I.L.I. became the fourth-largest underwriter of new life policies in the British Isles. Meanwhile, a chunk of the I.O.S. worldwide administrative operation was shifted to England to take advantage of some extra space and some extra time on the computer at International Life

House, I.L.I.'s new eleven-story center at Wembley Park, just outside London.

I.O.S. was also having legal troubles in Switzerland during these years. The great expansion of I.O.S. began at about the time the Swiss decided that the way to avoid overheating of their economy was to limit the number of foreigners allowed to work in Switzerland. Several hundred thousand workers, mostly Italian and Spanish, were denied renewal of their residence and work permits, and shipped home; Swiss companies that wanted to hire new staff from abroad were told to do without. Yet I.O.S. was growing steadily, with multilingual help, much of it non-Swiss.

For a while, the I.O.S. staff explosion was inconspicuous. In Geneva, as in Paris, Cornfeld had started by working out of his own apartment, on the seventh floor of 119 Rue de Lausanne, looking over the lake to the Alps. As I.O.S. grew, Cornfeld simply took over more and more apartments at that address, then whole floors, and finally the entire building. When I.O.S. headquarters employment reached seven hundred or so, questions began to be asked.

Again, it turned out that the letter of the law had been observed. The University of Geneva, like all European universities, has no money for scholarships. Students, therefore, have always been exempted from the requirement that foreigners must hold work permits. I.O.S. hired University of Geneva students. There being no requirements of attendance for those enrolled at the university, many of them were available full time. And when the supply of students ran out, I.O.S. imported new students. A lawyer might be hired in Munich or Rome, for example, brought to Geneva, and registered as a graduate student at the faculty of law, and then ushered to his office at 119 Rue de Lausanne; the university would not hear from him again. "We couldn't hire even one foreigner," Edouard Pictet of Geneva's Pictet & Cie says resentfully, "and they had hired seven hundred. That hurts."

Unlike the reinsurance gimmick in England, the student game in Geneva ended by being expensive to I.O.S. In early 1967, several hundred I.O.S. "students" were informed by the police that their residence permits would not be renewed, and, as a result, much of

Cornfeld's administrative apparatus had to clear out of Switzerland. Swiftly, I.O.S. secured the approval of the French Government to establish offices right across the border from Geneva, in the town of Ferney-Voltaire. Working twenty-four hours a day, under flood-lights all night, French workmen completed in sixty-three days several office buildings with working space for a thousand and a cafeteria with three hundred seats, called "The I.O.S. Chuck Wagon." This did not entirely solve I.O.S.'s problems, because all these people had to be rehoused, too—but living space of some sort, much of it in farmhouses in what is by no means a highly developed section, was found for everyone.

Young and mostly single (only 38 percent of the I.O.S. staff in Ferney is married), the I.O.S. "students" had recreation needs; and these, too, became a matter of corporate concern after a late party one night brought out the entire constabulary of the *pays de Gex* in and around Ferney. I.O.S. had bought some of its land in Ferney from an elderly woman who now owns the house where Voltaire spent his declining years, and she had become a friend of I.O.S. She agreed to let I.O.S. take the gatehouse of the Voltaire property and turn it into a club for employees. Beginning this spring the park around the great cynic's house will rock to sounds quite undreamed of in his philosophy.

The Swiss bankers were not quite through with Cornfeld, however. They exacted two further concessions: one, that he would disband his Swiss selling organization and in the future sell his securities in Switzerland only through the banks; and two, that while he could keep his executive offices at 119 Rue de Lausanne, he would immediately remove from his selling literature the statement that I.O.S. had its "headquarters and administrative offices in Switzerland, a country with a history of political, economic and monetary stability." I.O.S. Investment Program literature now lists the "sponsor and distributor" as "Investors Overseas Services, Bahamas."

Cornfeld says his relations with the Swiss are now improving, which must be true—they could hardly get worse. But little pieces of nastiness still occur. In December, for example, *La Suisse,* Geneva's tabloid newspaper, carried a story about a doubling of the venereal-disease rate in the *pays de Gex* since "a certain foreign company" crossed over to Ferney. I.O.S. investigated frantically, and found that, sure enough, there had been six cases of gonorrhea in the *pays de Gex* in 1966, and there were twelve cases in 1967.

I.O.S. had registered with the SEC as a dealer in 1960, in order to work on military bases outside the United States, and in 1965 Cornfeld moved into the United States itself. To prepare for the move, he bought (for $1,900,000) an 80 percent share of Investors Planning Corporation, his former employer.

I.O.S. reorganized the I.P.C. sales staff and stepped up the voltage of the sales pitch. Sales of ten-year programs rose from a monthly average of about $5 million in face value to a monthly average of about $18 million. "Quite apart from the fact that I'd worked there," Cornfeld said rather sadly last December, after the SEC had ordered him to sell I.P.C., "the really exciting thing to me was the demonstration that our success wasn't the result of our having no competition. As long as we were just working overseas, people could say we had a product no one else had, and our success was a special thing, like selling gumballs to the Pakistanis. Well, we came into New York, into the most competitive market in the world. The sales of the other mutual-fund dealers in New York stayed the same for two years— and our sales boomed." Meanwhile, of course, I.O.S. was selling its own nonregistered funds elsewhere in the world, and trading on the American exchanges. The SEC examined what it knew about the operations of this particular dealer, found the information inadequate, investigated, and then complained.

Some of the accusations seemed trivial—for example, that I.O.S. salesmen had illegally sold nonregistered securities on the island of Guam. (One of Cornfeld's New York lawyers, assigned to look into this charge, says with heavy sarcasm, "We had a man out there for weeks, interviewing gooney birds.") But some of the charges were very serious—for example, that I.O.S. had caused some of the funds owned by Fund of Funds to submit false information in registration statements to cover over illegal rebates of brokerage commissions to I.O.S.

The stickiest point of all proved to be another matter: the SEC insistence that I.O.S. disclose its customer lists and certain operating information that the Securities and Exchange Act requires from registered dealers. The reply from I.O.S. was that the law in many of the countries where it operates requires confidentiality in financial transactions; and that I.O.S. operations abroad were not subject to SEC jurisdiction. (I.O.S. had, however, made effective use of the SEC registration in its selling literature.) Cornfeld says that revelation of the I.O.S. customer lists would have been a serious breach of faith and dangerous to some owners of I.O.S. programs: "We have six heads of state among our clients, and many nationals of Iron Curtain countries."

People at the SEC, obviously acting on information from other government agencies, believe that the I.O.S. principle of confidentiality serves to conceal much "hot" money from criminal operations in Las Vegas and the Bahamas, and from misappropriation of United States AID funds in many underdeveloped nations. Nobody knows for sure how much hot money flows to I.O.S. Information gathered at the company's computer center in Nyon, up the lake from Geneva, indicates that a considerable I.O.S. business in the Bahamas is done on an anonymous basis. It seems at least possible that Cornfeld could not reveal names to the SEC simply because I.O.S. itself does not know and has no way of finding out who owns the numbered accounts in the Bahamas.

The Commission claimed that the Fund of Funds prospectus was misleading to potential customers. (Xerox copies of these SEC charges will be given to anyone on request, or even without request, by a number of Swiss and German banks.) The text of the prospectus showed, for example, that IIT and Fund of Funds had done far better than the Dow-Jones industrials, but only a footnote showed that part of the differentials reflected the fact that the funds and not the averages benefited from reinvestment of dividends. Without notifying the shareholders, I.O.S. had changed the prospectus of Fund of Funds to permit purchases from *any* investment company rather than, as originally stated, only from publicly held mutual funds. And while promising that the costs of acquiring shares for Fund of Funds would not exceed one percent of the investment, the prospectus had not announced that I.O.S. itself was rather greedily pocketing most of that one percent in its capacity as a dealer for the funds purchased. (Since the same commission would have been paid to somebody else, the customer's equity was not diminished—though it could have been enhanced by the waiver of the commissions.)

The SEC also interested itself in the question of what happened to the brokerage commissions I.O.S. controlled by virtue of its heavy purchases from mutual funds. Traditionally, mutual funds have rewarded the broker-dealers that sell their shares by directing other brokerage houses, which execute the funds' market orders, to give up some of the commissions to the broker-dealers. Not being a member of any exchange, I.O.S. was obviously not entitled to any such "give-up." But its bargaining position with the mutual funds whose shares it bought was obviously strong, and it used this strength to designate the recipients of brokerage business and give-ups.

The SEC went after the registered funds in an effort to get information about the extent of this "directed brokerage," and about what happened to it. The funds' prospectuses included statements from I.O.S. that none of these commissions or give-ups had produced benefits for I.O.S. or its affiliates or anybody associated with either. Other evidence, however, indicated that the brokers who got the commissions may have made arrangements with their banks to place large sums on deposit, interest-free, with Investors Overseas Bank in the Bahamas, a wholly owned I.O.S. subsidiary. The SEC also discovered that $750,000 of commissions had been credited to Martica Clapp, an attractive lady, Cuban by birth, Bermudian by citizenship, and Bahaman by residence. Her husband is Sam Clapp, a Boston lawyer who has had many and varied affiliations with I.O.S. enterprises. What, the SEC wanted to know, had Martica Clapp done to earn this money? And what had she done with it after she got it? No official reply was made by I.O.S. to these queries. Asked privately a few weeks ago, general counsel Edward Cowett said, "By reason of the fact that Martica and Sam are in the Bahamas they can be very helpful to us, and they have been. Sam Clapp is one of the cleverest tax attorneys I know. This is excess business to us—we have commissions coming out of our ears all over the place. And so long as we have these commissions to give up we'll give them to our friends." It is probably not an answer that satisfies everybody.

So far as public relations are concerned, the worst moment in the SEC investigation was the disclosure of a letter Cowett had written after a visit to the New York office of Investors Continental Services, which served as the general American operations center for I.O.S. until mid-1965. A carbon of the letter had been found in an I.C.S. file by an SEC gumshoe, who made a hand-written copy of it before handing it back to I.C.S. with a number of other original documents the agency wished to have I.C.S. photocopy for further study in Washington. No photocopy of this particular letter was ever received in Washington, and on subsequent examination it was found to have disappeared from the I.C.S. files. It read, in part, as follows: ". . . Whenever an incorrect commission statement comes in to New York, whenever a letter written on I.C.S. stationery by someone who is not [a] registered representative finds its way into the New York office . . . Hy [Feld, the I.C.S. New York manager] attempts to remove such commission statement, letters, or other papers from I.C.S. files. However, there is a strong probability that Hy will not be able to catch everything which should not be put into the I.C.S. files . . .

"As you are probably aware, the I.C.S. files are always open to complete examination by the N.A.S.D. [the National Association of Securities Dealers] or SEC. One improper paper in the file, if discovered, could lead to a complete investigation of the entire workings of I.C.S. Such an examination would include, in all probability, a review of all correspondence coming into the office over a protracted period. Since the correspondence in any period of three or four or five days is bound to include at least one daming [*sic*] letter, you can see that the results could be disastrous. . . ."

Cowett at first could not recall any such letter, but then Chairman Manuel F. Cohen of the SEC read the handwritten copy aloud to him at a private, informal meeting of I.O.S. representatives with the commission in September, 1965. With an expression that has been described as his Mona Lisa smile, Cowett replied, "It sounds like my letter."

Well, Cornfeld was asked recently, what does the letter mean? His answer was that the letter warned against allowing records of commissions earned by registered representatives of I.C.S. to be mixed up with records of commissions earned by other I.O.S. representatives, in other parts of the world. "It had no significance whatever," he insisted. "Ed's got an immoderate style. All he was saying was, 'You can wear two hats, but you can't keep them in the same closet.' Half our trouble with the SEC was that Ed kept telling the staff he was smarter than they were. They may have been schmucks, but they were the government."

Cowett is a slight and graceful man not yet forty, who has a rather raffish manner combined with intellectual tastes. He was an associate in a Wall Street law firm working for Dreyfus when he first met Cornfeld, who became his client when he opened his own firm in 1958. By 1960, Cornfeld was his biggest client, and in 1963 Cowett moved to Geneva to become an I.O.S. executive. Next to Cornfeld himself, he has probably been the most important man in the company. Roosevelt's "national funds" are mostly Cowett's invention. He is still outraged about the SEC's publication of his letter: "It's the closest thing to McCarthyism I know. Anyway, what do they mean accusing us of not keeping it in the files? If we hadn't kept it in the files how would they ever have found it?"

"But what *does* the letter mean?" he was asked.

"Do you know," Cowett said, "through the whole investigation nobody at the SEC ever asked me to explain what that letter meant!"

"Yes, but you're being asked now."

"The reason for that letter was that all commissions are processed in Geneva. So I.C.S. would receive commissions statements for somebody who is not a registered representative. He doesn't have to be registered, because he works for I.O.S. and sells Fund of Funds. But the commission statement is in the files in New York, where it shouldn't be. That's all there is to it."

In other words, Cowett's claim, like Cornfeld's, is that the letter refers only to a wholly innocent but unfortunate kind of clerical error.

The error would make it appear that sales commissions, which could legally be paid by I.C.S. only to its own registered representatives, were going to people not registered with the N.A.S.D. Those who wish to refer again to the letter will see that Cowett's explanation takes care of its first paragraph but not necessarily its second paragraph.

I.O.S. went to court to try to enjoin the SEC investigation, and lost. Cowett then returned to Washington and suggested to general counsel Philip Loomis of the SEC that there ought to be a settlement. Over a long and dreary half year, representatives of I.O.S. and the SEC worked out a compromise that would take the matter off the SEC docket, and in May of last year the deal was completed.

The order finally accepted by I.O.S. was a tough one. It barred the company and its affiliates and all its officers from any activity whatsoever in American securities markets. I.O.S. agreed to sell its American subsidiaries, I.C.S. and I.P.C., and to do no securities business whatever with American citizens or citizens of other countries who maintain residences in the United States. In order to insulate itself from all trading in American securities. I.O.S. began placing all orders to buy and sell through an independent bank in London. I.O.S. also agreed to respect that portion of the Investment Company Act which prohibits any such company from holding more than 3 percent of the shares of a publicly held registered diversified mutual fund. Finally, the SEC required I.O.S. to offer to all American military personnel and federal-government employees the right to a complete refund of any losses they had ever taken in Cornfeld's funds, including all sales charges and administration fees. I.O.S. sent letters to 4,000 American customers, and Cowett says that only a handful asked for their money back: "Of our 2,800 replies, 500 were just thank-you notes, people telling us how sorry they were they couldn't continue their I.O.S. investment plans. I'm thinking of having the 500 letters bound into a book for presentation to the SEC."

Cornfeld himself bounced back magnificently. "Gentlemen," he said to a meeting of the I.O.S. board of directors called immediately after the settlement was approved, "the SEC has just made a splendid new corporate policy for us." Announcements went out to the salesmen and customers implying that the settlement was a victory for I.O.S., upholding its thesis that its activities were not subject to SEC jurisdiction, maintaining the confidentiality of I.O.S. client lists, and liberating the Fund of Funds investment advisers from various governmental controls that had cramped their style. The German newspaper *Die Zeit* expressed surprise that I.O.S. had not cut all its ties with the United States long before, seeing that it was such a fine idea.

Actually, there is something to be said for Cornfeld's good cheer. Even before the SEC moved, I.O.S. was beginning to transfer Fund of Funds investments from publicly held mutual funds to "proprietary funds" in which Fund of Funds would be the only investor ("captive funds," the SEC calls them). The general idea was that men who were running successful publicly held funds would run special I.O.S. funds on the side. In some cases, this arrangement would enable I.O.S. to put money under the management of men whose publicly held funds were too small to absorb Fund-of-Funds-sized investments; it also, of course, would award to I.O.S. subsidiaries the management fees that otherwise went to the management companies running the publicly held funds. The deal with the individual managers involved paying them a share of the profits from appreciation of the portfolios they manage for Fund of Funds.

Cornfeld now has made such arrangements with eight young money managers. Among the first of them was Fred Alger, Jr., who in 1965, at thirty, had made Security Equity Fund the hottest thing in the industry. At the end of 1967, Alger was managing $82 million of Fund of Funds money, and his compensation for the year seems to have been about $1,250,000—not bad for an office with only six employees. Alger remembers his first contact with Cornfeld, in December, 1965: "He called me up to have breakfast with him, and told me that he was going to start a fund for me and call it the Alger Fund, so if it didn't go he'd know the so-and-so to blame."

The SEC order forced I.O.S. to liquidate the proprietary funds and they lost their United States registration; all of them, however, were instantly reconstituted in a nonresident Canadian corporate shell (which Cowett had organized and put aside for possible future use before the Canadians changed their laws on nonresident corporations in 1965: "You never know," Cowett explained recently, "when you may need a corporation"). As registered American investment companies, the I.O.S. proprietary funds had been subject to tax penalties if more than 30 percent of their income derived from short sales and trades in stock held less than ninety days. As foreign companies, they are relieved of such tax liabilities, which has made some of them much more active in the market.

One restriction on the operation of these funds was added, however, by the SEC: like all other I.O.S. subsidiaries, they were forbidden to do business directly with American registered brokers and dealers. Because of this order, all I.O.S. brokerage business is now directed through London & Dominion Trust U.K., Ltd., in England— or, more precisely, through a room with that name on the door, in a small office building at 27 Old Jewry, a block from the Bank of England. The floor of which this room is a part is leased to Arthur Lipper III, a slight young man with Rudolph Valentino features and soft black hair who set up his own New York Stock Exchange house last March, in part "to serve the most important and profitable client in the world."

In the London & Dominion room stand the teletype machines through which Alger and his colleagues in New York send their buy and sell "suggestions." By the terms of the SEC settlement, the proprietary funds cannot actually send "orders," because I.O.S. business cannot be done directly in New York. (Instead of teletyping "Buy 500 Polaroid," Alger will teletype "Suggest buy 500 Polaroid." This form is very carefully followed.) When the "suggestions" are received, London & Dominion teletypes Geneva for confirmation that I.O.S. does in fact wish to follow them. On receipt of the O.K., the men in the London & Dominion room turn toward a window separating them from an Arthur Lipper room, which holds a telephone switchboard for a three-way New York-London-Geneva leased wire plus teletype machines to the Arthur Lipper III offices in New York. Below the window is a space to permit the passage of messages. If the message from London & Dominion is a market order, Lipper (London) relays it instantly to Lipper (New York), where it is forwarded instantly to whichever broker is to execute the order. The

elapsed time between Alger's initial teletype and the arrival of the
order back in New York is usually no more than a minute or two.

London & Dominion is a small independent bank headed by Clin-
ton A. Redgrove, a large, bluff Englishman who is also a director of
I.L.I. (U.K.) and an adviser to Henry Buhl on the purchase of South
African securities for IIT. Its main offices are nearly half a mile away
from 27 Old Jewry, and Redgrove does not even pretend to supervise
the communications room. "It's a service we can do," Redgrove says,
explaining rather smoothly the function of that room in his business,
"because of our independent relationship with I.O.S. Freshfields,
our solicitors, cleared the arrangements with the SEC." For performing the service, Redgrove gets an annual fee (usually about $30,000)
and expenses. In addition, London & Dominion receives increasing
I.O.S. business—Redgrove was the broker, for example, when IIT
bought $10 million of gold during the talk about devaluation of the
dollar last December.

Thanks to the operation of the communications center in London,
Geneva now has absolute control over brokerage assignments. "Prior
to the SEC settlement," Cowett said recently, relaxing in Lipper's
handsome offices on the thirty-eighth floor of the spanking new 140
Broadway building in New York, "Alger would place his orders himself. Now I allocate all the brokerage." Lipper, who gets the largest
single piece of it, to pay his expenses as the communications center,
added helpfully, "The SEC has made I.O.S. an efficient operation for
the first time." Added costs for the leased wires run about $600,000 a
year, but the costs are easily paid through the brokerage commissions,
which, as Cowett pointed out, I.O.S. has coming out of its ears—indeed, the costs may be more than covered by the commissions just on
the *increase* in trading by the I.O.S. proprietary funds since their
change of legal domicile released them from the ninety-day rule. The
new communications operation is, perhaps, a prototypical I.O.S. effort: formed in pursuance of legality, it adheres absolutely to the letter
of the law, while the spirit is sorely oppressed. Surely the SEC, by
ordering complete insulation of I.O.S. from the American market, did
not intend to tighten Geneva's control over I.O.S. business in the
United States.

Criticizing I.O.S. is such fun and so easy that its critics rarely stop to consider the nature of the alternatives that have been offered to the upper-middle-class European with some capital to invest. In general, he has no place to go but one of a small group of banks that do not really compete against each other, that give him a limited range of services, and discourage nosy parkers who ask too many questions about what is being done with their money. "Their idea of managing money," Cornfeld says scornfully, "is to hire a $300-a-month clerk who shifts Nestlé's from one account to another so the bank can make two commissions."

It is certainly true that European banking practice has left equity markets thin and malleable and dominated by a few dozen families. Cornfeld has demonstrated that there are great pools of potential investment capital available in all the European countries for people who will go out and solicit it. The European banks, however distasteful they find Cornfeld's "American methods," will not long allow their fastidiousness to fence them off from the exploitation of this gold mine; indeed, several of them, including the Rothschilds, are already on the move and setting up funds to be aggressively promoted on the Continent. The real significance of the I.O.S. invasion is that it is creating a major new market for equity capital in Europe.

That this revolution should be wrought by Bernie Cornfeld is, to say the least, remarkable. Some day the tourist busses to the French Alps may stop for a moment while the guide points to the castle on the hill and identifies it as the Chateau de Pelly, where the financier Cornfeld performed his experiments. Children will be taught that he wore a blue beard. In the universities scholars will debate the importance of the contributions made by Cornfeld—you know, Bernie Cornfeld, the chubby boy with the stutter, *nebbish,* his mother worked as a nurse—remember? You may not believe it—sometimes Cornfeld himself has trouble believing it—but that's what's happening.

Index

About the Author

MARTIN PRAGER MAYER was born in New York in 1928; both his parents are lawyers. He was graduated in 1947 from Harvard, where he majored in economics and also studied philosophy and music.

After working as a reporter and editor for several publications he became, in 1954, a free-lance writer. He is the author of two novels and four reportorial studies: *Wall Street: Men and Money; Madison Avenue, U.S.A.; The Schools;* and *The Lawyers.* Mr. Mayer's articles on education, business, television, music, law and other subjects have appeared in *Esquire* (for which he writes a monthly column about music), *Harper's, Saturday Evening Post, Fortune, TV Guide, Better Homes & Gardens, Life, The New York Times Magazine, Horizon, Musical America,* and *Commentary,* among others.

From 1961 to 1965 Mr. Mayer was a member of the Panel on Educational Research and Development in the Executive Office of the President, and from 1962 to 1967 he was chairman of a New York City local school board. His book *Social Studies in American Schools* is based on his work as a consultant to the American Council of Learned Societies in 1961–62, and his report on international secondary education was published in 1968 by the Twentieth Century Fund, under the title *Diploma.* He is also the author of a biography, *Emory Buckner,* also published in 1968, under the auspices of the William Nelson Cromwell Foundation.

Mr. Mayer serves in various advisory or trustee roles for the University of Illinois Arithmetic Project, *Opera News,* the New York Pro Musica and the United Nations International School. He is married to the writer and scholar Ellen Moers. They have two sons, Thomas and James.

Format by Ellen H. Brecher
Set in Times Roman
Composed and printed by York Composition Company, Inc.
Bound by The Haddon Craftsmen, Inc.
HARPER & ROW, PUBLISHERS, INCORPORATED